C000042980

PUTTIN(

Divorce and remarriage in
biblical and pastoral perspective

Putting Asunder

Divorce and remarriage in
biblical and pastoral perspective

Stephen Clark

BRYNTIRION PRESS

Cover design:
Phil Boorman @ burgum boorman ltd

Cover photograph:
Haydn McCorriston

Published by Bryntirion Press
Bryntirion, Bridgend CF31 4DX, Wales, UK
Printed by WBC Book Manufacturers, Bridgend

Contents

Preface

This book is a modest attempt to deal with a subject of major concern at the present time. While its main emphasis is upon a biblical understanding of the issues involved, I have attempted, in the final chapter, to illustrate how the biblical principles might be applied.

The subject of divorce and remarriage can sometimes generate a fair amount of heat among God's people. What I have tried to avoid is to come to Scripture with my mind made up; rather, I have sought to work carefully through the biblical material and then to draw conclusions from it. This has presented me with the difficult question of maintaining a proper balance between the need to keep the argument flowing in a readable way and yet without sacrificing the detailed study of the biblical text. The detailed study is essential in a consideration of the subject of divorce, particularly because of the need to interact with, and to take account of, differing understandings of the biblical teaching. It is only by such detailed study that one can indicate why one interpretation is preferable to another. I have attempted to preserve the balance in the following way.

The main text of the book is reasonably straightforward and readily accessible to the average minister. It should not be too difficult to follow the argument and to see where it is going. The detailed argumentation that supports the thrust of the argument, including discussion of linguistic issues and technical matters, is found in the notes and appendices, or in the excursus to a chapter. It should be stressed that these are *not* token footnotes, put there for effect. They are essential to the argument that is presented, but would have cluttered the body of the text in an unhelpful way. However, they are essential to the book. Indeed, it is usually the case that the longer the note, the more important it is to read it. To have omitted the notes would have left the book hopelessly superficial. To have incorporated the notes into the main body of the text would have affected its readability. To have written two separate books would have meant that those for whom it has been chiefly written—working ministers—would probably have gone for the less technical version and would thereby fail to see how certain conclusions have been reached. Discussion on the subject of divorce at a ministers conference on the subject made it abundantly clear to me that very detailed argument is necessary to deal with some of the controverted issues. Moreover, given that the books on this subject by men such as William Heth and Gordon Wenham and Andrew Cornes have been considerably influential, it was important to interact with their views to explain why I think they are to be rejected. I carry on such debate largely in the notes.

Accordingly, it is suggested that the way to read the book is to read through the body of the text *without* reference to the notes, in order to get the general picture and not to miss the wood for the trees. Once this has been done, the text may then be re-read in conjunction with the notes. Alternatively, the reader might wish to read a chapter and then read the notes to the chapter, before proceeding to the next chapter and notes. If this course is followed, the reader will be spared endless cross-referencing and the tedium that would inevitably result. I should add that it is those chapters that deal with the biblical teaching, rather than with the English Law, where the notes are detailed, extensive, and all-important.

It remains for me to express my gratitude to numerous people without whose help this book would have been marred with many more imperfections than may already exist. To the Revd Graham Harrison of Newport I am grateful for finding time in his unbelievably busy schedule to read the bulk of the first draft and for making numerous helpful suggestions. It was at his invitation that I first gave an outline of the biblical teaching to the students of the Evangelical Movement of Wales Theological Training Course. The stimulating discussion on that occasion prompted a number of fruitful lines of thought and further enquiry. The Revd David Kingdon, Managing Editor of Bryntirion Press, made many helpful suggestions. Dr David Instone Brewer, Research Librarian of Tyndale House, Cambridge, was kind enough to respond to a number of queries and to give of his time to discuss some aspects of his work; that I disagree with some of his thinking in no way minimises the considerable esteem in which I hold his work. Miss Brenda Lewis, formerly of the Evangelical Movement of Wales, readily gave her advice on a number of hotly debated questions concerning the semantic range of certain Greek terms, as well as on a number of questions concerning Greek syntax. She has also spent many hours in editing a quite complex manuscript. Miss Mair Jones, formerly of the Evangelical Movement of Wales, also gave much of her own time to the Bryntirion Press in the production of this book. I am deeply grateful to both ladies. I am especially grateful to John Kendall, of the Faculty of the Evangelical Theological College of Wales, for being willing to give of his time to discuss certain exegetical questions relating to 1 Corinthians 7, as well as to respond to queries concerning certain Greek terms in that chapter. I am particularly grateful to him for drawing to my attention, at a very late stage in the writing of this book, a discussion conducted on the website 'B Greek'. That discussion served to confirm certain conclusions that I had already drawn. To Mr Bruce Ritchie, Solicitor, and Deputy Secretary (Professional Practice) Law Society of Scotland, I am deeply indebted for outlining to me the current state of the law north of the border. Naill Small, Solicitor, and Secretary of the Family Law Association of Northern Ireland, provided a similarly invaluable service with respect to the position in Northern Ireland. It is a pleasure to acknowledge my deep gratitude to these various friends and colleagues. They are in no way responsible for any errors or deficiencies in the book. Peter Birks, Regius Professor of Civil Law at Oxford University, was kind enough, in the middle of a busy Michaelmas term, to respond to a number of difficult questions concerning the *lex Julia de adulteriis* by sending me some published material of which I had hitherto been unaware.

To the church family at Noddfa Evangelical Baptist Church, Abersychan, my debt of gratitude is of a different kind. For their love, prayers, and support over the past seven years I am profoundly grateful. That their minister was sometimes absorbed in thinking through the debates over the exegesis of New Testament texts is, I believe, more than compensated for by the fact that a number in the church have been helped as a result of this study. If parts of it are somewhat technical, the overall purpose is that it may ultimately be of pastoral help to the people of God. The final stages of this work have been completed since becoming minister of Freeschool Court Evangelical Church, Bridgend. The officers and members have shown exceptional kindness to my family and to me, and their Christian fellowship has encouraged me as I have completed this work.

Most of all, my thanks are due to my dear wife Lynne, and to my children, Rachel, Robert, and David. Many an evening my absence from them to work on this book was borne gladly and patiently. Now that it has seen the light of day, I gladly dedicate it to them.

My prayer is that this work may be of some service and help to God's people in their pilgrimage to heaven.

PART I

Introduction

The subject of divorce acutely challenges the Christian Church in a variety of ways. To begin with, there is substantial disagreement as to what the Bible actually teaches on this subject. There is, for example, a range of views expressed by biblical scholars and theologians, as well as by more popular writers, as to what the Bible means by divorce and as to the consequences which it entails with respect to the status of divorced persons.[1] This diversity of understanding is often reflected by those with pastoral responsibilities within the churches, and thus expresses itself in a range of practice with respect to the treatment of divorced Christians and of remarriage after divorce. There is, therefore, a challenge to exegesis and theology, to pastoral care and church practice, as well as to inter-church relationships and unity. If we could but clarify understanding on the Bible's teaching, we should be better able to respond to this series of challenges.

However, the Church does not exist in a vacuum but is to bear witness within the society in which she is placed. When the divorce laws in force in that society collide with the requirements God makes of us, the Church inevitably faces another series of challenges. Ministers may be guilty of giving counsel which is totally impractical, while lawyers—even Christian lawyers—may give advice which leaves their Christian clients troubled in conscience and confused. In all of this, there is the danger that the Church will either absorb the spirit of the age and become indistinguishable from the world, or that she will adopt a siege mentality which will leave her like a fortress, sealed off from society and unable to help those of her members who face the anguish of divorce.

This book is a modest attempt to help to equip churches, and especially pastors, to face these challenges. It is impossible to do this without some knowledge of the law which applies in our society.[2] The present time is a convenient opportunity to address this in view of the fact that the divorce law of this country has recently undergone considerable changes.[3] (It should be made clear that

Parliament has enacted the new legislation, but the time of its implementation is subject to the Lord Chancellor's decision.) The significance of these changes lies in the fact that we now face, I believe, a situation more akin to that which was faced by the New Testament church than at any other period since the coming of Christianity to these shores. We are not the first generation of Christians to have to face the appallingly complex problems which result from seeking to uphold a very high view of marriage in a world where divorce is relatively easy to obtain. However, this being the case, it is essential that we do not make that situation more difficult by misunderstanding the New Testament teaching and thereby become guilty of imposing upon it a meaning which it does not bear. It is the writer's conviction that there has been long and widespread misunderstanding concerning one particular strand of New Testament teaching, particularly as expounded in 1 Corinthians 7, that has led to the present work being written.

Chapter 1
Divorce Law in England and Wales

On 4 July 1996, the Family Law Act 1996 received the Royal Assent and passed onto the statute book. Its passage through Parliament had been somewhat stormy, not least because certain of the Government's own backbenchers saw the 'no fault' principle of divorce to be a direct attack upon the family and upon 'family values'. This concern represented a failure to understand the purpose of the legislation and the philosophy behind it. The Family Law Act 1996—from now on we shall refer to it as FLA 1996—is not a revolutionary piece of legislation but the natural conclusion to a process of evolution that began in 1937. Prior to that date, a divorce could only be obtained upon proof of the adultery of one's spouse. This meant that divorce was based firmly upon the idea of a 'matrimonial offence'. However, the Matrimonial Causes Act 1937 allowed divorce on the grounds of a spouse's cruelty, desertion for three years, or supervening incurable insanity. As the Law Commission was to note in its 1966 report, *Field of Choice*, by allowing for supervening incurable insanity the 1937 Act had begun to breach the matrimonial offence principle.[1] Nevertheless, this was a fairly small breach. Another thirty years would elapse before the floodgates would open. Surprisingly, the Established Church was to play an important part in that development.

Prior to the passing of the 1937 Act, concerns had been expressed at the so-called 'Hotel cases', where a couple effectively agreed to divorce and evidence was 'manufactured' to prove the spouse's adultery.[2] This could only bring the law into disrepute and encourage one of the things the law purported to forbid, viz., connivance. The 1937 Act did not really address this kind of problem. However, in 1966 a committee appointed by the Archbishop of Canterbury to consider the question of divorce published its Report.[3] The Report argued for the abandonment of the matrimonial offence principle in favour of a principle of 'breakdown of marriage'. This principle was to become the sole ground of divorce under the Divorce Reform Act 1969. The philosophy of the law is well expressed in the Law Commission's Report, *Field of Choice*: '. . . when, regrettably, a marriage has irretrievably broken down, [a good divorce law will] enable the empty legal shell to be destroyed with the maximum fairness, and the minimum bitterness, distress and humiliation.'[4] Whereas the 1937 Act retained the matrimonial offence principle but allowed a slight breach, the 1969 Act swept aside the whole concept of matrimonial offence: henceforth, divorce would be granted upon proof of a state of affairs, viz., that a marriage had died, rather than on the proof of the state of a spouse's behaviour. The 1969 Act had introduced a 'no fault' divorce law and this was re-enacted by the Matrimonial Causes Act 1973.

The question naturally arises as to why FLA 1996 is regarded as such a new departure, in view of the fact that 'no fault' divorce has been in existence for the past twenty-five years. The answer lies in the fact that, although the 1969 Act introduced divorce on the sole ground of irretrievable breakdown of marriage, the existence of this state of affairs would be evidenced by one of five facts which would need to be proved to establish that the marriage had, in fact, irretrievably broken down. The five facts are as follows:

1. That the respondent has committed adultery and the petitioner finds it intolerable to live with the respondent.
2. That the respondent has behaved in such a way that the petitioner cannot reasonably be expected to live with the respondent.
3. That the respondent has deserted the petitioner for a continuous period of at least two years immediately preceding the presentation of the petition.
4. That the parties to the marriage have lived apart for a continuous period of at least two years immediately preceding the presentation of the petition and the respondent consents to a decree being granted.
5. That the parties to the marriage have lived apart for a continuous period of at least five years immediately preceding the presentation of the petition.[5]

Many observers failed to realise that the five facts did not constitute offences to be proved against one's spouse, but they were facts that would demonstrate that the marriage had irretrievably broken down. In view of this widespread misconception, it is easy to understand how such observers regard the FLA 1996 as effecting little short of a revolution in the divorce law.

FLA 1996 has removed the need to prove any fact that evidences irretrievable breakdown. The reasons for this should be fairly obvious. If I have to prove a fact in court, it should be open to my opponent to seek to challenge me. This is what litigation is all about. But the philosophy behind the 1969 Act was that divorce be attended with the minimum of bitterness, distress, and humiliation. It is quite clear that a prolonged cross-examination of one's spouse would hardly be in keeping with that philosophy. Moreover, if one of the spouses believed that the marriage had irretrievably broken down, it would seem to be rather futile for the other spouse to argue to the contrary. That being so, defended divorces under the legislation introduced in 1969 were to become extremely rare. Lawyers would advise against it. In any event, Legal Aid would only be available to defend a divorce in the most exceptional cases. Accordingly, if one's spouse alleged a fact that was not true, the other spouse would not be advised to defend the petition. Failure to challenge the allegation would not mean that one accepted it as true, since it would be the spouse who alleged the fact who would make the sworn statement that it was true. At most, what would be advised would be that one could 'cross petition': that is, the spouse who had received the divorce petition could also allege a 'fact'—usually of what is commonly called 'unreasonable behaviour'—and the divorce would, in due course, be granted. The facts which 'proved' the breakdown had become something of a sham. FLA 1996 has, accordingly, swept away the need to prove any such facts.

Although FLA 1996 received the Royal Assent on 4 July 1996, its provisions will only come into effect on such day(s) as the Lord Chancellor may appoint.[6] At the time of writing,[7] the part of the Act that deals with divorce and separation proper has not yet come into force. On 2 April 1998 the Parliamentary Secretary to the Lord Chancellor's Department stated the following in a House of Commons written answer to a parliamentary question:

17

The Government remains committed to implement Part II of the Family Law. A very extensive series, pilot testing a number of different models of information meetings, will operate until at least March 1999. It would be wrong to anticipate the results of these pilots . . . It would be safe to assume that the Lord Chancellor will be unable to implement Part II until at least the end of 1999 or even early in the year 2000.

Some observers think that this is an optimistic timescale. Unless and until Part II is implemented, the ground of divorce will continue to be that found in MCA 1973, and it will be necessary to prove one of the five facts. (At the time of going to press, it has become clear that the implementation of that part of the Act which deals with divorce has been deferred by the Lord Chancellor. It now appears to be unlikely that it will be implemented before 2001, if at all.) The main thrust of the new law is as follows.

Firstly, the philosophy behind the new law is spelled out quite clearly: the institution of marriage is to be supported and couples in difficulty are to be encouraged to save their marriages. Where a marriage has irretrievably broken down, it should be brought to an end with the minimum of distress to the parties and to any children who are affected, as well as seeking to promote as good a continuing relationship as possible between the parties and any children. This is to be done in as cost-effective a way as possible, while ensuring that risks of violence to any party or child are minimised.[8] This part of the Act is already applicable, having come into force on 21 March 1997.

The detailed provisions of FLA 1996 seek to implement this philosophy and these aims. Divorce proceedings are started by one or both of the spouses filing at the court a statement that the maker of it believes that the marriage has broken down.[9] No fact has to be alleged to support this belief. However, the person who makes the statement must, at least three months before making it, have attended an information meeting[10] and the marriage must be twelve months old before the statement is made.[11] The purpose of the information meeting is to provide information concerning matters that may arise under FLA 1996, and to give details of marriage counselling and to encourage a meeting with a marriage counsellor. Clearly, the hope is that help will be given which will prevent divorce proceedings being started by the making of a statement. However, where such a statement is made, a period of nine months must then elapse before an application may be made to the Court for a divorce.[12] This period is known as the period for reflection and consideration:[13] that is to say, it is not to be viewed simply as a period which must elapse, but as a period when the marriage may either be saved or when the divorce and its implications and consequences may be carefully pondered. There are provisions for extending this period[14] and for suspending it while reconciliation is attempted.[15] The Court may, on its own initiative or on the application of one of the parties, make directions concerning the need for the parties to attend mediation meetings.[16] Furthermore, the granting of Legal Aid to be represented in proceedings relating to family matters is conditional upon having complied with certain requirements relating to mediation.[17]

If, at the end of the period for reflection and consideration, one of the parties declares his belief that the marriage cannot be saved and applies for a divorce, the Court shall grant it, provided that certain requirements have been satisfied.[18] Very briefly, that is the main thrust of FLA 1996 with respect to divorce. It needs to be added that the provisions for a separation order are slightly different. The main difference is that whereas the statement which starts divorce proceedings cannot be filed at court until the marriage is twelve months old, a statement with respect to which an application for a separation order is made can be made within the first twelve months of the marriage.[19] Moreover, a separation order can be converted into a divorce order, but not before the marriage is two years old.[20] The main difference in the effects of a separation order and a divorce order is that remarriage after a separation order which has not been converted into a divorce would be bigamous and therefore illegal.

FLA 1996 is not, therefore, the attack upon the family and its values which some have alleged it to be. However, it does pose some very specific problems for Christian churches which seek to be faithful to the teaching of God's Word, as well as to Christians whose spouses start divorce proceedings. How these problems are to be faced depends, in large measure, on one's understanding of the teaching of God's Word. To that we now turn.

PART II

Chapter 2
The Old Testament Teaching

Whatever different understandings Christians may have of the Bible's teaching concerning divorce, all will be agreed that it has something to do with marriage! This being so, the proper place to begin a consideration of the Bible's teaching on divorce is with its teaching about marriage.

The divine pattern for marriage is laid down in Genesis 2:24.[1] Firstly, it is to be heterosexual: it consists of a man and a woman. Secondly, it is to be monogamous: the man will cleave to his wife, and they—that is, the one man and the one woman—will be one flesh. Thirdly, it is a permanent union: by becoming one flesh, the man and the woman have become a new unit. The entrance of sin could not but have implications for marriage. The entrance of death consequent upon sin meant that no marriage would be permanent, in that sooner or later death would sever the bond.[2] One does not read very far in Genesis before coming to polygamy,[3] extramarital sex,[4] and homosexuality.[5] Strangely, there is no specific mention of divorce, as such, in the Book of Genesis. The nearest we get to a mention of divorce is in Genesis 21:9-14. Hagar is specifically called Abram's wife,[6] and God tells Abram to heed Sarai's request to send Hagar away.[7] However, this having been said, it would be unwise to read too much into this passage. To begin with, Sarai was already Abram's wife before he took Hagar to himself. It is, therefore, something of a polygamous situation. Secondly, although Hagar is called Abram's wife,[8] it is clear that this was an arrangement whereby Hagar would become a surrogate mother for Sarai. It was not a normal marriage situation.[9] Thirdly, an enormous amount was at stake in Abram fathering a child through Sarai. Much of Genesis is concerned with the unfolding and development of the promise made in chapter 3:15. Genesis 9:26 'canalises' the promise to the line of Shem, while 12:1-2 further specifies that it is to be fulfilled in the line of

Abram. Chapter 15 is an enormously important chapter in the unfolding of God's plan. Abram believes God's promise that God will give him a son. In view of the divine pattern of marriage set out in 2:24, Abram's taking of Hagar, recorded in chapter 16, must be understood as Abram wavering in his faith in God's promise to him, since he seeks to bring about the fulfilment of God's promise in a way that is contrary to God's will. This is the reason for the exposition of the theological significance of this incident in Galatians 4:21-31. In view of these considerations, it would be wise not to attempt to construct any understanding of the Bible's teaching on divorce from this incident.

Mosaic legislation

For an understanding of the Old Testament teaching on divorce, attention has frequently been focused on Deuteronomy 24:1-4.[10] Clearly, these verses are extremely important for a number of reasons, not the least being that of the four accounts of Christ's teaching concerning divorce, three make some reference to the teaching of these verses.[11] However, we shall seriously distort the meaning and significance of this passage unless we place it in the context of the Mosaic legislation as a whole; and fundamental to that legislation was the seriousness with which it viewed sexual sin. For example, Leviticus 18 prohibits sexual relations with a range of blood relatives and in-laws (vv.6-18), forbids homosexual intercourse and bestiality (vv.22-23), and outlaws adultery per se (v.20). All of these offences carried the death penalty (v.29).[12]

Deuteronomy 22:13-29 is another important passage for understanding the total context in which Deuteronomy 24:1-4 must be understood. The thread which ties together the verses in this passage appears to be concern with the effects of sexual relations outside of marriage. Thus, verses 13-21 are concerned with a husband who suspects that his wife had lost her virginity to another man at some time before her marriage. If the allegation were proved to be unfounded, then the man would be punished, would have to pay financial compensation to his father-in-law, and would be forbidden ever to divorce his wife (v.19). Clearly, these provisions would have had a number of likely effects: men would think twice before making rash allegations, while women would be encouraged to retain their virginity and their parents would be encouraged to retain the evidence of their daughters' premarital purity.[13] If the charge were proved true, then divorce was not an option. The woman was to be stoned to death (vv.21-22). The death penalty was also to be exacted where a virgin pledged to be married slept with another man. The man and the woman were to be executed (vv.23-24). Divorce would be wholly out of the question. However, this was not to be the case where a man raped a virgin pledged to be married. In such a situation, the man alone was to be executed.

The case of a virgin who was not pledged to be married and who had sexual relations was to be dealt with somewhat differently. Deuteronomy 22:28-29 deals with this case, but so does Exodus 22:16-17. It would seem that the Exodus passage has in view the situation where the intercourse is with the virgin's consent, whereas the Deuteronomy passage suggests that rape may have taken place.[14] In the former case, the man would have to pay the bride price for virgins to the girl's father and take the woman as his wife. In the latter case, the man would have to pay a fixed amount—not a dowry but a penalty[15]—to the girl's father and marry her. However, he would be forbidden ever to divorce her (v.29).[16] In view of all of these considerations, it is clear that in the following situations divorce was not an option: where adultery had been committed; where there had been proven, consenting premarital sexual relations with a third party; where a husband's accusation of his wife's premarital intercourse with another man had been shown to be unfounded; and where marriage to a woman had followed her violation by the man who had raped her.

There are two other important passages we need to keep in mind before turning to consider the teaching of Deuteronomy 24:1-4. Numbers 5:11-31 deals with the situation where a husband suspects that his wife has had extramarital sexual relations. This may be either because he has good reason to be suspicious (vv.13-14a), or simply because he is a jealous husband (v.14b). Clearly, it would be undesirable for such a state of affairs to persist. Accordingly, this passage sets out a procedure to deal with the situation. The difference between the procedure set out here, and the requirement of Leviticus 18:29 and 20:10 that an adulterous wife be executed, indicates that the death penalty was only to be applied where the adultery was witnessed. This is confirmed by Deuteronomy 22:22, where it is specifically required that the couple be 'found sleeping' together; and also by the condition laid down in Numbers 5:13, that the procedure specified in the verses that follow should only apply where there was no witness to the suspected adultery.[17] The clear import of this passage is that an innocent wife would be unscathed by the ritual, but a guilty wife would come under a curse. However, it does not appear that the curse would terminate her life.[18] Here, then, was a case of adultery that did not lead to the death penalty. This passage is interesting for identifying a point which is so obvious, yet might easily be missed: there may have been many instances of sexual sins being committed which, if witnessed, would carry the death penalty, but which were not, in fact, witnessed by anyone. This is surely part of the reason for the provisions of Deuteronomy 22:13-21 as well as of Numbers 5:11-31. Deuteronomy 22:13-21 confirms the fact that Numbers 5:11-31 is not dealing with a husband who becomes suspicious of his wife having had premarital sexual intercourse, but is dealing with his suspicion as to something having happened after he had married her. Numbers 5:19 also makes this clear.

The second important passage as background to Deuteronomy 24:1-4 is Deuteronomy 21:15-17.[19] These verses make clear that polygamy was not outlawed under the Mosaic covenant. It is not uncommon for Christians to be perplexed by this fact, particularly in view of the clear teaching of Genesis 2:24. An analogy from English law may help to remove this perplexity and clarify the situation that obtained. There was a period in English law when certain gaming contracts were illegal:[20] that is to say, they were forbidden by the criminal law, and a punishment would be pronounced upon someone convicted of breaking that law. These contracts are no longer illegal, but they are classed by the law as 'unlawful': this means that although a gaming contract is no longer a criminal offence and the gaming community regularly transacts business, such a contract cannot be enforced in the courts.[21] The law does not now criminalise such contracts, but neither does it approve of them. It is in this light that we must understand the toleration of polygamy by the Mosaic law.[22] What this means, of course, is that it was not necessary for a man to divorce his wife in order to be able to marry another woman. He was always able, under the Mosaic law, to marry a second wife.

Deuteronomy 24:1-4

With this background in mind, we may now consider the teaching of Deuteronomy 24:1-4. The first thing to note is that the legislation's main concern is to prohibit a man from remarrying a wife whom he had previously divorced and who, having remarried, was subsequently widowed or divorced again. The NIV brings out this meaning very clearly and is to be preferred to those translations which suggest that the legislation is concerned chiefly with imposing an obligation on a husband to divorce his wife in certain circumstances.[23] Thus the main thrust of the passage is concerned not with the grounds of divorce, nor with the procedure for divorce, nor even with the effects of divorce, but rather with the consequence of remarriage after divorce. The main consequence was that the woman and her first husband might never thereafter be remarried. Such a thing would 'be detestable in the eyes of the LORD' and would bring sin upon the land (v.4).

It is important to note that this is not a piece of legislation whose intent is expressly to authorise the remarriage of divorced women. It would be more accurate to say that this passage envisages such a situation as a necessary incident or background to the behaviour which is expressly forbidden. In that sense, it is treated in a similar way to the divorce of verse 1: it is one of the events which form the context in which a certain course of action is prohibited. Having said this, we need to note that remarriage by the woman is not outlawed and, set against the prohibition of verse 4, is necessarily and implicitly permitted. Moreover, it would appear to be legitimate to infer that a divorced woman who had remarried and who had been subsequently widowed or divorced could remarry again.[24] The question must be asked, Why could she not subsequently remarry the first husband? The answer to this question turns chiefly on the significance of the following words in verse 4: 'her first husband, who divorced her, is not allowed to marry her again after she has been defiled. That would be detestable in the eyes of the LORD.' In what sense had she been defiled?

A number of possible answers have been given to this question, some emphasising that the divorce introduces an element of deformity or defilement, while others see the defilement as arising from remarriage after divorce.[25] There are good reasons for holding that anything which leads to sexual relations existing between a woman and more than one man, and between a man and more than one woman, is viewed by Scripture as an abnormality occasioned by the entrance of sin and its presence in the human race: see Leviticus 21:7,13-14.[26] The Mosaic law related this abnormality somewhat differently to different situations.[27] Thus, divorce per se constituted the barrier to a priest marrying a divorcee (Leviticus 21:7). In the case of a man who had divorced his wife, the divorce did not constitute the barrier to him remarrying her, but her subsequent remarriage to a third party would do so (Deuteronomy 24:4). Neither the divorce nor remarriage constituted a barrier to someone other than a priest or her former husband marrying her (Deuteronomy 24:2).

We may say, therefore, that Deuteronomy 24:1-4 is chiefly concerned with the prohibition, in certain circumstances, of the remarriage of a husband to his former wife, rather than with permitting a husband to divorce his wife. That prohibition arises from the abnormality which would exist if the woman had subsequently married another man. However, the abnormality would be rooted in the act that gave rise to the woman's second marriage, viz., the divorce by her first husband. Far from encouraging divorce, this legislation, properly understood, would make a man careful about divorcing his wife; for if he later regretted his action, he would be for ever debarred from reversing it if his wife had subsequently remarried. Having considered the main thrust of the legislation, we turn to three other features of it which call for consideration.

Firstly, as has been noted, the divorced wife was free to remarry. The Mosaic legislation knows nothing of divorce that could not be followed by remarriage. This is not to say that it encouraged it; it neither encouraged nor discouraged remarriage after divorce. However, it clearly did not expressly forbid it, but notes it as a possible consequence of divorce. The Mosaic legislation did not specifically address the question as to whether the original couple were still one flesh or not, or whether the new couple had become one flesh. However, there are compelling reasons for believing that divorce did end the one-flesh union.[28]

Secondly, implicit in Deuteronomy 24:1 is the requirement of the husband to give his wife a certificate of divorce. It appears that it was already assumed and accepted that there could be no divorce without such a certificate. While the wording of the passage clearly indicates that Moses was not introducing something unknown but alluding to something with which the people were familiar, it may nevertheless be inferred that there is an implicit command to give a certificate of divorce if divorce were to be effected. This point is clearly underlined in Isaiah 50:1-2, where the absence of a certificate of divorce is the sure evidence that the Lord had not repudiated his covenant with his people.

The third question arising from the Mosaic legislation is, What is the meaning and significance of the words 'something indecent' in verse 1? While it is easier to specify to what these words cannot refer than to assign a positive meaning to them, there are good reasons for believing that they refer to the situation where a man, for a number of possible reasons, no longer found his wife to be physically attractive.[29] The legislation is worded in such a way that it seems that Moses is not laying down a ground for divorce but, rather, is referring to those situations where divorce would take place.[30] This said, it would appear that the effect of this legislation would be the same for the 'something indecent' as it would be for the certificate of divorce: that is to say, that just as divorce would only be valid where a certificate of divorce would be given, so a divorce could only take place where the husband found 'something indecent' in his wife, as a consequence of which she no longer found favour in his eyes.

Malachi 2:14-16

If the prohibition of Deuteronomy 24:4 entailed an implicit recognition and toleration of divorce in certain circumstances and brought a measure of regulation to bear upon the whole matter, Malachi 2:14-16 makes it abundantly clear that the Lord did not approve of divorce. To understand the precise significance of this prophetic denunciation, it is important to keep in mind that Malachi is dealing with the divorce which the Mosaic legislation recognised. There may or may not be other good biblical arguments for saying that the Lord always hates divorce. What one must not do is to lift these verses from their historical context and seek to use them as a universal principle or, still less, as a slogan. The meaning of the verses is that the divorce which was practised by Old Testament Israelites was something which, while not expressly forbidden, was nevertheless found hateful by the Lord. The reasons for the Lord's hatred are given, and they confirm our understanding of the 'something indecent' of Deuteronomy 24:1. While there is dispute as to how the passage is to be translated, the following points are fairly clear. Firstly, the husband was guilty of a kind of treachery against, or betrayal of, the wife of his youth: 'you have broken faith with her . . . the wife of your marriage covenant' (v.14). (It should be noted that this verse refers to marriage as a 'covenant': this entails the fact that while marriage is a state and the fact of marriage confers a certain status upon the spouses, it also involves mutual obligations. Furthermore, it is the background to the Old Testament emphasis that Israel is the bride of the Lord.) Secondly, there was a ruthlessness involved in the husband's divorcing of his wife which amounted to violence against her: '"I hate divorce," says the LORD God of Israel, "and I hate a man's covering himself with violence as well as with his garment," says the LORD Almighty' (v.16).[31] Thirdly, as with, divorce involved action against the Lord as well as against another person; it had vertical, as well as horizontal, dimensions.[32] This entire passage is important not only for understanding the Old Testament teaching on divorce, but also for a proper appreciation of Christ's treatment of the Mosaic legislation.

It may be objected that the Old Testament does not have an entirely negative view of divorce and of the husband who initiates divorce. For example, appeal might be made to the Lord divorcing his people as proof that the Old Testament approved of divorce in certain circumstances. However, this argument cannot be sustained.[33] It might nevertheless be argued that the positive way in which the Scripture views the putting away of foreign wives indicates that divorce is not presented in an entirely negative light in the Old Testament (Ezra 9 and 10; Nehemiah 13:23-31), and that this fact should be borne in mind when interpreting Malachi 2:14-16. This, however, would be to misunderstand Ezra and Nehemiah and the action which they took, which must be understood in the light of the need to re-institute the place of the Mosaic law in the nation after a period of terrible judgement for its contempt of that law.[34]

One question we have not yet addressed is whether a woman could divorce her husband. A negative reply has generally been given to this question. However, there is clear evidence within the Old Testament that in certain circumstances a woman could obtain a divorce from her husband: that is to say, he would give the certificate of divorce in a situation where she wished to be divorced from him.[35] Two passages of Scripture are relevant: Exodus 21:10-11,[36] and Deuteronomy 21:10-14.[37] We shall first consider the verses in Deuteronomy, since—in some respects—they are the more straightforward to understand, and we shall then consider the passage in Exodus before seeking to draw some conclusions.

Deuteronomy 21:10-11

Deuteronomy 21:10-11 is dealing with the situation where an Israelite wishes to have as his wife a foreign woman who has been taken as a prisoner of war. Verse 11 permits such a marriage, but verses 12-13 lay out the procedure that is to be adopted. The last part of verse 13 envisages the marriage as having taken place: 'she shall be your wife'. There are good reasons for believing that verse 14 is laying down provisions which are to apply where the man finds the woman to be displeasing after she has become his wife.[38] In such a situation he must 'let her go wherever she wishes'.

This clause has a number of interesting features. First of all, it should be noted that the words 'let her go' may be understood to mean 'divorce her'.[39] Although she was originally a prisoner and could therefore have been treated as a slave, marriage has fundamentally changed everything. Therefore, if her husband becomes displeased with her, he cannot simply turn her into his slave, nor may he divorce her and then treat her as his own slave or sell her to someone else; rather, he must let her go wherever she pleases. The divorce severs any relationship between the two of them. The purpose of this legislation is, therefore, to protect the position of a slave who has become a wife from being returned to a position of servitude. Indeed, the procedure to be followed before she is married is designed to preserve her dignity as a person and to prevent her from being treated as an object of gratification: the mourning period referred to in verse 13 serves this purpose. This leads to the second interesting feature of this legislation: do the words 'let her go wherever she pleases' imply that the wife has requested the divorce and that the husband must accede to such a request? It is impossible to be dogmatic, but there are good reasons for suggesting a negative answer to this question. The inference to be drawn is that, having found the wife to be displeasing, he would no longer treat her as his wife and would probably wish to divorce her. In such a case, she is then a free woman in the same way as a non-slave wife who had been divorced would be free.[40] The question is not addressed as to what would happen if he tried to keep her as a slave, or sell her as a slave. Presumably, in those circumstances, she could take her case to the elders or to the judges, who would compel the husband to divorce her. In that case, while not possessing a right to divorce her husband, she would have the right to initiate the process whereby the husband would have to divorce her.[41]

Exodus 21:7-11

Like Deuteronomy 21:10-14, the passage in Exodus 21:7-11 is concerned with the position of servants or slaves. However, this passage differs from the deuteronomic legislation in that it is not dealing with a foreign woman.[42] It also differs in that the woman is sold by her father (verse 7a). In this respect it differs from the situation envisaged in Deuteronomy 15:12, where the woman sells herself into slavery. This is part of the explanation for the fact that, according to Deuteronomy 15:12, the female slave was to go free in the seventh year as a male slave would go free, whereas Exodus 21:7 states specifically that she is not thus to go free. The other reason for the difference between the Exodus passage and Deuteronomy 15:12 is the fact that the slavery in question in Exodus 21 is with a view to marriage. The situation envisaged is that of a poor man who sells his daughter into slavery with the expectation that her master will marry her, or that he will give her in marriage to his son. Matthew Poole's comments on verse 11 are admirable for their precise clarity:

> The sum is this, The master was either, 1. Willing to part with her; and then he was to let her be redeemed by herself, or any of her friends, but not by a heathen, verse 8. Or, 2. Willing to keep her; and then, as he had betrothed her, he was to perform all the duties of a husband to her, although he had another wife besides her, verse 10. 3. If he would keep her, and yet deny those duties to her, then as his fault was aggravated, so was his punishment; for now he cannot sell her, but must let her go freely, as in this verse.

Verse 8 is almost certainly dealing with the situation where the master of the woman, who had been sold to him as a slave with the expectation that she would be married to him, decides not to marry her.[43] Verse 9 is contrasting her status, if given to the master's son, with that of the wife of verse 4.[44] Verse 10 is anticipating difficulties which might arise if the master, having married the woman, subsequently marries another woman, particularly if that other woman was a free woman.[45] The legislation protects the first wife: the husband is not to defraud her materially or sexually.[46] Where he does so defraud her, she may leave him: 'she is to go free' (verse 11). It is this last verse which is allowing divorce to take place on the basis of the husband's behaviour. Indeed, it could be argued that here is a clear case of divorce for 'unreasonable behaviour'.[47] It would appear that, as with Deuteronomy 21:14, it is the husband who would give the certificate of divorce but, in the event of him refusing to do so, the woman could bring her plight to the elders or judges, who would compel him to give the certificate.[48]

To summarise

We are now in a position to summarise the Old Testament teaching on divorce. Divorce, like bigamy, fell short of the divine ideal of marriage. Though tolerated by the Mosaic law because of the hardness of men's hearts, it was hated by the Lord, and was treated by the Mosaic law as testifying to the abnormality which sin creates. The Mosaic law introduced certain restrictions on the remarriage of divorcees. However, these restrictions were not occasioned by the one-flesh union being still intact, since the act of divorce ended that state of affairs. Indeed, the divorce which was tolerated by the Mosaic law specifically allowed remarriage, subject to certain restrictions. Divorce required the giving of a certificate. This was the husband's act and would take place when he no longer was pleased with his wife because he no longer found her to be attractive. Where the husband would not divorce a wife with whom he was no longer pleased, but sought to treat her as a chattel, she could take steps to compel him to give her the certificate of divorce. The divorce tolerated by the Mosaic law was necessitated by the hardness of men's hearts, either because they no longer found their wives attractive and would therefore put them away, or because, no longer finding them attractive, they treated them shamefully and were compelled by the wives to give the certificate of divorce. It was the failure of many of Christ's contemporaries to realise this that shows how completely they had misunderstood the Old Testament teaching and how completely Jesus did understand it. To the New Testament teaching we must now turn.

———

Excursus
on the meaning of 'something
indecent' in Deuteronomy 24:1

During the time of Christ, there was considerable difference of opinion concerning the meaning of these words, one interpretation following Rabbi Shammai and the other following Rabbi Hillel. The Mishnah records the debate in *Gittin* 9.10:

> The House of Shammai say: 'A man should not divorce his wife unless he found in her something indecent, as it is said: "For he finds in her an indecent thing" (Deut. 24:1).' And the House of Hillel say: 'Even if she burned a dish for him, as it is said: "For he finds in her an indecent thing" (Deut. 24:1).'

Brewer (EN 1997; Non-Academic [1996-1999] Chapter 2) has pointed out that the Mishnah contains summaries of debates which are highly abbreviated to aid memorisation. The expanded version of this debate, as it would have been understood in the mind of a first-century Jew, is, according to Brewer, as follows:

> The school of rabbis who follow the teacher Shammai teach: 'If a man is basing his divorce on Deut. 24:1, he cannot divorce his wife for anything except indecency.' The school of rabbis following Hillel teach: 'The text of Deut. 24:1 also allows divorce on the grounds of any "thing", which included even a small thing like burning a meal, because the text contains both the words "indecent" and "thing".'

In the second century AD, Rabbi Akiba referred it to the situation where a man found a woman more beautiful than his wife. The same section of the Mishnah states:

> Rabbi Akiba says, 'Even if he has found another more beautiful than she is, as it is said (Deut. 24:1) "And it shall come to pass, if she does not find favour in his eyes".'

This means that three 'grounds of divorce' were discerned by the rabbis in this verse. The Shammaites emphasised the word 'indecent' and, on that basis, understood the reference to be to unchastity. The Hillelites, by emphasising the word 'something', added the second ground of divorce which was very wide-ranging, while Akiba emphasised a different part of the verse—'who becomes displeasing to him'—and gave yet a third reason for divorce. (It should be noted that Akiba lived in the second century AD. Whether he was the originator of the interpretation he held, or whether he was carrying on a traditional understanding of the words, it is difficult to say. From what we know of Akiba, it is more likely that this was his own interpretation.) Differences of understanding still persist amongst Christian writers as to the meaning of 'something indecent', though, thankfully, the differences are not as great as between Shammai and Hillel. Brewer (1996) understands it to refer to unfaithfulness on the part of the wife. Murray (1961) understands it to refer to some indecency or impropriety of behaviour which, while falling short of illicit sexual intercourse, may have consisted in some shameful conduct connected with sex life. Heth and Wenham (p. 230) quote Isaksson: 'Isaksson quite convincingly argues that the indecency here is a matter of the wife's having exposed her pudendum voluntarily or involuntarily. This arouses the husband's loathing (cf. 2 Sam. 6:12-20; Ezek. 23:18; also Exod. 20:26).' This is similar to Murray's view. Craigie, commenting on this verse, is more cautious and possibly more realistic in saying that it may have been a technical legal expression and then adding, 'the precise meaning is no longer clear'. He tentatively considers as a possible meaning some physical deficiency, such as, for example, the inability to bear children.

The words 'something indecent' translate the Hebrew words, *'erwāt dābār*. One of the difficulties in understanding this phrase is that it is used on only one other occasion in the Old Testament, in Deuteronomy 23:14, where it refers to the need to ensure that the Lord should find nothing unseemly in the camp. This concern is expressed immediately after regulations have been given for the covering of human excrement. The reference is, therefore, to something offensive and unpleasant, but not necessarily to moral defilement. This could support the idea that Deuteronomy 24:1 is referring to a husband who finds his wife to be offensive or unpleasant, possibly in a physical way. While it is true that the word *'erwâ* is used frequently in Leviticus 18 to refer to the naked-ness which is uncovered in sexual relations, and is also used fre-quently in Ezekiel 16 of nakedness, with connotations of shame, Murray and others are probably going too far in concluding from this that the words in Deuteronomy 24:1 refer to some shameful conduct on the wife's part. Craigie's caution is to be preferred. However, the following considerations may allow us to be some-what more definite than Craigie, while being less definite than Murray.

The wife of one's youth

Malachi twice refers to divorce as a breaking of faith with the wife of one's youth (Malachi 2:14-16). Proverbs 5 warns against being tempted by an adulteress. A sure preservative against being thus captivated by another woman is to be captivated by the love of one's wife (verses 19-20). The exhortation is given to rejoice in the wife of one's youth (verse 18). There are some striking similarities between Proverbs 5 and Malachi 2:14-15. Both refer to the wife of one's youth (Proverbs 5:18; Malachi 2:14-15), and both passages deal with an act of treachery against her. Proverbs 5 deals with a man's unfaithfulness as a result of being allured by an adulteress (verses 1-6), while Malachi is concerned with the suffering experi-enced by the wife as a result of being divorced by the husband, probably in order to marry a pagan woman (verses 11, 14-16). In the former passage, this unfaithfulness is related to failure to rejoice in the wife of one's youth and being captivated by another woman (verses 18-20), while in the latter passage it is related to being treacherous to the wife of one's youth (verses 14-15). In both pas-sages the Lord is witness to what happens (Proverbs 5:21; Malachi 2:14).

It seems quite reasonable, therefore, to link the divorce referred to in Malachi 2 with the husband's desire to marry another woman, i.e. 'the daughter of a foreign god' (verse 11). If Malachi 2:14-16 is read in the light of Proverbs 5, it becomes clear that Malachi was raising a protest against the prevalent practice among men of divorcing their wives for 'newer models'—in much the same way as one would, today, trade in an old car for a newer model. Part of the significance of Proverbs 31:30 lies in its implicit recognition of the fact that a man who marries a woman only for her charm or physical beauty will inevitably find that her attraction will, in time, fade. Since physical and sexual attractiveness are related, it therefore follows that a man who has married a woman solely on the basis of her physical attraction will find her no longer sexually attractive when her physical attraction has waned, and will not find her physically attractive when her sexual attractiveness has waned. The 'indecent thing', or the 'unseemly [or nakedness of a] thing' which the husband finds and which leads to his no longer viewing his wife favourably could well, therefore, refer to his finding her no longer physically and sexually attractive, possibly as a result of her age. He may find her 'nakedness' displeasing. This interpretation may find some support from those passages that deal with situations where a man is forbidden to divorce his wife.

Deuteronomy 22:28-29 deals with one of the situations where a man was not allowed to divorce his wife. This was the case where a man was obliged to marry a virgin whom he had raped. The sad episode of Amnon and Tamar, recorded in 2 Samuel 13, throws an interesting light upon the prohibition of divorce contained in Deuteronomy 22:28-29. It is quite clear from verse 13 that Tamar was not at all averse to marrying the man who was about to rape her. Moreover, it is clear from verse 16 that she hoped that Amnon, having raped her, would do the honourable thing and marry her. After all, a pagan prince had once shown this honour to a woman who had been forced (Genesis 34:1-12). However, verse 15 informs us that, having tasted forbidden fruit, Amnon hated Tamar with greater intensity than he had lusted for her. It is surely sound psychology that a person may come to loathe the very thing for which he has craved. A man who had had to marry a woman whom he had raped might subsequently find her physically and sexually offensive and wish to divorce her. He was forbidden to do so. But this may confirm our interpretation that the usual case where divorce would take place was where a man found his wife to be physically and sexually displeasing. The interpretation that is being suggested is that which A. W. Pink gives in his treatment of these words: 'it would appear that the allusion was unto some physical defect or disease which caused her to "find no favour" in her husband's eyes' (Pink, p. 230). Where I go beyond Pink is in suggesting that the ageing process may sometimes have had something to do with this, and in seeking to demonstrate this from passages such as

Proverbs 5:18-20; 31:30, and Malachi 2:15, whereas Pink's conclusion is reached 'by a process of elimination' (Pink p. 230).

The Revd David Kingdon has suggested to me that *dābār* is suggestive of an act rather than a state, and that the exposure by the wife of her pudendum would be an act, but physical unattractiveness would be a state. This being the case, Isaksson's interpretation may be preferable to the one I am proposing. My response to this suggestion is as follows. First of all, this is trying to build too much upon the meaning of the Hebrew term *dābār*. Indeed, the fact that the phrase *'erwat dābār* occurs on only one other occasion in the Old Testament (Deut. 23:14), and that there it manifestly refers to a state of affairs rather than to an action (though, admittedly, the state of affairs results from an action), would favour more the interpretation I am proposing than that advanced by Isaksson. This point notwithstanding, the phrase has to be understood against the totality of the Old Testament teaching rather than in a narrowly lexical manner.

The interpretation offered thus far also finds support from Exodus 21:10-11. This important passage for the whole subject of divorce has been already examined in this chapter (pp. 32-3), where it is argued that it provided the basis for a woman to request her husband to divorce her if he was depriving her of food, clothing or conjugal duties. What is significant, for present purposes, is the fact that the husband might be guilty of such behaviour if he had married a second wife and preferred her to the first. Thus, he might reach the stage where he no longer found his first wife attractive and for this reason would deprive her in various ways. If so, she could get a divorce from him. It is easy to see that it is only one step removed from this for the husband to divorce her before he marries the second woman. This would be exactly the kind of situation envisaged in Deuteronomy 24:1 and Malachi 2.

Dabney's view

R. L. Dabney (pp. 408-10) understands *'erwat dābār* to denote some kind of personal deformity or disease. However, his understanding of the Mosaic legislation is that it is to be closely related to a society in which young women were reared in comparative seclusion and marriages were arranged by intermediaries. Thus, the bridegroom may have had little opportunity to become acquainted with his bride-to-be. To quote Dabney:

When she was brought to him at the nuptials, if he found her disfigured with some personal depravity or disease . . . which effectively changed desire into disgust, he was likely to regard himself as swindled in the treaty, and to send the rejected bride back with indignity to her father's house. [She thus became a wife in name,] yet without a husband, she drags out a wretched existence, incapable of marriage, and regarded by her parents and brothers as a disgraceful encumbrance. It was to relieve the wretched fate of such a woman that Moses' law was framed (p. 409).

It is clear that according to Dabney's interpretation the marriage was never consummated.

It is plain that Moses' law contemplates the case, only, in which no consummation of marriage takes place . . . The same fact appears from the condition of the law, that she shall in no case return to this man, 'after she is defiled', i.e. after actual cohabitation with another man has made her unapproachable (without moral defilement) by the first. Such was the narrow extent of this law (p. 409).

In the light of this, Dabney understands Christ's teaching in Matthew 19:3-9 as effecting a repeal or abrogation of the Mosaic teaching on this matter. He gives two reasons for his position. Firstly, because of the changed social customs relating to marriage in our Lord's day and, secondly, because of the appalling perversion of the Mosaic teaching which then prevailed.

Dabney's understanding of the type of divorce permitted by Moses is that it could only occur where the marriage had not been consummated. However, this interpretation can hardly be sustained in the light of the teaching found in Deuteronomy 22:19,29. The situation dealt with in verses 13-21 of this chapter is where a man takes a wife and, after the marriage has been consummated, accuses her of having lost her virginity before her marriage. Verse 19 specifies what is to happen where she has been proved innocent: since the husband has given a bad name to an Israelite virgin, he is to be fined a hundred shekels of silver, which are to be given to the girl's father. This, however, is not all: the man is forbidden to divorce her as long as he lives. If the Mosaic divorce could only be effected where a marriage had not been consummated, there would be no point whatsoever in the prohibition of verse 19, since verse 13 specifically tells us that the marriage *had* been consummated. This would be an absolute bar to divorce in any circumstances, let alone those envisaged in verses 13-19. In other words, the words of prohibition are somewhat pointless and redundant. But if Moses allowed divorce where a marriage had been consummated, then the prohibition of verse 19 makes perfect sense: it is saying that *in this set of circumstances*—where an Israelite virgin had been slandered—a husband was forbidden to do what otherwise he might have done. Such a slander became an absolute bar to divorce.

Dabney would be on sure ground were he to say that the divorce allowed by Moses included the situation where a man is displeased with his bride before he consummates the marriage. Deuteronomy 22:13-21 only considers what is to be done when an accusation is made *after* the consummation of the marriage. There are only two possible outcomes: if the girl is proved to be innocent, then verse 19 applies; but if she cannot establish her innocence, then she is to be stoned to death (vv.20-21). What is not considered by this passage is what is to happen when the husband expresses displeasure *before* consummation. It may well be that in such a case the man could divorce the woman. However, Dabney is clearly mistaken in confining the Mosaic divorce legislation to such a case.

This becomes yet more clear when we turn to verse 29 of the chapter. In this situation it is precisely because sexual relations have taken place that the man is to marry the woman. Because he has raped (violated) her he is obligated to marry her, and he is not permitted to divorce her 'as long as he lives'. Quite clearly, if divorce could only be effected when a marriage had not been consummated, it would seem strange that Moses felt it necessary to prohibit divorce in these two cases for as long as the man was alive. The fact that Moses refused to allow divorce to take place in these specific instances indicates a background in which divorce was permitted in other cases in which marriages had clearly been consummated. It was thus necessary, for this reason, to exclude these two cases where the actions of the men concerned had exposed the women to appalling humiliation.

The specific and explicit prohibition of divorce in the two cases we have considered implicitly assumes that divorce was not forbidden in other cases. Thus, for example, where a woman 'not pledged to be married' (Exod. 22:16) consented to the seductive advances of a man, he was required to pay the bride price and marry the woman. However, in this situation there is no prohibition against his subsequently divorcing her, as there is in Deuteronomy 22:29.

There is a second reason why Dabney's interpretation of *'erwat dābār* must be rejected. He fails to see the significance of the fact that in Leviticus 21:13-15 the high priest is forbidden to marry a widow, or a prostitute, or a divorced woman. A prostitute had obviously had previous sexual relations. So had a widow, but with this important difference: she had been married, had had sexual relations, but the marriage was no longer in existence. Divorce fits neatly into this framework and, as we have already had occasion to note, what these verses are concerned with is the abnormality resulting from sin (see notes 26 and 27 to this chapter). The entrance of sin created the abnormal situation where a woman might have sexual relations with more than one man: for example, a widow who remarried. Deuteronomy 24:1-4 specifically states that if the divorced woman becomes the wife of another man and is subsequently divorced or widowed, her first husband is not allowed to remarry her. It seems strange, to say the least, to understand Moses as having in view a second husband who divorces his new wife *before the consummation of the marriage*. The juxtaposition of the divorced woman with a widow suggests a similarity with Leviticus 21:7,14.

Thirdly, as we shall see when we come to consider Matthew 19:3-9, Jesus interpreted the Mosaic legislation as allowing the divorces of his (i.e. Moses') day, but also as actually permitting the men of his own day to put away their wives: 'Moses permitted you to divorce your wives because your hearts were hard' (verse 8). As against Dabney, we may thus say that Jesus understood the teaching of Moses to apply to divorce that took place after a marriage had been consummated.

The ritual of Numbers 5
Two important questions remain to be answered with respect to the meaning of the phrase *'erwat dābār*. Both questions concern the

position of a wife who had undergone the ritual prescribed in Numbers 5:11-31. It is assumed by Murray (1961) and Pink (p. 229) that divorce would not apply in a case where a husband suspected his wife of adultery, since the appropriate course of action would be to follow the procedure laid down in Numbers 5:11ff. However, questions which need to be asked, but which I have not seen addressed elsewhere, are these: might a wife who had been shown to be innocent be subsequently divorced, and might a husband divorce a wife who had been cursed as a result of the ritual? We shall consider each in turn.

Since the legislation contained no prohibition of a husband divorcing a wife who, having undergone this ritual, had been shown to be innocent, one may conclude that a husband who no longer found his wife attractive was not forbidden from divorcing her according to the procedure found in Deuteronomy 24:1. What he was not allowed to do was to divorce her on the basis of continuing suspicions of adultery after she had been exonerated of any such charge. Rather, he would be divorcing her because of the fact that he no longer found her to be attractive. The ritual would have removed the ground for jealousy but would not necessarily mean that the husband might not, at some subsequent point, wish to divorce his wife. The absence of any prohibition of his divorcing her after she had been proved innocent is not insignificant when placed alongside Deuteronomy 22:13-21. That passage also deals with a husband who makes an accusation against his wife, and sets out a procedure for establishing innocence or guilt. Where she is proved innocent, the husband is specifically forbidden from subsequently divorcing her (v.19e), for he has *falsely* accused her. But Numbers 5 contains no such prohibition. Is this not significant?

What if the ritual led to her coming under a curse? This is a difficult matter to determine. I have earlier referred to Wenham's (1981) view that the judgement found in verse 27 included barrenness of womb. Verse 28 appears to lend support to this interpretation. This being so, we may link this with Craigie's understanding of '*erwat dābār* as being a reference to a physical deficiency, such as the inability to bear children. (Craigie refers to a possible parallel found in an Old Assyrian marriage contract.) A number of important comments need to be made concerning this observation. Where a cursed wife was subsequently divorced, one is dealing with an adulteress who is divorced. It is not true, therefore, as many writers have sought to argue, that adulterers and adulteresses were always put to death under the old covenant. Nevertheless, the divorce would have been not on the specific ground of adultery but, rather, on the physical deficiencies or deformities of the wife, which resulted from the curse (see vv.21-22). Moreover, such a woman was not dealt with as an adulteress—although she was one—because to be treated as such by the Mosaic law required the evidence of the two witnesses and issued in the death penalty.

An analogy from English law may help to elucidate this point. It is quite common for the prosecuting authorities to decide against prosecuting an individual on the basis that the evidence against him is not strong enough, the standard of proof *in the case of a crime* being that the charge must be proved beyond all reasonable doubt. Or it may be that the individual is prosecuted but acquitted. However, since in *civil* proceedings the standard of proof is that something must be proved on a balance of probability, it is perfectly possible for someone to be ordered to pay compensation for an act that a criminal court has decided the individual was not proved guilty of committing. This is exactly what happened in the celebrated case, in the USA, of O. J. Simpson.

It is possible to argue that a husband had found his wife's adultery, exposed by the ritual of Numbers 5, to be 'something indecent' and thus a basis for divorcing her. There are, however, cogent reasons for believing that this was not the type of situation which Deuteronomy 24:1 was intended to deal with, even though it might be held to cover such a situation. Jesus specifically stated that the Mosaic legislation found in Deuteronomy 24:1-4 was necessitated by 'the hardness of your hearts' (Matt. 19:8). Mark, as well as Matthew, records these words of Christ. However, Matthew also refers to Joseph's decision to divorce Mary as being because he was a righteous man (Matt. 1:19). Significantly, the term for 'righteous' (*dikaios*) can connote faithfulness to one's covenant obligations. It would be unthinkable for Matthew to describe Joseph's decision to divorce his wife as being prompted by such covenant faithfulness if it was for the same kind of situation which Jesus said demonstrated the hardness of men's hearts. (I do not mean that *dikaios* always denotes covenant faithfulness. For a very good discussion

44

of 'righteousness' see Piper.) It would appear that the Mosaic law did not forbid a man to divorce his wife after she had been proved innocent according to the ritual found in Numbers 5, or after having been cursed by it. However, it appears reasonable to conclude that greater light is thrown upon the background to Deuteronomy 24:1 by Exodus 21:10-11 and by the type of situation envisaged in Malachi 2:11, 14-16, than by Numbers 5:11ff.

Before passing from Numbers 5, comment ought to be made on verse 28. This verse appears to lend support to the view that the curse would result in childlessness. In the light of Craigie's reference to an Old Assyrian marriage contract which appears to have regarded childlessness as a reason for divorce, it may be that barrenness was a species of the genus of the 'something indecent' to which Deuteronomy 24:1 refers.

At this point it should be noted that I take a very different view of the meaning of *'erwat dābār* from that expounded by Brewer (*Tyndale Bulletin* 47.1 [1996] pp. 1-25). He states:

> Divorce is specifically referred to in Deuteronomy 24:1-2 as the proper remedy when one's partner was unfaithful. This ground for divorce could only be applied to women, because the permissibility of polygamy meant that adultery by a man could not be a ground for divorce (p. 10).

Brewer is right in saying that adultery by a man with an unmarried woman could not be a ground of divorce because of the permissibility of polygamy. However, it is difficult to see how he can sustain the position that divorce was the proper remedy for the man where his wife proved to be unfaithful. If the act of adultery were witnessed by two witnesses, then the woman was to be executed. If such evidence were not forthcoming but the husband had his suspicions—perhaps as a result of being told by one witness or by two witnesses of having seen the wife in a compromising situation which fell short of adultery—then the appropriate course of action was for the woman to be subjected to the ritual of Numbers 5:11ff.

It is true that a tractate in the Mishnah, *Sotah*, deals in some detail with the ritual of Numbers 5, but—as Brewer himself notes—one must distinguish the Mosaic law from rabbinic comment and interpretation. *Sotah* addresses some interesting questions that arise from Numbers 5:11ff. but which are not considered in the passage. For example, what was to be the position where a woman admitted, en route to the place where the ritual would occur, that she had been guilty of adultery? What would be the position if she were unwilling to undergo the ritual? In both of these cases, the Mishnah prescribes that the husband shall divorce the wife.

While this provides important background to the situation that obtained while Christ was upon earth, and against which his teaching on divorce is to be understood, it is nevertheless important to stress that this was not the primary kind of situation envisaged in Deuteronomy 24:1. Fundamental to our Lord's teaching is the fact that Deuteronomy 24:1 was in the nature of a concession, made necessary on account of the hardness of heart (Matt. 19:8*a*; Mark 10:5). Christ contrasted his teaching with that of Moses. (The evidence and detailed argumentation for this last assertion will be found in the next chapter.) In both Matthew 5:32 and 19:9, Christ allows a man to divorce his wife where she has been guilty of *porneia*. (I am using the phrase 'allows a man to divorce his wife' in a very general way. I shall seek, in due course, to demonstrate that Jesus never set out to give grounds for divorce. Moreover, the meaning of *porneia* will be considered in the next chapter, as will the reason for the exception which Christ laid down.) This is stated to be the one exception: in all other situations Christ's teaching is that the divorce Moses legislated for would involve adultery. This must mean that divorce was allowed by Moses for reasons other than adultery and, this being so, it must follow that *'erwaṯ dāḇār* is not referring primarily to adultery.

The fact that the LXX translates *'erwaṯ dāḇār* by the words *aschēmon pragma* does not necessarily entail the belief that the phrase cannot be equivalent to, or be translated by, *porneia*. What is important to note is the fact that this is a very literal rendering of the phrase and preserves something of the difficulty that attaches to it. (I am grateful to Revd Philip Eveson for the observation that the LXX of the Pentateuch tends to be quite a literal translation.)

PART III

The New Testament Teaching

Chapter 3
The Teaching of
the Gospels

The teaching of Jesus on divorce has been interpreted in diverse ways within the Christian Church and has generated considerable controversy.[1] We are, indeed, walking through a minefield. This being so, there is wisdom in first taking a general 'aerial' view of the landscape of Christ's teaching, before beginning to pick our way carefully through the details. At the very least, we may establish areas of agreement between rival interpretations, and this may help us to consider the details—where disagreement often arises— with greater objectivity. Hopefully, this may promote clearer understanding of what Jesus taught.

General considerations and background

The specific teaching of Jesus on the subject of divorce is found in four passages of Scripture, all of which are in the Synoptic Gospels.[2] The passage in Mark 10 is parallel to that found in Matthew 19. Thus, there are three occasions when Jesus is recorded specifically as having given instruction on this matter. While there is other material in the Gospels that provides background to Christ's teaching, it will be useful, before considering that material, to note the general thrust of what he taught. The following points seem fairly clear.

Firstly, on no occasion did Jesus seek to set out grounds for divorce. Quite the contrary! His concern was to stress that divorce would, except in certain circumstances, involve adultery and should not take place save in those exceptional circumstances. Luke 16:18 is quite unequivocal on this point: 'Anyone who divorces his wife and marries another woman commits adultery, and the man who marries a divorced woman commits adultery.' Mark says pretty much the same (Mark 10:11-12). If, for the moment, we ignore the exceptions or 'exceptive clauses' found in Matthew's Gospel, we shall find that the teaching recorded there is virtually identical to that found in Luke and Mark. Thus, ignoring the exception, Matthew 5:32 reads as follows: 'But I tell you that anyone who divorces his wife causes her to become an adulteress, and anyone who marries the divorced woman commits adultery.' Likewise, if we ignore the exception, Matthew 19:9 reads as follows: 'I tell you that anyone who divorces his wife and marries another woman commits adultery.' Jesus' teaching is strongly 'anti-divorce' and 'pro-marriage'.[4]

Secondly, Jesus' teaching does contain an exception to his general teaching.[4] While the precise wording and import of the exceptions which Matthew records will be examined in detail later in this chapter, it is important to note, at this stage, that such exceptive clauses exist. As far as Christ's teaching is concerned, controversy mostly revolves around the understanding of these exceptions. At the risk of oversimplifying what is a complex debate, it may be said that one cluster of interpretations tends to ignore the exceptive material, or explain it away, or fit it into an already established interpretive grid; while in rival interpretations an opposite tendency may be discerned, namely, to emphasise the exceptive clauses. It is essential, therefore, that we treat individual passages as building blocks and thereby synthesise the biblical teaching. It may be that this will lead to a minimising of the diversity of interpretations.

Having said this, we need to note the third general consideration. This is that the exceptive material found in Matthew's Gospel is not put in the form of providing a ground for divorce, but constitutes an exception to Christ's teaching that the man who divorces his wife causes her to become an adulteress and will himself, should he remarry, be an adulterer.[5] Therefore, even when making an exception, Jesus does so in such a way as to demonstrate that his concern is with the fact that the man who divorces his wife thereby creates a situation that will involve adultery. The exception to that rule is where the wife has already, in some way, been unfaithful.[6] In such a case, the adultery has already taken place.

Christ's teaching ought not to be understood in a vacuum, but must be placed in the context in which it is found. We need to consider the general religious background against which his teaching is to be understood, as well as the specific context of those passages in which he deals with divorce. A number of areas need, therefore, to be considered. First, and by far the most important, is Jesus' attitude to the Old Testament in general, and to the Mosaic law in particular. The Gospels make it overwhelmingly clear that Jesus regarded the Old Testament, considered as a whole, as being the Word of God, and viewed its constituent parts—right down to the very words—as being spoken by God.[7] This being the case, Jesus treated the Old Testament as possessed of an inherent and unique authority.[8] Christ's view of the Old Testament means that he regarded traditions not found within the Old Testament itself—whether merely human traditions, or traditions which, it was claimed, stemmed from Moses—as not possessed of inherent authority. The value of any such tradition would always have to be considered in the light of the Old Testament.[9] Thus, in the Sermon on the Mount, Jesus is at pains to stress that his rejection of what had become traditionally accepted religious teaching did not mean that he had come to destroy the Law or the Prophets.[10] Accordingly, his teaching on divorce in Matthew 5:31-32 involves a rejection of the traditionally accepted position. If, therefore, we are to understand Christ's teaching aright, we must grasp what the traditionally accepted teaching was. However, more needs to be said concerning Christ's view of the Old Testament. For it is one thing to say that he accepted its divine origin, nature and authority, and that he had not come to destroy it, but we would be seriously mistaken if we were to assume that this means that he had come just to reaffirm the Old Testament teaching. As we shall see, the evidence is plain that he did not teach that it was to be applied after his coming in the same way as it had been before his advent.

Jesus' understanding of his relationship to the Old Testament is best understood by reference to his words in Matthew 5:17. He has come to fulfil the Law and the Prophets. This means that the Old Testament reaches its goal and climax in him and, as a consequence, its relevance and application undergo a profound change with his coming into the world.[11] That it is God's Word that he has come to *fulfil* means that there will be continuity between the New Testament and the Old Testament; that he fulfils the Old Testament inevitably means that there will also be discontinuity. Thus, we must avoid two common errors when considering the relationship of the Old Testament teaching on divorce to Christ's teaching on divorce. The first danger is so to stress the continuity that Jesus is regarded as doing little more than repeating the Old Testament teaching.[12] The other danger is to drive a wedge between the Old Testament and Christ, so that there are no connecting links between what he teaches and what the Old Testament teaches.[13] Both of these extremes are wrong and fail to perceive the complexity of the relationship between the two Testaments.

The question of Christ's view of the Old Testament naturally leads on to a consideration of the rabbinic disagreements concerning divorce. These also formed part of the background to the context in which Jesus' teaching must be understood.[14] Rabbinic debate centred on differing interpretations of the meaning of the words 'something indecent' in Deuteronomy 24:1. The school of Shammai taught that the words referred to unfaithfulness on the wife's part, while the school of Hillel interpreted the words much more widely, allowing a man to divorce his wife if she had spoiled a dish of food![15] There are good reasons for believing that Jesus did not approve of either of these approaches.[16]

If the Old Testament law and the rabbinic debates are two important elements in the background against which we must understand Christ's teaching, a third important fact to take into account is that Palestine was, at this period, an occupied territory, and the Jews were a subjugated people. This is a very important part of the background to the four Gospels, and lies behind a not inconsiderable amount of teaching found within them.[17] Its immediate relevance to the subject of divorce arises in connection with the penalties and punishments laid down in the Mosaic law for sexual sins. Could the Jews in Palestine implement these and, if they could, would they be implemented? The answers to both of these questions are important for an understanding of the historical context within which Jesus lived and taught, and are relevant to an understanding of the significance of some of his words. A number of complex issues are connected with these questions. There are good reasons for believing that, at the time when Jesus ministered, the death penalty could not be imposed for sexual sins, and that Jesus did not approve of the death penalty for such sins.[18]

It is essential for us to grasp both the historical context and the immediate and wider biblical context in which Jesus' teaching is found, in order to safeguard against the very real danger of making Christ's teaching on divorce answer questions which were not of immediate concern to him. Frequently, Christians have resorted to verses in the Gospels to find answers to questions such as the following: Did Jesus ever allow divorce and, if so, on what grounds? Did Jesus permit remarriage after divorce? These are, of course, burning questions upon which the Church of Christ needs to know the mind of her Master. However, they are *our* questions; examination of Christ's teaching may well demonstrate that they were not *his* questions. And if this proves to be the case, we shall inevitably go astray in our exegesis if we seek to make the relevant texts speak to issues that are outside their universe of discourse. This is not to say that we shall seal up our Lord's teaching as having relevance only to the situation in which he found himself. What it does mean is that we must first clarify what his teaching was, by setting it in its context. Once we have done this, we may then ask how his teaching—intended to deal with one set of questions—applies and relates to a different historical context and to *our* set of questions. With this in mind, we need now to turn to a consideration of the relevant texts.

Treatment of Jesus' teaching found in specific passages

Luke 16:18

There are at least three reasons why it is proper to consider this verse before looking at the material in Matthew and Mark. Firstly, the teaching found here is compressed into one verse and is, therefore, succinct. By contrast, Matthew 19:3-11 and Mark 10:2-12 are extended treatments of divorce and raise a number of other issues not found in Luke 16:18. Furthermore, those passages convey Christ's teaching as a response to a trap question set by the Pharisees and, as we shall see, Christ's teaching in those verses has to be considered in the light of the particular question with which he was faced. In Luke 16:18, however, his teaching is not conditioned by such a consideration. Secondly, while Matthew 5:31-32 is a fairly compressed statement, it contains an exception. There is real value in first ascertaining Jesus' teaching apart from any exceptions, so that we may be clear as to what it is that he is allowing as an exception. Thirdly, while Luke is evidently not the earliest

Gospel to be written, it was, it would seem, written for a Gentile Christian, Theophilus (1:3), with the aim of setting out the Church's belief concerning the acts and teachings of Jesus. As the gospel had penetrated into the Gentile world, here was the basis for the instruction that was given to Gentile Christians.

Context

Initially, it may seem that this verse bears no relationship to the surrounding verses. However, closer examination reveals that this verse fulfils a specific purpose by being placed where it is. After telling the Parable of the Shrewd Manager [or Unjust Steward] (16:1-12), Jesus goes on to explain that it is impossible to serve both God and money (v.13). This provokes something of a hostile reaction from the Pharisees because they loved money (v.14). Jesus then describes the Pharisees as those who justify themselves in the eyes of men. God, however, knows their hearts, and what is highly valued among men is detestable in God's sight (v.15). This point will be expounded and illustrated by Jesus in the story of the rich man and Lazarus (vv.19-31). Here is an example of a man who was rich (v.19; cf. v.14) and who was, presumably, highly valued among men (cf. v.15*b*). However, he finds himself rejected by God and in torments (vv.23-26). The life he has lived has brought him to this position and led to this judgement being passed on him (v.25; cf. v.15*b*). How might he have avoided ending in such a tragic way? In precisely the same way that his brothers may avoid the torments of Hades (v.28a). The way is set out in verse 29: they must heed Moses and the Prophets. Evidently, this is what the rich man had failed to do, and his plea in verse 30 suggests that his brothers are not heeding Moses and the Prophets either. This ties the story not only back to verses 14-15, but also to verses 16-17. The Pharisees, like the rich man, have had Moses ('the Law') and the Prophets. There is an inviolability to the Law (v.17), which means that to evade its teaching and demands—as the Pharisees were doing—will inevitably lead to one being rejected by God (v.15). This is precisely what had happened to the rich man.

Yet, while the Law is inviolable, this does not mean that it is permanent: the Law and the Prophets were *until* John.[19] Since John's day, the good news of the kingdom of God has been proclaimed and everyone has been pressing into it: that is, everyone but for the

54

Pharisees and their ilk. Thus, the poor man has entered, but the rich man has been excluded. Verses 16-17, particularly when read together with verses 29-31, indicate that one's attitude to the Law and the Prophets reveals what will be one's attitude to the kingdom of God. Clearly, if one has embraced the message of the Law and the Prophets—which has pointed forward to an eschatological reality—then it follows that one will embrace the reality which fulfils the Law and the Prophets. By the same token, rejection of the message of the eschatological kingdom demonstrates that one has never, at heart (v.15), embraced the message of the Law and the Prophets. Jesus uses precisely this argument elsewhere.[20] Thus, while ordinary people, and poverty-stricken people, were entering God's kingdom, the Pharisees were not; their attitude to the Law and the Prophets was all wrong, and thus they could not accept the message of the kingdom. All the while they were highly esteemed among men, but detestable in God's sight. Verses 16-17, therefore, fit very neatly between verse 15 and the story of the rich man and Lazarus (vv.19-31).

But what of verse 18, and the reference to divorce? If this verse were omitted, would not the story of the rich man and Lazarus follow on quite naturally from verse 17? How is the subject of divorce relevant at this point? The answer is that a number of links make this subject highly appropriate at this point. The first is a verbal link with the word 'detestable' in verse 15. There are clear echoes here of Deuteronomy 24:4.[21] According to this verse, it would be detestable before God for a woman, having been divorced and remarried, and then subsequently widowed or divorced, to be married again to her first husband. Having referred to the Pharisees as a group who were detestable before God, Jesus goes on to assert that their divorcing of their wives constituted adultery. It was not only their attitude to money that was offensive to God. Their divorce practice was equally offensive. Liefeld's comment on this verse is appropriate: 'This brief excerpt from Jesus' teaching on divorce and remarriage is included as an example of one aspect of the law the Pharisees tended to minimize.' Just as the rich man was representative of the Pharisees in their love of money and in their evasion of the challenge of the teaching of the Law and the Prophets, so their lax approach to divorce was also contrary to the demands of the Law and the Prophets.[22] And this was detestable before the Lord. Had they properly understood the teaching of the Law and the Prophets, they would then be prepared to accept the eschatological fulfilment of the Law and the Prophets in the kingdom of God. The ethic of the kingdom of God with respect to divorce is the teaching found in verse 18. Thus, Jesus' teaching on divorce not only links back to verse 15 and to the condemnation of the Pharisees, illustrated by the case of the rich man, but it also links in with the teaching found in verses 16-17 concerning the role of the Law and the Prophets and their relationship to the kingdom of God. In effect, Jesus is saying that the Pharisees have not adhered to the requirements of the Law and the Prophets in the matter of divorce, and in that, whatever men have thought of them, their behaviour is detestable to God. But now, even the concessions allowed by the Mosaic law will no longer apply, because of the coming of the kingdom. The coming of the kingdom will drastically alter the situation with respect to divorce. This is what verse 18 is concerned with, and it is to the exegesis of this verse that we must now turn.

Exegesis

Three questions need to be addressed at this point. What did Jesus say? What did he mean? Why did he say what he said?

The first question is easily answered. The NIV rendering is: 'Anyone who divorces his wife and marries another woman commits adultery, and the man who marries a divorced woman commits adultery.' The only possible alteration is in the second half of the sentence, which is rendered by the AV, for example, as follows: 'and whosoever marrieth her that is put away from [her] husband committeth adultery'. The slight variation, 'from [her] husband', is accounted for by different manuscript readings.[23] The meaning is unaffected, whichever reading is adopted, save that the longer reading seems to suggest that the woman referred to in verse 18*b* is the same as the woman in verse 18*a*.[24]

But what did Jesus mean? The question may appear to be somewhat superfluous, since the answer seems perfectly straightforward: any man who divorces his wife and marries another woman commits adultery, and whoever marries the woman divorced from her husband commits adultery. A moment's consideration, however, suggests a number of questions that indicate that, if straightforward, Jesus' words are disarmingly so; there is much more that lies beneath the surface. To begin with, why is there no mention of either of the two women involved committing adultery? What is the position of the woman who marries the man who divorces his wife, and what is the position of the woman who, having been divorced by her husband, then marries another man? Both women are evidently within the scope of the discussion, but nothing is said about either of them being guilty of adultery. Jesus, quite simply, does not address that question, and whatever inferences we may wish to draw, it remains a striking fact that he does not address it. Still more striking is the fact that in part *b* of the verse Jesus says that whoever marries a divorced woman commits adultery. Jesus does not specify that the man is himself married and is taking a second wife, or that he has himself been divorced. Accordingly, he may be a single man. He is singled out as being guilty of adultery, while the woman is passed over. This is surely significant and raises a number of important points.

Firstly, we must not regard individual sayings of Christ on divorce as setting out his comprehensive teaching on the subject. Consideration of Christ's teaching on divorce can easily be bedevilled by this false hermeneutical approach, which then requires us to twist other passages to fit into a doctrine of divorce that has been prematurely formulated on the basis of an individual text. Moreover, if we find that there are questions that Jesus did not address, it may be useful to ask why. In the present instance, there appears to be a perfectly straightforward answer. Jesus is pointing out that what is highly esteemed amongst men is detestable before God. What was detestable was the way in which men were adopting a cavalier approach to marriage and taking a lax view of divorce. Palestinian Judaism was very much a male-dominated society,[25] and Jesus is taking issue with this outrageous abuse of women, and doing so in the context of it being contrary to the Law and the Prophets, and to the kingdom of God which has now been inaugurated.[26] That is the specific focus of his concern, rather than publishing a manual on divorce. The men who were regarded—and who regarded themselves—so highly, were not so regarded by God; in his eyes they were adulterers.

Two further points need to be made. Firstly, Jesus is specifically dealing with a class or category of people: the Pharisees. Their whole approach to divorce was wrong, and Jesus is pronouncing a wholesale condemnation of their practice. Two things follow from this. The first is that we need to understand the absolutist nature of Jesus' remarks in their context. His teaching in this verse admits of no exceptions. Elsewhere, we may find that there are, or are not, exceptions to this absolutist teaching. What we must not do is to say that because this verse contains no exception, then there cannot be any. For Jesus is here addressing a specific evil, and that is the evil of which the Pharisees were guilty. The second thing that follows from the fact that Jesus is here making a wholesale condemnation of the Pharisaic practice of divorce concerns part *b* of the verse. I shall advance the thesis, and seek to elaborate and defend it further when considering the teaching in Matthew's Gospel, that Jesus redefined adultery. Behaviour that undermined or repudiated the sacred nature of the one-flesh union instituted in marriage in general, and in individual marriages in particular, constituted adultery. This follows from the fact that, as we have already argued in the notes to chapter two (see pp. 222-3), the one-flesh union was ruptured by divorce.[27] (This point will be developed further later in this chapter.) Consequently, the man who divorced his wife and married another woman was no longer one flesh with his first wife. If, according to a fairly widespread understanding, what constitutes adultery is for a *married* person in a one-flesh union to have sexual relations with a third party, then clearly the man in verse 18*a* cannot commit adultery, because he has *already* divorced his wife and severed the one-flesh union. This is probably why many consider the one-flesh union to be permanent and only broken by death. But we have already noted (see p. 46 and note 28, pp. 222-3), and will later demonstrate, that Jesus did not teach this. How, then, was the man of verse 18*b* guilty of adultery? The answer lies in the fact that Jesus is defining adultery in a broad way. The essence of the sin lies in the repudiation of marriages and in the repudiation of an individual marriage. This explains how the man in part *b* of the verse may be guilty of adultery even though he may never have been married before this point. He is part of the whole corrupt, male-dominated system.

The second point to be made about this verse concerns the fact that what was acceptable under the Mosaic law is not permissible within the kingdom of God. Under the Mosaic covenant, divorce followed by remarriage did not constitute adultery. In the kingdom of God, it does.

Finally, note should be taken of the fact that no mention is made of the certificate of divorce. This is a striking omission, given the fact that the Jews paid particular attention to it,[28] and that mention is made of it in each other account of Christ's teaching. The explanation is probably as follows. While the whole context in which the verse is found is thoroughly Jewish, Luke was not writing for a Jewish, but for a Gentile, audience. In particular, it appears that he approaches questions of Jewish law from the perspective that that law is no longer binding upon the Church of God.[29] Consequently, while he is eager to expound something of Christ's teaching on divorce which had passed into the teaching and experience of the Church, he does so without burdening the teaching with those accoutrements which were relevant only to Jews. Thus, the absence of reference to the certificate of divorce makes the theological point that Jesus' teaching, called forth in one context, is of relevance in other contexts. This is the rule of the kingdom of God.

In sum, therefore, Jesus is making a wholesale condemnation of the prevailing practice of divorce. He categorises both the man who divorces his wife and marries another woman, and the man who marries the divorced woman, as adulterers. Although this condemnation of divorce arose in the context of the prevailing Jewish practice, it is the basis for the things which Theophilus has been taught and is relevant in a Gentile and, therefore, a wider context (1:4). The strongly absolutist nature of the teaching here does not necessarily entail the proposition that for a man to divorce and remarry, or for a man to marry a divorced woman, will always constitute him an adulterer. However, whether any such exception to the strongly absolutist teaching found in Luke 16:18 is to be allowed will depend upon whether Jesus himself admitted any exception.[30] This inevitably leads us to the material found in Matthew's Gospel, and to this we must now turn.

Matthew 5: 31-32

Context

These verses occur in what is commonly called 'The Sermon on the Mount'. Volumes have been written on these three chapters of

Scripture; it will be necessary to confine our comments to a few brief remarks. Firstly, running through the Sermon is an exposition of the nature of life in the kingdom of God, in contrast to the Pharisaic and scribal misunderstanding of it which was current in Jesus' day.[31] Secondly, Jesus fulfils the Old Testament Scriptures, and life in the kingdom is therefore inextricably linked to one's relationship to him.[32] Jesus' teaching in this sermon is set very much in the context of his time, but *the Sermon itself* contains indicators that Jesus is looking further ahead and that the teaching he lays down is intended for future generations also.[33] The foregoing points entail the proposition that there will be both continuity and discontinuity between the Old Testament and Jesus' teaching.[34] Thus, while it is true that Jesus contrasts his teaching with the misunderstandings of the Old Testament which were current in his day, it is also the case that there will be significant differences between his teaching and that of the Old Testament.[35]

Matthew 5:21-48 consists of a series of contrasts or antitheses between the scribal and Pharisaic misunderstanding of the Mosaic law and the true meaning of it. In particular, Jesus appeals to his own authority in describing the kind of life that will be lived by the citizens of the kingdom of heaven.[36] A number of common threads seem to run through the misunderstanding that characterised the scribes and Pharisees. Evidently, they were concerned with legal correctness and, therefore, with an external compliance to the law of Moses. One must not commit the act of murder; one must not commit the act of adultery; one must ensure that a proper certificate of divorce is given; one must ensure that oaths are kept; justice must be exact (v.38), and one must make sure that neighbours are loved and that enemies are hated. By contrast, Jesus is less concerned with being on the right side of an external law, but much more concerned with being right in one's whole attitude before God. Of course, the scribes and Pharisees would say that the way to achieve this would be by being legally correct. But that is precisely Jesus' point. First, the scribes and Pharisees had mangled the law into something that they could quite easily obey by limiting its demands to external matters. Accordingly, the real meaning of the law needed to be reasserted. Secondly, the law was eschatological and found its fulfilment in Christ. Righteousness was therefore inextricably linked to him and his accomplishment, and would lead on to a life that would express the demands and values of the kingdom of heaven. One thing that characterises the kingdom is that Jesus' disciples are not to ride roughshod over, or be vindictive towards, the 'wrong sort of people'. Reconciliation must be effected with offended brothers, and wrongs must be righted with adversaries (vv.23-26); enemies are not to be hated (v.43), nor is one to do the bare minimum when commandeered by Roman officials (v.41).[37] It is in this kingdom context that Jesus' words concerning divorce are to be understood.

It is quite clear that verses 31-32 are a continuation of verses 27-30. Two features of verses 27-32 demonstrate this. Firstly, verses 27-30 are concerned with adultery and how to avoid committing it. Verse 32 links divorce with adultery. Verse 28 says that adultery may be committed by a look. Verse 32 declares that adultery can be committed by the giving of a divorce certificate. Secondly, the introductory formula to verse 31 differs from the words of introduction to every other pair of antitheses in verses 21-48.[38] Although verse 31 introduces the subject of divorce, Jesus has not yet finished with his treatment of adultery. Accordingly, before we turn to verses 31-32, a number of comments need to be made on verses 27-30.

The first thing to note is that Jesus is dealing with sin committed by men rather than women: it is the man who looks lustfully at a woman who has committed adultery with her in his heart.[39] In verses 27-30, the woman is a passive victim of the rapacious look of the man. Secondly, nothing is said of the marital status of either the man or the woman. It is 'whoever looks'[40] on a woman[41] with lust who has already committed adultery with her in his heart. Jesus is, therefore, giving a radically new definition of adultery. There is such a thing as 'heart adultery'. At this stage, the woman is simply an object—a victim, one may say—of the man's lustful look. He has committed adultery with her in his heart. If we follow through on the definition of adultery which we inferred from our treatment of Luke 16:18, we may say that what the man is doing is contrary to the divine institution of marriage. God has ordained that sexual desire be fulfilled *within* marriage, but the man Jesus describes is, in his heart, sexually desirous of the woman *outside of* marriage. It is in this that the sin of adultery consists, not simply in the act of intercourse between someone who is already in a one-flesh union with a spouse and another party. That is an example of adultery, but it does not exhaust the definition. The point of verses 29-30 is that this heart adultery may so easily lead on to the act of sexual intercourse with one who is not one's spouse, and even with one who is the spouse of another. As we have seen, rabbinic Judaism did not regard the act of sexual intercourse between a married man and a single woman as adultery; but if the woman was married, then *she* was guilty of adultery, whatever the marital status of the man. It is clear that Jesus is here probing and exposing the nauseating hypocrisy of his day. Evidently, visual lust or illicit desire was very much a male sin. (It still is! Tabloid newspapers know this well, which is why they have nude women photographed, but not nude men.) Contrary to the prevailing view of his day, Jesus describes men as adulterers, but passes over the women. Where illicit physical relationships take place, it would seem from verses 27-30 that Jesus is regarding these as usually the result of male desire.[42]

It may be objected that the logic of the interpretation offered of these verses would demand that one regard as an adulterer an unmarried man who sexually desires an unmarried woman, and restrains himself from any physical sexual contact until they are both married, though he longs for the consummation of their relationship in sexual union. Would this not be a *reductio ad absurdum*? The simple answer is that Jesus is not entering into a casuistical analysis of the kind that asks, When is adultery not adultery? but is exposing a vice that was prevalent in his day, as it still is. Simply to look at a woman to lust after her is, in effect, a denial of God's ordinance of marriage. There is no knowing where such lust may lead and what tragedy it may entail. It is simply not the case that Jesus is here dealing with the battles which courting couples may have with their emotions. To try to undermine the case that has thus far been presented by an appeal to such a *reductio ad absurdum* is ruthlessly to lift Christ's words from their context.

As we saw in Luke 16:18, it is evident that Jesus was concerned with male sexual exploitation of women, especially when it hid under the pretence of conformity to the Mosaic law. That was exactly the evil that was addressed in Luke 16:18, and it is the evil that is addressed in Matthew 5:27-29. It is that evil that is the immediate context to verses 31-32, and it is now time for us to turn to these verses.

Text

The only textual issue that needs to be addressed arises from the fact that certain manuscripts lack the words, 'and anyone who marries the divorced woman commits adultery'. Both AV and NIV have the words, and it is noteworthy that NIV makes no reference in its footnotes to the presence of the shorter reading. The reason for this is that the longer reading is so well attested and that there is no strong argument for accepting the shorter reading. Accordingly, the text underlying the AV and NIV should be accepted as authentic.[43]

Exegesis

As we have seen (see note 38), the presence of the particle *de* links these verses with the immediately preceding verses, and yet indicates that something new is being considered.[44] What Jesus is about to deal with is related to the question of adultery. It is specified in verse 31: divorce.[45] The traditionally accepted teaching, in antithesis to which Jesus will set his own teaching, is summarised in verse 31: 'whoever puts away his wife must give her a certificate of divorce'. Three features stand out in this verse. Firstly, we are still in the realm of male dominance: it is the *man* who is putting away his wife. Secondly, there is no mention of any reason as to why she is being put away. Thirdly, the one thing needful when putting away one's wife is that she be given a certificate of divorce. From these three features a number of things may be inferred. We may infer that the traditionally accepted teaching was concerned not so much with the rightness of divorce as with simply carrying out the right procedure.[46] Moreover, it would appear that the purpose of the legislation found in Deuteronomy 24:1-4 had been buried under a concern with procedural minutiae. We may also be tempted to infer that divorces were being effected unilaterally by men, without the women having any say. However, it may well be the case that the men were treating their wives in such a way that the wives were requesting divorce. The men were not really concerned about the behaviour that was leading to this request but with the need to ensure that legal technicalities were then observed.[47] This approach had become acceptable to the people of Jesus' day.

In verse 32 Jesus advances his own teaching *in contrast to that found in verse 31.* The particle *de* in this verse is adversative and is employed to point the contrast between verses 31 and 32. It will be useful initially to omit the exceptive words in this verse and, once we have grasped the overriding impact of Jesus' teaching, to study what he meant by his words of exception.

The first important feature to observe is that Jesus is clearly describing the woman as something of a victim. Two elements of verse 32*b* make this clear. First, it is the man who *makes* her to become an adulteress.[48] Secondly, the words translated 'to become an adulteress' (NIV) or 'to commit adultery' (AV) are in the passive voice in the Greek.[49] The latter part of the verse—'and anyone who marries the divorced woman commits adultery' (NIV)—has the words 'commits adultery' in the middle voice, and here the words in the middle voice must bear an active meaning.[50] The effect of the passive is that the woman is made to suffer the repudiation of her marriage: this is what is meant by her being made to suffer adultery, while the man who subsequently marries her is himself implicated in the undermining and repudiation of her first marriage or of the institution of marriage.[51]

However, Jesus makes an exception to the principle that her first husband caused her to suffer adultery: 'except for marital unfaithfulness' (NIV); 'saving for the cause of fornication' (AV). Two issues must be addressed: what do these words mean, and why are they in the verse? Each question is crucial to a proper understanding of Christ's teaching on divorce.

There are two aspects to the first question. What do the words 'except for' mean, and what does 'marital unfaithfulness' denote? Various meanings have been assigned to the words 'except for', but there is no good reason for changing from the meaning assigned by AV and NIV.[52] However, the word translated 'marital unfaithfulness' has generated considerable diversity of opinion. At least four different understandings of the term may be seriously argued for. Some of these understandings can be further subdivided.

The first influential line of interpretation contends that *porneia*, the Greek word that is used, refers to unlawful marriages. There are two forms of this understanding: the 'rabbinic view', and the 'mixed marriages view'. The rabbinic view understood *porneia* to denote marriage within the prohibited degrees found in Leviticus 18:6-18, whereas the mixed marriage interpretation understands the term to denote the marriage of a Jew to a Gentile.

Another interpretation argues that the word refers to a betrothed person having sexual relations with a third party before marriage. This would be similar to what Joseph must have assumed had happened with Mary.

A third understanding equates the word with the 'something indecent' of Deuteronomy 24:1. This interpretation further divides three ways. Some argue that the reference in Deuteronomy 24:1 was to something similar to our 'unreasonable behaviour', and that Jesus was endorsing this as justification for divorce. Others understand the term in Deuteronomy 24:1 to refer to sexual unfaithfulness of some kind, and that Jesus is therefore endorsing this as a justification for divorce. A third group—understanding the term in the same way—go on to argue for a preteritive view of Jesus' words: 'sexual unfaithfulness notwithstanding'.

The fourth view—and the one I believe to be correct—is that Jesus is not endorsing Deuteronomy 24:1 at all. Rather, he is referring to sexual misconduct, and such misconduct is an exception to the principle that a man who puts away his wife causes her to suffer adultery and the man who marries her commits adultery.[53]

Clearly, the meaning of this term is crucial, but assessment of the merits of the differing understandings involves a fair amount of technical discussion, and the reader is therefore referred to the Excursus at the end of this chapter. Jesus is saying that whoever puts away his wife, except in the situation where she has been guilty of illicit sexual intercourse, causes her to suffer adultery. The exception is a real exception, and illicit sexual intercourse may be understood to cover the kinds of situations dealt with in Leviticus 18. Thus homosexuality and bestiality would be covered. In saying this, I do not mean that such sins were being committed by the people of Jesus' day; rather, sexual infidelity is a general category that would include the kinds of behaviour condemned in Leviticus 18.

Before drawing inferences and conclusions from this verse, we need to address the second question that arises, which is this: why did Jesus allow this exception? It is important to state the question precisely in these terms, and not in the terms in which it is sometimes expressed. Not infrequently the question is posed thus: why does Matthew include exceptive words in his Gospel? Such a question may be perfectly acceptable. The Gospel writers evidently wrote with different purposes in mind, and arranged their material to suit their particular purpose or purposes. A comparison of Luke 1:1-4 with John 20:30-31 demonstrates that these two writers had different purposes in view. Luke was aware of existing material, and clearly both Luke and John included material not found in the other Gospels and excluded material that is found elsewhere. Similarly John tells us that he omitted material which did not suit his purpose. The orthodox doctrine of Scripture, that the Bible is God's inspired Word, is perfectly consistent with the fact that the human authors' personalities and purposes were involved in the writing of Scripture.[54] Moreover, it is indisputable that the Evangelists sometimes used their own words in reporting sayings of Jesus. The very fact that Jesus would have preached in Aramaic but the Gospels are written in Greek made this necessary. This may then mean that the choice of one Greek word, instead of another that could equally well have translated the Aramaic, may be used to bring out a particular emphasis that suits the Evangelist's purpose.

All of this is perfectly acceptable. But not infrequently more lies behind the question, Why did Matthew write the exceptive words? One or both of two beliefs may lie behind that question. The first is that Luke and Mark record the *real* teaching of Jesus, as opposed to Matthew's gloss upon it. What this means, of course, is that one is being selective with the text of Scripture. From Luke and Mark one constructs Christ's teaching on divorce. Matthew's exceptive words do not readily fit with that teaching. Accordingly, one looks for reasons for Matthew's addition of the exceptive words. Methodologically, one could with equal justification construct Christ's divorce teaching from Matthew and then ask why Mark and Luke omit the exceptive words. If it be replied that Mark and Luke are consistent with each other but that Matthew is the joker in the pack, the response must be as follows. Matthew has more to say about divorce than Mark and Luke, and it may be that methodologically it is safer to begin with Matthew and then consider Mark and Luke. Secondly, if this argument were accepted, we should end up approving the approach characteristic of a certain type of liberalism that routinely regarded John as unhistorical because it is so different from the Synoptic Gospels.

The second belief that lies behind the question, Why does

Matthew include these words? actually obtrudes through the question: they are *Matthew*'s words, not Christ's. While accepting that the Gospel writers may use their own language to record teaching, I believe Murray is wholly right to regard the belief that the words are Matthean additions to be inconsistent with the orthodox doctrine of Scripture. There are many reasons why this belief is unnecessary, unacceptable, and mistaken.[55] One is accustomed to theological liberals saying that the teaching in one Gospel contradicts that found in another, and that therefore only one—if either—accurately reports Christ's teaching. But for evangelicals to resort to such a methodology to harmonise accounts is a counsel of despair. Of course, it may be said that Matthew is simply clarifying Christ's teaching for a different type of situation. Quite apart from the dubiety of such an argument, what is wrong with this approach is that one is already committed to an understanding of Christ's teaching without considering all the data. Christ's words must be allowed to stand within Matthew's Gospel, and it must be determined what purpose they serve *there*. Then, when all the Gospel material has been considered, we must seek to find out the reasons for differences between the Gospels. Instead of this approach, a very different one is adopted. Because the exceptive clause is not found in either Mark or Luke, it is assumed that Matthew has, for his own reasons, softened the original absolutism of our Lord's pronouncements on divorce. This approach is *forced* to find reasons for the exceptive clause, and then downplays the effect of that clause because it is not found in Mark and Luke. It is, therefore, a case of being selective with the data, or at least giving greater weight to the sayings on divorce as recorded in those two Gospels. I shall resist the temptation to charge those so guilty with having an agenda to work to and a case to prove!

To return, then, to the question, Why are these words of exception uttered by Christ? What purpose do they serve? It seems obvious and almost tautologous to say that Jesus intended them to be understood as an exception to the principle he enunciates in verse 32. After all, it would appear to be fairly obvious that if a man discovers that his wife has slept with a lot of different men in the previous six months, he is hardly making her suffer, or commit, adultery if he divorces her. He has not made her do what she has freely chosen to do. The exceptive words hardly seem necessary. Yet the very fact that many Christian writers *do* believe in the illegitimacy of divorce suggests that this is not so obvious to everyone and that these exceptive words are all-important. Moreover, it is important to remember the context of Christ's words. He is contrasting the righteousness of the kingdom with that of the Pharisees. Divorce was a reality in Jesus' world. He condemns the practice that prevailed as involving adultery. This is undoubtedly the general picture. However, he does not mean to burden the conscience of a disciple who discovers that his wife is sexually unfaithful. Jesus is giving instruction to his disciples, and he means them to live very differently from the Pharisees (Matt. 5:1,20). Since the Pharisees and teachers of the law appear to have had a lax approach to divorce, Jesus sets the standard of the kingdom in contradistinction to that lax view. However, he did not mean them to understand that a divorce for a reason other than that generally countenanced by the Pharisees, that is, a divorce where the wife had been guilty of *porneia*, came under his condemnation.

The importance of this is twofold. Firstly, there is rabbinic evidence that a man who knew his wife to be guilty of adultery *had* to divorce her.[56] Jesus certainly does not command such action to be taken, nor does he frame his teaching simply to suit existing practices. On the contrary, much of the Sermon on the Mount is quite antithetical to accepted Jewish ideas of the time. Moreover, Christ's repeated words, 'But I tell you', underline the fact that he was teaching by his own authority and not with reference to the teaching of others. This must mean that he really believed and taught that divorce for *porneia* would not involve the divorcing husband in causing his wife to suffer adultery. Accordingly, at one level, he was not disapproving of a disciple who, according to the custom of the time, divorced a wife guilty of *porneia*. But at another level, it may be said that Jesus is subverting that practice: for that practice was adhered to *in terms of the Old Testament*. As we have seen earlier, and we shall see this again in Matthew 19 (and the point will be developed in the Excursus to this chapter), Jesus is not approving of the divorce that was tolerated by Deuteronomy 24:1. Therefore he is not endorsing an interpretation of the 'indecent thing' as including a wife's *porneia*.

Superficially, therefore, Jesus' teaching in Matthew 5:32 would not have been *perceived at the time* to be exceptionable or revolutionary. His Jewish hearers would probably have lined him up on this issue with Shammai and assumed that the exception covered the case where a man was expected to put away his wife. But those with eyes to see beneath the surface of his words would realise that Jesus was not endorsing Shammai but setting up his own teaching as the eschatological fulfilment of the Law and the Prophets. When the last vestiges of the old theocracy and old order had passed away, Christ's disciples would know that though the provision contained within the Mosaic covenant for dealing with the sexual sins of a wife no longer existed, there was provision in the kingdom of God for someone who found it intolerable to continue in a marriage to a woman who had been guilty of sexual infidelity. He could divorce her.

This understanding of the purpose of the exceptive words in Matthew 5:32 fits both the immediate context and the longer-range view which, we have seen, is not entirely excluded from the Sermon. It is to be preferred to two other explanations that are regularly given. The first explanation is that this was to relieve the consciences of Jewish Christians who were compelled by their Jewish community to divorce their wives who were guilty of *porneia*, but felt unable to do so because of Christ's prohibition of divorce. The exceptive words allowed them to deal with this situation. Needless to say, this explanation tends to be tied to a belief that the words are Matthew's and not Christ's, and it is built upon an understanding of Jesus' teaching on divorce gathered chiefly from Mark and Luke. The criticisms already made of those foundational beliefs obviously apply to the superstructure built thereon. Moreover, the belief that Jesus trimmed his teaching to suit the Jewish beliefs of the time can only be seriously and consistently held by those who *mis*read the Gospels. That evangelicals have sometimes overemphasised the differences between Jesus and his Jewish culture cannot be denied, and the trend of the last twenty-five years to understand Jesus in his Jewish context is obviously right and important. But it surely is to ignore large chunks of the Gospels to say that Jesus accommodated his teaching to suit prevailing Jewish thinking and belief.

The second explanation of the purpose of Christ's words maintains that Jesus was substituting divorce for the death penalty. This explanation has the merit of emphasising the discontinuity motif found in Matthew 5:17-20, although it has to be added that those who hold this view think more in terms of *abrogation* than of eschatological fulfilment, and approach the continuity/discontinuity tension in terms of an anachronistic classification of the Law into moral/ceremonial/civil categories.[57] The inadequacy of this explanation lies in its failure to understand the historical context in which Jesus ministered. We have already seen in the previous chapter and in the notes to that chapter that, in general, the Old Testament had very strict procedural requirements for the implementation of the death penalty, and that there were specific requirements where that penalty was to be exacted for sexual sin. The Mishnaic tract *Sotah* had considerably developed some of these requirements, and it was against this background that Jesus ministered. Furthermore, we have seen that there is good evidence to believe that the Jews could not, at this stage in their history, exact the death penalty for sexual sin. As a subjugated people, this would have been tantamount to treason.

Accordingly, if we are to make sense of Jesus' teaching, it has to be by understanding it in the context of his day. The Qumran community had, of course, opted out of the Jewish society of the day, and evidently regarded the situation as so corrupt as to merit divine judgement. Accordingly, they awaited divine vindication, when the proper order of things would be established. By contrast, Jesus functioned within the Jewish society of his day. Yet he too believed and taught that judgement would fall on the Temple, on Jerusalem, and therefore upon the whole Jewish religious set-up. However, because he was the eschatological fulfilment of the Law and the Prophets, his perspective upon the society of his day, its need and the divine remedy, was fundamentally different from that of the Qumran community. Accordingly, we should not understand the exceptive words as effectively endorsing the Old Testament moral law but abrogating the civil law. Rather, we should understand that Jesus is declaring himself to be the eschatological fulfilment of the Old Testament, and therefore many of its standards and structures will undergo profound transformation. Thus, he is not so much abrogating the death penalty for sexual sin, as implicitly saying that that whole order—which, as a result of Roman domination, had begun to break down—would, because Jesus was its fulfilment, pass away.

We may now draw some provisional conclusions from Jesus'

teaching in Matthew 5:32. Divorce was obviously outlawed by Jesus because of the adultery that would thereby be entailed. Since adultery is sin and is contrary to the kingdom of God, it follows that divorce is likewise against the righteousness of God's kingdom and is therefore forbidden. However, since adultery is not entailed by the husband divorcing his wife for *porneia*, such a divorce is not, per se, contrary to the righteousness of the kingdom of God. That being so, it is not forbidden. Jesus does not command it, nor does he commend it. But he does not forbid it. And since the ethics of the kingdom are the very highest, we should not see Christ's non-prohibition of it as on a par with the Mosaic concession of divorce. Jesus' permission of divorce is *not* a concession to any hardness of heart on the part of the divorcing party. Consequently, although Jesus is *not* setting out to give grounds for divorce, one is warranted in inferring from his words that a husband may divorce his wife where—but only where—she has been guilty of *porneia*: that is, of illicit sexual intercourse. This amounts, therefore, to a ground of divorce.

More controversially, we are warranted in saying that the divorce envisaged by Jesus would have the same consequences as that envisaged by his hearers and contemporaries. Clearly, Jesus is making a wholesale attack upon the prevailing Jewish practice of divorce. But he is *not*—contrary to many who teach otherwise—attacking the Jewish *concept* of divorce. We shall see later that the relationship between the New Testament and the Old Testament is far more complex—one might almost say, subtle—than is often realised. There *is* continuity as well as discontinuity, and it is imperative that we do not seek to squeeze the nature of the inter-relationship of the two Testaments into a mould that is exclusively continuous or discontinuous. The prevailing Jewish understanding of the *effects* of divorce was in line with that of the Old Testament. We have already noted (and I shall seek to demonstrate in due course) that the argument that remarriage after divorce always involved abnormality, because the one-flesh union of the first marriage persisted until death, is mistaken. Divorce ended the marriage, and the divorced woman was free to remarry, as was the divorced man. Jesus has declared that such divorce is unjustifiable, and because it amounts to an unjustifiable repudiation of the marriage it entails adultery. But it is not unjustifiable where the wife

71

has been guilty of sexual sin. That being so, the marriage is ended, but *not* unjustifiably. It is true that Jesus does not consider the question of remarriage. But within the terms of his discourse, there is no reason to question the fact that the husband, no longer being one flesh with the divorced wife, and not being guilty for having ended the marriage, was free to remarry. There can be little doubt that our Lord's hearers would have understood him as permitting remarriage in such circumstances.

Writers who endorse a 'no remarriage' position simply fail to understand Matthew 5:32 in its context. Of course, those who argue that the main burden and thrust of Jesus' teaching in this verse is to allow a man who divorces his wife for illicit sexual intercourse to remarry, also misunderstand the verse. Jesus is teaching that for men to divorce their wives always entails adultery *except* in one situation. However, from that teaching it may be legitimately inferred that such a man may remarry if he is in that situation. The 'no remarriage' view entails the understanding that the verb *apolyō* is being used differently in verses 31 and 32, and that we are supposed to understand this. In the Jewish context in which the Sermon was preached, the divorce referred to in verse 32 would have had to be effected by the giving of the certificate of divorce. Jesus is saying that this will entail adultery, *except* where there has been *porneia*. In other words, the technical requirement of the giving of the certificate could not prevent the husband from causing her to suffer adultery, except where she was already guilty of *porneia*. The point is that, in that specific case, the giving of the certificate would have effected the divorce, and *in that situation*, given Christ's exceptive words, there is no reason to doubt that the certificate had ended the marriage. The husband is now free to remarry if he so desires. In fact there is every reason to expect him to do so.

Two things are not addressed in this verse and, at this stage, inferences cannot therefore be drawn about them. The first concerns whether the woman divorced for *porneia* might remarry. Jesus does not address this issue. It was the rabbinic understanding that she was denied to her paramour.[58] There is nothing to indicate Jesus' view of this, though in the absence of evidence to the contrary it might be assumed that he agreed with this. But a definite view on this question cannot be formed at this stage of the -

investigation. Secondly, Jesus does not address the evidential requirements to justify a husband in his belief of his wife's *porneia*.

We have devoted a considerable amount of space to the meaning of verse 32, and particularly to the exceptive words. It has been essential to do this because it is the exceptive words that generate a great deal of controversy. Moreover, it has been necessary to consider the exceptive phrase in some depth before considering the exceptive words in Matthew 19:9. Dispute has raged over the meaning and application of the exceptive words in this verse. However, it has not always been sufficiently realised by those who take opposite views of the matter, that the question of the rightness of remarriage after divorce for *porneia* is not to be decided exclusively by the syntax of the exceptive words in Matthew 19:9. This question has to be considered in the light of what Jesus understood to be the effects of divorce. Although we shall exegete Matthew 19 in its own terms and context, one test of the rightness of that exegesis will be that it can be properly harmonised with Luke 16:18, Mark 10:2-12, *and with Matthew 5:32*. With these thoughts in mind, it is time to consider the largest unit of Jesus' teaching on divorce: Matthew 19:1-12, and Mark 10:1-12.

Matthew 19:1-12; Mark 10:1-12

Both of these passages are evidently recording the same incident and conversation. However, there are significant differences between the two accounts. It is important to note that there are quite a number of differences. Too frequently, attention has fallen upon the fact that Matthew has an exceptive clause which is missing from Mark. Different explanations are then sought for this difference, and the differing explanations tend to be related to the different views that are taken of divorce. A better way of dealing with the differences would be to exegete each passage and then to attempt to give a coherent explanation for *all* the differences between the passages. Although it is not intended at this point to foreclose the issues, it is worth observing that it may be found that the differences touch larger issues than that of divorce. If we ask the wrong questions of the text, it follows that we will get wrong answers and may well be guilty of forcing Scripture to fit our own agenda.

In view of the above, we shall first consider Matthew's teaching, and seek to draw some inferences from it. We shall then do the same with Mark and, having done so, address the differences between the two accounts and consider whether provisional conclusions need to be amended. When all has been done, we shall seek to integrate *all* the Gospel material upon the subject and to draw firm conclusions as to Jesus' teaching on the subject of divorce. In view of the widely accepted view of Marcan priority, it might be thought that the material in Mark should be considered *before* Matthew. However, as we have just dealt with the material in Matthew 5, it is preferable to consider Matthew 19 before Mark. Furthermore, when we come to consider Mark 10, we shall find that he has condensed the conversation between the Pharisees and Jesus. This being so, it is better to begin by studying the fuller account in Matthew.

Matthew 19:1-12

Context

The passage begins by informing us, 'When Jesus had finished saying these things, he left Galilee and went into the region of Judea to the other side of the Jordan.' Thus Matthew introduces this account by telling us two things: *when* it occurred and *where* it occurred. It occurred 'when Jesus had finished saying these things'.[59] Matthew repeats this phrase, or a phrase similar to it, on numerous occasions to mark the end of a unit of teaching given by Jesus.[60] However, we are not to think that what follows is necessarily sealed off from the unit of teaching which has just been completed. The unit of teaching will be distinct from, but not necessarily unrelated to, the events that follow. In the present case, it will be seen that there are some fairly important lines of connection between Matthew 19:1-12 and what has preceded this passage. Chapter 18 contains teaching given by Jesus in response to two questions. In verses 2-20 we have Jesus' response to the question, 'Who is the greatest in the kingdom of heaven?' while verses 22-35 are a response to Peter's question, 'Lord, how many times shall I forgive my brother when he sins against me? Up to seven times?'

In reply to the disciples' first question, Jesus takes a little child as an illustration of the need for a spirit of humble dependence instead of arrogant self-assertion (vv.2-4). Such a spirit will be

expressed in the welcome given in Christ's name to a little child
(v.5). The significance of this, of course, lies in the fact that many of
Jesus' contemporaries would have tended to despise little children.[61] Indeed, there are indications that Jesus' disciples were still
somewhat of this outlook.[62] The fact that Jesus regarded such
children as important leads on to his solemn warnings against leading such little ones who believe in him to sin (vv.6-10). In this connection, Jesus sets forth the need for an uncompromising attitude
to sin within oneself, illustrating this by the graphic portrayal of the
need to cut off the offending hand or foot and to pluck out the
offending eye. We have here, of course, the same illustrations that
he has already used in the Sermon on the Mount, in the very section where he has dealt with adultery and divorce (5:29-30). We
have already seen that Luke and Matthew have emphasised the
fact that Jesus is condemning a practice which effectively devalued
and downgraded women. Likewise, in this passage Jesus is challenging the view that regarded children as of little consequence.
Jesus goes on to illustrate this truth with a story about the lost
sheep. One lost sheep may appear to be of less value than ninety-
nine sheep that are accounted for. However, no farmer would think
like that, but would leave the ninety-nine for the one lost sheep.
The effort expended by the farmer conferred significance on the
sheep, and, at the same time, the significance of the sheep to the
farmer was the reason that he expended the effort. Jesus draws the
lesson from this in verse 14: if individuals matter so much to our
heavenly Father, then it ill behoves us to treat individuals shoddily
or lead them into sin.

This last point is then developed and applied in verses 15-20 in a
particularly challenging way. Jesus is dealing with the situation
where a brother has sinned against us. What he says is that every
effort must be made *both* to restore the offending brother *and* to
restore the damaged relationship. Indeed, the two belong together.
Jesus goes on to consider the possibility that such efforts will be to
no avail. In such a case, the offending brother is no longer to be
regarded as a brother but as someone outside the Christian community. This section is, of course, famous for the fact that it is one of
the two occasions when Jesus refers to 'the church'. What may be
gathered from this is that although he is addressing an immediate
situation, he is also looking further ahead to the time when the

church will have an identity distinct from the structures of Judaism. In this connection, verses 16-17 are a fascinating example of the way in which the 'continuity/discontinuity' motifs are treated in Scripture. Verse 16 contains a quotation from Deuteronomy 19:15. The following verses in Deuteronomy 19 clearly set this requirement in something of a judicial context. As we have previously seen, Jesus was happy to function in a context where the theocracy had broken down. Moreover, he taught that he was the eschatological fulfilment of the Law and the Prophets. The fact that in Matthew 18:17 Jesus refers to the church provides eloquent testimony to this fulfilment motif. However, there is place within this eschatological community for provisions that applied to the Old Testament theocratic community of God's people. Clearly, while the church is exercising what might be termed a judicial function in verse 17, it is not judicial in the sense in which Deuteronomy 19:15 is judicial, nor could it be judicial outside of the theocracy. This is a good example of the way in which the New Testament fulfilment of Old Testament teaching and institutions is far more nuanced than is allowed for by a straight line of continuity or a simple break of discontinuity.

In view of the teaching given by Jesus in this section, it is not surprising that Peter poses the question that he does in verse 21. Jesus goes on to explain that our forgiveness should know no limits. In the light of verses 15-18, it is clear that the expression and bestowing of forgiveness can only take place where repentance is expressed. Jesus then tells an unforgettable parable that elucidates the basis upon which relationships are to be conducted in the kingdom of heaven: they are to be modelled on God's compassionate treatment of us. It was after finishing *these* sayings that the passage on divorce occurs. The juxtaposition of these two passages is full of significance. To begin with, after the teaching found in chapter 18, there is almost something obscene about the question posed by the Pharisees in 19:3. Having already noted the lax view of marriage and divorce held by some of the Jewish teachers, we immediately realise that we are in a different world from that of the kingdom of God. Secondly, if honesty and openness are important in relationships, and if there is need for compassion and forgiveness modelled upon God's compassion and forgiveness, then where might this teaching be more applicable than in marriage? If our interpretation of Matthew 19:1-12 contradicts the emphases found in chapter 18, then we should immediately suspect that our interpretation is mistaken.

Having said this, however, we must also avoid the danger of allowing the immediate context of chapter 18 to shackle our interpretation of chapter 19 so that it contradicts what we have already learned from Matthew 5:32. In this connection we need to note the following. In 5:27-30, Jesus taught that we must be ruthless and radical in dealing with sinful tendencies. That teaching is identical to what we have in 18:8-9. In 5:27-30, this demand is set out in connection with the temptation to commit adultery. In verse 32, as an example of causing someone to commit adultery, Jesus cites the man who divorces his wife. We have seen that there is one exception, and that is where the wife is guilty of *porneia*. In such a case, adultery will not have been entailed by the husband's action and, presumably, in view of the teaching found in 5:27-30, this points up the extreme gravity of what the wife has done. After all, if men are warned to pull out their eyes and cut off their hands and feet rather than succumb to sexual sin, it follows that for the woman to succumb to sexual sin is also an extremely grave matter.

In other words, as we approach Matthew 19, it is imperative to keep in mind the searching challenges found in chapter 18: the maintenance of right attitudes to others, right relationships, a heart of mercy. At the same time we must also keep in mind the teaching found in Matthew 5:32 that *porneia* on the part of the wife is sufficiently grave for the husband to divorce his wife without thereby incurring sin himself. If, however, the husband's spirit falls below the standard set forth in chapter 18, then he will be sinning.

The second important contextual consideration is also found in verse 1: 'he left Galilee and went into the region of Judea to the other side of the Jordan.' The significance of the location lies in the fact that this area was governed by Herod Antipas. This fact has a fourfold significance. First of all, Antipas had himself divorced his wife, the daughter of the Nabatean king Aretas, in order to marry Herodias. Secondly, however, Herodias had also 'divorced' her husband Philip, who was Antipas' brother, in order to marry Antipas.[63] Thirdly, it was in this area that John the Baptist had exercised his powerful ministry; and, fourthly, it was precisely for challenging Antipas' marriage to Herodias that Antipas had him imprisoned and Herodias finally brought about his execution. In view of these considerations, and in the light of the fact that Jesus elsewhere describes Antipas as 'that fox' (Luke 13:31f.), it is pretty obvious that a question about divorce in this area could be extremely and politically sensitive.

The last contextual point to note occurs in verse 2. In view of the preparatory nature of John the Baptist's ministry, it is quite possible that many in the crowds that followed Jesus in this area had earlier come under the influence of John's ministry. It will be seen that this possibility is of considerable significance in understanding the question posed by the Pharisees in verse 3.

Exegesis

Verse 3 records the question that gave rise to Christ's teaching on divorce in this passage. However, we are informed that the Pharisees were not so much concerned to elicit Christ's teaching for their own benefit as, rather, 'to test him'. The idea conveyed is that the Pharisees are intent upon trapping Jesus.[64] The trap is laid by the question they pose in verse 3. On the surface, the question is inviting Jesus to declare where he stands in the rabbinic debate as to the legitimate grounds for divorce. As we have already noted, there was disagreement between Shammai and Hillel over the meaning of Deuteronomy 24:1. As one recognised by others as a rabbi,[65] it was perfectly natural for Jesus to be asked his views upon this matter. But this hardly constituted a test or a trap.[66] The whole point of a trap is that it is unseen. Thus, the question posed *conceals* the trap that is laid, and it is intended to elicit a response by which Jesus will be taken in the trap. Matthew has revealed the nature of the trap in verses 1-2. If Jesus espouses a position similar to that of Shammai, it would not be difficult for the Pharisees to ensure that Antipas and Herodias heard of this.[67] Since John had lost his liberty, and ultimately his life, for pronouncing upon Antipas' marriage to Herodias, there was surely good reason to believe that Jesus might share a similar fate if he espoused Shammaite views. Indeed, Jesus would have been more at risk. A pronouncement whose implications would be hostile to Antipas' marriage would be viewed as politically insensitive and subversive, given the way that John had been dealt with. For a teacher of Jesus' standing to take up a position hostile to the marriage would have been tantamount to issuing a daring challenge. However, to take up a position which might

78

implicitly legitimise the marriage would make him appear vulnerable in the eyes of the crowds. After all, faithfulness had cost John
his life. If Jesus were effectively to legitimise the marriage, then it
would appear as if John's death was a foolish and unnecessary
waste. How would the crowds who had heeded John's message be
likely to respond? It would be similar to an Ulster Unionist politician, prior to the 1998 Good Friday Agreement, saying in a
staunchly loyalist area that the Battle of the Boyne (1689), the clos-
ing of the gates of Londonderry by the apprentice boys, and the
loyalist deaths since 1969, were all the result of loyalist folly. Any
politician saying that would lose credibility overnight amongst the
loyalist community.

So the Pharisees intend to impale Jesus on the horns of a very
cruel dilemma: either to be consistent with what he has said in the
past and be in trouble with Antipas and Herodias, or to keep on the
right side of Antipas and Herodias but lose favour with the crowd.
Added to this is the fact that the Pharisees would be sure to pounce
on the least sign of Christ being inconsistent with his own teaching,
and would be certain to seek to tease out his views if he replied in
an evasive way. It was an exceedingly well-laid trap.

Jesus begins his reply in verse 4. It is essential to note that he
answered his questioners as well as their questions. The fact that he
had been asked a trick question should put us on notice that he will
not necessarily give a straightforward reply.[68] The words, 'Haven't
you read?' fulfil a number of purposes. First of all, Jesus is not
replying to their question in his own words. He uses words from
the Old Testament that were accepted as canonical by all the religious groupings within Judaism. Accordingly, if the Pharisees wish
to make anything out of what is said in verse 4, they will be taking
issue against their own Scriptures and against themselves. Jesus is
on safe ground to quote from Genesis. Secondly, the words function
in this verse in a similar way to the words, 'But go and learn what
this means' (9:13). These words constituted 'a rabbinic formula
used in a slightly sardonic way to administer a gentle rebuke to
those who needed to go and study the text of Scripture further.
Jesus' opponents, who prided themselves in their knowledge of
Scripture and their own conformity to it, needed to "go and learn"
what it meant.'[69] Thirdly, Jesus is going behind the teaching contained in the Sinaitic legislation to the foundational teaching found

in Genesis. What is the material to which he draws his questioners' attention? It is, first of all, a reference to Genesis 1:27: 'at the beginning the Creator "made them male and female"'.[70] Reference to this verse in connection with marital matters was not unknown to the Judaism of this period.[71] Nevertheless, at this point it serves a specific purpose in Jesus' reply. By quoting Genesis 1:27, he is drawing attention to a number of things. Firstly, he is preparing for the emphasis in verse 6 that God has an involvement in marriage, since it was he who differentiated between male and female as the necessary precondition to the institution of marriage in Genesis 2:24. There was a strong tendency amongst many of Jesus' contemporaries to view marriage as no more than a merely human contract.[72] Verse 4 thus prepares for the 'religious' dimension to marriage laid down in verse 6. Secondly, this quotation makes clear that the one-flesh relationship alluded to in verse 5 is a relationship of equals. The question posed by the Pharisees—was it lawful to divorce one's *wife* for any and every reason?—clearly expressed something of the tendency of men to treat their wives as less than equals. By quoting Genesis 1:27 before considering Genesis 2:24, Jesus was implicitly drawing attention to woman's equality with man before God.[73] The fact that he quoted Genesis 1:27 first also serves to demonstrate that the account in Genesis 2, of the creation of woman *after* the man and *for* the man, does not imply inferiority on the woman's part.[74] Moreover, Jesus' words in verse 4 clearly indicate that the original differentiation of male and female as equal before God is still the divine will.[75]

In verse 5, Jesus gives the second quotation from Genesis, and this, together with the words already quoted in verse 4, forms the basis for the teaching he will give in verse 6. The words, 'for this reason' (*heneka toutou*) are, of course, part of the quotation from Genesis 2:24.[76] In Genesis, they refer back to Adam's words in verse 23. It is significant that in that verse Adam says, 'This is now bone of my bones and flesh of my flesh.' Although the woman had been taken out of the man and, in that sense, was bone of his bone and flesh of his flesh, it is because she has been brought to him as his bride (verse 22) that she is now bone of his bone and flesh of his flesh. This prepares the way for the statement in verse 24 that they will become one flesh. There is unity, identity and equality specified in verse 23*a*, and diversity specified in part *b* of the verse: 'she shall be called *woman*, for she was taken out of man.' There is also diversity of role implied by the fact that she came out of the man, and by the fact that Adam named her.[77] It is *for this reason*—that is, because of the equality and identity, coupled with the diversity—that man, who cannot find the help he needs in the animals, 'will leave his father and mother and be united to his wife, and they will become one flesh'. According to the Genesis account, a unique dignity is conferred upon the woman: she is able to be to the man what no other creature, and no other man, can be to him. It is precisely because he finds himself in the woman that he 'will leave his father and mother'.

These words are important for two reasons. Firstly, they assert that the man will exercise a certain initiative in the formation of a marriage: it is *he*, not the woman, who will leave father and mother. Obviously, the woman leaves as well. But it is the man who will initiate. Secondly, in the light of the importance which the Old Testament attaches to the child/parent relationship, the fact that the man will leave them for someone else is quite staggering. After all, in a very real sense, he is their flesh and blood. However, the one-flesh union between husband and wife will be a closer bond than that of parent and child. One cannot properly assess the seriousness of divorce without appreciating the unity which exists between husband and wife, and one cannot properly appreciate that unity without assessing the significance of the fact that it takes precedence over the parent/child relationship. There is something further to add: the man who takes the initiative in leaving his parents is the one who is to 'be united to his wife'. He not only takes the initiative in leaving his parents, but it would appear that, in a very real sense, he is the one who is to be united to his wife. Of course, she is united to him; but the way the verse is worded indicates that the man has a responsibility in being united to his wife. The irony of the situation can now be appreciated. The Pharisees ask if it is lawful for one's wife to be put away for every reason or cause: Jesus replies by saying that for *this cause* a man shall be joined to his wife. They are asking if there are many reasons for divorce: he replies that there is one immense reason for staying together.

It will be useful, at this stage, to pause to consider the implications of all this. We have noted the tendency amongst Jesus' contemporaries to regard the man as possessed of rights which the woman did not have. These rights were being exercised in the matter of divorce. However, Genesis 2:24 teaches that the man has *responsibilities* towards his wife, and that these are bound up with keeping a marriage together rather than splitting it apart.

There are a number of differences between the wording of the quotation in verse 5 and that found in Genesis 2:24, but they are of no major significance.

In verse 6a, Jesus draws a conclusion from these two quotations: 'So they are no longer two, but one.'[78] A husband and wife have become a new unit; any suggestion that the man may think and act in disregard of his wife is, therefore, a complete denial of this fact. Having drawn this inference, Jesus now begins to provide something of an answer to the Pharisees' question: 'Therefore what God has joined together, let man not separate.' This is an absolutely crucial verse. To begin with, this ends Jesus' response to the Pharisees' first question and becomes the springboard for their next question. Secondly, this verse is regularly quoted in the debate about the biblical teaching on divorce. It is critical, therefore, that every word is carefully weighed and that we are crystal clear as to what it was that Jesus was saying. 'Therefore' (*oun*) has a logical force: that is, what Jesus says in verse 6b is nothing but the logical outworking of what has preceded. What has preceded, of course, has been the teaching of Genesis that from the beginning onwards it has been the Creator's will that mankind consist of male and female who, though equal, are differentiated and have different roles. This underlying unity expressed in diversity is the reason why the man will take the initiative in separating from his parents to become joined to his wife so that these two persons will become one flesh. There is thus a divine will and a human initiative in marriage. This being so, the logic of the situation is that 'what God has joined together, let man not separate'. Jesus is asserting in the clearest possible way that marriage is *not only* a human agreement. It *is* that, because the man joins himself to his wife. But it is more: God joins them together.[79] Clearly, there is no joining together by God if the man does not leave his parents and is not united to his wife. But when he does that, it is the divine will that they are joined as one. This being so, 'what God has joined together, let man not separate'. What does this last clause mean?

We have seen that, in verse 6, Jesus is giving his answer to the question posed by the Pharisees. Asked if it is lawful for one to put away one's wife for every reason, he has replied that there is one great reason for the man to be glued to and faithful to his wife. He then says that it is the divine will, and it is a divinely accomplished fact, that they have been joined as one. Therefore, man should not split apart this unit that now exists. Jesus is clearly teaching that the book of Genesis logically entails a prohibition of divorce: 'let man not separate'. It is essential to recognise that Jesus is *not* saying that it is metaphysically or ontologically impossible to separate what God has joined together; rather, he is saying that it should not be done.[80] In view of the fact that Jesus is now responding to the question posed by the Pharisees, it inevitably follows that Jesus regarded a husband's putting away his wife as separating what God had joined together. Man should not do this, but it is nevertheless a tragic possibility, and this possibility is actualised when a man puts away his wife.[81]

Certain observations and inferences should now be drawn from the teaching thus far in this passage. Firstly, Jesus has skilfully avoided being trapped. Secondly, he has set out the divine will with respect to marriage, as found in Genesis. Thirdly, he has drawn out the implications of the divine will for divorce. He has implied that divorce ruptures the unity which God effects;[82] it is something that is inconsistent with the divine will and should not be done. Jesus has certainly not distanced himself from John the Baptist, but neither has he done anything other than assert the teaching of the Old Testament, which the Pharisees themselves claimed to respect. In no way could they level a charge against him to Antipas. Moreover, he has pointed out to the Pharisees their lack of understanding of Scripture. He has turned a potential threat upon himself into an attack upon them. For the purposes of constructing a biblical theology of divorce, it must be stressed that Jesus has made it abundantly plain that the one-flesh union is 'breakable' by an act of divorce.

The Pharisees, however, dare not leave it there. Had they done so, their plan would have been foiled and they would have felt humiliated. Nor did they need to leave it there, for there was teaching in the Old Testament on the subject of divorce. And everyone would know that the way in which their question was put was an invitation to Jesus to declare where he stood on the interpretation of Deuteronomy 24:1. So it was natural for them to pursue the matter. They may have been unable to answer what Jesus had said. But in view of what he had said, they might be able to embarrass him by asking him to relate what he had said to the Mosaic legislation. Hence their question in verse 7. It is important to note that this is a very different question from that which they had initially asked. In verse 3, they were really concerned with ascertaining Christ's view as to *what* were the grounds for divorce. In verse 7, they ask *why* there was provision for divorce.[83]

What was the purpose of the Mosaic legislation? A number of features in this question need to be noted. First of all, it is clear that the Pharisees professed a very high view of the Mosaic law. Their question is meant to force Jesus into a corner. In effect, they are saying something like this. 'You have taught that the early chapters of Genesis entail a prohibition of divorce. But Moses—who wrote Genesis—commanded that a certificate of divorce be given. He could not have done that if divorce was contrary to the divine will, since Moses was God's mouthpiece and declared God's will. We prefer Moses' understanding of the situation to yours. If what you say is right, how can you square it with Moses' teaching?' That is what the question is all about. The second feature to note is that the Pharisees ask why Moses 'command[ed]' the giving of a certificate of divorce? Since the only specific use of the term 'certificate of divorce' (*biblion apostasiou*) in the Mosaic law is in Deuteronomy 24:1, it is clear that their question is concerned with the purpose of that part of Scripture. Incidentally, it also confirms our Lord's assessment (in Matthew 5:31) of their approach to these matters. Their question may indicate that they believed that Moses commanded divorce in certain circumstances or, alternatively, that the most important aspect of the Mosaic legislation on divorce was the requirement of the giving of the certificate. In view of the words at the end of the question, 'and send her away' (*kai apolysai*), it is probable that they regarded Deuteronomy 24:1 to be implying a command to divorce. At the same time, they would have regarded the certificate with great seriousness.[84]

This question forms the background to some of the most important teaching to be found in the Gospels, not only about divorce, but also about the Mosaic law. We need to bear in mind that Jesus' words in verse 8 are dealing with a much wider range of issues than only divorce. Moreover, they are the prelude to the teaching given in verse 9, which is equally wide-ranging. In verse 8, Jesus explains that it was because of the hardness of their hearts that Moses permitted them to put away their wives, but that from the beginning this was not so. The Pharisees, as we have seen, regarded themselves as Moses' disciples.[85] Moses was God's mouthpiece and gave God's law to Israel. This made Israel a unique and special nation, and the Pharisees, as the self-appointed guardians and custodians of the law, regarded themselves as having an extra-special position within the nation. However, Jesus is now saying that the Mosaic legislation on divorce was necessitated by the hardness of heart of the people. By saying, 'the hardness of *your* hearts',[86] Jesus is explaining that the Mosaic legislation had in view not only Moses' contemporaries but Israelites for generations to come thereafter. If it was true that God gave Israel his law because they were a special people, it was equally true that their uniqueness lay not in the fact that they were more righteous than other nations.[87] Some aspects of the law that came by Moses bore eloquent testimony to the people's sinfulness and hardness of heart. In effect, Jesus is saying that the law was given to Israel because of her sin. This, of course, is a massive seam of New Testament theology which is developed by Paul.[88] Its origins go back to Jesus, and even further, to the Old Testament itself.[89] Moses had to permit divorce because of the hardness of heart of the people. Accordingly, the Pharisees were fundamentally mistaken in understanding the Mosaic permission of divorce as ideal, still less as imposing an obligation to divorce. Incidentally, Jesus is here implying a criticism of the Shammaites who, while interpreting 'the indecent thing' of Deuteronomy 24:1 quite strictly, went on to assert that divorce was obligatory.

Jesus goes on to explain that 'it was not this way from the beginning'. He is doing two things here. Firstly, he is interpreting the Old Testament *historically*. Genesis 1 and 2 set out God's ideal for marriage, and this has implications for divorce. Deuteronomy comes much later, and what it says cannot undo the ideal set out in Genesis. Something has happened between Genesis 2 and Deuteronomy 24 that means that Moses has to allow a less than ideal state of affairs. But this permission does not overthrow the ideal. Carson has drawn attention to the need to follow the Bible's 'story line' and to interpret it in the light of that story line.[90] This is a good example of the need for such interpretation and warns us against isolating biblical material on divorce from its context. However, as we have seen (see note 75), by using the words 'from the beginning' rather than 'in the beginning', Jesus is teaching that the Genesis material is still the ideal and sets forth the will of God on this matter. In this one verse, Jesus has accomplished a number of things. Firstly, he has answered the Pharisees' question as to the reason for the Mosaic legislation on divorce. Secondly, he has avoided interpreting the legislation in such a way as to land himself in difficulty with Antipas. Thirdly, by referring to the divine ideal, he has avoided bringing himself into disagreement with John the Baptist. Fourthly, he has implicitly criticised the Shammaites and, *a fortiori*, the Hillelites. Fifthly, he has drawn attention to Israel's sinfulness and, in particular, the sinfulness of the Pharisees. Sixthly, he has implied that one of the purposes of the Mosaic law was to restrain sin or some of the complications to which sin gives rise, and has therefore implicitly criticised the widely held view that the Mosaic law in its entirety was the blueprint for life.

In one sense, the conversation could have ended at that point. However, in verse 9, Jesus develops what he has said yet further and rounds off this part of the discussion. This verse is possibly the most controversial verse on divorce found in Jesus' teaching and, arguably, in the whole Bible. Inevitably, attention is frequently focused on the exceptive phrase, some arguing strongly that it does not permit remarriage after divorce, and others arguing equally strongly that it does. Rather than take up sides and then argue for the position taken, we shall proceed as we have done thus far, seeking to exegete the meaning of Jesus' words, to explain their significance and function in their context, and then—*and only then*—to ascertain what bearing they might have upon our own day and age.

Verse 9 is a difficult verse. There are textual problems, and problems of translation. The problems of translation relate both to the meaning of words and to the syntax of the sentence. Since this verse has occasioned much controversy and is clearly crucial to an understanding of Jesus' teaching, no apology should be needed for putting it, as it were, under the microscope in order, as far as is humanly possible, to remove all doubt as to its meaning. There are good reasons for accepting the reading that, as we shall see, can support the NIV rendering of these words.[91] But what do the words mean? As with our treatment of Matthew 5:32, it will be helpful to consider the verse apart from the exception in order to grasp its overriding teaching. Once we have done so, the exception may then be considered.

It is probably best to translate the conjunction *de*, and not to treat it simply as a connective which does not need to be translated. By so doing, we are more likely to appreciate the fact that Jesus is continuing in this verse from what he has just said in verse 8.[92] While the particle is clearly adversative in verse 8, it carries the meaning of 'and' in this verse, being linked with the last part of verse 8 but containing further development by Jesus. The words *legō de hymin* (= and I say to you) are clearly uttered to emphasise what Jesus is about to say, and suggest that he is not now simply interpreting Old Testament teaching but speaking on his own authority. The words are reminiscent of the repeated formula, *egō de legō hymin* (= but I say unto you), which Jesus had used in the Sermon on the Mount. What Jesus says is that whoever puts away his wife and marries another commits adultery. This, of course, is identical with what he says in Luke 16:18. A number of important features should be noted. The Pharisees had asked Jesus what was lawful. That was clearly a reference to the Mosaic law. John had rebuked Antipas for doing that which was unlawful. In terms of the Mosaic law, as we have already observed, Jesus did not give a direct answer to the question. However, he now asserts that to divorce and remarry is tantamount to adultery. In saying this he would have shocked the Pharisees but have said nothing that would have alarmed Antipas. It would have shocked the Pharisees because, as has already been observed, the Jews did not regard it as adultery for a man to have a second wife. Bigamy may not have been commonly practised at this period, but it was not forbidden. Accordingly, Shammai may have regarded divorce except for sexual infidelity as not permitted by the Mosaic law, but that does not mean that he would have regarded a subsequent marriage as adulterous. For even if he viewed the husband as still married in the eyes of God to the first wife, he was not forbidden from having a second wife (since polygamy was permitted). Accordingly, the wrong consisted in divorcing for an illegitimate reason. What Jesus said would therefore have shocked his hearers.

However, it does not follow that Jesus was giving his opponents ammunition that Antipas could use against him. It is one thing to say that an act is adulterous. It is another thing to say that it is 'wrong and unlawful'. It may appear that this is to split hairs and make a distinction without a difference. A moment's reflection should demonstrate that this is not the case. There is an important distinction and difference between saying that a relationship is adulterous and saying that it is unlawful. Clearly, for Jesus to cate-gorise such divorce and remarriage as adulterous meant that he viewed it as a breach of the seventh commandment and as sin. No doubt, his hearers would have understood it in this way. But it is perfectly consistent to say that an immoral character such as Antipas would take great exception to being told that what he had done was wrong and unlawful, and yet not be overly concerned at being called an adulterer.

The point may be illustrated as follows. The British Royal family has recently gained notoriety for the extramarital affairs of some of its members. They have admitted as much in public. Journalists may draw attention to the fact that they have committed adultery. That is one thing. But if the Archbishop of Canterbury started preaching sermons in which he were to say that these people had done what is unlawful before God and sinful, and that they are therefore wicked people, my guess is that there would immediately be a storm of protest. They may admit that they have committed adultery, but the temperature is raised the moment one says that what they have done is wrong and wicked. A man may admit to being homosexual. A Christian minister may refer to the man as such. There is no problem; the man may well glory in the fact. The trouble begins when the minister says that the man is therefore wicked. It is one thing for, say, the Archbishop of Canterbury to refer to the adultery within the Royal Family. No doubt, he regards it as sinful behaviour, but problems will only arise for him if he articulates that belief.

That is precisely the difference between John the Baptist's treat-ment of Antipas' divorce and remarriage and Jesus' words in verse 9. We shall note in Mark's Gospel that these words were spoken to the disciples in the house. However, in Matthew there is nothing to indicate that the Pharisees did not hear what Jesus said. Unless we are to regard him as being virtually suicidal at this point, and as walking straight into the trap he had skilfully avoided thus far, then it seems that the kind of explanation of Jesus' words which I have offered must be accepted.

We should also note that in referring to remarriage when he has been asked about divorce, Jesus is linking remarriage very closely to the divorce that was being practised in his day. Men were putting away their wives out of a desire for other women. This would confirm our understanding, given in the previous chapter, of what really lay behind the need for the Mosaic legislation. But whereas the Old Testament permitted that, Jesus now calls it adultery. This must mean that *he* is not permitting it. Accordingly, Jesus is saying a number of things here. Firstly, he is setting his own teaching on a par with that of Moses and, indeed, with that of God himself. Secondly, he is *not* so much abrogating the Mosaic teaching as fulfilling it. With the coming of the one to whom Moses pointed, the concession to men's hardness of heart no longer applies. This must imply, firstly, that in the eschatological kingdom there is provision to deal with the problem of men's hardness of heart by changing the heart; and, secondly, that Jesus is redefining the people of God as no longer consisting of the nation of Israel but of those whose hearts are renewed in the eschatological kingdom which he has come to inaugurate. Thirdly, Christ being the fulfilment of the law and the one in whom the eschatological kingdom is realised, it inevitably follows that not only are the people of God being redefined, but the nation of Israel and its structures and laws received from Moses will no longer be the determining features and characteristics of the people of God. Attention too frequently focuses on the narrow issue of divorce in this verse, and the even narrower issue of the exceptive material, with the result that these huge theological realities and claims are totally missed. But it is a feature of the Gospel writers—and particularly of Matthew and John—that individual 'motifs' become paradigms by which the eschatological fulfilment of the Old Testament is exemplified.[93] It is not insignificant that Jesus' teaching on divorce in Matthew 5:31-32 and in Luke 16:18 is in the context of eschatological fulfilment of the Old Testament in the kingdom of God.

What then did Jesus mean by the words 'except for marital

unfaithfulness'? The word translated 'marital unfaithfulness' is *porneia*. This term is examined fairly comprehensively in the Excursus to this chapter, and the reader is also referred to the earlier discussion of Matthew 5:32 and to the relevant notes on that term. However, two further questions arise which must now be considered. First, there has been dispute as to the meaning of the words translated 'except for'. Secondly, considerable debate has been occasioned by the question as to whether the exceptive words apply only to the divorce or if they also include the remarriage. We shall consider each question in turn.

The words 'except for' translate the Greek *mē epi*. It has been argued that these words may mean either that Jesus is not considering the matter of *porneia* or that he is saying, 'notwithstanding *porneia*'. In either case, Jesus is not giving an exception: in the former case, he is simply not commenting upon the issue; in the latter, he is saying that even where the wife has been guilty of *porneia* a husband will be guilty of adultery if he divorces and remarries. Obviously, this is a vital matter to resolve, since either of these meanings leads to a very different conclusion from that which one reaches if the words mean 'except for'. It is submitted that the arguments that have been advanced to support either of these meanings are unconvincing and that *mē epi* is correctly rendered by 'except for'.[94] The phrase is intended to allow an exception to the teaching that Jesus is setting forth.

But to what does the exception refer? Here we undoubtedly come to the heart of the debate as to whether Jesus allowed remarriage after divorce. The question has often been put thus: do the exceptive words relate only to the divorce or do they relate also to the remarriage? Murray believes that they apply to divorce and remarriage, while Heth and Wenham, and also Cornes, believe that they only relate to the divorce. There is a sense in which this is an unfortunate way of putting the question. What Jesus is saying in this verse is something like this: whoever divorces his wife and marries another woman commits adultery, but a man does not commit adultery when he divorces his wife for *porneia* and marries another woman. There are compelling reasons for believing this to be the teaching of Jesus as over against the 'no remarriage' view espoused by Heth and Wenham and by Cornes.[95]

It will be useful to pause to consider what Jesus is teaching in verse 9 and what inferences may be drawn from his words. Firstly, he is teaching that the Mosaic law has reached something of a terminus. Whereas that law did not regard divorce and remarriage as entailing adultery, Jesus emphatically did regard it as so doing. This radical change results from his eschatological fulfilment of the Mosaic law. One greater than Moses had come! Secondly, where divorce was on the basis of illicit sexual intercourse, then neither the divorce nor subsequent remarriage by the man whose wife had been the guilty party would involve him in adultery. Jesus was neither commanding nor commending divorce for such a reason, nor was he encouraging remarriage. But neither was he forbidding or discouraging it. Thirdly, in view of his setting aside the Mosaic concession, Jesus' permission of divorce and remarriage was *not* occasioned by the hardness of heart of the men. Accordingly, we are not to understand divorce as a failure to live up to the teaching that Jesus had given in chapter 18 on the need for forgiveness. No doubt, that teaching must be implemented in the spirit in which a man would put away his wife, and we have already seen that Joseph exemplified this in his dealings with Mary. However, just as Matthew 18:17 deals with the removal of an individual from the congregation because his behaviour strikes at the very heart of the church, so 19:9 permits divorce where the wife has been guilty of behaviour which undermines the marriage. And *porneia* is such behaviour. Since adultery is sin (which, as we have seen, is defined by Jesus as consisting in the repudiation of marriage), it is clearly forbidden by Jesus for a man to divorce and remarry except where his wife is guilty of *porneia*, since this, *de facto*, undermines the marriage. But since sin will not be entailed where the husband puts his wife away because of her *porneia*, it inevitably follows that Jesus is implicitly allowing divorce and remarriage in such a case. Furthermore, although Jesus is claiming that the eschatological kingdom has already been inaugurated, by referring to *porneia* and divorce he is making it plain that it has not yet come in its fulness. The already/not yet tension, which runs through the New Testament, is found, in embryo, in Matthew 19:9. Thus, whereas in the beginning there would have been no divorce (for then there was no sin), divorce is permitted in this present era of the kingdom. But it is not now permitted in the way that it was before the inauguration of the kingdom of God by Jesus.

Of course, Jewish custom demanded that a man put away his wife where she had committed adultery, and Augustus had enacted a law demanding the same.[96] This has led numerous writers to the view that Jesus only allowed the exception in Matthew 5:32 and Matthew 19:9 because of this situation.[97] But this is both an unwarrantable position and is based on a flawed hermeneutical procedure. If we take the second criticism first, the writers who argue for this position have already concluded from Mark and Luke that Jesus never permitted divorce. Having formed their view from the teaching of those Gospels, they then have to 'explain' the exceptions in Matthew. As we have already seen, by the same token someone else might formulate his view on the basis of Matthew and then explain the 'absence' of the exceptions. Rather, we should establish the teaching of each Gospel and then—and only then— seek to frame an integrated theology. Secondly, even if this procedure were valid, it would fail to explain why neither Mark nor Luke mentions the exceptive material. It will not do to say that Matthew recorded it because of Jewish sensibilities at this point, for, as already pointed out, Augustus had enacted a law on this matter (see note 96). Therefore, it was not only in Jewish communities that there was an obligation to divorce where adultery had been committed. The *lex Julia de adulteriis* required the same of those who were under the Roman law. If the type of argument advanced by Heth and Wenham were sound, viz., that the exceptive material in Matthew was Matthew's comment necessitated by the Jewish law, then one would expect Mark and Luke to have added such an exception because of the Roman law. Even if this argument were valid to explain why Jesus allowed divorce—and it is not valid—it would manifestly fail to explain why he should then have permitted remarriage. It is submitted that while the Jewish insistence that a husband divorce an adulterous wife provides background material to the New Testament, it does not explain Matthew's exceptive material. The real reason why this argument is so used is because of a prior commitment to the belief that nothing other than death can break a marriage; hence Jesus' views on divorce and remarriage. The exceptions have to be twisted to fit into that grid. Once accept that Jesus taught that divorce ended marriage and that *porneia* is a species of adultery, and there will be no difficulty in explaining the exceptive material. While not endorsing the school of Shammai, Jesus is legitimising divorce for *porneia*, but is doing so by his own authority, and not with reference to Moses.

It remains to consider verses 10-12. Some who argue that verse 9 does not allow remarriage argue that these verses support their position.[98] It will become clear that I do not share that view. What will also become clear is that these verses contain important teaching concerning the eschatological kingdom, and preoccupation with the light these verses throw on the exceptive clause of verse 9—important though that is—can easily blind us to matters of momentous importance upon which Jesus was pronouncing.

In verse 10, the disciples exclaim, 'If this is the situation between a husband and wife, it is better not to marry.' The first question to answer is, To what are the disciples referring when they say, 'If this is the situation between a husband and wife . . .'?[99] The disciples may well be referring to all that Jesus has been saying, but it seems that they are especially referring to his words in verse 9. As we have seen, Jesus' words amount to a condemnation of divorce *and remarriage*, except where there has been sexual infidelity on the wife's part. Accordingly, they are referring to Jesus' implied ban on divorce and remarriage. As we have seen, divorce entailed the possibility of remarriage. In condemning the one, Jesus inevitably condemned the other, and vice versa. They find Jesus' words somewhat surprising, not to say shocking. Why was this so? It is sometimes said that the interpretation which we have put forward would not have been too shocking since, in some of its details, it was not too different from Shammai's position. Accordingly, the shock of the disciples must indicate that Jesus meant something different and that we have, therefore, misunderstood him.

But this does not necessarily follow, and there are good reasons why the disciples would have been shocked at what Jesus had said.[100] That we have not misunderstood his meaning in verse 9 becomes clear when we go on to consider what the disciples say in verse 10: 'it is better not to marry'. A more literal rendering of this verse would be, 'it is not expedient to marry', but the meaning is well brought out by the use of the comparative 'better'.[101] Heth and Wenham believe, as does Cornes, that the disciples are referring to Jesus' new definition of divorce, which categorises all divorce, except for unchastity, as wrong, and which absolutely forbids—in all cases without exception—remarriage after divorce. But it is difficult to see how the disciples' words make sense if that is their meaning. A man who divorces but cannot remarry is in a similar, though not identical, position to an unmarried man. Apart from the fact that he has experienced marriage, he is now returned to the position which he knew before marriage. Accordingly, he would *not* be in a better position by not marrying in the first place, but in a similar position. Why would it have been better for him not to have married? But if the disciples have been shocked by Jesus' implicit prohibition of *divorce* and *therefore of remarriage*, their words make perfect sense: a man who marries is thereby committed to something from which he is not allowed to be released. Now the disciples could argue that an unmarried man was in a favourable position compared to that of a married man, precisely because a single man is not bound by that inviolable commitment and is 'free'.

In verse 11, Jesus replies that not everyone would be able to accept such a saying, but only those to whom it would be given. It is important to understand to which 'saying' Jesus is referring. There are two possibilities. The first is that he is referring back to his own saying in verse 9. This would then mean that the only people who could accept such a saying would be those who possessed the ability to abide by Jesus' teaching on divorce and remarriage. Those to whom it is given would not be a select group of disciples but all disciples in the kingdom, since the lifestyle they espouse is essentially something which they are empowered to do. Heth and Wenham espouse this view and link it with verse 12. The reference to those who make themselves eunuchs for the sake of the kingdom is to those who will not remarry after divorce out of regard for the kingdom: that is the choice they make, but they are empowered to do so because it has been given to them. According to Heth and Wenham, this confirms their understanding of verse 9, since verse 12 demands that these people do not remarry. This, they claim, is what verse 12 is referring to. While Cornes believes that the 'saying' referred to in verse 11 is the disciples' statement in verse 10, he takes the same view of verse 12 as Heth and Wenham. Does the saying refer to verse 9 or to verse 10? I think that there are good reasons for referring it to the disciples' words in verse 10, rather than to Jesus' words in verse 9.[102] This will become clear from our study of verse 12.

Verse 11 contains something of a shock to the disciples, which we might easily miss. In verse 10, they are not extolling the single state; rather they are expressing their amazement at the teaching of Jesus. The measure of their amazement is gauged by the fact that on their understanding of it—that is, the teaching of Jesus—the single state would be seen as preferable to marriage. Jews routinely considered the married state to be both natural and the norm and, therefore, the single state as patently unnatural and abnormal. The following quotation brings this out fairly clearly:

> Christian tradition is that Jesus Himself did not marry. This is in fact a deduction from silence: it is not explicitly stated in the Gospels that He was not married. In rabbinic texts, however, an argument from silence would suggest the reverse: it was so unusual for rabbis not to marry that such a fact would probably have been mentioned. Thus a Jew reading the Gospels might assume that Jesus was married, a Christian that He was not . . . [An] assumption [developed in Christianity] that there is an ideal greater than marriage, whereas in the Jewish tradition this would be very unusual.[103]

While this is not the most felicitous way of expressing matters, and while I believe that the New Testament indicates that Jesus was not married, this quotation does emphasise that the single state was somewhat abnormal, and not just unusual, for the Jews. This being the case, it is remarkable that Jesus not only does not dismiss the disciples' words but also refers to the single state as something given to some (*hois dedotai*). What was regarded as abnormal is, according to Jesus, a gift to some.

This is then explained in verse 12. The AV and the NIV bring out the fact that the connective particle *gar* (= for) functions in this verse as a conjunction which links the verse with verse 11, and is not just a stylistic connective which can be left untranslated. Verse 12 will describe those 'to whom it has been given' as accepting the saying that it is better not to marry. Jesus identifies three categories of such people and links all of them together by virtue of the fact that they are all 'eunuchs'. The NIV, by translating the last clause of the sentence dealing with eunuchs with the words 'and others have renounced marriage', has somewhat robbed the verse of its force

(emasculated it?!), whereas the AV retains the force of the original.[104] Whatever the meaning of the clause, we shall see that there is
a considerable impact in the way in which it is worded, and this
should be retained in translation. What exactly did Jesus mean? To
answer this, we need to address the following questions. First,
what is the meaning of the word 'eunuch' in the sentence, and of
the phrase 'being made a eunuch'? Secondly, what was the impact
and significance of the reference to eunuchs, and how would it
have been understood by Jesus' hearers? Thirdly, what part does
the saying play in the flow of the argument? We shall examine each
question in turn.

The noun translated by the word 'eunuchs' includes within its
semantic range those who are castrated and those who, without an
operation, are incapable of procreation. The verb refers to the act of
castrating.[105] Origen, one of the Church fathers, actually castrated
himself as a result of his literal understanding of this verse. The
general view that has prevailed is that the second occasion when
the verb is used in verse 12 refers to the forgoing of marriage.[106] Let
us examine the three references to eunuchs in the verse. Jesus is
relating what he says about eunuchs to verses 10-11, that is, to the
theme of marriage. Thus, the reference to those who are born
eunuchs is to those who, because of their physical (or psychologi-
cal?) condition at birth, will never be able to consummate marriage.
It clearly does not refer to being married, for everyone is born
unmarried, and everyone at birth is incapable of consummating
marriage. Since Jesus is only referring to some, he must mean that
some are born such that they will never be able to consummate
marriage. The second reference is to those who have been made
eunuchs by men. This almost certainly refers to men who, because
they have been castrated, are incapable of consummating marriage.
Those who cared for women of a harem would come into this category. It is possible that, by a process of extension, this clause could
denote those who, by circumstances into which they are forced by
others, are unable to marry. However, it is doubtful if this is the
intended meaning. Cornes' reference to those who have been
seduced by those in the gay community is almost certainly an
example of reading into the text something which would not have
been intended by Jesus, though it *may* possibly be a legitimate
application of the teaching.

The question naturally arises as to whether we are to understand Jesus as shifting the meaning of the words on the third occasion. I do not think so. He could have said that some choose, for the sake of the kingdom, to be unmarried, but he chose to speak of men making themselves eunuchs. We should not tone down the force of this language. The pressure to tone down the force of Jesus' language arises from a concern to avoid Origen's grotesque misunderstanding of the words. But we are not limited to the stark alternatives of a literalistic understanding or else an understanding that explains the phrase as a choice to remain unmarried. There is a third option: retain the stark language and understand it as an extremely vivid figure of speech. This is exactly what we do with Jesus' words concerning plucking out offending eyes and cutting off offending hands. Here is similar language. The whole point about the eye and the hand is that they have God-given and noble functions. However, sin can so affect them that drastic action is needed. Likewise, man's sexual drive is God-given and noble; however, it can be affected by sin. In such a case, drastic action is called for. Accordingly, Jesus is here referring to the suppression of the sexual drive within man, a suppression which reduces his desire for sexual union in much the same way as if he had been castrated. This understanding avoids a crass literalism but also avoids bleeding away the force of the imagery. It is not just that a man chooses to remain unmarried; he makes a drastic renunciation that leaves him incapable of marrying.

It may appear that this understanding supports the 'no remarriage after divorce' view. Jesus had forbidden it; accordingly, his disciples who have divorced for *porneia* are to deal drastically with their sex drive in order to remain single. While superficially plausible, this understanding cannot be sustained.[107] What Jesus is saying is that some people—who are neither born eunuchs nor made eunuchs by men—will choose to remain unmarried for the sake of the kingdom of God. Jesus must be referring to men who are not devoid of sexual drive. But he must also be referring to a fairly special group. There are a number of reasons for saying this. First, he is only referring to some, not to all. Secondly, he has already referred in verse 6 to Genesis 2:24, where the union of man and woman in marriage continues to be the divine ideal. Thirdly, in view of the previous point, the divinely ordained way for dealing with sexual drive is *not* to suppress it but to express it in marriage. Other biblical teaching indicates that the stronger the sexual drive, the more important this becomes.[108] Thus, while Jesus is referring to those who are not devoid of sexual drive, it is evidently the case that that drive is not so insistent that it is desirable and wise to be married. Certain demands of the kingdom of God lead to the suppressing of this desire on the part of those who are so gifted and who are able to accept this saying.

To whom is Jesus referring? Evidence from elsewhere in the New Testament supports the belief that he is referring to disciples who, possessing the necessary gift from God, choose to forgo marriage for the sake of the kingdom of God. Paul appears to place himself in this category in 1 Corinthians 7:7, while making it perfectly clear that not everyone is thus gifted. It may be thought that the language of castration is singularly inappropriate for someone who has received the ability to remain single. Surely someone so gifted would not need to take drastic action to suppress his or her sex drive. Nor, it could be argued, is such language appropriate to someone who, presumably, would not be sinning by being married. However, neither of these criticisms will withstand scrutiny. To begin with, we are not to think of someone with the 'gift' to remain single as being totally devoid of sexual drive. Such a person is not in the same position as someone who was born a eunuch or who has been castrated by men. While Paul speaks of his gifting in 1 Corinthians 7:7, he speaks in 1 Corinthians 9 of 'rights' which he had forgone. Amongst those rights was the right to 'take a believing wife along with us, as do the other apostles'. This was a right that Paul denied himself. He did so because he had the gift to do so. In the light of 7: 8-9, it would have been folly, and tempting God, to have decided to remain unmarried had he not been so gifted. But his words towards the end of chapter 9, in verses 24-27, demonstrate that the forgoing of his rights required discipline on his part, and that discipline is expressed in language which has affinities with the vivid language used in Matthew 18:8-9 and 19:12. Moreover, Paul's words in verse 23, 'for the sake of the gospel', bear affinities with Matthew 19:12, 'for the sake of the kingdom'. With regard to the second criticism, it is indeed true that it would not be sin—i.e., breaking a command of God applicable to all men—for Paul to have married. On the other hand, true discipleship requires that the whole of our life be offered up to Jesus, and that we seek first God's kingdom, and lose our lives for Jesus' sake and the gospel's sake. In this respect, given that Paul possessed the giftedness to remain single, and in view of the commission that was given to him, he could only live out the good and perfect will of God for him by remaining single. In that respect, the language of cutting off the hand and eye, and the language of castration, are not inappropriate.

It is very easy for us to miss the impact that these words must have had upon Jesus' disciples. We have already seen that marriage was regarded as the norm. We need also to remember that the Mosaic law excluded from the assembly of the Lord those who had been emasculated either by crushing or cutting. For Jesus actually to refer to someone emasculating himself for the sake of God's kingdom would have been shocking, notwithstanding the fact that this was not to be taken literally. It would have sounded almost like an attack upon, or denial of, the teaching of Moses. However, Isaiah had looked forward to the day when the eunuch would not complain that he was only a dry tree, and there would be a place for the eunuch and the foreigners within the Temple (Isaiah 56:3-5). It is surely possible that while Jesus is, on the one hand, appearing to stand in contrast to the Mosaic law, he is, on the other hand, announcing the fulfilment of the Isaianic prophecy. The reference to becoming a eunuch for the sake of the kingdom may well resonate with Isaiah 56:3-4 and bear affinities with the kind of teaching found in Matthew 11:4-5—God's promises through the prophets were now being fulfilled. Indeed, whereas Isaiah promises that there will be a place for the eunuch, Jesus is positively asserting that some will become eunuchs for the sake of the kingdom. Clearly, the Isaianic reference appears to be to a literal eunuch; but in terms of their lament that they were unfruitful, those who would make themselves eunuchs would be no different. The kingdom has come, and with it profound changes.

But Jesus is doing something yet further in this verse, which he has already done in verse 9. It is one thing to say that the kingdom has come. But the divine ideal is that of male and female united in marriage. The fact that some are still born eunuchs, while others are made eunuchs by men, indicates that the kingdom has not yet fully come. There is, indeed, realised eschatology here, but it is certainly not over-realised eschatology. And the fact that some will make themselves eunuchs for the sake of the kingdom indicates that before the kingdom has fully come—indeed, in order that it may fully come—there will be a call to sacrifice. The eunuch saying fits perfectly within the context of the wider issues of the already/not yet tension of the eschatological kingdom and the continuity/discontinuity motifs. The final saying, 'The one who can accept this should accept it', powerfully reinforces the challenge inherent in Jesus' words, while guarding the church against the false asceticism against which she later needed to be warned (1 Tim. 4:3).

I have sought to demonstrate that there is good reason for understanding the eunuch reference to be to those who, possessing the gift, remain unmarried. However, the case for understanding this reference to be to those who remain unmarried after divorce has been powerfully and persuasively argued by Heth and Wenham. Drawing on the work of Quesnell and Dupont, they present a fairly detailed and technical argument, based upon Matthean style, that the reference must be to singleness after divorce. While powerfully presented, the arguments adduced are seriously flawed and will not withstand detailed criticism.[109]

Our study of Matthew 19:1-12 is now concluded. In due course, the question of how Jesus' teaching is to be applied will need to be considered. Before this can be done, it will be necessary to study the material found in Mark and to account for the differences between Matthew and Mark.

Mark 10:1-12

General

While Mark's teaching will be considered in its own light, and his particular emphases will be highlighted, there will obviously be a certain amount of overlap between this passage and Matthew 19:1-12. This being the case, in order to avoid tedious repetition and duplication, the reader will be referred, at numerous points, back to the relevant comments on the same material in Matthew's Gospel. After concluding our study of this passage, an attempt will be made to account for the differences between Matthew's account in Matthew 19 and Mark's account in this passage. Nevertheless, it will also be appropriate at various points in the exegesis to draw attention to those differences between Matthew and Mark for which an explanation will be needed.

Context[110]

Verse 1a is concerned with questions of geography and location— 'Jesus left that place'. The place was Capernaum (9:33) which was in Galilee. Leaving Galilee, Jesus entered 'the region of Judea and across the Jordan'.[111] There is a threefold significance in the setting.

First,

> Mark's account of the Galilean ministry is terminated with chapter 9. From this point forward the narrative moves swiftly and relentlessly towards its inevitable climax in Jerusalem. Verse 1 is a summary passage, reporting a further stage in the journey toward the Judean capital and the resumption of a public ministry.[112]

Secondly,

> The itinerary marks a return to the Jordan region where John the Baptist had conducted his ministry and had suffered imprisonment and martyrdom. If Jesus had been associated with John for any length of time it is possible that in coming to southern Judea and Perea he was returning to an area and people he knew well. His reputation in these areas is attested by chapter 3:8, although it is not clear whether it was established by direct knowledge or report.[113]

Thirdly, he was entering the territory of Herod Antipas. The remarks that were made when dealing with Matthew 19, concerning the significance of the crowds and of the fact that Jesus was in Antipas' territory, need to be borne in mind here (see pp. 77-9).

The second part of verse 1 sets the ensuing controversy over divorce in the context of Jesus teaching the crowds.[114] As Lane comments, 'In both Judea and Perea Jesus began teaching crowds of people once more, resuming a public ministry which had been discontinued some time before He left Galilee (Ch. 9:30).'[115] It is in this context of public teaching in Judea and Transjordan that the Pharisees came to test Jesus with a question (v.2). As we saw when considering Matthew 19, the place and the people are the background against which we are to understand the test. The fact that in Mark the Galilean ministry terminates at the end of chapter 9 may indicate that we are intended by Mark to under-stand that Jesus was here being confronted by a more sophisti-cated breed of Pharisee than he had encountered in Galilee. This may receive confirmation from the fact that whereas, in Matthew 26:73, Peter is told that his accent gives him away as having been with Jesus of Galilee (v.69), in Mark 14: 70 he is told, 'Surely you are one of them, for you are a Galilean.' There were noticeable differences between Galileans and Judeans, and the Judean Pharisees would have been more of a challenge than the Galilean Pharisees.

Exegesis

Verse 2 informs us that the Pharisees came and asked Jesus a ques-tion, in order to test him.[116] I have already referred to the fact that the test was a trap set by the Pharisees.[117] While Mark has arranged his material in such a way as to emphasise the test which was being set Jesus by the Judean Pharisees, the wording of the Pharisees' question in verse 2 is such as to emphasise to Mark's readers the trap which is being set in Antipas' territory. The question does not concern the rea-sons for which a man may divorce his wife, but whether it is lawful to do so at all.[118] Phrased in this way, the question is indeed strange, since it was clearly not unlawful, in terms of the Mosaic law, for a man to put away his wife. In view of the fact that the Pharisees agreed that it was lawful for a man to divorce but were divided as to the situations which would justify it, we are, as it were, being put on notice by Mark that something is missing from this question. This is not a conclusion reached by comparing this passage with Matthew 19. Rather, it is arrived at by recognising that otherwise the question was hardly a test at all. Indeed, as Brewer has pointed out, 'It would be obvious that the question posed in Mark was an abbreviation, because otherwise it was absurd. If they had really asked Jesus, "Is it lawful for a man to divorce his wife?" he would have humiliated them by saying, "Yes, of course it is lawful—it is written in the Law."'[119] Why was the question abbreviated? Brewer finds the expla-nation in the nature of the Mishnah. He writes:

> Jesus was invited to take part in a debate, which was well known in the Jewish world. We find a record of that debate in the Mishnah, which is a collection of early Pharisaic writings. The

name 'Mishnah' means 'to repeat' or 'to memorise', because it was originally the memorised summaries of the important debates on the meaning of the Law. These summaries are often highly stylised and abbreviated to aid memorisation. Any details or phrases which were obvious to a first century Jew are omitted. We find the same kind of abbreviation in many Gospel passages, especially in Mark, though Matthew and Luke are often less abbreviated, and John is sometimes quite verbose!

Brewer understands Mark to be recording the invitation that was given to Jesus to declare where he stood vis-à-vis the rabbinic debate of the time: 'Any first century Jew would have mentally added [the phrase "for any and every cause"].'[120]

I do not think, however, that Brewer's explanation adequately accounts for the rather strange wording of the Pharisees' question.[121] Some other explanation must be sought. The following is a suggested resolution of this difficulty. It is unlikely that Mark's largely Gentile readership would be very interested in debates and differences internal to Palestinian rabbinic Judaism. They would be far more interested in how the Old Testament applied to them in their situation and how Jesus, as the one true Lord, dealt with situations fraught with conflict, and what help this could give them as they faced their own situations of trial and conflict. Moreover, in an Empire in which—as we shall see in the next chapter—the divorce situation was chaotic, there was real need for the Church in this situation to know the mind of her Master. Mark's account concentrates on bringing out those features which will best serve this purpose and, accordingly, it is unnecessary for him to quote all that the Pharisees said to Jesus.[122]

In verse 3, Jesus directs his questioners to the teaching of Moses by posing a counter question: 'What did Moses command you?' By forcing them to state the Mosaic teaching, Jesus is avoiding the trap that has been set for him. He is forcing them to declare what their Scriptures teach. Which Scriptures? Is Jesus here referring to the first five books of the Bible, or is he referring to the specifically Mosaic legislation? From the Pharisees' reply in verse 4, it is clear that they understood the reference to be to the specifically Mosaic teaching, whereas Jesus' words in verses 5-6 indicate that he had in mind the entire Mosaic corpus. In verse 4, the Pharisees declare that

Moses 'permitted' a man to write a certificate of divorce and send his wife away.[123] Evidently, they have declared their own position vis-à-vis the question which Mark has recorded them as posing: they believe it is lawful for a man to put away his wife because Moses permitted it. Clearly, Moses would not have permitted something that was unlawful. In verse 5, Jesus gives the reason for this part of the Mosaic legislation. As we noted in our study of Matthew 19, the Mosaic legislation was occasioned by the hardness of the men's hearts. But from the beginning of the creation, this had not been so: the divine ideal is set forth in the same way in which Jesus set it forth in Matthew 19:4-5, by referring to Genesis 1 and 2. This is what Jesus is saying in verses 6-8*a*. In 8*b* Jesus draws the same inference that we saw him draw in Matthew 19:6*a*. In verse 9, he says what he said in Matthew 19:6*b*.

In terms of the test that the Pharisees set him, Jesus has said nothing that is not found in the Old Testament, or that may not be legitimately inferred from the Old Testament. If he is in difficulty with Antipas as a result of what he has said, then all who accepted the authority of Moses would be in difficulty—which would be a very large proportion of the Jewish population of Palestine! Indeed, the Pharisees would hardly be likely to risk putting many of their own kind in the dock. So Jesus' answer would give the Pharisees no ammunition to give to Antipas to fire at him on their behalf. That Mark's readers had to be prepared to suffer like their Master is something Mark has made very clear in his Gospel; but it is also very clear from a passage like this that there is need to be wise in the way one conducts oneself before a hostile world.

Verse 10 tells us, 'When they were in the house again, the disciples asked Jesus about this.' Away from the Pharisees and the crowds, the disciples want him to elaborate on what he has said, namely, that the Mosaic legislation was a temporary measure occasioned by men's hardness of heart. We are to understand their question as expressing a desire for more light from Jesus upon this matter. In verse 11, Jesus says exactly what we have in Matthew 19:9, apart from the exceptive clause.[124] The verse expresses an absolute prohibition of divorce. In verse 12, Jesus says exactly the same of the woman who divorces her husband and marries another man.[125] The differences between this account and Matthew's account will be explored in the next section. But it is appropriate to ask two questions at this juncture. The first is, Did Mark intend his readers to understand Jesus to be absolutely prohibiting divorce and remarriage? And the second, Is the reference to the woman divorcing her husband something which Jesus said, or is it added by Mark? We shall take up each question in turn.

The first thing that needs to be borne in mind is the fact that Mark has not fully recorded the Pharisees' question. But that will obviously affect his recording of Jesus' answer. Indeed, his omitting of material from the question serves his purpose of highlighting a specific aspect of Jesus' answer. If the question specifically addressed the issue of what grounds will justify divorce, then it might make sense to have an answer in the terms, 'These are the cases in which divorce may take place.' But it would be entirely out of place where the question concerns not the grounds of divorce but the lawfulness of it; either it is lawful, or it is not. Of course, the Pharisees were concerned with the question of the grounds because of the acute disagreement between the Shammaites and Hillelites over this issue. But Mark's Gentile readers would not be interested in this, and so the question, as recorded by Mark, turns simply on the lawfulness, according to the Old Testament, of divorce. Jesus' reply to the Pharisees is, basically, that divorce was not unlawful, under the Mosaic economy, but that this did not express the divine ideal. The Mosaic provision was occasioned by men's hardness of heart, but from the beginning it was not so. Jesus then goes on to reassert the divine ideal: what God has joined together, let not man separate. In effect, he is implying the same kind of distinction that we noted earlier with respect to English law: the fact that something is not outlawed and forbidden does not mean that it is approved and lawful. We noted the example of gaming contracts, which, while not illegal in the sense that they are criminalised, are not lawful in terms of their recognition in the courts. In effect, Jesus is saying that Moses had to deal with men as he found them; but how men were was not in line with the divine ideal. Jesus' answer, as recorded by Mark, is conditioned by the question put to him, as recorded by Mark. That question concerned the legitimacy of divorce, and Jesus now declares that there is no longer a place for the Mosaic divorce provision. This point is further emphasised in the conversation with the disciples, where Jesus categorises divorce and remarriage as adulterous.

At this point, two important features of Mark's treatment deserve comment. The first concerns one of the emphases of his Gospel as compared and contrasted with Matthew. Matthew regularly emphasises that Jesus and the kingdom he inaugurates are *the fulfilment* of the Old Testament. Mark, by contrast, though not denying this emphasis (see, for example, 1:1-3,11,15), seeks to bring out the fact that this will inevitably entail the abrogation of aspects of Old Testament teaching, and even a return to a situation which obtained before some of the Old Testament legislation came into being. For example, in Mark 7:1-23, the controversy Jesus had with the Pharisees about hand-washing is recorded. Mark, like Matthew, represents Jesus as contrasting the requirements of God's Word with the demands of human tradition. Jesus upholds the former and criticises the Pharisees for nullifying God's Word by their tradition. But Mark brings out an emphasis that is missing from Matthew. In verse 19, we read, 'In saying this, Jesus declared all foods "clean".'[126] Matthew does not mention this. The point is, of course, that Mark is emphasising that, in principle, Jesus' teaching *had the effect* of abrogating *aspects* of the Mosaic law. Clearly, Jesus' teaching did *not* have the effect of abrogating everything that Moses taught, because in verses 9-13 he identifies Moses' teaching with the command of God that applies to his hearers. What is happening is that those *temporary and provisional* aspects of the Mosaic law were being set aside. These, of course, were the very things that served as 'badges and boundary markers' in the Judaism of the period, and caused so much difficulty in the early church.[127] Certainly, Peter had to learn that all food was clean in order to appreciate the big lesson that the gospel is for all people and table fellowship is possible with all believers. Paul's letter to the Romans massively emphasises that the gospel is universal in its scope and not confined to the Jewish people. But these lessons have obvious implications for aspects of the status of the Mosaic law. Mark's dependence upon Peter, and his links with Paul and with the church at Rome,[128] would mean that this emphasis on abrogation of the Mosaic law as a result of the coming of Christ would be both natural for Mark and not wasted on his readers. This being the case, in chapter 10 he emphasises that Jesus has set aside the Mosaic law. This case becomes all the more compelling when one bears in mind some of the connecting links between Mark 7 and Mark 10.[129]

The second point to bear in mind is that in verse 9 Jesus implicitly forbids divorce, and does not address the question of remarriage until verse 11. Verses 11-12 are but the elaboration and unfolding for the disciples of what is found, in embryo form, earlier in Jesus' conversation with the Pharisees. Accordingly, if we understand verses 11-12 to be absolutely prohibiting divorce and remarriage, then we must understand verse 9 to be absolutely prohibiting divorce. There is *no* exception to it. Were a woman to commit adultery many times with many different men, it would be utterly forbidden for the man to divorce the woman. It is not only remarriage which is being forbidden; verse 9 forbids divorce. If we say that the idea that Matthew has Jesus allowing remarriage after divorce is flatly contradicted by Mark, and therefore it cannot be that Matthew is to be understood as allowing remarriage, we must also say that Matthew allowing divorce for *porneia* is also flatly contradicted by Mark. Mark does not allow divorce at all. A standard answer to this is that Matthew was making allowances for those Jewish Christians who were compelled, by their Jewish culture, to divorce. Mark's readers did not face this problem. Quite apart from objections which we raised concerning this treatment of Matthew's Gospel, this explanation fails to take account of the fact that the *lex Julia de adulteriis* required men to divorce their wives if they had committed adultery.[130] So why does Mark not include an exception as does Matthew?

The common explanation advanced by writers such as Heth and Wenham fails to consider the implications of the *lex Julia* for the exceptive clause. If Mark is recording Jesus as absolutely prohibiting divorce, then the following are entailed. First, Matthew's Gospel and Mark's really are in hopeless contradiction at this point. This consideration alone is wholly unacceptable to those who espouse an evangelical and biblical doctrine of Scripture. Secondly, Mark is teaching that a man must not divorce his wife if she fornicates with many different men, if she enters into homosexual relationships with other women, or even if she is guilty of bestiality. The man must not separate what God has joined together. Thirdly, the man must maintain the marriage in the very teeth of the requirements of the *lex Julia*. Christians are being called to flout *that law*, which was enacted to preserve public morals, and face the consequent penalties for their disobedience. If people are hesitant to accept these entailments, perhaps they might agree that a different understanding of Mark's teaching might make better sense.

I propose the following. Since divorce for *porneia* was not within the scope of the discourse initiated by the Pharisees, as recorded by Mark, Mark does not record Jesus' exceptive words. The reason for this is that he is concerned to emphasise the effective abrogation of parts of the Mosaic law, and the need to maintain high standards of marriage and not resort to easy divorce. Easy divorce was commonplace in the Roman Empire, and Mark faithfully records Jesus' teaching as relevant to that issue. Just as Mark records Jesus as upholding the command to honour parents but as also setting aside the food laws, so he records Jesus as upholding the law forbidding adultery but as setting aside the law which permitted divorce. However, Mark would understand his readers to approve of the *lex Julia*, and to take for granted that it was permissible to put away for *porneia*. In Mark 7:21, *porneia* is described by Jesus as defiling, and he is, therefore, reported by Mark as having a serious view of it. Those guilty of moral defilement, now, are not to be treated as they would be under the Mosaic law, but Mark's readers would understand that the moral defilement which strikes at the heart of a marriage may become the basis of divorce.

There is good reason to believe that the words of verse 12 were uttered by Jesus and not supplied by Mark. The reader is referred to earlier comments, when dealing with Matthew 19, where it was pointed out that the attributing of words purportedly coming from Christ's own lips to the Gospel writers raises serious questions as to whether those who say such things have abandoned the evangelical doctrine of Scripture. In the present passage, there are good contextual reasons for believing that Jesus' words *to his disciples* in verse 12 were a reference to Herodias.[131] Of course, Mark has a very good reason for recording these words, because of the prevalence in the Empire of women divorcing their husbands.[132] The words of Jesus were not so relevant to a Jewish readership and, therefore, Matthew does not record them. These words of Jesus throw further light on his reason for quoting Genesis 1:27. The equality of the sexes meant that what was reprehensible in the man was equally reprehensible in the woman.

Differences between Matthew and Mark

Attention frequently falls on the absence of the exceptive clause from Mark and on its presence in Matthew. However, there are numerous differences between the two accounts, and the best explanation is one which will explain *all* the differences. That explanation is to be found in the different purposes of the two Gospel writers. Matthew is concerned to bring out the fulfilment motif and to show how this leads to continuity and discontinuity between the Old Testament and Jesus' teaching. The kingdom has already, but not yet fully, come. Thus, there will still be situations where divorce is permitted, but the Mosaic toleration of divorce has no place in the eschatological kingdom. Writing for a Jewish Christian readership, Matthew preserves the rabbinic-debate background to the question put to Jesus by the Pharisees. By contrast, Mark is writing for a Gentile readership, which would not be interested in rabbinic debates but would be very interested in knowing how to be faithful to Jesus in a hostile world. Having knowledge of the Old Testament, but not of Palestinian Jewish customs, they would be interested in having some kind of background to the question as to which parts of the Old Testament would still apply to them and which parts had been effectively abrogated. Accordingly, Mark emphasises the setting aside of the Mosaic legislation and, as a consequence of this, underlines the fact that the easy divorces in the Empire were contrary to God's will. The issue of *porneia* was not under consideration and did not need to be mentioned.

Conclusions

Jesus attacked the easy divorces of his day. His teaching on divorce was addressed to that situation. He saw no justification for such divorces and taught that the situation allowed by Moses would no longer apply in God's kingdom. The same standards would be required of both men and women, and the only time that, according to Jesus, a man might divorce was where his wife was guilty of *porneia*. Since the same standards were expected of women, it follows that Jesus implicitly did not condemn a woman who divorced because of her husband's *porneia*. He did not specifically address this issue, since it was not the context in which he ministered. But this conclusion is legitimately inferred from his teaching.

Excursus
on the meaning of *porneia*

The difficulty with the term *porneia* is that it has a fairly wide semantic range and may, therefore, bear a wide range of meanings. In determining which is the appropriate meaning, the interpreter of Scripture has to consider a number of factors. Clearly, the limits of the semantic range of the term need to be fixed; this having been done, the rendering which best fits the context should be chosen. However, this procedure raises hermeneutical questions, for a high view of Scripture requires us to understand the term not only in its immediate context but also in the wider context of the teaching of Scripture as a whole. But this might lead to exegesis of the verse in question being straitjacketed and hijacked by a theological understanding already gained from other passages of Scripture. In grappling with the meaning of a verse, it is clearly important to ask why the verse is there. However, it is possible to employ such a question so that the answer demands that a particular meaning be assigned to a term. The meaning of the term is then fixed by the purpose assigned to the verse. But there is a sense in which one must grasp the meaning of a verse or a term before one can enquire into its function. What all of this demonstrates is that linguistic expertise may not be sufficient to interpret a controverted text: the very fact that experts in New Testament Greek are divided over the meaning of *porneia* in Matthew 5:32 is eloquent testimony to this observation.

The reasons for understanding *porneia* in verse 32 to mean 'illicit sexual intercourse' or 'illicit sexual activity' are overwhelming. Lexically, this meaning is assigned to the term. Thus, BAG give the meaning of *porneia* as follows: 'prostitution, unchastity, fornication, every kind of unlawful sexual intercourse'. It is thus used in the following: Romans 1:29; 1 Corinthians 5:1; 6:13; 2 Corinthians 12:21; Galatians 5:19; Ephesians 5:3; Colossians 3:5. It is distinguished from *moicheia* in Matthew 15:19 and Mark 7:21, though *moicheia* appears as *porneia* in Sir 23:33. BAG cite Matthew 5:32 and 19:9 as examples of the sexual unfaithfulness of a married woman, and 1 Thessalonians 4:3 as an example of illicit sexual intercourse. BAG note that the words *ek porneias gennēthēnai* are used to describe an illegitimate child. Thayer states that the term is properly used to denote illicit sexual intercourse in general. The LXX regularly employs the term and its cognates in this way. Thus, the Hebrew *zᵉnût* and *zᵉnûnîm* are translated by *porneia*. *Zânâ* and *taznût* (only used in Ezekiel 16 (9 times) and 23 (11 times)) are translated by *porneia, porneuō* and *ekporneuō*. In many—though not all—of these cases, the reference is not just to isolated incidents of illicit intercourse but to a pattern of promiscuity or prostitution. Certainly, *ekporneuō* carries the idea of abandoning oneself to, or glutting oneself with, sexual lust.

To understand *porneia* as referring to sexual immorality makes perfect sense of the exception in Matthew 5:32. Jesus is saying that if a man divorces his wife, he will cause her to suffer adultery. Clearly, where the woman is herself guilty of sexual immorality, she has already committed adultery, since illicit sexual intercourse is a clear repudiation of the one-flesh union that lies at the heart of marriage. If *porneia* is not understood in this way, we are left with the following anomalous position: if a man divorces his wife—even though she has frequently had intercourse with different men in the last year, or regularly had intercourse with another man—he causes her to suffer adultery. This, of course, is an incredible understanding of the verse, but one must so understand it unless one accepts that Jesus is making an exception where the wife has been guilty of illicit sexual intercourse. It may be objected that this assimilates the meaning of *porneia* and its cognates to *moicheia* and its cognates, whereas there is clearly a distinction between the two word-groups. But this is not so, for a number of reasons. First, if adultery is understood in the narrow sense of repudiation of a specific marriage by one of the spouses, then *porneia* has a wider range of meaning, since it includes intercourse between two unmarried people. If we accept the wider definition of adultery that appears to be demanded by Matthew 5:28—that is, that anything which is hostile to the institution of marriage is a form of adultery—then it is clear that *porneia* is a species of which *moicheia* is the genus. Secondly, illicit sexual activity is to be widely defined. It includes homosexuality, bestiality, etc. Indeed, it would appear that the sins referred to in Leviticus 18 would be covered by the term. However, before deciding that this is the meaning of the term in this verse, we need to examine all the other possibilities.

111

The 'unlawful marriages' view

The first view to be considered is the one designated by Heth and Wenham as the 'unlawful marriages' view. There are two forms of this, the first being that *porneia* in Matthew 5:32 is a reference to a marriage within the prohibited degrees, and the second that it refers to mixed marriages.

a) *Prohibited degrees*

In support of this view, it has been pointed out that in Leviticus 18:6-8 the Hebrew term *zᵉnût*, which is translated in the LXX by *porneia*, refers to the prohibited degrees of consanguinity and affinity. Bruce, Fitzmyer and others find support for this usage of the term in the New Testament: 1 Corinthians 5:1; Acts 15:20, 29; 21:25. Commenting on the use of the term in Acts 15, Bruce states:

> [*porneia* is] here intended not in the common sense of the word (for abstention from that was in any case stringently enjoined on all Christians) but in the sense of transgression of the degrees of consanguinity and affinity prohibited in Leviticus 18:6-18. These mutual prohibitions were basic to the Jewish marriage law and have been an article of Christian canon law from the time of the Jerusalem decree.[133]

Fitzmyer extends this argument.[134] Like Bruce, he sees the use of *porneia* in Acts 15 as an application of the Holiness Code of Leviticus 17–18 to Gentile Christians. He goes on to note that the Damascus Document found at Qumran applies the Hebrew term *zᵉnût* to the prohibited degrees in Leviticus 18:13. Since this is translated by *porneia* in the LXX, Fitzmyer concludes that any Palestinian Jew of the first century BC and AD would understand *porneia* to refer to *zᵉnût*. This being so, the argument in support of this translation proceeds on the basis that this rendering best fits the purpose of the passage. Mark and Luke both contain absolute prohibitions of divorce. This was the same teaching as that recorded by Matthew. However, the Christians for whom Matthew was writing included Gentile Christians who had, prior to their conversion, married within the prohibited degrees. They felt precluded from ending these unions because of Jesus' absolute prohibition of divorce. Accordingly, Matthew added the exceptive words to bring out the true meaning of Jesus' words in a context very different from those in which they were first uttered. Thus, the absolute prohibition of divorce stands, but Jesus never meant to approve of incestuous marriages. Such a problem would not have arisen in a strongly Jewish context. But when it did arise, Matthew—whose Gospel is the most Jewish of the Synoptists'—added the exceptive clause. Supporters of this position point to its lexical support, its suitability within the context of Matthew, and its consistency with the rest of Jesus' teaching.

However, there are cogent reasons why the 'unlawful marriages' view is untenable. As we have already noted, it leaves Jesus saying that any husband who divorces the most debauched of women is thereby causing her to suffer adultery. This, as we have seen, is incredible. It is accepted that the term may translate the Hebrew *z^enût*. However, before severely limiting the term to such a narrow meaning, there must be powerful contextual considerations to require such a meaning. With the greatest of respect to proponents of this view, they appear to be guilty of assuming what they need to prove. Far from marriages within the prohibited degrees being a problem for Gentile Christians within the early church, the New Testament evidence is the exact opposite. Thus, in 1 Corinthians 5:1ff., Paul says that the immorality which has occurred is of a kind which did not even exist among pagans. The meaning is quite clear: not even pagans behaved like this. If that were so, then how did it arise that Gentile Christians found themselves already in incestuous marriages? It will not do to say, as Heth and Wenham do, that pagans would not marry within the prohibited degrees of consanguinity, but might marry within the prohibited degrees of affinity, because Paul is evidently dealing in 1 Corinthians 5 with a case of affinity, *not* consanguinity. The man had had his father's wife, not his mother! What evidence we do have in the New Testament concerning incest, is that it was virtually unheard of amongst pagans. Moreover, if this had been an issue in the early church, it is scarcely conceivable that the only mention of it should have been by way of Matthew's exceptive clauses. Therefore, while it is true that *porneia* may refer to an incestuous marriage, there are weighty reasons for rejecting such a limited understanding of the term in Matthew 5:32.

It ought also to be noted that the instances where the New

Testament is alleged to use the term with reference to an incestuous marriage are not altogether straightforward. For example, it is possible that the incestuous brother in 1 Corinthians 5 had not married his stepmother, but was having sexual relations with her. (The phrase 'to have a woman' or 'to have a wife' (*gynaika echein*) was a euphemism for having sexual relations.) The sin referred to in 1 Corinthians 5 is then that of having sexual relations outside of marriage (fornication), and sexual relations of a particularly wicked kind (with one's stepmother!). If so, it is '*aggravated* fornication' that Paul is dealing with, not an incestuous marriage. Clearly, he would have been as unsparing in his condemnation of the latter as of the former.

The decision of the Council of Jerusalem, recorded in Acts 15, raises a number of complex questions. If it is accepted that the letter sent from Jerusalem was intended to secure the compliance of Gentile Christians with the sensibilities of their Jewish brothers as an act of Christian fellowship and spiritual expediency, then—as this interpretation admits—the letter is of limited application. But does this mean that a Christian is free, today, to marry within the degrees of consanguinity forbidden within Leviticus 18? If not—and Bruce's reference to Canon Law leaves one feeling that supporters of this view would not be happy with such a situation—then one cannot say that the letter is only concerned with conciliating offended Jewish Christians. Indeed, the language of Leviticus 18:24-30 indicates that the matters dealt with in that chapter were of relevance to the Israelites not only for a limited period. This, of course, leaves one with the problem as to why a reference to *porneia* should have found its way into a letter dealing largely with 'ceremonial' issues. (In using the term 'ceremonial', I am not suggesting that the Mosaic Law adopted the anachronistic classification of its regulations into moral/civil/ceremonial. Rather, I am using the term to describe the kinds of things that might create tension in Jew/Gentile relationships—things that were not, per se, binding upon Gentile believers, but that Gentile believers might observe for the sake of those relationships.) The simplest solution would appear to be as follows. The letter requires the Gentile Christians to refrain from eating idol meats, eating blood, and eating food that was not kosher. The reference to *porneia* arises from the fact that there was, in the Gentile world, a clear link between eating food offered to idols and engaging in fornication—a link that arose through cult prostitution. Thus, in 1 Corinthians 8, Paul begins his treatment of eating food sacrificed to idols; but in dealing with this issue he goes on to consider the whole problem of immorality (10:6-8). The reason, therefore, for the inclusion of *porneia* in Acts 15 would have been that there was always the risk of being sucked back, through partaking of meat offered to idols, into the licentious lifestyle which accompanied much idol worship. This being the case, the argument that sees Acts 15 as forbidding unlawful marriages is considerably weakened. If the interpretation I have offered is correct, it means that the New Testament does not use *porneia* to refer to an incestuous *marriage*. (The reference in 1 Corinthians 5 should not be understood to be a reference to marriage.)

Before we turn from this interpretation, two further points need to be made. Firstly, the interpretation is built upon a reconstruction of the *Sitz im Leben* (life setting) of Matthew's Gospel, a reconstruction which is not only *not* supported by evidence, but flies in the face of what evidence there is. Secondly, it is not necessarily the case, as Heth and Wenham contend, that Roman law forbade marriage within prohibited degrees of consanguinity but not of affinity. They build their case upon a section in Gaius's *Institutes* (Gaius 1:18-23; 2:31). However, this matter is not as straightforward as Heth and Wenham assume, as a brief consideration of certain aspects of Roman law should make clear. Barry Nicholas observes:

> ... in the Empire there emerge two 'schools' to which most if not all of the leading jurists of the first two centuries of the Empire seem to have belonged. They were founded ... by two leading jurists of the reign of Augustus, Capito and Labeo, but took their names from two subsequent heads, Massurius Sabinus ... and Proculus ... We are driven to the conclusion that the doctrines of each school must have been an accumulation of the opinions of successive heads of the school on different problems.[135]

The 'classical' period of Roman law covers the period of the 'Principate', 27 BC to AD 284. It was in this period that Gaius lived and worked.

115

Internal evidence suggests that he completed the *Institutes* soon after the death of Antoninus Pius (AD 161) . . . Since he refers to the leaders of the Sabinian school as 'our teachers', [it seems reasonable to say that he was a follower of Massurius Sabinus]. It has been suggested that he was a provincial, but all that we can reliably infer is that he was not accepted as a member of the select group of leading jurists . . . there must have been many lesser lawyers outside this group; Gaius was probably one of these . . . rescued from oblivion by the simplicity and clarity of his exposition in the *Institutes*.[136]

The reason Nicholas draws the inference that Gaius was not one of the select group of leading jurists is found in the following observation: 'He is never mentioned by any classical writer, in spite of the jurists' liking for citing each other's opinions.'[137] Thus, we have a lesser jurist who belongs to one of two leading schools. The great value placed upon his *Institutes* (such that it makes them part of the staple diet of every Roman law student) is due to their 'unique importance because they provide the only evidence for the classical law which we can with reasonable certainty believe to be free from alteration either by post-classical editors or by Justinian's compilers'.[138] Clearly, this fact makes the work invaluable. However, what it does not mean is that we can ascertain the Roman law by reading Gaius in the way in which we can discover the new divorce law in this country by reading FLA 1996.

In contrast to Heth and Wenham's quotation of Gaius, it may, in this connection, be valuable to quote the following words from Justinian: 'A civil law marriage is contracted by Roman citizens who are united according to law.' It is clear from Justinian's work that the words 'according to law' rendered illegal a marriage between close blood relatives or those related by marriage. Justinian lived in the sixth century AD. He was responsible for the codification of Roman law, known as the *Corpus Iuris Civilis*. This included the *Digest* or *Pandects,* and the *Institutes*. The *Corpus Iuris Civilis* was a somewhat unsystematic legal code; the *Digest* was a collection of juristic writings, and the *Institutes* a fairly basic textbook which owed much to Gaius's *Institutes*. While it must be borne in mind that the members of the commission responsible for the compilation of the *Digest* 'were to abridge and alter as much as was necessary to ensure that the work contained no repetitions, no contradictions, and nothing that was obsolete',[139] and that it therefore expressed the law as it stood in Justinian's day, it should, nevertheless, be pointed out that nearly two thousand books were read in order to compile the *Digest*, and that these were reduced to 150,000 lines, leaving a book which, as Nicholas observes, is 'one and a half times the size of the Bible'.[140] It is, therefore, somewhat precarious for Heth and Wenham to assert, simply on the basis of extracts from Gaius's *Institutes*, that degrees of affinity were not prohibited in Roman law, particularly when leading Roman lawyers take a contrary view on the basis of the work of Justinian. For example, Buckland—whose stature as an authority on Roman law none would question—states the following: 'Still more important were the bars created [to marriage] by relationship *and affinity*' (italics mine). Buckland goes on to expound the bars created by degrees of affinity:

> *Affinitas.* Connexion by marriage. One party to a marriage might not afterwards marry an ascendant or descendant of the other or, in later law, a brother or sister in law. Nor might one marry a person who had been betrothed to one's parent or child. There were other analogous rules. In all these cases a union conflicting with the rules was void: in some it was punishable and in those under the rules as to relationship and the like it was treated as incestuous.[141]

It is clear from Buckland's reference to 'later law', when it was forbidden to marry one's brother-in-law, that the other prohibited degrees of affinity applied at an earlier stage. Since Gaius states that one could marry one's brother-in-law or sister-in-law or, in certain circumstances, a stepsister or stepbrother, Heth and Wenham conclude: 'For Roman law, affinity seems to have been no legal impediment to marriage.'[142] However, while it is true that in allowing marriages between brothers-in-law and sisters-in-law the Roman law was wider in what it allowed than the Holiness Code (cf. Leviticus 18:16), this does not alter the fact that, in the earlier Roman law, marriage was forbidden between ascendants and descendants by blood or marriage. In the later Empire it was forbidden to marry a deceased wife's sister or a deceased husband's brother. What this means, of course, is that Heth and Wenham have misunderstood the significance of what Gaius says; they have failed to see, for example, that a marriage between a man and his stepmother was forbidden. This being the case, 1 Corinthians 5:1 is almost certainly referring to sexual relationship rather than to marriage, and it explains why Paul castigates such behaviour as falling below the standards of pagans.

The development of the Roman law may be traced in Jolowicz, which is the leading work on the historical development of Roman law. A detailed treatment of the Roman law of marriage—as, indeed, of most other aspects of Roman law—will be found in Buckland's *Textbook of Roman Law,* which is an encyclopaedic study (but not for the faint-hearted), and in Corbett. Helpful background material on Gaius and Justinian will be found in Nicholas. On the compilation of the *Digest,* reference should be made to Honoré, who differs somewhat from Nicholas in his understanding of the way in which it was compiled.

b) *Mixed marriages*

The second form the 'unlawful marriages' view takes is that *porneia* refers to marriage to a person whom one is prohibited from marrying because of that person's national identity. The *porneia* of Acts 15 is understood in this way, and Jesus' exception relates to a man in such a mixed marriage putting away his wife. This is the kind of situation that occurred during the days of Ezra and Nehemiah (see Ezra 9; Nehemiah 13:23-27).

But this interpretation is really quite unsustainable and impossible. To begin with, the Mosaic law did *not* forbid all mixed marriages, and the Old Testament recognised some marriages that were strictly forbidden by the Mosaic law (see chapter 2, note 34, above). Secondly, the fact that the Mosaic law distinguished between nations from whom one could not choose a marriage partner and those where one was not thus forbidden, indicates that it would have been impossible to apply a blanket condemnation to all mixed marriages *and* be faithful to the Old Testament. Thirdly, there is absolutely no evidence elsewhere in the New Testament that there was a problem with mixed marriages. Quite the contrary! Thus, in Acts 16:1 we are introduced to Timothy, whose mother was Jewish but whose father was Greek. If the reference to *porneia* in Acts 15 denotes a mixed marriage, then it was singularly inept of Paul to choose as one of his travelling companions a product of a marriage forbidden by the Jerusalem letter!

Moreover, we are asked by this interpretation to believe that there is but *one* ground where Jesus does not absolutely forbid divorce, and that is where one of his disciples ends up married to a Gentile. It is true that the Sermon on the Mount is addressed to a living situation in which the people were living under the Mosaic law and observing Jewish customs. That being so, it is difficult to see why Jesus would need to single out a mixed marriage: if this was to be a problem in the Christian community, it would become so at a later stage, when the gospel would have penetrated further into the Gentile community. It may be argued that the exception was a Matthean addition to deal with just such a situation. The problem with arguing in this way is that, while addressed to the Jewish context of Jesus' day, the Sermon on the Mount is clearly looking further ahead. Thus Matthew 5:17-20 indicates that the eschatological kingdom will radically affect the application of the law to the lives of Jesus' disciples. No doubt, many patriotic Jews would have been outraged by Jesus' words in 5:38-47, but he did not trim his message to accommodate their nationalistic sensibilities.

The simple fact is that the New Testament records the expansion of the gospel into the Gentile world as being the occasion of integration between Jews and Gentiles in Christ and in his Church. That there were tensions and problems none will deny. But what is significant is that nowhere does the New Testament suggest that there were problems in mixed Jew/Gentile marriages. In the absence of any evidence to suggest otherwise, there is no reason to believe that the reference to *porneia* in Acts 15 is to mixed Jewish/Gentile marriages. Indeed, as we have seen in the reference to Timothy, there is good reason to exclude this understanding. And if Acts 15 cannot be pressed into service to support this meaning, it is difficult to see how *porneia* can be understood in this way in Matthew 5:32.

In considering arguments that might support this view, Heth and Wenham note the following linguistic points. The term *porneia* is used in Jubilees 30:7,10-11, where a daughter of Israel's 'marriage with a Gentile is no better than fornication'. The LXX uses *ekporneuō* to describe Israel's playing the harlot with the daughters of Moab.

Moreover, Heth and Wenham note that the Temple Scroll from Qumran forbids the king from marrying a foreigner, and they accept Daube's arguments for extending this prohibition to all the people. But all of this manifestly fails to prove the point.

Let us examine each of these arguments in turn. The quotation from Jubilees demonstrates that the semantic referent of *porneia* in that passage is 'fornication'. This is, as it were, the underlying meaning of the term, which has to exist for the comparison to hold. All that Jubilees proves is that a mixed marriage is compared to *porneia*. This no more fixes the meaning of the term than does the fact that the New Testament sometimes employs *porneia* and its cognates, and the Old Testament the equivalent Hebrew terms, as a metaphor for spiritual unfaithfulness to the Lord. Furthermore, one must ask if Jesus and the apostles approved of the theology found in this part of Jubilees.

The reference to *ekporneuō* in Numbers 25:1 is similarly unconvincing. To begin with, there is good reason to believe that the passage recounts *both* spiritual *and* physical adultery. Thus Wenham himself, in his excellent *Tyndale Commentary*, makes the following observations on verses 1-2: '"Play the harlot" has both a physical and a spiritual sense. Sacred prostitution was a common feature of Canaanite religion; through it some of the Israelites were allured to participate in pagan sacrifices and "bowed down to their gods".' Furthermore, Wenham comments on verse 6 as follows: 'Up to this point intercourse with foreign girls had taken place outside the camp. Now under the nose of Moses and the other people, Zimri showed his contempt . . .' What this means, of course, is that Numbers 25 is recording a situation of widespread spiritual and sexual failure, both of which were related to each other. But that fact hardly allows us to fix the meaning of *porneia* in Acts 15, and then read that meaning back into Matthew 5:32. After all, Ruth was a Moabitess, and an ancestor of David and of Jesus. The real import of the prohibition of certain mixed marriages in the Old Testament concerns the people of God not marrying those who are pagans. As we saw in the previous chapter, exceptional cases were allowed, where the woman gave herself up to the Lord. The New Testament equivalent to, and application of, these prohibitions is that Christians should marry 'only in the Lord'. But, as we shall see in the next chapter, a Christian was specifically forbidden from separating from an unbelieving spouse.

The reference to the Temple Scroll proves nothing at all. The simple fact of the matter is that there are major differences between Christianity and the teachings believed by the Qumran community. While the Dead Sea Scrolls provide fascinating background material to the Gospels, it would be perilous in the extreme to refer to them to fix the meaning of a much controverted New Testament verse, when there are excellent reasons for understanding the verse in another way.

Finally, with respect to this interpretation, it should be pointed out that the examples of narrow and specific meanings cancel each other out. Even if Jubilees did assign a narrow meaning to *porneia*—which, as we have seen, it does not—the problem would be that it also translates *z^enûṯ.* in the LXX rendering of Leviticus where the prohibited degrees are considered. All of this means that the term has a wide semantic range. By understanding the term in a general sense, one will find that many of the narrow and specific usages of the term may well be included in Matthew's exception, and only those that can be shown not to fit will be excluded. I am suggesting that mixed marriages is one meaning that does not fit.

Before turning to the next possible interpretation, it may be worth noting that the understanding of *porneia* as a reference to idolatry may be linked with the 'mixed marriages' view. It is true that *porneia* can be used metaphorically to denote spiritual unfaithfulness in idolatry. It is easy to see how an Israelite or Jew married to a Gentile could find himself joined to an idol worshipper. By extension, one may then say that this could apply to the situation where a Christian is married to a pagan who engages in gross idolatry. There are numerous reasons for rejecting this interpretation. First, Jesus is saying in verse 32 that the man who divorces his wife will cause her to suffer adultery, except where he does so for the cause of *porneia*. It is difficult to see how the woman worshipping an idol could be an exception to the husband causing her to suffer adultery. We need to remember that Jesus is *not* giving grounds for divorce, but describing the consequences of divorce *except* in this one situation. Secondly, whatever faults Palestinian Judaism of the Second Temple period suffered from, it seems quite certain that for the Pharisees to approve marriage to pagan idolaters was not one of them. Exclusivism rather than syncretism was the sin that Jesus regularly pinpointed in the religion of his day. If one looks ahead to the situation that would obtain when the gospel penetrated Gentile culture, and the problem of Christians being married to non-Christians had to be considered, it has to be said that the New Testament makes it quite clear that *this* situation was not one that Jesus addressed when he was upon earth.

The 'betrothal' view
The next meaning to consider is what Heth and Wenham denominate the 'betrothal' view. This understands Jesus' exception for *porneia* to be referring to sexual infidelity on the part of a person after having been betrothed, but before marriage had been consummated. The New Testament itself, of course, refers to this type of situation in Matthew 1:18-19. A number of comments need to be made about this view. Firstly, it is perfectly possible that *porneia* could include this type of case without being confined to it. Jewish marriage customs were such that betrothal was of greater significance than our engagement to marry. Thus, as Heth and Wenham point out, the following passages indicate that a betrothed person was already regarded as a husband or wife: Genesis 29:21; Deuteronomy 22:23-24; 2 Samuel 3:14; Matthew 1:18-25. This being so, Heth and Wenham dismiss Murray's rejection of this interpretation, claiming that he fails to understand the status of a betrothed person. This seems somewhat harsh on Murray, and Heth and Wenham fail to consider certain aspects of the status of a betrothed person. For example, in 2 Samuel 3:14, not only does David describe Michal as his wife whom he has betrothed to himself, but Ish-Bosheth orders that Michal be taken from her husband Paltiel. If Paltiel is Michal's husband, then Michal is Paltiel's wife. But David calls her his wife. This means that Michal has two husbands, and so here is a case of polyandry. It is probably better to understand the use of the term 'wife' of a betrothed person as an example of proleptic language. Thus we may say that the Queen of Great Britain was born in 1926, though, of course, she was not the queen then. Similarly, when someone exchanges contracts to buy a house, he may then call the dwelling 'my house'; but, strictly speaking, that is only true on completion of the sale and purchase. Betrothal should be understood in these terms.

The Old Testament background is not altogether clear at this point. Deuteronomy 22:13-21 deals with the case of a man who alleges that his bride had already lost her virginity. If proof of her virginity could not be found, she was to be stoned. If the proof was produced, the man was fined and thereafter barred from divorcing her. Deuteronomy 22:23-24 deals with a betrothed person who consents to intercourse with a man other than the man to whom she is betrothed. In that case, both were to be executed. The procedural requirements referred to in the previous chapter—that is, two witnesses, etc.—would have to be satisfied for execution to take place. Verses 25-26 deal with the case of rape. A girl who had lost her virginity but not been caught in the act would have lost her proof of virginity and be dealt with under the provisions of verses 20-21. Accordingly, there was no provision under the Old Testament for divorce in this type of case. However, a number of questions arise. What if the girl became pregnant during the betrothal period, but the man to whom she was betrothed claimed that he was not the father? This is exactly the situation in Matthew 1:18-19. It may be thought that the ritual of Numbers 5 would then be carried out. Heth and Wenham seem to suggest that this was the case.

However, there are two difficulties with this understanding. First of all, Numbers 5 appears to be dealing with a marriage that has been consummated and not with a betrothal type of situation. Secondly, there is evidence in the Mishnah that the Numbers 5 ritual could not be effected where the woman was betrothed but not married. Thus, *Sotah* 4.1 reads: 'A woman that is betrothed or that awaits levirate marriage may not drink [the bitter water] or receive her Ketubah: for it is written, "When a wife . . . ".' This quotation is important for a number of reasons. Firstly, it specifically distinguishes the Old Testament use of the word 'wife' from a betrothed person; to that extent, Heth and Wenham's criticism of Murray as not understanding the status of a betrothed person is harsh, and their view perhaps over-confident. Secondly, it specifically excludes the betrothed person from the ritual of Numbers 5. On the other hand, it is difficult to reconcile this quotation from *Sotah* with the following quotation from the same source: 'All agree that [the priest] may not take account of her concerning a time before she was betrothed . . .' (*Sotah* 2.6). Presumably, a husband could not, some time after the consummation of marriage, make allegations against his wife relating to the period between betrothal and consummation, because there was already provision in Deuteronomy 22:13ff. for such a situation. Accordingly, this quotation suggests that the ritual could be applied in a betrothal situation. If so, this is probably the public disgrace referred to in Matthew 1:19. Accordingly, it would appear that, in the New Testament era, divorce was an alternative to forcing a woman to undergo the ritual of Numbers 5. This would seem to be confirmed by *Sotah* 4.2, which states that a woman who admitted that she was unclean was not to drink the bitter water, nor was a woman to be forced who refused to drink. *Sotah* provides that such were to be divorced.

The situation of Joseph appears to be this. Mary could not be executed because there were no witnesses, for the obvious reason that her child had been miraculously conceived and was not the result of fornication. Joseph, however, did not know this before the angelic announcement. Hence, he could either put her through the ritual or divorce her quietly. The *ritual itself* would have been something of a humiliating experience for any woman, especially if she were innocent. One has only to think of what a police suspect feels like during an intimate body search to appreciate that an innocent woman would have found the whole procedure profoundly distressing. But it would be extremely unlikely for a man to put her through this unless he had very strong grounds for doing so. Presumably, a woman who had been impregnated by her betrothed might be prepared to suffer the indignity of the *act* of the ritual in order to be vindicated by the *result of the ritual*. Presumably, honest men would prefer to do this than quietly to divorce the betrothed; for in the latter case, there would always be the feeling that the man was afraid of the truth. There would, however, be an exception: the man who truly loved his betrothed, and was filled with concern for her, would prefer to put her away quietly than have her humiliated and shamed. Prior to the angelic announcement, Joseph could only believe that Mary would be shamed. The term *dikaios* (righteous), while having a wide semantic range, could certainly convey the idea of being faithful in a covenant relationship and being faithful to the other party to that relationship. In certain contexts it might carry overtones of 'mercy'. This appears to be the case with Joseph and, hence, he was willing to divorce Mary quietly. (I do not mean, as some wish to argue, that the 'righteous' word-group always means this, but that it may sometimes include this idea. For a thorough and valuable discussion of the meaning of the term 'righteousness', see Piper.) Furthermore, it was probably the case that, in the event of Joseph divorcing Mary quietly, she would have kept any 'Ketubah' or marriage settlement, whereas this would not be the case when a woman was divorced after having been shown to be guilty of sexual unfaithfulness.

Brewer argues (Brewer, Non Academic) that the situation Joseph faced brings into sharp focus the differing approaches of the school of Shammai and the school of Hillel. The betrothal could have ended in one of two ways. Joseph could have alleged sexual infidelity on Mary's part. In the absence of witnesses, this would have necessitated the public trial envisaged in Numbers 5. This was the Shammaite kind of divorce. Alternatively, Joseph could have chosen the Hillelite divorce, which was something he could effect privately, possibly with the help of a rabbi to draw up the divorce certificate. This, in fact, is what Joseph chose to do.

As we have seen, BAG refer to an illegitimate child as *ek porneias*. It would seem that a betrothed person who had sexual activity with another person was guilty of *porneia* and, given the status of a betrothed person, divorce could be effected. The question, however, is this: should the exception of Matthew 5:32 be confined to this meaning of the term? There are strong reasons for answering in the negative. First, we need to remember that Jesus is *not* setting out grounds for divorce, but is castigating a husband who divorces his wife as causing her to suffer adultery. There is one exception: where there has been *porneia*. The weakness of the exclusive 'betrothal view' should now be clear. According to this view, a man who divorces his betrothed, who has engaged on but one occasion in sexual activity during her betrothal period, will not cause her to suffer adultery. However, a man who divorces his wife, who has slept with many different men on numerous occasions, will cause her to suffer adultery. There is absolutely no sense in such an interpretation. There is undoubtedly an agenda that lies beneath this interpretation, and it is as follows: a consummated marriage effects a one-flesh union that only ends in death. To put away a wife—and assuming she marries again—means that she will in the eyes of men be married to husband number two when in the eyes of God she is still married to husband number one. There is a word for this:

adultery. Thus, for a husband ever to divorce his wife will lead to adultery. But this will not be so in the case of a betrothed person. The one-flesh union has not been effected. Accordingly, where she has been sexually unfaithful, the man may put her away. Should she marry the man she has slept with, she will regularise the situation.

But this really is an impossible way of understanding Christ's words of exception. We have seen in the previous chapter that the one-flesh union *can* be broken—by divorce. This, itself, is a repudiation of the marriage. But where the wife commits *porneia*, she is effectively repudiating the marriage; therefore, by divorcing her, the husband is not causing her to suffer something, because she has already actively done that which undermines the marriage. Furthermore, this interpretation fails to understand the words 'his wife' (*tēn gynaika autou*) in verse 32. As Murray points out, if the exceptive words relate only to a betrothal situation, then the word 'wife' is being used in a number of ways in two verses that are juxtaposed. Verse 31 is clearly referring to a consummated marriage. For the betrothal interpretation to work, verse 32 must be understood in one of two ways.

The first possibility is that Jesus has changed the meaning of *tēn gynaika autou* in verse 32, so that in that verse it means something quite different from the identical expression in verse 31. In verse 31, it means a wife to a consummated marriage, whereas in verse 32 it means a betrothed woman. To say the least, this is stretching credulity, and appeal to Jewish marriage customs and to a handful of references where a betrothed person is called 'wife' hardly makes this more believable. Apart from the fact that the references to a betrothed person being a wife are in a context where the meaning is quite clear, and that Matthew 1:19 is almost certainly proleptic, some evidence within the text would be needed to show that the meaning of a phrase is shifting from the meaning in the previous verse. Moreover, the Gospel writers are not averse to using specific language to denote a betrothed person (Matt. 1:18; Luke 1:27; 2:5). If Jesus were referring to a betrothed woman who was unfaithful, then this could have been put beyond all dispute by describing her as someone pledged to be married. Verse 32 would then read, in translation, something like this: 'Anyone who divorces his wife causes her to suffer adultery, save that a man may put away the woman betrothed to him where there has been *porneia*.' As verses 31-32 stand, the betrothal view is hardly the natural way of understanding verse 32, and there is overwhelming reason for not accepting this as the meaning.

The second possible way of establishing the 'betrothal' interpretation—given the difficulties in understanding *tēn gynaika autou* differently in verse 32 from verse 31—would be if it could be demonstrated that *porneia* in verse 32 can only mean unfaithfulness on the part of a betrothed person. But we have already seen that the semantic range of *porneia* is such that this cannot be so, and that this use of the term is not at all common. This being so, the conclusion appears irresistible that it is not possible to confine the exception in verse 32 to a case of unfaithfulness on the part of a betrothed woman.

It may be argued that Jesus is dealing with the case of a married woman whose premarital *porneia* comes to light after she has been married. Although I have not seen this interpretation defended, I am grateful to the Revd David Kingdon for drawing to my attention the fact that there have been those who have understood *porneia* in this way. I am given to understand that the late Basil Atkinson held this view.

This seems to me to be a quite untenable interpretation. To begin with, there is nothing in the text to indicate that this was Jesus' meaning. Secondly, this view leads to the absurd position that one may divorce one's wife where one discovers after marriage that she was guilty of *porneia* before the marriage, but one may not divorce where the *porneia* occurred after the consummation of the marriage. It seems difficult to resist the conclusion that this view regards premarital *porneia* as being more serious than post-marital *porneia*. Thirdly—as was pointed out in the exegesis of Matthew 5:32— Jesus is not setting out grounds for divorce but is explaining the effects and entailments of divorce. It really is impossible to suggest that a man who puts away his wife for post-marital *porneia* causes her to suffer adultery, whereas the man who divorces his wife for *porneia* which, he discovers, she was guilty of before marriage, does not cause her to suffer adultery.

'Something indecent'
We turn now to the interpretation which understands *porneia* to

denote the 'something indecent' of Deuteronomy 24:1. Clearly, if this understanding can be proved to be correct, it will then be necessary to consider which of the subdivisions of this position is the right one. However, if it can be shown to be incorrect, then *all* the subdivisions and permutations of this position will fall with it.

Superficially, at a linguistic level, this interpretation would seem to be very weak indeed. The LXX rendering of the Hebrew *'erwāṯ dābār* in Deuteronomy 24:1 is *aschēmon pragma*. If the exception of Matthew 5:32 were referring to the same thing, then one might expect either that the LXX rendering of Deuteronomy 24:1 would use *porneia*, or that Matthew 5:32 would use *aschēmon pragma*. This is, however, a somewhat simplistic approach for two reasons. First, there was considerable debate in Jesus' day as to the precise meaning of *'erwāṯ dābār*. If Matthew 5:32 simply repeated the LXX rendering of those words, it might be thought that no further light was being shed on the matter by Jesus. Secondly, as Heth and Wenham point out,

> there is no direct relationship between the divorce vocabulary in the Septuagint and the terms used in the New Testament. The verb *chōrizō* is used in the New Testament for 'divorce' but never means this in the LXX even when the LXX uses it in other senses. *Apolyō* means 'divorce' in Matthew 1:19; 5:31-32, etc., and is used with many other nuances in the New Testament. But in the divorce passages it replaces the LXX *exapostellō* (Deut. 22:19, 29; 24:1, 3; Jer. 3:1, 8; Is. 50:1; Mal. 2:16), which is never used in this sense in the New Testament.

This being the case, it follows that it is possible that the different Greek terms may have the same semantic referent and thus be equivalent in meaning. Secondly, as Heth and Wenham also point out, the LXX translates the Hebrew *dābār* by either *logos* or *pragma*, but *logos*—which is the word used in Matthew 5:32—appears eight times as often as *pragma*. Heth and Wenham go on to argue that the school of Shammai transposed the *'erwāṯ dābār* of Deuteronomy 24:1 into *dᵉḇar 'erwâ* (Mishnah, *Gittin* 9.10) and this, they claim, corresponds almost exactly with the wording of Matthew 5:32.

Since those with widely differing understandings of Jesus' teaching on divorce believe that *logou porneia*s in Matthew 5:32 is equivalent to *'erwāṯ dāḇār* in Deuteronomy 24:1, it is essential to evaluate very thoroughly the arguments in support of this position. This understanding of the words of exception must be rejected because of Jesus' own assessment of the material found in Deuteronomy 24:1. Detailed consideration of Christ's teaching found in Matthew 19:3-12 is found elsewhere in chapter 3 (pp. 74ff.). However, at this stage, attention is drawn to verse 8. Jesus specifically states that the Mosaic permission of divorce in Deuteronomy 24:1 was a concession to the hardness of men's hearts. Therefore, if in Matthew 5:32 Jesus is effectively allowing divorce for the same reasons as Moses permitted it, then we must say that Jesus is making a concession to the hardness of heart in just the same way as Moses did. Not only does this fail, as we shall see later, to fit into the flow and structure of Jesus' argument in Matthew 19:8-9, but it also tells against Jesus' teaching on the kingdom being the eschatological fulfilment of the Law and the Prophets. We have already seen that Jesus' teaching in Luke 16:16-18 is to the effect that a radical change has occurred with the coming of the kingdom, and that this has fundamentally changed the Mosaic toleration of divorce. If, however, Jesus is permitting divorce for the same reason as Moses permitted it, the whole eschatological framework of Jesus' teaching on the kingdom is undermined.

It may be objected that in Matthew 5:17-20 Jesus has stressed that he has come to uphold the Old Testament teaching, and that in verses 21ff. he is declaring the true meaning of the Old Testament as over against a traditional misunderstanding. Thus, he allows an exception to his prohibition of divorce in line with Moses' toleration, but he rejects the Pharisaic misunderstanding and abuse of the material found in Deuteronomy 24:1. This is the position argued for by Crispin. However, as we have already noted, Matthew 5:17-20 is *not* teaching that Jesus has come to uphold the *Mosaic law*. Jesus has not come to pull the Old Testament to pieces, but neither has he come simply to reaffirm all of it. He has come to *fulfil* it. Thus, there is both continuity *and* discontinuity between his teaching and that found in the Old Testament. Furthermore, as we noted in the previous chapter, and also in this chapter when considering Matthew 19:3-12, there was variety within the Old Testament, and the permission of divorce in Deuteronomy 24:1 was not the Old Testament ideal.

The kingdom inaugurated by Jesus *does* emphasise the ideal. In this sense, therefore, we can understand Jesus to be doing two things in Matthew 5:31-32. Firstly, he quotes the traditional understanding of divorce, which he means to correct. *Even within the terms of Deuteronomy 24:1-4 that traditional approach was fundamentally mistaken.* This was because, as we have already seen, the purpose of that legislation was to prevent a woman who, having been divorced, was remarried and then subsequently divorced or widowed, from being married again to the first husband. That was the purpose of the legislation. It regulated an existing practice by recognising as mandatory the giving of the divorce certificate, and prevented the abomination of returning to the first husband after subsequent remarriage. In so doing, the woman was being afforded a degree of protection. But, in Jesus' day, this legislation was being regarded by many as providing men with carte blanche to divorce their wives, and we have already seen that Jesus was addressing this situation both in Luke 16 and in Matthew 5. Moreover, within the wider context of the Old Testament—the Law and the Prophets—divorce was not viewed favourably. Thus, in Matthew 5:31, Jesus is drawing attention to a perverse understanding both of Deuteronomy 24:1 and of the Old Testament teaching. The traditional understanding was a perversion of the Old Testament. Then, in verse 32, he sets forth the kingdom teaching—to which the Old Testament pointed—as the basis upon which his disciples were to live. Thus, he not only corrects the Pharisaic misunderstanding of the Old Testament, but also, by fulfilling the Old Testament teaching, makes plain that the concession found in Deuteronomy 24:1 no longer applies. Accordingly, *porneia* does not mean *'erwāṯ dāḇār*.

There are two possible arguments that may be advanced to refute what I have said above. Neither of these is, I believe, convincing. The first argument is that the hardness of heart to which Jesus referred was the hardness of the wife's heart in being unfaithful to her husband. In a personal conversation with Brewer, in which I indicated that Jesus' reference to hardness of heart indicated that he was contrasting his teaching with that of Moses, Brewer responded by saying that Jesus was contrasting the situation that obtained at the beginning, before sin entered, with the situation with which Moses had to deal. That situation was one where a wife might be unfaithful, and a husband could then divorce her.

Jesus allowed the same basis of divorce as Moses. Thus *porneia* = *'erwāt dābār*. This was discussed more fully when dealing with Matthew 19:9. However, the following observations are in order. First, this is a somewhat unusual way of understanding the reference to 'hardness of heart'. Though Murray is not specific on this point, it is clear—as we see more fully in our consideration of Matthew 19—that he understands the reference to be to the hardness of heart of the men who divorced their wives, not to that of the wives who were being divorced. Lane, commenting on Mark 10:5, says, 'The force of [Jesus'] pronouncement here and in the following verses is to obliterate the Mosaic tolerance.' Cornes quotes Lane approvingly; yet it appears from Cornes' references to Murray that he disapproves of Murray's understanding of the teaching on divorce, which is quite different from his own. It seems that all are agreed that the 'hardness of heart' refers to the men. This has certainly been a fairly standard understanding of this phrase. When dealing with Matthew 19, I sought to demonstrate that the words 'hardness of heart' can only refer to the men. If that can be established, then Brewer's argument cannot be sustained.

The second possible line of attack upon the position I have advanced is to argue that Deuteronomy 24:1 contains a number of 'grounds' of divorce. In referring to hardness of heart, Jesus was referring to one (or possibly two) of the two (or possibly three) grounds for which Moses allowed divorce. However, Jesus was now sweeping these away and only allowing divorce for one of the reasons contained in the verse, namely, that which was equivalent to *porneia*. We have already seen that the Shammaites argued that 'indecent' was the vital word, and that this referred to unchastity. The Hillelites emphasised the word 'something', and believed that there were added reasons for divorce. Akiba, in the second century, emphasised 'who becomes displeasing to him', and therefore found a third ground of divorce. According to the position I am now criticising, Jesus was effectively lining himself up with the Shammaite position. This being so, there is eschatological fulfilment which makes no concession to men's hardness of heart—the discontinuity motif—but there is also continuity with the Old Testament. Can this argument be sustained? I think not. Let us deal with the Akiba case, first of all. He said in the second century AD, 'Even if he has found another more beautiful than she is, as it is said

131

(Deut. 24:1) "And it shall come to pass, if she does not find favour in his eyes'" (*Gittin* 9.10). In recent times, Hilton and Marshall, having commented upon *'erwāt dābār*, go on to say:

> Note, however, that our passage begins with another phrase—'if she finds no favour in his eyes'. From our text we cannot tell if this is an *alternative* reason for divorce or an *additional* reason for divorce: does it mean either she has done something wrong *or* she finds no favour in his eyes, or does it mean *both* she has committed adultery or incest *and* she finds no favour in his eyes? From the biblical text it is impossible to tell (p.121). [It should be observed that Hilton and Marshall understand *'erwāt dābār* to be a reference to sexual sin.]

It is difficult to see how the above position can be sustained in view of the fact that Deuteronomy 24:1 specifically says that she finds no favour in his eyes 'because' of the 'something indecent'. It is *because* he has found *'erwāt dābār* in her that she no longer finds favour in his eyes. This being so, there is no basis in the text for the belief that there is a ground for divorce additional to *'erwāt dābār*. It might be said that verse 1 contains superfluous language unless one allows for two different grounds: evidently the finding of something indecent within his wife causes the husband to view her less favourably, otherwise he would not divorce her. By allowing for two distinct grounds one removes this superfluity of language: one ground is based on something in the woman—there is something indecent in her; the other ground is based on the husband's feelings—he no longer views her favourably. But this does not follow. Evidently, the husband no longer views her favourably: if he did, he would not be divorcing her. The words *'erwāt dābār* specify those situations where, not viewing her favourably, he might divorce her. On the basis of the meaning I argued for in the previous chapter, viewing her unfavourably because she could not cook would not be a sufficient reason to divorce her. So the words are not superfluous. In divorcing her, the husband was admitting that he had cooled in his affection towards her and this was not because of something blameworthy in her. Hence Jesus' words about hardness of heart. As far as I am aware, the three grounds for divorce were not contended for in Jesus' day, Akiba's interpretation coming later.

Moreover, Akiba's influence was such that a school of rabbinic interpretation grew up which laid great emphasis on every letter of the text and drew extremely far-fetched interpretations from it.[143] His interpretation of Deuteronomy 24:1 is an example of this. Accordingly, it is highly unlikely that Jesus' words could have been understood against that background. Even if evidence is forthcoming that this position had been canvassed in Jesus' day, the arguments adduced thus far demonstrate that it was really a nonstarter. Moreover, Jesus' words in Matthew 19:8 indicate that the *entire* scenario envisaged in Deuteronomy 24:1, and not only part of it, was necessitated by the hardness of men's hearts. In view of these considerations, the attempt to assimilate Jesus' use of *porneia* to *'erwāṯ dāḇār* of Deuteronomy 24:1, and allowing this as a reason for divorce in contradistinction to the ground of 'she finds no favour in his eyes', must be regarded as a failure.

What of the view that Jesus is siding with the Shammaites as over against the Hillelites, and that this may mean that he is allowing for divorce for unchastity—'something *indecent'* - but not for the Hillelite reasons—'*something* indecent'? Whatever the merits of this view, it is abundantly clear that this cannot be used as the basis of an argument that Jesus is distinguishing two different grounds for divorce *within* the phrase *'erwāṯ dāḇār*: that is, that Moses allowed one of them for the hardness of heart and that this would no longer apply; but the other ground was not necessitated by hardness of heart and Jesus would still allow this. The dispute between the Shammaites and the Hillelites centred on the meaning of *'erwāṯ dāḇār*. If Jesus had taught that the phrase covered two situations, then he was effectively lining himself up with Hillel. The Hillelites accepted the Shammaite belief that the phrase included unchastity; but they taught that it also included other things. There is no way that Jesus' hearers could possibly have understood him to be saying that he accepted the Hillelite exegesis of the phrase, but that henceforth only the Shammaite understanding would be allowed. It is clear that Jesus is referring to the Mosaic legislation in Deuteronomy 24:1 as a whole and is categorising all of it as necessitated by hardness of heart. That being so, the second argument in favour of assimilating *porneia* to *'erwāṯ dāḇār* also fails.

What of the linguistic argument that *porneia* = *'erwāṯ dāḇār*? Heth and Wenham are correct to point out that the fact that the LXX does not use *porneia* in Deuteronomy 24:1 does not necessarily mean that *porneia* is not an equivalent term in the verse in question, and their appeal to different divorce terminology in the New Testament from that which is used in the LXX demonstrates that the case for *porneia* meaning *'erwāṯ dāḇār* certainly has to be considered. However, the following points are apposite. Firstly, the hermeneutical considerations outlined above tell decisively against the equivalence of *porneia* with *'erwāṯ dāḇār* in this verse. Secondly, the fact that the New Testament uses different divorce terminology from that employed in the LXX cannot be used as the basis for an argument that the New Testament may use a different term to denote *'erwāṯ dāḇār* from that used in the LXX. The reason for saying this is as follows. The verb *exapostellō*, which is the LXX term for divorce and which is rendered in Matthew 1:19 and 5:31-32 by *apolyō*, is (despite the fact that it is never used in the New Testament to denote divorce) not a difficult word. Its semantic range is fairly clear, as is its meaning in individual cases. By no stretch of the imagination is *'erwāṯ dāḇār* an easy phrase to understand. While the term *'erwâ* is used many times in the Old Testament to denote nakedness, and frequently to connote something shameful, *'erwāṯ dāḇār* is a notoriously difficult phrase, occurring on only one other occasion in the Old Testament, and on that occasion with no connotation of sexual shame. So the analogy with divorce terminology does not really hold. It may be said that *porneia* is hardly a straightforward term, as the length of this Excursus demonstrates. But, again, the analogy does not hold. *Porneia* may be used in a wide variety of ways, and careful consideration is needed to understand its meaning in a given context. But the various meanings it may carry—that is, its semantic range—are fairly clear. The difficulty with *'erwāṯ dāḇār*, however, is precisely to know what the two words, taken together, actually mean; it is not simply a case of running through the semantic range and identifying the appropriate referent. Moreover, there is a clear equivalence between *exapostellō* and *apolyō*. Quite apart from the matter of divorce, both terms can mean 'send away'. It is easy to see, therefore, how both terms can refer to the act of a husband sending away his wife. Furthermore, Heth and Wenham are, with respect, quite simply wrong when they say, 'there is no direct relationship between the divorce vocabulary in the Septuagint and the terms used in the New Testament'. The LXX terminology used to denote the divorce certificate is *biblion apostasiou* in Deuteronomy 24:1. Matthew uses *apostasion* in Matthew 5:32, while in 19:7 he uses the fuller *biblion apostasiou*. Mark also uses the fuller phrase in Mark 10:4. So there is clearly an equivalence. But this is not the case with *porneia* and *'erwāṯ dāḇār*.

The LXX rendering of *'erwāṯ dāḇār* is *aschēmon pragma*. The adjective *aschēmōn* is used in Genesis 34:7 to denote the 'disgraceful' thing which Shechem had done in lying with Israel's daughter. The noun *aschēmosynē* is used in Exodus 20:26 to denote the nakedness which would be exposed in going up the steps to the Lord's altar, while the term is used in Leviticus 18:6-20 with sexual connotations, as it is in Leviticus 20. Abbott-Smith points out that the noun is used frequently in the LXX as a euphemism for *hē aischynē*, which means 'shame' or 'shameful deed'. The word *aschēmōn* is formed by attaching the negative prefix *a* to *schēma*, which means form (and for which *morphē* is a synonym). Thus, Abbott-Smith gives the following meaning: '1. shapeless; 2. uncomely, unseemly'; while Thayer gives: 'a) deformed; b) indecent, unseemly: 1 Cor. 12:23 (opp. to *euschēmōn*).' BAG define the meaning thus: 'shameful, unpresentable, indecent (opp. *euschēmōn*). The word is applied especially to sexual life in Dio Chrys. 23 [40], 29 . . .' *Euschēmōn*, to which *aschēmōn* is the opposite, means 'proper, presentable, seemly, decorous, comely', and the adverbial form *euschēmonōs* is employed in Romans 13:13 ('let us behave decently') and in 1 Corinthians 14:40. The neuter plural form of the adjective is used in 1 Corinthians 12:24 of one's presentable parts. From the foregoing, it appears that the meaning of *aschēmon pragma* is as difficult as *'erwāṯ dāḇār*. While *aschēmōn* and its cognates may connote shame attendant upon the exposure of one's nakedness, the term has other connotations as well, and may be rendered in English as 'uncomely' or 'unseemly [matter]'—which takes one no further than the English rendering of *'erwāṯ dāḇār*. The meaning of the phrase in Deuteronomy 24:1, therefore, has to be determined by an in-depth consideration of the Old Testament teaching, such as we attempted in the previous chapter. What can be said is that the semantic range of the phrase is wider than *logou porneias*. In view of the conclusions reached in the previous chapter as to the meaning of *'erwāṯ dāḇār*, and the hermeneutical considerations touched on in our treatment of Christ's teaching concerning the reason for the

Mosaic concession, *logou porneias* should not be regarded, in Matthew 5:32, as equivalent to *aschēmon pragma*.

It only remains to note that those who argue that by *logou porneias* Jesus is referring to *'erwāṯ dāḇār* of Deuteronomy 24:1 differ considerably amongst themselves as to what Jesus meant to teach by these words of exception. Some argue for the 'no comment' or 'preteritive' understanding of the phrase: that is to say, that Jesus is declaring that divorce involves adultery, but in saying this he states that he is leaving *logou porneias* out of his universe of discourse. Accordingly, we can draw no conclusion from the exceptive phrase. We have already seen that *parektos* cannot be made to bear this meaning in the phrase. *A fortiori* one must reject the understanding which says that Jesus declared that divorce would lead to adultery *even for the cause of the indecent thing of Deuteronomy 24:1*. Crispin argues that Jesus *was* making a genuine exception, and that this was for the same reason for which Moses allowed divorce—the 'indecent thing'. Crispin goes on to reason that since sexual sin carried the death penalty, the indecent thing must refer to something akin to our 'unreasonable behaviour'. However, we have already seen that the phrase cannot bear that meaning, nor can Jesus be endorsing the Mosaic concession. Finally, Brewer also regards the words as a genuine exception and understands them to refer to sexual unfaithfulness. This was essentially the Shammaite position. While I believe that the words are genuine words of exception and that *logou porneias* refers to sexual unfaithfulness, this is *not* what *'erwāṯ dāḇār* means in Deuteronomy 24:1. Jesus is *not* endorsing the Shammaite position, which was based on an understanding of words in Deuteronomy 24:1, but is introducing something completely new. If the resultant teaching on divorce is, at points, similar to that of Shammai, the resemblance is only superficial. Jesus' teaching is built upon an entirely different foundation.

Chapter 4
The Teaching of Paul in 1 Corinthians 7

Introduction

Evangelicals who believe that Jesus allowed divorce and re-marriage for sexual infidelity have long been divided over the question as to whether Paul allowed another ground for divorce in 1 Corinthians 7:15. Some have argued that this verse allows divorce for desertion,[1] while others have said that it teaches no such thing.[2] Those who believe that it allows for divorce in cases of desertion differ amongst themselves as to the type of situation with which Paul is dealing.[3] Strictly speaking, our concern is not to take sides in this debate but, as with the Gospel material, to exegete Paul's words and then to draw conclusions from it. We should never approach a passage of Scripture to ascertain whether it establishes one of a number of positions, since this may well limit our understanding of the text. In looking for answers to our questions, we may fail to see the writer's questions; indeed we may miss altogether what the passage is saying because we are forcing it to address a situation with which it was not concerned. I think it will become clear that this wrong approach to Scripture is well illustrated in the way writers have approached 1 Corinthians 7:15, and that the difference over whether or not the verse allows divorce for desertion is based entirely on a misunderstanding of the situation into which Paul was writing. If we are to avoid that misunderstanding, it is essential to say something about the general background to the letter and the particular background to chapter 7.

Background of 1 Corinthians

The Corinthian Church
Background information on the founding and make-up of the Corinthian church is found in Acts 18:1-17, and in 1 and 2

137

Corinthians. From 1 Corinthians 1:22-24 it would appear that the church was comprised of both Jews and Gentiles, and this is borne out by what we are told in Acts 18. Acts 18 suggests that Paul's mission in Corinth was largely unsuccessful amongst the Jews (vv.6,12), but this has to be counterbalanced by what we are told in verses 7-8. It is possible that some of the Gentiles who made up the church had been God-fearers in the synagogue. The fact that 1 Corinthians is liberally sprinkled with Old Testament references and allusions suggests that the church was fairly well versed in Old Testament teaching, and the most likely explanation for this is that such knowledge had been acquired in the synagogue.[4] At the same time, there are enough references in this first letter to indicate that a fair number of the Gentile Christians had been converted from outright paganism.[5] In particular, it is quite clear that some of the believers had been converted from a fairly debauched and immoral lifestyle: some in the church had been sexually immoral, and guilty of adultery, homosexuality, and male prostitution.[6] Corinth was a notoriously wicked city, and while we must not make the mistake of assuming that every man had been a brothel keeper and every woman a prostitute, it is, nevertheless, the case that some had been converted from a sexually immoral life and now had to live out their new life in Christ in this evil society. The church at Corinth, then, was largely Gentile, but it contained Jewish believers as well as Gentile believers, some of whom had had contact with Judaism, and others whose background was pagan. Socially, there were not many with positions of influence and power in society.[7]

The city of Corinth was, of course, part of the Roman Empire. The significance of this, for present purposes, lies in the fact that the people to whom Paul's letter was written were governed by, and subject to, Roman law. It is essential to bear this in mind when considering 1 Corinthians 7. As has been observed, the question is frequently posed as to whether 1 Corinthians 7:15 allows divorce for desertion. This question presupposes an understanding of desertion and divorce which is quite at variance with the Roman law applicable at the time in question.[8] It will, therefore, be necessary to say something about the Roman law of marriage and divorce.

Roman law of marriage and divorce

Barry Nicholas summarises the Roman institution of marriage as follows:

> There are few Roman institutions which differ so fundamentally from their modern counterparts as marriage. From the legal point of view marriage is to us a status, the creation and termination of which are closely regulated by law, and which not only founds a number of rights and duties between the parties but also to some extent affects the relationship of the parties to the rest of the world. A Roman marriage, on the other hand, was very largely a social fact, about the creation and termination of which the law had very little to say, and which had almost no effect on the legal condition of the parties . . .
>
> Roman law imposed . . . conditions as to capacity to marry . . . but subject to these conditions all that was required for a valid marriage was a manifestation of a common intention to be married. And what constituted an intention to be married, as opposed to an intention merely to live together, was a question of fact, of social convention. Similarly, the intention must be manifested in some act, but what this act must be, except that it need not be consummation, was again left to be settled as a question of fact. There were, of course, social ceremonies which customarily accompanied a marriage, and which would in the normal case leave no doubt as to the existence of the requisite intention, but none of these ceremonies was legally necessary.[9]

Accordingly, at the time of the Empire when 1 Corinthians was written, as long as a couple possessed capacity to marry,[10] were not within the prohibited degrees,[11] and consented,[12] then marriage was effected by living together with the intention of doing so as husband and wife.

What were the legal consequences of marriage? This is, indeed, a complex subject that developed from the time of the early Republic to that which obtained by the end of the Empire. An adequate treatment of this subject presupposes and requires a knowledge of the Roman law of persons, which is beyond the purpose and scope of the present study.[13] However, it will be necessary to draw attention briefly to some of the salient features of the Roman law of marriage.

At the time of the Twelve Tables,[14] 451/450 BC, marriage was accompanied by what was called *manus*. This meant that the wife came under the power or *potestas* of her husband or of his *paterfamilias*. This would then give her the same rights of succession to her husband as would be possessed by any children they might have. However, even at an early stage, *manus* was distinct from marriage.

Manus was created in one of three ways. For patricians, there was an involved ceremony called *confarreatio*, while a far more common way of creating *manus* was by way of *coemptio*, which was a ceremony not dissimilar to that by which a person might acquire ownership of property. *Coemptio* was open to plebeians. The third method was *usus*. Both *confarreatio* and *usus* were complicated ceremonies, and it was very easy for a defect to arise. However, a defect would be cured if a woman remained married for a full year; she would then be *in manu* to her husband. The Roman jurist, Gaius, pointed out that if she wanted to avoid being *in manu* to her husband, she should absent herself from her husband for three consecutive nights during the first year of marriage. Of course, a defective ceremony of *confarreatio* or *coemptio* was the same as no ceremony. This brings out the fact that *manus* was distinct from marriage but would come into existence by *usus* unless the wife heeded the advice of Gaius.

The distinction between marriage and *manus* was such that, as the law developed, by the time of the Empire it had become rare for women to be *in manu* to their husbands. Accordingly, a wife stayed under her own *paterfamilias* if she had one, and if not, did not come under any *paterfamilias*. Whichever was the case, the husband had no rights over her property and, consistent with this, she was to maintain herself. She was no longer agnatically related to her husband or to her own children. (What this means is that if she were under a *paterfamilias* she was regarded as a descendant. Being *in manu* to her husband had the same effect and would have implications for inheritance. This 'agnatic' relationship to her husband did not exist if she were not *in manu* to him.) Thus, in the 'free marriage' situation that obtained during the time of the Empire, the wife owned her own property, was in no way subject to the control of her husband, and the notion of joint ownership was virtually unknown. However, it was customary for a woman, or her father or anyone else, to make a gift to the husband-to-be on the occasion of the marriage. This was called *dos* and was the subject of a number of rules depending on the kind of *dos* it was. Nevertheless, the husband did not benefit greatly from this gift, and from the early Empire it was laid down that the husband could not sell immovable property in Italy without his wife's consent, and could not mortgage it even with her consent.

It has been necessary to emphasise some of the consequences of the Roman law of marriage in order to dispel some of the myths which persist concerning the status of married women during the New Testament era. As Grimal comments,

> There was an ever-increasing relaxation of constraints, woman was acquiring personal freedom, and fathers no longer arranged marriages for their daughters against their wishes . . . Instead of a union imposed upon the young people and settled by a contract that ignored their wishes, we now find marriage based on the mutual consent of the contracting parties and lasting only by virtue of their joint desire to keep it in existence.[15]

Since marriage required no formality or ceremony, it followed that no formality was needed to end the marriage. Thus, the Roman law of divorce was very different from the Jewish practice of the giving of a certificate, or the English law, which requires a decree of the court to effect divorce and to end the marriage.

> Since Roman marriage depended for its existence merely on the parties living together with the intention of being married, it could equally be brought to an end by the free will of either or both. And just as no formality was needed for the beginning of a marriage, so also none was needed for its termination. All that was necessary was some evidence of intention.[16]

Divorce was therefore effected either by mutual consent (*divortium bona gratia*) or by one party to the marriage unilaterally ending it by an act of repudiation, which was called *repudium*.

> . . . a marriage was terminated by any manifested intention by either party no longer to be married. The resulting uncertainty in some cases as to whether a union was (or was still) a marriage would seem to us intolerable, but would be of much less importance in Rome where the legal consequences of marriage were, as we shall see, very few.[17]

141

So fundamental was this unfettered freedom of divorce that even an agreement not to divorce was void as being incompatible with the Roman idea of marriage.[18]

. . . it was from the second century BC onwards that habits changed—to such an extent that, towards the end of the Republic, divorce had become extremely frequent and constituted a serious threat to the stability of family life.

Ancient authors have preserved the memory of certain particularly scandalous divorces, whose only object was to ensure a completely free life for the female partner. We have Seneca's famous remark about the woman 'who counted the years of her life, not by the number of consuls, but by the number of her husbands' . . . Considerations of self-interest seem to have played an even more important part in the increase of divorce than the desire to enjoy life to the utmost. Being in practice in control of her own fortune, a woman felt little inclination to allow it to be used for the benefit of a man who, in many cases, was less well off than she. Women preferred to seek mates who could be expected to make them heirs within a reasonable period, or whose personal fortune offered them hopes of still greater luxury. It also seems that in Imperial times, Roman women were reluctant to accept the trials and vexations of motherhood. This hastened the rupture of unions which were only temporary, since their continuance was not made necessary by the presence of children. So, in Imperial times, it was often a case of wives divorcing their husbands, not, as formerly, of husbands divorcing their wives.[19]

It all sounds very familiar!

Attempts were made to lessen the instability of family life, which was resulting from the free and easy divorce of the Empire. Thus Augustus enacted the *lex Julia de adulteriis*, which penalised the most common ground of divorce, adultery, and which required that notification of the divorce to the wife be in the form of a letter before seven witnesses.[20] There were other discouragements, but it is quite clear that divorce continued to be fairly free and easy.

This background is quite important to 1 Corinthians 7. It is possible to concentrate attention on the internal life of the

Corinthian Church and to reconstruct the life setting into which Paul wrote his letter, without taking into account the background of the society in which the Corinthian Christians were called to live out their lives.[21] But quite apart from the fact that it is obvious that these young Christians were not living in hermetically sealed bubbles, 1 Corinthians itself puts us on notice that some of the Corinthians' difficulties were related to the problem of living for Christ in a pagan society.[22] It is important to bear in mind that this observation may well have relevance to chapter 7, and recognition of this fact will save us from viewing the background context too narrowly. The Roman law background has been important for another reason: it demonstrates that desertion, if accompanied with the appropriate intention—and in most cases this would be so—constituted divorce. Thus, the question as to whether 1 Corinthians 7:15 allows divorce for desertion is seen to be a non-sense question, akin to asking if the present King of France is over 50 or under 50. Since France has no king, there cannot be a yes/no answer to that question, just as there cannot be a yes/no answer to the question, Did Paul allow divorce for desertion in 1 Corinthians 7:15?

Background to the Letter
1 Corinthians was written in response to a report Paul had received from members of Chloe's household about the church situation in Corinth (1:11; 5:1; 11:18), and in reply to a letter the Corinthians had written to Paul (7:1; 8:1; 12:1). In chapters 1–6 Paul deals with the issues raised in the report he has received, and in chapter 7 he begins to deal with the questions raised in their letter to him, each matter raised by them being introduced by the words, 'Now about . . .' This is a general analysis of the letter's contents, since in the second part of the letter Paul can still touch upon matters raised in the report (11:18).[23] From Paul's words in 5:9, it appears likely that Paul had written an earlier letter which we do not have, and Fee argues that the Corinthians' letter to Paul is prompted by, and is in response to, the lost letter which Paul had written.[24] Whether 5:9 is a reference to an earlier letter or to 1 Corinthians itself,[25] what is not in dispute is that Paul's letter is written partly in response to matters raised by the Corinthians. What this means, of course, is that Paul's words must not be understood in a vacuum, but against

the background of the life of the church and, where he is responding to their letter, against the background of the questions they
have asked. That raises difficulties in interpreting the text, since we
do not have their letter but must try, as best we can, to reconstruct
what it is that they were saying. Nowhere in the letter is this more
important—or more difficult—than in chapter 7.

Context
Chapter 7:1 almost certainly contains a quotation from the
Corinthians' letter—'It is good for a man not to marry'—and verses
2ff. are Paul's response to that.[26] NIV gives a misleading translation.
Paul quotes the Corinthians' words, which were that it was good or
beautiful not to have sexual relationships.[27] In verse 2 Paul explains
that each husband and wife should have sexual relationships with
their spouse. In verse 4, he explains that each spouse's body
belongs to the other. Underpinning verse 4 is the one-flesh unity
which exists in marriage and to which Paul refers in Ephesians
5:31.[28] Paul understands marriage to be a unity of two people which
extends to the physical and sexual realm. He clearly believes there
to be an equality, in that each spouse's body belongs to the other.[29]
In verse 5 he prohibits each spouse from 'depriving' the other. In
the context of the preceding verses, this is obviously a reference to
depriving the other spouse of sexual relations.

As we noted in chapter 2, the word translated 'deprive' is the
same term as is used in the LXX of Exodus 21:10.[30] The importance
of this lies in the fact that Brewer believes that the Jewish marriage
contracts, which were based on Exodus 21:10, provide the background to part of 1 Corinthians 7, and that in this chapter Paul
applies the Old Testament teaching on divorce to the Corinthian
situation. Thus, Jesus dealt with the legislation found in Deuteronomy 24:1, while Paul refers to the three grounds of divorce
which, Brewer believes, were found in Exodus 21:10-11. I think
that Brewer has certainly broken new ground in this area, but he
wishes to draw inferences which the evidence does not justify.[31]
Paul allows a concession to his prohibition of 'depriving', but it is
a concession which is strictly defined and limited: it must be by
mutual consent and it must be for a limited period of time.[32] With
pastoral realism, Paul tells them to come together again or Satan
would take advantage of their lack of self-control. In verse 6, he

144

stresses that what he has said about sexual 'fasting' is a concession and not a command. He wishes that all men were as he was—that is, unmarried—but acknowledges that each man has his own gift from God.

Verse 7 is something of a 'bridge' with verses 8-9, where Paul addresses the 'unmarried' or those who have been 'widowed'. Paul is probably quoting from the Corinthians' letter in verse 8 and then responding to them in verse 9, just as he had done in verses 1-2.[33] He acknowledges the importance and the strength of sexual desire in some people, and for those, if it is good to remain unmarried, it is better to marry than to burn. In view of what he has said in verses 2-6, it is obvious that he would expect those who marry to have sexual relationships with each other.

Exegesis

Although we shall exegete verses 10-16, it will be necessary to look, first of all, in greater detail at one aspect of verse 8: what is the identity of 'the unmarried'[34] to whom Paul refers? I believe that there are good reasons for holding that Paul is referring here to a group that included those who had already been divorced. Since—as shall be seen—in verse 10 Paul lays down that a believer must not divorce another believer, and says in verses 12ff. that a believer may not, except in certain circumstances, divorce an unbeliever, it is reasonable to infer that in verse 8 Paul is including those who had been divorced *before* they had been converted.[35] Thus, in verse 8 Paul addresses a group which included certain divorcees. His instruction to them in verse 8 is almost certainly a quotation from their letter to him. He agrees that it is a good thing if they remain unmarried, as he was. However, verse 9 qualifies this agreement with what the Corinthians were saying and is another example of the 'Yes, but' type of argument which Paul employs in this letter.[36] His instruction to them is that it is better to marry than to burn. It is sometimes assumed, from this verse, that Paul had a very low view of marriage; that he was, in effect, saying that marriage was only a preferred option to sexual frustration, and that its only real value is to be found in its removal of sexual tension and frustration. This is a serious misunderstanding of Paul's teaching, for the following reasons.

First, if Paul were to have held such a low view of marriage, he would have been out of line with the rest of the biblical teaching, with its positive view of marriage. Secondly, he would have been contradicting his own teaching, for it must be acknowledged that in Ephesians 5:22-33 we find possibly the most exalted view of marriage anywhere in the Bible. A positive view of marriage is also set forth in 1 Timothy 5:14. (It is obvious that I accept the Pauline authority of Ephesians and of Timothy. Indeed, I believe that not to do so is to have departed from the biblical and evangelical doctrine of Scripture.) Thirdly—and in terms of understanding 1 Corinthians 7, this is the most important point—Paul is responding to the Corinthians' letter. It was *they* who were saying that it was good not to marry. Paul does not disagree outright, because there was a very real element of truth in what they were saying. After all, Paul was himself unmarried. But it was not the whole truth and, in the context of the Corinthian church, it was a dangerous half-truth if not corrected by other elements of truth. Paul appeals to *those other considerations, which were supremely relevant and important in the Corinthian context.* And *one* important aspect of truth is that marriage *is* the God-ordained way of removing sexual tension and frustration. There is a realism about Paul's teaching which we should not be too 'spiritual' to fail to acknowledge. That would be to be guilty of the same over-realised eschatology to which some of the Corinthians had succumbed.

The significance of the teaching found in verse 9 for the question of divorce lies in the fact that Paul tells the unmarried of verse 8 that if they cannot control themselves, it is better to marry than to burn. Included in the unmarried were certain divorced people: those who had been divorced before they had been converted. Paul's teaching is that while it may be good for such to remain unmarried, they were not forbidden to remarry and, furthermore, where they were 'burning', it was better to marry than to remain unmarried and to burn with passion. This is a very important point to grasp. While practical application is dealt with in the next chapter, attention is drawn, at this point, to the fact that Paul is here addressing the vexed question as to what is the position of a person who was divorced before being converted. Answers to this question usually divide along familiar lines. On the one hand, there are those who say that in view of the fact that the Christian is a new creation, what happened in his unconverted past is irrelevant at

146

this point, and he may therefore marry again. On the other hand, there are those who say that marriage is a creation ordinance and that conversion is not relevant to the question as to whether such a person may be married. Those who take this latter view are then divided amongst themselves between those who will not allow remarriage in any situation and those who allow remarriage where the divorce was on account of *porneia*. The position I am advocating is different from both, although it has more affinities with the first approach than with the second. Paul specifically addresses the question, and this means that we are not left having to infer an answer from general principles. The believer is free to be married.

It is appreciated that this may appear to be an unfamiliar interpretation, and for that reason some may well feel uneasy with it and hesitant to accept it. Indeed, with one exception, I am not aware of any studies which argue the case in this particular way, though there may be such studies of which I am unaware.[37] However, the following arguments are, in my view, conclusively in its favour. In verses 10-11, as we shall see when those verses are considered in detail, Paul deals with the question of divorce and remarriage amongst believers. He reproduces the teaching Jesus gave when he was upon earth. In verses 12-14, Paul allows divorce for reasons for which Jesus did not allow divorce. The fact that Paul is saying something different from that which Jesus said is specifically acknowledged by Paul. The reason for this is that he is dealing with a type of situation with which Jesus did not deal when he was upon earth. Thus, verses 10-13 include a repetition of Christ's teaching on divorce and remarriage, and also teaching on a new type of situation concerning divorce and remarriage, which had to be specifically identified as such. The point of verses 12-13 is that they deal with divorce and remarriage in circumstances sufficiently different from those considered by Christ that Paul's teaching adds something to that which is recorded in the Gospels. He needs to identify this so that his readers can recognise what is going on. This should become clearer when we come to consider those verses.

However, in verses 8-9 Paul is dealing with a type of situation entirely different from any touched upon by Christ. Since he is neither reaffirming the teaching of Christ nor developing it, but dealing with something utterly different, he does not need to preface his remarks with the words 'not I, but the Lord', nor with words 'I, not the Lord'. The presence of those words in verses 10 and 12, respectively, alerts us to the fact that those verses bear a special relationship both to each other *and* to the teaching Jesus gave when on earth. Their absence from verses 8 and 9 informs us that we are dealing with something quite different. And what is different is the fact that verses 8-9 include in their consideration a person outside of God's covenant who is married to another person outside of the covenant. One divorces the other. Some time later, one of these—it could be either the divorced or the divorcer, or both, since divorce could be by mutual consent—is converted and comes within the covenant. Here is consideration of a Christian who was divorced before becoming a Christian. What is the marital status of this person in the eyes of God and in the eyes of the church? He or she is unmarried and may be married.

It is unthinkable that there were no such persons in Corinth, and that in a chapter which deals with a range of difficult questions concerning marriage and divorce this question would not have surfaced. An analogy with our society may help at this point. Given the high divorce rate in England and Wales, it is not at all uncommon for churches to admit into their membership people who were divorced before they were converted. It is a fairly common problem encountered in pastoral practice for such a Christian to wish to marry another Christian. If it is a common problem to us, it was surely so for the Corinthians. Moreover, we should not underestimate the significance of the fact that someone who had been married and had enjoyed a fairly normal and happy sex life would, on having been divorced, have married again. It is perfectly possible that misunderstanding of Jesus' teaching, as passed on as part of 'the traditions' by Paul, may have led some of Paul's readers to have assumed that it was 'good' to remain unmarried. However, in view of having experienced a sex life within marriage and in view of the prevailing sexual temptations within Corinth, it would not be at all unlikely for sexual frustration—'burning'—to be experienced. Hence Paul's words in verse 9. This could be true of widows also, as well as of those who had never been married, particularly if they had engaged in premarital sexual activity before having been converted. These considerations, together with the linguistic considerations dealt with in note 35, lead, in my view, to the understanding that Paul dealt decisively with the question of the person divorced before conversion. Incidentally, it should be noted, in passing, that Paul understood divorce to end the marriage, so that a divorced person was 'unmarried'.

There are two vital things to note in verse 10. First, Paul is giving a command.[38] Secondly, he underlines the command by saying that it is not he, but the Lord, who is giving the command. What he means by this is that he is about to repeat a command which the Lord Jesus gave during the days of his earthly ministry.[39] The reason why Paul says this will become clear when we come to verse 12. The command is that a wife must not separate from her husband. Two questions arise: first, what does Paul mean? and, second, why does he say it? If the command that Paul is giving is recorded in the Gospels, then the only place where Jesus refers to a woman not leaving her husband is Mark 10:12. This raises a number of interesting considerations.

First, Jesus was clearly referring, in Mark 10:12, to a woman not divorcing her husband.[40] In this verse, if Paul is repeating that teaching, he must also be prohibiting a wife from divorcing her husband.[41] Paul is reaffirming the strong 'pro-marriage' and 'anti-divorce' stance of Jesus. However, he then qualifies this in verse 11. Paul anticipates what would be the case if she does 'separate'. This second part of verse 11 is regularly understood by those who hold to 'no remarriage after divorce' as meaning that if the woman does divorce, she must not remarry. This brings the teaching, it is claimed, perfectly into line with the teaching of Jesus, who forbade divorce and remarriage. However, it is claimed, Jesus did allow an exception to divorce, but allowed no exception to his 'no remarriage' rule.[42] But this interpretation does not do justice to what Paul actually says. Paul lays down a command that the woman must not separate. He then addresses the situation if she does separate, in language which is quite general and is not tied to her doing so in a case of *porneia*. There may be numerous reasons why she separates. If Paul were repeating Christ's teaching, we should expect him to refer to *porneia* as the reason for separating; but he does not do so. Indeed, by going on to speak of the possibility of reconciliation, Paul is almost certainly making it clear that the one situation *not* in view is where the husband has been guilty of *porneia*.[43]

What this means is that Paul is here making something of a concession occasioned by pastoral realism. This is quite different from the exceptions Jesus made, which were *not* a concession to human weakness nor yet a concession necessitated by pastoral realism, but a genuine exception to the rule he laid down. But Paul is here countenancing the possibility that, in some cases, believers will not attain the ideal. In such a case, that less-than-ideal state is carefully circumscribed. She must remain unmarried or be reconciled to her husband. What does Paul mean?

We argued in an earlier chapter that divorce ends a marriage so that each spouse is then unmarried. Paul's language in verse 11 would appear to confirm that the marriage has been ended by the woman's separating, which, as we have seen, in Roman law constituted the act of divorce. However, a careful consideration of Paul's words indicates that he is saying the exact opposite and that the marriage is still intact. According to Jesus, divorce ended the marriage relationship, whether justifiably or not. Where there was *porneia*, the divorce was justifiable and the divorcing party was free to remarry. That was Jesus' concept of divorce. In this verse, the separating spouse is not to remarry, which means that we are not dealing with *porneia*. But that must mean that we are not dealing with a straightforward divorce; for if Paul, as a concession to pastoral realism, were allowing such a thing, he would *not* be re-affirming Christ's teaching, since Jesus did not make any such concession. What Paul is doing is acknowledging that in some cases a believer may separate from her spouse. If so, it must be abundantly clear that this falls short of divorce, by her remaining unmarried or by her being reconciled. Here then is a case of separation that falls short of full divorce. It may be asked, How is this repeating the Lord's command, since Jesus did not deal with such separation? and why does Paul call the woman 'unmarried'?

The answer to both questions is reasonably straightforward. Paul repeats the Lord's prohibition of divorce. By allowing separation that cannot lead to remarriage, he is emphasising that he is not making a concession in the area of divorce and is therefore most emphatically upholding what Jesus taught. If in verse 10 he is prohibiting separation rather than divorce, then he is *a fortiori* prohibiting divorce and thereby upholding Jesus' teaching. In the first part of verse 11, he makes clear that the separation that might occur must never be regarded as divorce, since she must remain unmarried.

But if Paul is only dealing with separation in verse 11, why does he call her unmarried? Before answering this question, it should be pointed out that those who take the 'no remarriage after divorce' position are also in difficulty with this verse. The whole basis of their case is that, in the eyes of God, the couple is still married. Accordingly, if verse 11 is referring to divorce, rather than just separation, how can Paul call the woman 'unmarried' when, in God's eyes, they are still married? Presumably, the 'no remarriage' supporters would reply by saying that they are unmarried in the eyes of the law but are married in the eyes of God. Brewer—who certainly believes that remarriage after divorce is permissible—has a variation on this by saying that in the eyes of the Roman law they would be unmarried but according to biblical law they were still married. There are problems with both of these interpretations. If in the eyes of the Roman law they were unmarried, we might expect Paul in verse 11 to say that the wife must marry or be remarried. But Paul does not say this. Indeed, Brewer argues that the word translated 'be reconciled' was a technical term used in Greek marriage contracts to refer to the reconciliation of separated couples.[44] Furthermore, it is inaccurate to say that separation per se constituted the act of divorce. It had to be accompanied with the intention to end the marriage. No doubt, in almost all cases where separation occurred, it was accompanied with the intention to end the marriage. But Brewer's reference to Greek marriage contracts indicates that this was not always so, and the whole point of Paul's words in verse 11*a* is to emphasise that this separation was not an act of divorce. The reference to the woman being 'unmarried' is probably best understood by reference back to verses 2-5. To be living under separate roofs, not to be living as husband and wife, and to be 'depriving' one's husband, contrary to the teaching Paul had already laid down, was—in effect—to be unmarried. Obviously, to Paul, marriage was more than a bare legal concept, and this comes through in what he says in verse 11.

But why does Paul refer to this issue? Presumably, it had been raised by the Corinthians in their letter. One theory is that whereas some were no longer having sexual relations as a result of an over-realised eschatology, others had either gone further, or were tempted to go further, by leaving their spouses altogether. Since there was a problem with so-called 'eschatological women', Paul addresses the women first.[45] Plausible as it may sound, this theory fails to account for all the evidence.[46] It is more likely that separations or divorces were being envisaged for a variety of reasons. Paul reaffirms the Lord's command but, given the need of the situation, he makes a concession as something of a 'holding job', carefully circumscribing the concession and giving a clear enough hint that he would expect the wife to be reconciled and not to stay separated.[47] Then, at the end of verse 11, Paul applies the same teaching to the man.[48]

In verse 12, Paul addresses a different group: the rest. He has addressed all the married in verses 2-5, the unmarried in verses 8-9, and the married, again, in verses 10-11. Who can 'the rest' possibly be? Verses 12-13 make it clear that he is addressing a mixed marriage of believer and unbeliever. Thus, verses 2-5 apply to all marriages, whether of two believers or of a believer and unbeliever. Verses 10-11 address issues specific to the marriage of two believers, while verses 12-14 deal with a mixed marriage. This must mean that what Paul has said in verses 10-11 applies only to a marriage of believers; but since this was a reaffirmation of Christ's teaching, it follows that his teaching on this issue was intended only for marriages of those in the covenant community.[49] This last point is underlined by Paul's words in verse 12 that he, not the Lord, is now about to speak. He is putting us on notice that what he is about to say cannot be found in Jesus' teaching, precisely because Jesus did not address this type of situation. Again, we are right to believe that Paul is addressing teaching in reply to questions which the Corinthians have raised. His prohibition of a believer divorcing[50] the unbeliever suggests that he had been asked about this. Why? Verse 14 probably supplies the answer. The believers feared contamination from the unbelieving spouses, and their misunderstanding referred to in 5:9-10 may have exacerbated this fear. It is possible that some had abstained or were intending to abstain from sexual relations with their spouses for fear of contamination. Thus Paul writes as he does in verses 2-5. Others may have felt that they needed to go further and leave their spouses altogether: hence Paul's words in 12-14. Moreover, it is possible that conversion had led on to some very real tensions within numerous Corinthian households, and that the believing spouses assumed that the easiest solution was divorce. There were probably different reasons why believers were wishing to leave their unbelieving spouses.

What is interesting in these verses is the absence of the concession found in verse 11, but the presence of a qualification that is missing from verses 10-11. Paul's teaching here is of an all-or-nothing nature: it is divorce or full cohabitation. He does not countenance separation. But what he says in verses 12-13 is conditional upon the unbelieving spouse being willing to live with the believer: the believer is not to divorce *if* the unbeliever is willing to live with the believer. What if the unbeliever is unwilling to do so? The usual answer is that verse 15 deals with that situation. However, there are good reasons for believing that verses 12-15 are dealing with three, not two, types of situation.

The main thrust of verses 12-13 is that a believer must not divorce an unbeliever who is willing to live with him/her. Verse 15 concerns the situation where the unbeliever departs. We have already seen that, according to Roman law, divorce could be effected by a unilateral act of repudiation—*repudium*—or by mutual consent. Verse 15 is dealing with a case of repudiation. But while the main thrust of verses 12-13 is that the believer must not divorce an unbeliever who is willing to live with him/her, what if the unbeliever is unwilling so to do and wants a divorce? This is the third type of situation. Since the prohibition of divorce is conditional on the unbeliever being willing to live with the believer, it is, therefore, a warrantable inference to draw that the believer will *not* be prohibited from divorcing where the unbeliever is unwilling to live with the believer. It is true that Paul does not enlarge upon this or expressly spell it out. But it is difficult to see how the conclusion can be resisted that divorce is possible in such a case. Some of the words Paul uses would be utterly redundant if he were not implicitly allowing divorce. If Paul is not implicitly allowing divorce, then he could have written as follows: 'If a woman has a husband who is not a believer, she must not divorce him.' The words 'and he is willing to live with her' add something to the sentence; they qualify, somewhat, the prohibition. The objection that the case of an unbeliever who is unwilling to live with the believer is covered by verse 15 does not really stand up to scrutiny. It was a commonplace of Roman law that divorce could be effected by repudiation or by consent. Accordingly, Paul's readers would pick up the implied permission to divorce, in certain limited circumstances, contained in verses 12-13.

Two questions arise at this point. The first is, In what circumstances might the believer divorce? Secondly, given the pastoral importance and implications of this permission, why does Paul not spell it out but only leave it to be inferred? After all, can a doctrine be built upon inferences?

There are two types of situation where the believer may divorce, both of which are covered by the fact that the unbeliever is unwilling to live with the believer. The first is a fairly clear case: the unbeliever tells the believer that he would like a divorce. There may not be animosity and, for a variety of reasons, he does not wish to end the marriage by an act of *repudium* but wishes for the marriage to end by consent. He may wish to go with another woman; he may have tired of his wife; he may be unhappy with her having her new-found faith; he may be wanting her to engage in sinful actions in which she is unwilling to engage. The point is that he does not want to continue the marriage. In such a case, since the divorce is the action of both parties, the divorce is as much her act as his. That being so, verses 12-13 imply that the believer may divorce, i.e. agree with the unbeliever that the marriage is over. The believer is not to hold out so that the unbeliever resorts to an act of *repudium*.

The second type of situation is related to the first. Let us imagine that the unbeliever exercises force to compel the believer to commit sin. What is the believer to do in such a situation? The answer is surely supplied by a consideration of the fact that if the two of them reside under the same roof, that hardly constitutes agreement to live with someone as a spouse, *which is the kind of living together that Paul has in mind in verses 12-13.*[51] Surely more is involved. Pagan men and women were quite ready to divorce each other. Paul explains in verses 12-13 that, for the Christian married to an unbeliever, that is no longer an option. But there is an exception, namely, where the unbeliever is unwilling to live with the believer as a spouse. Thus, if the unbeliever were to brutalise the believer, the believer could divorce. Indeed, given Paul's words in 7:2-5, it would appear that the withholding of sexual relationships might also be construed as a refusal to live with the spouse *as a spouse*. Of course, selfish sexual demands and exploitation would mean that the unbeliever was being as one-sided in this realm as if he were to deny his spouse. In such a case, the believer would not be forbidden to divorce.

It may be objected that, whereas we have argued that verses 12-13 contain indications that divorce by consent is possible, what is now being said amounts to *repudium*. But such an objection fails to come to terms with the fact that someone who is virtually compelled to follow a course of action may well say that the action is really the responsibility of the person who has forced them in that way. For example, the English law of divorce under the Matrimonial Causes Act 1973 recognises 'constructive desertion' as a fact that evidences irretrievable breakdown of marriage. This is the situation where a spouse's behaviour is so bad that the other spouse feels compelled to leave the matrimonial home. In such a case, the Court *construes* the act of the spouse who leaves as the act of the other spouse: hence the term, *constructive desertion*. Where the husband says that he wants a divorce, Paul is implying that the wife may consent, and vice versa. But actions are as important as words; and where the actions of a spouse are such that they declare that spouse's unwillingness to accept and live with the other spouse as a spouse, then the believer may divorce. If this were not so, one would be left with the ridiculous situation that a woman could agree to a divorce of a husband who mildly explained that he wanted a divorce, but she would be compelled to live with a husband who might beat her, degrade her, etc.

The second question is concerned with the fact that Paul does not spell this out. Why? There are a number of possible reasons. Firstly, it is undoubtedly the case that his emphasis falls on the fact that the believer is *not* to divorce. Secondly, this emphasis may well have been due to the fact that the Corinthians had asked him whether it was right and necessary to divorce their unbelieving partners because of the danger of contracting defilement. Thirdly, Paul could assume that his readers—familiar as they would have been with the distinction between *repudium* and *divortium bona gratia*—would have understood this qualification to his prohibition *without* the need for him to spell it out. If it be objected that this goes way beyond the teaching of Jesus, we must reply that Paul has put us on notice, in verse 12, that this will be so. This is because he is addressing a state of affairs not addressed by Jesus.

At this point, it is worth pausing to point out that this gives a realism to Paul's teaching. To tell a woman that she must submit herself to regular and systematic beating from her husband, to being compelled to perform degrading sexual acts, to living with a man who treats her far worse than his dog, because Jesus only allowed divorce for *porneia*, is to be guilty of a terrible misunderstanding of biblical teaching which might well cause untold misery and suffering. Jesus' teaching was addressed to a specific situation, and it is quite unwarrantable to universalise a general law which applies to cases with which Jesus was not dealing. (Incidentally, it is worth pointing out that a man who compels his wife to submit to sexual degradation might well be guilty of *porneia*, though it is doubtful if this type of case was considered by Jesus in his exceptive words. In any event, verses 12-13 would allow divorce in such a case.)

Verse 14 explains that, far from the believer contracting moral defilement from the unbeliever, the believer has a sanctifying influence upon his or her spouse and their children. This thought is introduced as a reason why the believer should not divorce if the unbeliever is willing to live with the believer. The reference to the children is all-important. What would happen to them if the believer were to separate? Children would be under the power of the *paterfamilias*, who would either be the father or his *paterfamilias*.[52] A divorce could, therefore, have implications for the influence of the believer on the children, as well as upon the unbelieving spouse; there was every reason to stay with the unbeliever if he were willing to live with the believer. But what if the unbeliever departed? This is the situation envisaged in verse 15. In such a case the believer is to let him go.

It is unfortunate that our English translation does not pick up undertones that are present in the Greek. The same verb is used as was used by Jesus in Matthew 19:6, and in Mark 10:9.[53] In those verses Jesus had said, 'What God has joined together, let not man separate' or 'let not man put asunder.' In verse 15 Paul says, 'If he put asunder, let him put asunder', or 'If he separate, let him separate.' The contrast with the teaching of Jesus is, therefore, quite stark and arises from the fact that Paul is addressing a different situation. It is not that Paul is approving of the unbeliever's act, but he is saying that the believer should not stand in his way. There is almost something decisive and final about the believer letting the unbeliever depart. This is brought out by the next clause: 'A believing man or woman is not bound in such circumstances.' These words have generated considerable controversy and a range of interpretations. The only interpretation which adequately fits the context is that Paul is telling the believer that the divorce is to be accepted by the believer, *who is no longer bound in marriage to the unbeliever.*[54] The call to live in peace in the remainder of the verse is a call to submit to the will of God in the situation and to enjoy the peace which comes from such submission.[55]

Verse 16 also has occasioned considerable debate as to whether it expresses optimism or pessimism. If the former, then it may be understood to refer back to verses 12-14, as an additional reason for continuing the marriage with the unbeliever. In effect, Paul is then saying, 'Who knows? You may be the means of salvation for your spouse.' The pessimistic interpretation understands Paul to be overcoming the anxious scruple of a believer in accepting the divorce. Underlying Paul's words is the assumption that the believer might be thinking that if the marriage were kept together, the unbeliever might be saved through the believer's witness. Paul is countering this thought with the question, 'How can you know whether you will be the means of your spouse's salvation?'—the idea being that it is idle speculation to assume that you will be such an instrument for good. Accordingly, since we are called to peace, and there will be no peace if you seek to maintain the marriage, and, in any event, you have no guarantee that your spouse will be saved, accept the divorce.

Which is right? The answer is that both are right and both are wrong. One is naturally reluctant to believe that Scripture is ambiguous and that opposing meanings may be read out of a text.[56] However, where the writer intended that there should be an ambiguity, we should not attempt to iron out the folds of a text so that it gives a smooth and straightforward meaning. There *are* examples in the Bible of what appears to be deliberate ambiguity.[57] Might not this verse be another example? I think so. In that case, Paul is reminding his readers that God has called them to live in peace. If the unbeliever is willing to live with the believer, then the believer is to accept this, live in peace with the unbeliever and do nothing to force a division. The unbeliever is sanctified by the believer. And who knows? The believer may be the means of the unbeliever's salvation. But if the unbeliever departs, the believer is not desperately to attempt to stop this, but is to remember that God has called him to peace. He is to accept the situation. After all, he has no warrant to believe that he will be the means of his spouse's salvation. Verses 15*d* and 16 thus apply to all of verses 12-15*c*, but they apply differently to the two situations envisaged.[58] The pessimistic strain in verse 16 is not absolute in its reference to verse 15; for Paul is not saying one cannot know whether the unbeliever will ever be saved. That, of course, is true, but it is not what Paul is saying. What he says is that the believer does not know if he or she will be the means of the unbeliever's salvation. Indeed, since God has called us to peace, and the wider biblical context indicates that God's Spirit delights to work in an atmosphere of peace,[59] it could be argued that there will be more likelihood of the unbeliever being won after he has left.

All of the above is confirmed in verses 17-24. Paul's basic teaching is that one's life setting is something assigned to us by the Lord, and something to which we are called. This being so, Paul's rule—which, as he makes clear in the last sentence of verse 17, is a universal rule which he is specifically applying to the Corinthians' situation—is that each believer should retain the place in life assigned to him by the Lord and to which the Lord has called him.

This relates back to verses 2-16 in the following way. Married people should function as married people and not abstain from sexual intercourse within marriage (vv.2-5). As a concession, Paul allows abstention for a limited period of time if it is for prayer and by mutual consent (vv.5-6). In verse 7, while expressing a wish that all would be like him—i.e. unmarried—he quickly goes on to stress that these matters are determined by God, who gifts some in one way and some in another. This reference to gifting clearly refers to the strength of sexual drive, which is an indicator whether one should marry or not. This becomes clear in verses 8-9, where Paul says that the unmarried should remain unmarried as he was, but if they could not control themselves they should marry, for it would be better to marry than to burn. What this means, of course, is that one should accept the life setting in which one finds oneself, but part of that life setting is one's own temperament and giftedness from God. Therefore, someone who is unmarried but is burning should realise that it is better to marry than burn and should not, therefore, remain in that unmarried state. In verses 10-11, Paul tells married Christians to stay together. But if separated, the separating spouse should either remain in that condition or be reconciled. In verses 12-13, Paul tells believing spouses not to divorce unbelieving spouses, if the unbeliever is happy to live as a spouse with the believer. But if the unbeliever is not willing to live as a spouse, this is part of the life setting in which the believer finds himself. He may divorce the unbeliever. He is called to peace, and there will be no peace if he tries to keep up the semblance of a marriage that, because of the unbeliever's behaviour, is nothing but a sham. Moreover, what makes him think that he will save the unbeliever by continuing to live under the same roof? In verse 15, Paul tells the believer that if the unbeliever departs, he is to accept this as the life setting to which God has assigned him. Thus, he may accept the divorce.

In verses 18-19, Paul gives another example of life situations that are not changed by conversion. The person who was already circumcised when called into the life of faith should not become uncircumcised, and the person who was uncircumcised should not become circumcised. Thus Paul is saying that one's racial and cultural background is also part of the life setting assigned to one by the Lord, and is to be accepted as such. What counts is obedience to God's commands. That, of course, raises problems because, as any first-century Jew would have said, circumcision is one of God's commands. Lying behind Paul's words, therefore, is a profound theological land-shift, which has been effected by the coming of Christ and has implications for what constitutes a life of obedience. And that is worked out in chapter 9, where it is clear that Paul saw that there were exceptions to the rule he laid down in all the churches, and those exceptions were based on obedience to Jesus Christ and commitment to his gospel. Paul's words in 9:19-23 stand as something of a contrast to what he says in 7:17-20. They alert us to the fact that the rule formulated and applied in 7:17-20 must not be understood in absolutist terms, which admit of no exception. (Compare Acts 16:3 and Galatians 2:1-3 to see the same flexibility in Paul.)

Paul puts this point beyond all dispute in verse 21. Being a slave was part of one's life setting. But it is clear that Paul regards freedom as preferable to slavery. Thus, a Christian slave should obtain his freedom if he can. And the variety of ways in which a slave might become free was such that this was something that might 'happen' to him or something he would take an active part to initiate.[60] Thus, a believer married to an unbeliever who was unwilling to live with him *as a spouse*, was not forbidden to divorce, either by mutual agreement or by constructive repudiation. Where the unbeliever effected divorce by leaving, this was something that happened to the believer, who was no longer bound or enslaved.

Wider issues and questions that arise

A number of important questions arise from the exposition that has been offered of 1 Corinthians 7:8-16. Undoubtedly, the most pressing question concerns the meaning of verse 39. On first reading, this verse might appear to teach that nothing can break the marriage bond while husband and wife are both alive. If this be so, then clearly the interpretation offered of earlier verses in this chapter would be contradicted by verse 39, and this would necessitate a revision of the exegesis which has been offered. Furthermore, the teaching of Romans 7:1-3 appears to be very similar to that found in verse 39. Since the context of the verses in Romans is so different from that of 1 Corinthians 7, it may be thought that this emphasis on the indissolubility of the marriage bond was evidently something patently obvious to Paul, and something he was concerned to impress upon the people of God.

For a number of reasons, Romans 7:1-3 merits separate attention, and it is addressed in Appendix 3. First, it is right to deal with 1 Corinthians 7:39 in the present chapter, since we have been concerned with 1 Corinthians 7 throughout this chapter. To consider Romans 7 in the present chapter would be to bring in material that is, strictly speaking, extraneous to the passage under consideration. Secondly, as Appendix 3 makes clear, in Romans 7:1-3 Paul's concern is with the place of the Mosaic law in the Christian economy, and the subject of marriage is introduced by way of illustration. By contrast, 1 Corinthians 7:39 occurs in a chapter which has been immediately and directly concerned with questions relating to marriage. In the third place, as I argue in Appendix 3, Paul's treatment of the marriage relationship in Romans 7 is in terms of the teaching of the Mosaic law: in 1 Corinthians 7, Paul is speaking as an apostle of Jesus Christ (vv.10,12,25,40; cf. 14:37; 1 Tim. 1:12-17).

For these reasons, we shall confine ourselves, at this stage, to a consideration of 1 Corinthians 7:39.

A number of general comments are in order before seeking to exegete the verse. First, it is not at all uncommon to meet statements in Scripture which, if taken in their most absolute sense, might contradict statements found earlier in the same portion of Scripture. Thus, 1 John 3:6, understood absolutely, clearly contradicts 1 John 1:8. Similarly, 1 Corinthians 14:34, if understood to require total silence on the part of the women, contradicts 11:5. It is part of any responsible approach to exegesis to demonstrate how such seemingly contradictory verses fit together. Secondly, what must be avoided is a pre-commitment to an understanding of one verse which leads one to 'force' another verse into such a prematurely constructed theological system. Those who seek to harmonise biblical passages must resist this ever-present temptation. The better course of action is to exegete each passage in its context. When this is properly done, it will be seen that each passage fits together.

Thirdly, this caveat against an improper approach to harmonisation notwithstanding, two important considerations must be borne in mind. A letter such as 1 Corinthians was intended to be read 'sequentially'. This being so, it is important to study it sequentially. Methodologically, it is better to work one's way through a chapter and seek to ascertain how later material fits with earlier material than to allow the last but one verse of the chapter to shackle exegesis of earlier verses. Naturally, if exegesis of the later verse throws into question the exegesis of the earlier material, it may well lead to the need to revise and correct the earlier exegesis. After all, if the Corinthians could misunderstand Paul's writing to them and need a corrective from him (1 Cor. 5:9-11), then it is perfectly possible that we shall make mistakes. Thus, later material in a letter, while not shackling exegesis of earlier material, might well prove a useful check and monitor on exegesis of earlier material. The second consideration to be borne in mind concerns understanding gained from earlier exegesis of a wide range of biblical material. If certain conclusions have seemed inescapable and have been confirmed by study of other passages, a verse which might appear to overthrow that understanding has to be weighed against the total weight of material already studied.

The significance of the last point resides in the fact that, if verse 39 teaches that the marriage bond is indissoluble while the two spouses to a marriage are alive, it will not only contradict our exegesis of the earlier part of the chapter but will also contradict our exegesis of Christ's teaching. It will mean that divorce, even in the case allowed by Jesus (that is, for *porneia*) does not break the marriage bond. We have already seen that Jesus taught that the gravity of divorce lay in the fact that it separated, or put asunder, what God had joined together. We have seen that this means that Jesus taught that divorce would break the marriage bond. Therein lies its iniquity. It is only permitted by Christ where one of the spouses has been guilty of behaviour which strikes at the heart of the marriage bond. Furthermore, we have had occasion to note that Paul's words in verse 12 necessitate the understanding that, with respect to the situation envisaged in verses 12ff., he will say something considerably different from what he has said in verses 10-11. In those verses he has taught that the marriage bond between the husband and wife must not be broken. In verse 15, we have noted that he must be saying something different from his words in verses 10-11. The difference is to be found in the words 'is not bound'; they must mean that the marriage bond is broken. This background understanding cannot be ignored in coming to verse 39.

It is interesting to note that Fee believes that verses 39-40 refer back to the earlier part of the chapter, and that verse 39 is reiterating that there is to be no remarriage after divorce. To say the least, this is a surprising treatment of this verse. Verse 25 begins a fresh section which, while not unrelated to the earlier part of the chapter, is certainly distinct from it. The last clause of verse 40 appears to refer back to verse 25. In that verse Paul designates himself as 'one who by the Lord's mercy is trustworthy'—words clearly echoed in 1 Timothy 1:12ff., where they refer to Paul's specific service of Christ. Here in verse 40 the clause clearly appears to be a self-conscious remark by Paul concerning his own spirituality as a possible counter to 'pneumatic' individuals in Corinth. This last observation shows that the verse has some affinity with 14:37, though in the latter case it is clear that we are in the realm of commandment and obligation, whereas in 7:40 Paul is rounding off a section which has had more to do with wise judgement than authoritative command (cf. v.25).

The importance of the fact that verses 39-40 round off the section which begins with verse 25 lies in the fact that Paul is concerned in this section with matters somewhat different from those that concerned him in verses 1-24. In the earlier section, he considered the subject of marriage and divorce fairly comprehensively: the position of those divorced before they were converted (vv.8-9); those married to believers (vv.10-11); those whose unbelieving spouses are willing or unwilling to live with them (vv.12-14), and those whose spouses divorce them by repudiating the marriage (v.15). Having moved on from that section and having been concerned with a different matter, it would be surprising for Paul to sum up the teaching on divorce in verse 39.

It is true that there is an asyndeton in verse 39: that is to say, there is no connective particle towards the beginning of the verse. Greek uses these so liberally that they are often left untranslated. Their absence is noteworthy, and the asyndeton in verse 39 could mark the beginning of a new paragraph.[61] Moreover, Fee draws attention to an 'ABA' pattern of argument in chapter 7, as well as in other passages of 1 Corinthians. This type of argument begins with a general statement, is followed by an explanatory digression, and concludes with a very specific response to the problem. Fee believes that this pattern accounts for the fact that verses 39-40 sum up the entire chapter. On the other hand, there are important verbal linkages between verses 39-40 and other verses found in the section that begins with verse 25.[62] These verbal linkages demonstrate that what is known as an *inclusio* exists here. Furthermore, as the exegesis should make clear, it is possible to understand the section beginning with verse 25 in such a way that verses 39-40 naturally conclude it, without having reference to the earlier part of the chapter.

Verse 25 alerts us to the fact that Paul is now going to deal with 'the virgins'.[63] Considerable effort has been expended by commentators to ascertain precisely to whom this word refers. The interpretation offered here tentatively follows that of Fee, who understands this to be a reference to those who are betrothed to be married.[64] According to Fee's understanding, certain 'pneumatic' individuals in the church at Corinth were pressurising betrothed couples not to go through with their marriages. This was giving rise to all kinds of difficulties. Accordingly, Paul is responding to this type of situation, which resulted from the ascetic tendencies of some who were suffering from a heavy dose of 'over-realised eschatology'.

Paul begins his treatment of this issue somewhat differently from the way in which he had dealt with divorce and separation earlier in the chapter. There, he was laying down a command (verse 10). Here, he is offering counsel (verse 25).[65] To be true, it is the counsel of an apostle of Jesus Christ and, as such, is to be regarded somewhat differently from a piece of good advice that a friend might give. As an apostle of Jesus Christ, writing under the inspiration of the Holy Spirit, the counsel is divine counsel. Nevertheless, it is counsel that Paul is giving, not commands, and there is an important difference between a divine command and divine advice or counsel. This observation requires a necessary distinction to be made, and prompts a question that must be answered. It is important to distinguish counsel not only from commandment, but also from mere permission to do something or toleration of a particular practice. There is a tendency for some to understand Paul's teaching in parts of this chapter to be akin to the Mosaic toleration of divorce. However, this is quite mistaken. Moses regulated an existing evil, and Jesus made clear that the coming of the kingdom removed that toleration. By contrast, the kind of language Paul uses in this section demonstrates that he is not tolerating evil.[66]

The question which must be answered is this: are there no commands to be found in this part of the letter, or is it all counsel? The answer to this question is that while there *are* commands (verses 29-31 partake of this character), these are by way of general application to *all* the church, and it is clear that Paul is universalising at this point.[67] However, when dealing with the specific matter raised by their letter, Paul lays down guiding principles. But he so balances the alternative courses of action, and allows such a range of options, that (with one notable exception, which we shall consider in due course) his response is in terms of what may be the best course of action for his readers, rather than what is absolutely required of them. This fact signals and confirms what he says in verse 25, namely, that he is giving counsel rather than issuing commands. Moreover, that he takes into account the circumstances and inner attitudes of his readers (e.g. verses 36-37) makes it abundantly clear that we are not here in the realm of absolute obligation. The

164

importance of such considerations and observations to the whole question of biblical ethics should not be overlooked.

Verse 26 informs us that the counsel Paul gives is given in the light of 'the present crisis'.[68] The meaning of this phrase has been the subject of considerable debate. I believe that there are sound reasons for holding that it does not refer to the entire eschatological period inaugurated by the coming of Christ, nor to the woes immediately preceding the second coming of Christ, but rather, that it denotes a particular period of trial or tribulation impending for the Corinthian Church.[69] This being the case, the counsel that Paul gives is controlled somewhat by the Corinthians' circumstances. In similar circumstances that counsel is valid. What must not be done is to universalise rules of behaviour from counsel given to believers who were facing a very specific situation. Paul's 'I think that it is good . . .' in verse 26 is almost certainly a quote from the Corinthians' letter and is another example of the 'Yes, but' type of argument which, we have already noted, is employed frequently in this letter. The 'but' part of the argument which qualifies the 'yes' part of the argument is picked up in verse 28. Thus, in verse 26 Paul agrees with the Corinthians, and in verse 28 he qualifies his agreement. However, in verse 26 he is not only agreeing with the Corinthians, but is also reaffirming the principle which he has laid down in verse 17 and which, he tells us in that verse, he lays down in all the churches. The fact that verse 27 follows verse 26 in the same way that verse 18 follows verse 17, with abrupt questions marked by asyndeton, indicates that at this point the Corinthians' stance bears a similarity to that of Paul. However, the general principle which Paul reaffirms, with respect to the subject under consideration in verses 25ff., is qualified in a specific way, which indicates that Paul's whole perspective is very different from that of the Corinthians. He is holding the position that he is *because of the present crisis*. By contrast, some of the Corinthians were adopting this position because of their ascetic tendencies.

But what is the position that Paul is adopting in verse 26? It is for a man to be as he is, or to stay as he is.[70] In verse 27, he illustrates this with respect to the matter in hand. The NIV translation of these verses is thoroughly misleading: there are a number of reasons why Paul is not here referring to divorce. First, if he were dealing with divorce, he would be referring back to verses 10-15. But he has only just begun a new section. To the argument that verse 26 reaffirms the principle laid down in verse 17 and therefore inevitably links verse 27 with the previous section, the reply must surely be that, as we have just noted, Paul is introducing a new consideration which relates to that principle in verse 26. Secondly—and this consideration tells decisively against the view that Paul is here dealing with divorce—in verses 10ff. Paul was laying down commands: in this section he is giving counsel. To be true, as we shall note, verse 27 is expressed as a command. Nevertheless, this command is used as the background to set up the advice he is going to give, and that advice is such that it cannot relate to a married couple. This being so, verse 27 cannot be relating to divorce. Thirdly, the words Paul uses are not the words of marriage and divorce but those of contractual obligation.[71] Paul is telling those who are betrothed not to seek to be released from the engagement, and those who are not thus betrothed not to seek to be so. In effect, verse 27a should read, 'Are you bound to a woman? Seek not to be loosed.'[72] Therefore, this verse is not dealing with divorce. Nevertheless, from Paul's Jewish background it might be thought that this is a 'quasi-divorce' situation, particularly in view of the fact that Joseph was minded to put away Mary, to whom he was betrothed. The Roman law of divorce, however, assumed that marriage had taken place, and to that extent, in a betrothal situation, divorce was not an option.

The Roman law of engagement was fairly straightforward:

> Anciently, in Rome as in Latium generally, this took the form of reciprocal stipulations or *sponsiones* (whence the word *sponsalia* meaning *betrothal*). The parties would normally be the intending husband or his paterfamilias, and the paterfamilias of the intended bride. This practice was discontinued in Rome earlier than in Latium, where it lasted until Roman citizenship and with it Roman law were extended to Latium during the Social War. In the classical period [and 1 Corinthians was written during this period] mutual promises to marry created no legal obligation, so much so that to stipulate for a penalty to be paid in the event of marriage not taking place was held to be *contra bonos mores*.[73]

However, the presence in the church at Corinth of those from a Jewish background would have probably meant that they would view with grave concern an approach to betrothal that was less than serious. It is unlikely that Paul's remarks in this part of the letter are addressed to Jewish Christians who had come under the influence of the ascetic tendencies of 'pneumatic' people. Marriage was such a firmly embedded idea in Judaism that it is unlikely that the over-realised eschatology would have found a fertile breeding ground amongst Jewish believers.

Paul then considers those who are not in such a position and advises that they should not seek a bride.[74] He immediately qualifies this advice in verse 28: 'But if you do marry, you have not sinned.' The question that arises at this point is as follows: Which part of verse 27 does verse 28 qualify? It may seem fairly obvious that Paul is here qualifying the latter part of verse 27: having advised against seeking a bride, he now says that it is not sin to marry. However, it is submitted that there are reasons for believing that verse 28 qualifies the whole of verse 27 and, by implication, verse 26. The position of those envisaged in verse 27a is that, in a sense, they are neither married nor unmarried, but betrothed. To stay as they are would not mean that they would be married but that they would continue in a betrothal situation, neither clearly unmarried nor married in the proper sense of the word. It is quite possible that 'pneumatic' people in Corinth were pressurising such couples not to go through with their marriages. It is clear from verse 36 that there were those who were betrothed who were not happy with this, and who wished to complete the betrothal by being married: 'he should do as he wants'. Moreover, those from a Jewish background and those who had been influenced by the synagogue could be expected to take a very negative view of such a laissez-faire approach to betrothal. However, because of the impending crisis, Paul believed that there was wisdom in continuing as one was. In the case of the betrothed, this would mean *not yet* to marry; and in the case of the unbetrothed, not to seek a bride. Paul is *not* saying that the betrothed should continue for ever in that condition but, *because of the present crisis*, a man should stay as he is. That is to say, *everyone* should stay in their present circumstances and not seek a change in their life situation, but particularly where such a change could lead to greater trouble. Thus, Paul is adopting a kind of 'wait and see' approach. Implicit in his advice is the fact that, after the crisis, those who had stayed betrothed could marry, just as those who were not betrothed could marry.

Thus, there are three options, not just two, for the betrothed. Option 1 is to break the engagement. This is forbidden by Paul in verse 27, and this prohibition is not mere counsel but a command, being expressed in the imperative mood.[75] The second option, which is the one that Paul counsels, is to stay as one is (verse 26). For a betrothed person, this means not yet to marry but to stay betrothed, and for a non-betrothed person, not to seek a bride. The third option is for the betrothed person to go through with the marriage, and for a non-betrothed person to get married. Paul specifically states that it would not be sin for this third option to be pursued. It is clear from the reference in verse 28*b* to 'the virgin', which is a feminine noun, that the 'you' of verses 27 and 28*a* refers to the man. Verse 28*b* balances verse 28*a*. It should be noted in passing that whereas Paul refers to the man in verse 27*a*, he does not expressly balance this with a reference to the woman in this part of the passage.

It is clear that at this point Paul has introduced teaching that is missing from verses 8 and 9. In those verses he has quoted the Corinthians to the effect that it is good to remain as they are, but has immediately qualified this counsel by saying that it is better to marry than to burn. There he has made no reference to 'the present crisis'. Why is this so? It is probably impossible for us to answer this question with certainty, because of the difficulties that we face in reconstructing the background to Paul's letter and the particular matters to which he was responding. However, we did note that verse 8 is probably referring to *all* the unmarried—or possibly only the 'demarried'. The interpretation I have preferred is the one which sees the unmarried of verse 8 as including those who have never been married as well as the 'demarried'—with a special reference to the widows. Paul is now making a special case of the betrothed. It is possible that those who had been married may have been under a greater tendency to suffer from burning. Furthermore, the complete change which would be brought about by a betrothed person being married might have made it more difficult for them to cope with the pressures of married life in the present crisis than would have been the case for those who had previously been married. It is the troubles that the married are going to face in this time of crisis which influences Paul in the advice he gives (verse 28c).

Verses 29-35 are in the nature of a parenthetical elaboration and amplification of what Paul has said in verse 28c.[76] As such, we need not be detained by a consideration of these verses, since the argument that is being presented is unaffected by them. At a number of points, where the meaning of these verses does have a bearing on the argument, they are touched on in a number of the notes to this chapter.

In verse 36, Paul picks up again the thread of the issues facing a betrothed couple. Verses 36-38 are amongst the most difficult in the whole of this chapter and, indeed, in the whole of the letter. The difficulty arises from uncertainty as to whether Paul is here addressing the man betrothed to a virgin or addressing her father. Before considering this question, attention should be drawn to a vital consideration, one which I have not seen addressed in any treatment of these verses but which is essential to a proper understanding of them. If Paul is here dealing with the man who is betrothed to the virgin, then the interpretation offered of verses 26-28, viz., that there are three options rather than only two, is absolutely demanded by what Paul says in verses 36-38. If there are only two options—that the betrothed marry (verses 36, 38a) or that they break off the betrothal (verses 37, 38b)—then Paul would be favouring option 2 in verses 37,38b, in direct contradiction to what he has said in verse 27. In that verse he commanded that a man should not seek to be released from his commitment to the woman; but in verses 37 and 38b he is actually saying that it is better to break off the arrangement than to marry. Accordingly, verses 37 and 38b can be harmonised with verse 27 in two ways: *either* by saying that there are three options open to the betrothed couple, one of which Paul expressly forbids, another of which he does not disapprove, and the third of which—subject to certain considerations and qualifications—he favours; *or* by saying that verses 36-38 must be dealing with a different situation from that considered in verses 27-28. We shall shortly consider the various interpretative options for verses 36-38, but it is worth noting at this point that the interpretation offered of verses 26-28 will assist in understanding some of the difficult language of verses 36-38, as well as enabling us to understand verse 39 in its proper context.

The two main possibilities that face us are that verses 36-38 are *either* dealing with the question of a father giving his betrothed daughter in marriage or withholding her, *or* with a betrothed man going on to marry his betrothed virgin or not going ahead with the marriage. The arguments are finely balanced, but I believe that there are good reasons for holding that Paul is still continuing with the same situation with which he was concerned in verses 26-28.[77] In verse 36, Paul amplifies what he had said in verse 28*a* and *b*. Where the man believes that by not marrying he is behaving improperly to the virgin to whom he is betrothed,[78] where he or she has reached a certain stage in life that makes it all the more appropriate to go through with the marriage,[79] where the man believes that he ought to marry her,[80] and where he wants to marry her,[81] he should do so. He will not be sinning. In verse 37, Paul amplifies what he has said in verse 26. In a very tortuous sentence, where numerous conditions are specified, Paul advises that the man should 'keep his virgin'.[82] This difficult phrase does *not* mean that the man break off the engagement, nor that the couple continue the rest of their lives engaged but not married; rather, this is Paul's way of advising the 'wait and see' policy of verses 26-27. In verse 38, Paul sums up the position with respect to these two possibilities *as they bear on the man*. In verses 36-38, the entire discussion has focused on what the *man* decides.

In verse 39, Paul addresses the woman. Two essential things must be observed if the interpretation of verse 39 is not to be skewed. First, the preceding context has *not* been a discussion of the relationships of husbands and wives, but that of betrothed couples. Indeed, even were one to opt for the interpretation that verses 36-38 were addressing the father of a virgin rather than the fiancé of a virgin, the point is the same: Paul has not been dealing with husbands and wives in verses 36-38. The second essential consideration is that Paul is only speaking here of the woman. To say the least, if his concern in this verse were with the indissolubility of marriage per se, then this is a strange way to express it. If it be said that Paul uses similar language in Romans 7:1-3, the reply must be made that in those verses Paul's argument demands that he use an illustration which stresses the fact that the wife is bound to the husband. (Further on this, see the consideration of those verses in Appendix 3.) However, if we understand verse 39 to be continuing the subject dealt with in verses 25ff., verse 39 makes perfect sense. In verses 36-38, Paul is amplifying the situation as it concerns the man's decision. Verse 38 concludes this, and thus Paul uses—as Fee notes—the strong inferential conjunction 'so then' to sum up the argument. In turning to the woman in verse 39, he is balancing somewhat his treatment of the man in verses 36-38. But the focus of his concern for the woman and what he says to her is sufficiently different from what he has said in verses 36-38 to account for the asyndeton.

Paul's concern in verse 39 is to answer the question, What is the position of the betrothed woman? That he uses the word for woman, rather than the word virgin, does not demand that he is here not addressing the virgins. There are good reasons for holding that he is still dealing with a virgin.[83] In the context of the argument, Paul is asserting that she is bound to the man to whom she is betrothed for as long as he lives. We noted that in verse 28*b* Paul balanced what he had said of the man in verse 28*a*. However, he did not balance what he had said of the man in verse 27*a* and *b*. Verse 39a perfectly balances what Paul had said in verse 27*a* and *b*. There he had insisted that the man who was betrothed was not to seek to be released from his obligations. This point has been elaborated in verses 36-38. Paul is now saying something similar of the woman. She is bound to her man[84] for as long as he lives. This does *not* mean that she is to continue the rest of her life engaged but unmarried. Rather, during the 'wait and see' period she is still bound in betrothal to him. She will only be released on his death. But why does Paul express himself thus? It is impossible to dogmatise, but it may well have something to do with the impending distress. It may well have been that the distress was more likely to entail the death of the man than of the woman. Thus, the woman is bound to her man during the wait-and-see period. Should he die, she would be free to marry another man. This explains why, at the end of a passage dealing with virgins, Paul considers the possibility of the virgin being a 'quasi-widow'. Moreover, the fact that widows were singled out for special mention in verse 8, whereas there is no such special treatment of widowers, and the statistical likelihood that there would be more women in the situation envisaged in verse 39*b* than men,[85] makes it perfectly natural for Paul to express himself as he does in this verse.

Of course, none of this means that married couples should view their marriages as breakable. The indissolubility of marriage is not Paul's concern in verse 39. Clearly, it is possible for those who believe that Paul allowed divorce in certain circumstances to argue that, in verse 39, Paul is teaching the indissolubility of marriage but is not dealing with the exceptions to that teaching. Indeed, I understand verses 10-11 not to be considering the exception to the prohibition of divorce that Jesus allowed. However, it is submitted that by carefully exegeting verses 25ff. it is not necessary to seek to harmonise verse 39 with earlier conclusions. Rather, verse 39 stands in its own right as dealing with a betrothed woman in the special circumstances Paul is considering, rather than with the indissolubility of marriage. Neither the indissolubility of marriage nor the situations where divorce is permissible come within Paul's universe of discourse in this verse.

Verse 40 completes this section. It clearly flows on from verse 39. The presence of the connective *de* towards the beginning of verse 40 and the fact that the verse is dealing with the situation of the woman who, staying betrothed, is then bereft of her man, makes clear that Paul is continuing from verse 39. But verse 40 demands that he is *not* summing up the entire chapter, but only the section beginning with verse 25. In the first place, verse 40*a* repeats the word 'judgment' with which, in verse 25, Paul notified us that he is giving counsel rather than laying down a command. If he were concluding the entire chapter, one would expect a stronger word. On the other hand, given that he began this section with the word 'judgment', it is natural for him to conclude with it. It rounds the section off nicely. Secondly, in verse 40*b*, Paul's reference to his belief that he thinks that he too has the Spirit of God fits neatly with his reference to his judgement in verses 25 and 40*a*. Were he summing up the entire chapter, where he has given commands as well as counsel, one would have expected stronger language (cf. 14:37). The more moderate language tells against this. Accordingly, the exegesis offered of verses 8-15 is not undermined at all by the teaching of verse 39.

The second obvious and burning question concerns the fact that Paul forbade a believer to divorce another believer, but allowed a believer to divorce an unbeliever in certain circumstances and to accept the divorce situation where the unbeliever divorced the believer. It almost appears that there is a double standard, and this prompts the question as to why there were different rules for a mixed marriage and for a marriage of two believers.

The first thing to say is that Paul has already indicated in this letter that certain situations require a believer to behave towards an unbeliever differently from towards a believer: in 5: 9-11 there is a fairly clear example of this. The dynamic of the Holy Spirit within the lives of Christians makes a radically different lifestyle possible for them. Moreover, such a lifestyle is obligatory for them (6:19). There is a radical distinction between the church and the world (1:23-24; 2:14-16; 5:12-13; 6:1-2; 14:23). This being the case, two things follow. First, one must not expect the world to behave like the church, and therefore one must not withdraw all contact from the world (5:9,10,12). Secondly, the church is to behave differently from the world and, if individuals fail to do so, then the church must deal with those individuals (5:11,13). In 7:10-11 Paul is addressing a Christian couple. The Holy Spirit indwells both of them and both are to live a life different from that of the society around them. Accordingly, divorce is not an option for them. The reason for this is that neither should behave in a way that would justify divorce, nor should either have resort to divorce in a situation where divorce would not be justifiable. We shall return to this point.

However, in verses 12-15, Paul is addressing a believer married to an unbeliever. The unbeliever neither accepts the lordship of Christ nor experiences the indwelling of the Holy Spirit. Of course, this does not mean that the unbeliever is a veritable demon. In 5:1 Paul has already indicated that pagans can have standards, and the wider biblical context supports the doctrine of God's common grace by which unbelievers can be enabled to be good husbands and wives. Moreover, the sanctifying influence of the believer is such that the unbeliever may even be happy that his or her spouse is a Christian. But it may not be like that. The unbeliever might resent the believer being a Christian and might seek to compel the believer to sin. The unbeliever might deprive the believer in the area of sexual relations. The unbeliever might—as unbelievers did in those days—simply tire of his spouse and leave for someone else. None of this behaviour is to be expected of a believer. Accordingly, a different set of circumstances existed in a mixed marriage from that in a marriage of believers, and Paul took account of this. This is the reason for the teaching in verses 12-15 being different from that found in verses 10-11.

In the wider biblical context this is not at all unusual. The call to live at peace with all men and to turn the other cheek does not mean that the rulers of a country are to cave in to every aggressor who seeks to take control of their country. Relationships are a two-way affair. A believer may seek to live as peaceably as possible with a work colleague, but if the colleague is pugnacious, intractable, and downright difficult, there may well be limitations to what can be done to improve things between them. But in the church, the believer is relating to other believers. Two believers acknowledge the lordship of Christ and are indwelt by the same Holy Spirit. They both acknowledge their solemn obligations and they have an ability to live up to those obligations. This is why Paul's words in 7:11 must be handled very carefully.

Tensions may arise in the best of Christian marriages. Divorce is not an option, and that becomes clear from the fact that the separating spouse must remain unmarried or be reconciled. But we must not think that Paul is envisaging the possibility of two Christians living in mutual hostility or in cold or polite indifference to each other. His teaching on the Lord's Supper in 11:17-33, and on love in chapter 13, has profound implications at this point. Christ's teaching in Matthew 5:21-26 and 18:15-35 is applicable to *all* believers, including a Christian couple who are separated. Accordingly, Paul must be understood as implying in verse 11 that reconciliation will take place. His teaching in 6:1-4 suggests that other believers in the church will be able to help the couple to be reconciled. Clearly, this may not be the matter of a few moments, but where the couple is working towards reconciliation, they are moving in the right direction. However, where there is a complete unwillingness and refusal to face one's Christian responsibilities, then pastoral and church discipline may well be necessary. Ultimately, of course, a professed believer's attitude may be such that he has to be put out of the church. At that point, the principles of verses 12-15 come into operation, rather than verses 10-11. Of course, excommunication really is a last resort, only to be used after strenuous efforts have been made to right matters. Nevertheless, it *is* a last resort, and a church should not shrink from such a step where it is necessary, and where it would enable a believer to divorce the excommunicated spouse and maintain a clear conscience.

A third burning issue concerns whether the divorced believer may remarry. The answer must surely be yes. The argument in the body of the text and developed in the notes is that the divorce has ended the marriage. If the divorce is along the lines of verses 12-13, then Paul has regarded it as justified, and if it is in terms of verse 15, the believer is to accept the situation. The argument that has been adduced is that Paul must be saying something more than what he says in verse 11. That something more is that the believer is no longer bound in marriage and is, therefore, free to remarry. Fee's argument that Paul is concerned with not changing status really is irrelevant. That is accepted. But *if* there is a divorce, then the status *has* changed. Of course, Paul does not go on to speak of remarriage because that would be outside his universe of discourse. But it is both a legitimate and necessary inference to draw from his teaching.

A fourth question arises from the interpretation that has been offered. It is as follows. It has been argued that Jesus' teaching only applied to the covenant people of God. However, that teaching allowed divorce for *porneia*. In a mixed marriage, Paul allowed more reasons for divorce. He did not allow wider reasons for divorce in the case of a marriage between two believers. However, if one spouse behaves like an unbeliever, then, ultimately, the church may discipline the unbeliever; and the believer, regarding his spouse as an unbeliever, will be free to divorce. But if a believer is guilty of *porneia*, one does not have to go through such a discipline procedure before obtaining a divorce. Does this not suggest that the New Testament envisages a believer committing *porneia*, but not committing those things for which Paul allows a believer to divorce an unbeliever? Worse, does it not lead to the conclusion that a believer who commits *porneia* is not necessarily viewed as an unbeliever, but that someone who simply insists on being unwilling to continue a marriage is to be viewed as an unbeliever? Does this not lead to monstrous miscalculation of moral values?

The answer to this objection is as follows. Jesus was largely addressing the problem of divorce in a male-dominated society. His comments in Mark 10:12 were almost certainly occasioned by Herodias' behaviour. Jesus was calling a halt to the prevailing practice of his day. He allowed divorce for *porneia*. However, he was addressing a 'trans-covenantal' situation, which applied to the Jews of that period as well as to his own disciples. In that Jewish society Jesus allowed a man to put away his wife for *porneia*. Jesus was *not* addressing the question of the discipline of the church. Clearly, Christians guilty of *porneia* may need to come under church discipline. In certain circumstances, response to that discipline could be of such a nature that excommunication might ultimately need to be effected.

Paul, by contrast, is not addressing a trans-covenantal situation. When reproducing the teaching of Jesus he does not refer to the exception of *porneia*, precisely because Christians are to avoid such behaviour. Nevertheless, were a believer to be guilty of *porneia* it is quite clear that Paul would not think that the church could ignore the situation. But the general point is that believers are to remain happily married. An unbeliever may want to get out of a marriage. *One* way in which he might demonstrate that is by being guilty of *porneia*, but there are many other ways. Now if a believer were to be guilty of such behaviour, discipline may well be called for, and the believer then be free to divorce. While discipline may be called for in the case of *porneia*, it so strikes at the heart of a marriage that the innocent spouse does not need to await discipline of the guilty spouse before divorcing him or her.

The genius of New Testament ethics lies in their ability to uphold moral absolutes and yet allow a believer to function in the society in which he finds himself. This is what 1 Corinthians 7 is partly about, and this approach to ethical matters is applied specifically to the question of divorce. The relevance of all this to our present-day situation is the subject of the next chapter.

PART IV

The Application
of Biblical Principles

Chapter 5
Practical Considerations

The New Testament consistently sets before Christians the very highest demands of marital faithfulness. These demands are such that divorce is, as a general principle, something that is never to be considered. Undergirding this ethical imperative is the glorious fact that the believer is indwelt by the Holy Spirit and that all the resources of God's grace are available to equip the believer for living the Christian life. Divorce is, therefore, not only disobedience to a categorical imperative but a practical denial of a glorious indicative. There is one exception to this principle, and that is where the other spouse is guilty of sexual infidelity. In such a case divorce is permissible, though not mandatory. The reason why it is permissible is because the guilty spouse has both desecrated the sacred bond of marriage and has put the other spouse in a situation where divorce is part of God's provision for dealing with the situation. The divorce is not sinful per se, but it testifies to a situation that has been affected by sin. The gravity of sexual infidelity and the gravity of a Christian being guilty of this are underlined by the permission of divorce in such a situation. We do well to remember that God views sexual infidelity in such a serious manner.

In addition to allowing divorce in such an exceptional situation, Paul allows for separation that does not amount to divorce. This is less than the biblical ideal, but it may be a lesser evil in certain circumstances. However, just as the Mosaic law tolerated divorce and yet discouraged it, so this Pauline exception is couched in such a way as to discourage separation and to encourage reconciliation. Such a separation must fall short of the divorce that allows remarriage. The pastoral implications of this are considerable. Clearly, such a separation is not cause for church discipline in the narrow sense of that term. But it is cause for church discipline in the wider sense of pastoral care and concern. If two Christians are living separately, surely that less-than-ideal state should exercise the whole church in general and those charged with pastoral care in particular. Furthermore, Paul's treatment, in 1 Corinthians 11, of the implications of the Lord's Supper for believers' relationships with each other, and his treatment of Christian love in chapter 13, have important applications at this point. Similarly, our Lord's words in Matthew 5:23-24 have an important bearing on the matter.

The importance of this wider biblical teaching is that Paul is *not* envisaging in 1 Corinthians 7:11*a* the case of two believers who are separated remaining in a state of mutual hostility or of mutual indifference. It is submitted that such a state of affairs should not be allowed to persist between any two believers in a church. Where such a state of affairs were to exist, church discipline according to the pattern of Matthew 18:15-19 would then be appropriate. Clearly, it is essential to bear in mind that discipline is an aspect of pastoral care, and anything which smacks of punitive justice, when two believers are struggling to get together, is wholly out of the question. Moreover, the effect of the whole situation upon any children must be carefully borne in mind. Furthermore, it should be stressed that the situation envisaged in Matthew 18:15-19 is the ideal way of dealing with a problem in relationships. Clearly, one of the difficulties that we often face in church life is that the teaching of Christ in this passage has been honoured more in the breach than in the observance. When a serious problem between two believers surfaces, perhaps after months or years of festering, it is impossible simply to go to Matthew 18:15-19 and seek to apply its teaching in a wooden kind of way. The failure of the individuals to obey that teaching, and the failure of the church to be living by it, will be part of the problem which the church has then to address, as well as the problem between the two believers. What this means is that churches cannot approach the problem of marital failure in church members in a vacuum.

The proper approach to such difficulties is in the context of the church being faithfully taught the Word of God and seeking to live obedient to that Word. The discipline of the church exists against the background of this rich emphasis upon the rule of God in the church by means of his Word. Moreover, while the teaching of Matthew 18:15-19 has relevance to a husband/wife relationship, the unique nature of that relationship demands that pastoral care and discipline be exercised with the utmost sensitivity. These caveats notwithstanding, where two believers have a strong misunderstanding, or even where they quarrel over an issue, the fact that they are Christians should mean that they will seek to resolve their difficulty even before the day is out (Matt. 5:23-26; Eph. 4:26-27). Perhaps more accurately, they should be able to deal with any wrong spirit within themselves that day, so that they are in a position to give attempts at reconciliation the very best chance. Where that is not so, and the matter gets into the public domain— as it does, where separation takes place—then the pattern of Matthew 18 is followed precisely to bring the spouses to the point where they should have been in the first place. If one of them persists in an attitude that is wholly inconsistent with that of a Christian profession, then the ultimate step of excommunication has to be taken. Of course, it may take much time and require much patience to see reconciliation effected. However, where the spouses are clearly struggling to obey the Lord and are moving in the right direction, excommunication is out of the question, though some discipline may still be necessary for a number of reasons. However, where there is a complete unwillingness to do the Lord's will, the drastic step of excommunication may have to be taken. This will mean that the excommunicated spouse is no longer to be treated as a believer but as an unbeliever. This suggests that 1 Corinthians 7:12-15 will then apply, rather than the teaching of verses 10-11.

There may be cases where two believers are separated but are not living in mutual hatred or mutual indifference. In such a case, although it is less than the biblical ideal, their church standing would not be affected. Of course, where a believer has been guilty of unacceptable behaviour which has forced his spouse to separate, that behaviour must be addressed. It is possible that such a case could also lead to excommunication, although it must be stressed that this must again be a very last resort.

One problem that can arise is that of a believing, separated spouse simply going to another church. Realism and sensitivity are indispensable requirements of pastoral care and practice. However, where someone seeks to evade the demands of biblical behaviour simply by removing to another church, it would—as a general principle—be incumbent upon that other church to discuss the matter with the first church. This is a huge area concerning the nature of church unity and inter-church relationships, and it is impossible to develop it in detail without reference to these wider issues. This is a subject that requires urgent attention, in a day and age in which a proper understanding of the nature of the Church is often woefully lacking. It is, however, an issue that belongs properly to ecclesiology or the doctrine of the Church and, for that reason, will not be pursued in this study.

The believer who is married to an unbeliever should neither separate nor divorce. He should do all in his power to be as accommodating as possible to the unbeliever. The apostle Peter clearly envisages the situation where a believer may win an unbelieving spouse (who may not be at all easy to live with) by consistently godly living (1 Pet. 3:1-2). However, where the unbeliever wishes to divorce and is clearly set upon this course, the believer has to allow this to happen. If the unbeliever files for divorce, the believer should not engage in an acrimonious dispute. Where the unbeliever deserts the believer and has no intention of returning, the believer is free to petition for a divorce. Where the believer is treated by the unbeliever in such a way that it is manifest that he or she is not content to live with the believer, even though remaining under the same roof—e.g. where the unbeliever beats the believer, forces the believer to sin, issues an ultimatum, expresses the intention to cease from sexual relations with his or her spouse—the believer is free to divorce. In all of these cases, the believer may subsequently remarry.

These are the general principles that are to be applied, given the English law of divorce. Yet even where there is ground for divorce, the believer is not bound to divorce, and even where he or she cannot continue to live in the same matrimonial home, it is possible to obtain a decree of judicial separation rather than a divorce decree. Even where divorce takes place, the believer should do everything in the spirit of Christ, as well as consider all of the wider issues of children etc. It would be essential, as well, for the believer's pastor to be informed at the outset of the full situation. Clearly, the Christian should take the provisions concerning mediation and attempts at reconciliation built into FLA 1996 seriously.

What of the situation where a Christian was divorced before he was converted? I have sought to argue that this situation is covered by 1 Corinthians 7:8-9. The Christian is to accept the life situation in which he was called. If he were already divorced, he must not think that he has to try to unscramble his past in order to make it good. Whatever has been the mess of his past, now in Christ he should seek to live a new life to the glory of God. To remain unmarried is good and right, but it is not obligatory to do so. Moreover, if the believer is burning, he should see that as an indication that he should marry, since it is better for him to do so than to burn. Clearly, where the believer has already remarried before he is converted, he is in the position envisaged in 1 Corinthians 7:12ff. and should do all in his power to make the marriage as happy as possible. Whatever the sins that accompanied the divorce and remarriage, he is now a new man in Christ. The basic principle of 1 Corinthians chapter 7 applies, viz., that one is not to seek a change in one's status simply because of conversion. Clearly, this principle has limitations. For example, the owner of a chain of betting offices who is converted will certainly need to seek a change of employment. This may well have implications for employees. But marriage is a different relationship, and for the Christian then to seek to contract out of the new marriage because of sin that may have been involved with it would be to be guilty of compounding his sin. Given the state of Corinthian society, it is almost certain that amongst the converts there would have been remarried divorcees. There is no hint in the letter that such believers are to leave their new spouses. Indeed, it is quite possible that *some* of those addressed in chapter 7 verses 10-15 were exercised particularly along this line. Paul's response is quite clear.

What is to be the situation where the believer was divorced before he was converted, but neither he nor his spouse has subsequently remarried? Should the believer seek to be reconciled and thus undergo a fresh marriage ceremony? The question is not specifically addressed in the New Testament, but the general principles that have been inferred might help in this situation. To begin with, it is not wrong to continue in an unmarried state (1 Cor. 7:8). But just as verse 9 acknowledges that marriage is a better option in some cases than others, this might be one of them. If the marriage failed largely because of the believer's past behaviour, now that he is a new person in Christ, might he not seek to put things right by going back to his spouse and making a go of things? Could he not seek to demonstrate the reality of his new life in this way? Where children have been traumatised as a result of the divorce, for the husband and wife to get together again may be the one thing needful to help those children. After all, even in the Old Testament, this was possible if the divorced woman had not subsequently remarried. However, where either has subsequently remarried or then been divorced or widowed, it is submitted that since it would be abomination to return to the first wife under the old covenant, *a fortiori* it would be an abomination to do so under the new covenant. The reason for saying this is not because Deuteronomy 24:1-4 is directly applicable now; rather, the 'abomination' terminology of the Mosaic legislation appears to deal with things that are universally contrary to the divine will.

However, the believer must not be unwise. It may be that to return, if neither has subsequently remarried, would be a disastrous course of action. Moreover, one has to consider the prohibition of marrying an unbeliever (1 Cor. 7:39). If someone is converted after divorce, they are in a less-than-ideal state, since marriage is to be permanent. Just as death is abnormal in that it is as a result of sin entering the world, so divorce is also the result of sin. Since a widow was not to marry an unbeliever, would it be right for a believer to return to an unbelieving spouse? It is submitted that while this situation bears some affinities with that of a widow, there is also a difference, in that the former spouse may be struggling to bring up children alone, and may even be exposed to the temptation to marry someone wholly unsuitable. This being so, it is submitted that one is here faced with the 'lesser-of-two-evils' type of situation. Hard and fast rules are impossible to apply, but general principles are to be applied, and they will relate differently to different situations.

In dealing with the range of practical cases that arise, we have to admit that sin creates complexities. Prior to the Fall, divorce would not have existed. The presence of divorce testifies to the fallenness of the present order of things. One aspect of this is that there will always be a range of moral dilemmas about which it is impossible simply to appeal to a clear-cut rule, much though we may lament this fact. In such a case, the following principles should be borne in mind. Firstly, undue dogmatism is wholly out of place. Secondly, the believer should be persuaded in his own mind and conscience (Rom. 14:5*b*,23). Thirdly, we should not make our conscience the yardstick for such a believer, nor should he seek to impose his views on others (Rom. 14:5*b*,13-23). Genuine, conscientious differences over this matter should be accepted (Rom. 14). Even where a church may regard a remarriage as adulterous, it should not refuse to accept the brother who thinks differently. Nor should he be disciplined (Rom. 14), if it is clear that he has acted in all conscience out of a respect for God's Word and believes that remarriage is permissible. Likewise, the believer has to realise that his acceptance by the church does not entail acceptance of his interpretation of biblical teaching at that point. It may be perfectly possible for such a believer to be remarried in another church or in a registry office and continue in full membership of his church. Similarly, churches united in their commitment to the Word of God and the gospel must recognise differences at this point, just as they do over other matters. All the while, we should be seeking greater light from God's Word and hold to the promise of Philippians 3:15-16.

It may be feared that the practical applications suggested in this chapter would, if followed, open the floodgates to a new latitudinarianism. This would be completely to misunderstand what has been said. Faithfulness to Scripture is what is requisite. But the Scriptures are concerned not only about principles but also about people. It is the genius of the New Testament teaching that the believer is to function in the situation in which he finds himself rather than in some non-existent, ideal state. The approach suggested in this chapter is built upon the exegesis of Scripture. The argument presented is that Scripture itself sets out a position that is far removed from the kind of black and white approach that has too frequently characterised evangelicals. All too often they have been governed more by a spirit of fear and a worldly moralism than by the teaching of the Word of God.

Specific examples

To move from the realm of biblical principles and their general application to that of specific examples is to discover just how complex and tragic real-life situations can be. If it is a failure of some books on divorce, written from a pastoral perspective, that they consider too quickly practical considerations and allow these to determine or influence the understanding of Scripture, it can be an equal, though opposite, danger for biblical scholars to write books on divorce which are utterly remote from reality. I fear that Heth and Wenham, as well as Cornes—whose books on divorce have had considerable influence—are guilty of this.

I shall seek, in the remainder of this chapter, to consider a number of concrete, practical cases, and how they should be approached. *All* the cases considered are actual, real-life situations. I have disguised the identity of the persons concerned and, in a number of cases, have slightly altered the details, in order to ensure that the parties concerned will not identify the cases, and that their identity should not be revealed to those who know them. Some of the cases were encountered within legal practice, while others have been encountered in pastoral work, either by myself or by colleagues. I should stress that none of the cases concerns members of any churches that I have pastored. The final preliminary point concerns the distastefulness of the details of some of the cases. I am mindful that there are things about which believers should not even speak, and I certainly have no desire to shock or to nauseate. On the other hand, the Scriptures themselves deal frankly, if discreetly, with sins which are described as an abomination. In order to apply the biblical teaching, it is essential to follow the scriptural pattern of being both frank and discreet.

Case 1

Mrs X is a pleasant Spanish lady who is married to a Scotsman and lives in England. She has four sons. She became disillusioned with the Roman Catholic Church in which she had grown up, and had attended the meetings of a number of 'Christian' cults, but concluded that no group could ever really know the truth. In her mid-thirties she encountered evangelical Christians and was wonderfully converted. Her husband did not share her new-found faith but was not antagonistic to her on account of her faith. However, over the years he had been physically violent towards her, sometimes in an extreme way. Having been converted, Mrs X resolves to live a Christlike life before her husband in the hope of winning him. However, he still has occasional outbursts of violence towards her, though not nearly as extreme as in the past. More concerning is the fact that he has become emotionally abusive. Living an extravagant lifestyle, he has virtually forced her out to work, so that she can help fund his extravagant tastes, in spite of the fact that she has heavy demands as a mother. Sometimes her children have to occupy themselves after school because both Mrs X and her husband are out at work. Mrs X is extremely unhappy with the situation for herself

186

and her children, but continues in the hope of winning her husband. Meanwhile, he promises both her and the children a special summer break. However, at the time that the holiday should be paid for, Mr X buys a fantastically expensive computer, thus denying any possibility of a holiday to Mrs X and the children. At this point, his physical violence has been increasing, and Mrs X seeks pastoral advice. She is advised to seek to talk her husband into reason, but under no circumstances should she contemplate divorce. She talks with Mr X, but this only inflames him against her.

When a child in Spain, Mrs X had been routinely and regularly sexually abused by her grandfather from the age of about eleven to fifteen. Many times he raped her. Mrs X's husband knows this but, after she has shared with him her concerns about his treatment of her, he contacts the grandfather to come and visit them in the summer. Mrs X goes into profound depression and is admitted to hospital. While in hospital, two of Mrs X's children are taken into care, while the other two are cared for by Mr X. In hospital, Mrs X forms a friendship with another patient, who is schizophrenic. He is discharged before her; on her discharge, she goes to live with him. Shortly afterwards, one of the children with Mr X commits suicide. She remains psychologically scarred, and her children all turn out badly.

This is a tragic case, where Mrs X was given very bad pastoral advice. She should have been advised to consider the needs of her children as well as her own needs. If after discussion with her husband there was no improvement in the marital situation, steps should have been taken to initiate divorce proceedings, either to encourage the husband to change or to end the marriage. The result of the advice she was given has been tragedy all round.

Case 2

Mrs A was a Christian before she married Mr A, who was not a Christian at the time of the marriage and is still not a Christian. Recently she has discovered that he has been watching videos of men and women engaging in sexual activity with animals. Mr A left one of these videos, inadvertently, in the living room. Mr and Mrs A have two children, a boy aged nine and a girl aged twelve. Mrs A is at work for a few hours three evenings a week, during which period Mr A looks after the children. Mrs A seeks advice from her pastor. He advises as follows.

It was a great mistake for Mrs A to marry a non-Christian, but the pastor accepts that at that time Mrs A had no reason to believe that her husband had perverted tastes. The pastor advises that she must deal with the situation as it is. She must protect her children. If the local authority were aware of the fact that the children could be exposed to such video material, they might insist on Mr A leaving the home or the children being taken into care. Moreover, Mrs A feels utter repugnance towards her husband and feels she could no more have sexual relations with him now than if he had slept with another woman. Her pastor advises her that her husband's behaviour is such as to justify her divorcing him on the basis that he is hardly consenting to live with her as a husband.

Case 3
Mr and Mrs B are both Christians in their early fifties. Mr B had a somewhat legalistic upbringing. Mr B has never been very concerned about the sexual aspect of marriage, but for the last nine months there has been no interest on his part whatsoever. During that time Mrs B has, on two occasions, discovered her husband masturbating. The first time she said nothing, not letting Mr B become aware that she knew of the situation. On the second occasion, she became extremely distressed and confronted Mr B about this. He was very upset and explained that he had always felt that there was something 'dirty' about a husband and wife having sexual relations. She persuades him to seek pastoral advice.

This is a very sad situation, which required quite a number of pastoral sessions, in which Mr B had to be educated as to the biblical teaching on the rightness of sexual relations between a man and his wife. This experience convinced the pastor that there was need to give biblical teaching upon this subject to his congregation. This was done in separate all-male and all-female Bible studies, where passages from Proverbs were studied. Mr and Mrs B now have a relatively normal relationship.

Case 4
Mr and Mrs C have been professing Christians for many years. In their mid-forties, they have two teenage children. Mr C has a

reputation for being a very spiritual and prayerful man. In fact, he is a womaniser, and in fifteen years has had sexual relations with as many different women, many of them married women. On one occasion, Mrs C was telephoned by one of Mr C's paramours, who dropped fairly clear hints that she had had sexual relations with Mr C in Mr C's home while Mrs C was away. On another occasion, the husband of one of Mr C's sexual partners called at the house and spoke his mind very plainly to Mr C as to what he really thought of him, and threatened him with violence. This was in front of Mrs C's children. Mrs C has kept this to herself for years, always believing that Mr C would change. Eventually, she divorces him and remarries.

Mrs C clearly has good grounds for divorce and may remarry. The worrying aspect of this case is that for so long she continued as if everything was all right. The question has to be asked as to whether, when it became clear that Mr C was a womaniser, she should have confided in the leaders of her church. All the time that Mr C was womanising, he was continuing to play an active part in church affairs and was regarded as a fine Christian. His children appear immunised against vital Christianity, and it is not hard to understand why. Obviously, sensitivity was needed, and after the first occasion that Mr C committed adultery, one can understand that Mrs C wanted to keep the matter secret. However, by the time that her children were exposed to the fact that their father was living an utterly hypocritical life, some firm action was needed. Significantly, in this case, Mr C never once apologised to Mrs C. Her idea of forgiveness was, therefore, less than the biblical idea, which requires that repentance precedes forgiveness.

Case 5

Mr and Mrs H are not Christians. Mrs H had a religious upbringing and goes to a local minister for advice. Her husband has served time for manslaughter. Recently, in a rage, he held a loaded shotgun to her head and threatened to blow her brains out. She has it in the back of her mind that God will punish her if she separates from her husband.

Clearly, Mrs H may divorce her husband. He is hardly consenting to live with her as a spouse. Moreover, the fact that they are both unbelievers limits somewhat the biblical teaching on divorce as it applies to them.

There are many other situations I could cite. However, the brief number of cases I have given should be sufficient to demonstrate how utterly remote from reality is the approach of those who categorically forbid divorce, and how seemingly harsh and arbitrary is the approach which allows divorce, but insists that the divorced person is still married, in God's eyes, to the spouse who has been divorced.

Appendix 1
The Perspicuity of Scripture

One of the Reformation's great emphases was *sola scriptura* (Scripture alone). A necessary corollary was that the Bible was the 'people's book'. Luther questioned the belief structure of the medieval church by appealing to the plain meaning of Scripture. Tyndale's concern in translating Scripture was to ensure that the ploughboy would be able to read it. In their controversies, the Reformers did not appeal to some hidden knowledge reserved for the favoured few, but constantly set forth Scripture in its plain sense as over against some of the wildly allegorical interpretations that had been advanced. In the present day, concern has been expressed that this doctrine is being obscured by the emergence of a scholarly, as distinct from an ecclesiastical, magisterium. This has led to a questioning of confessional evangelical understanding of the doctrine of justification by faith and has clouded the debate over the ordination of women. Clearer understanding of the semantic range of certain Hebrew and Greek terms and scholarly reconstruction of the nature of the Judaism of the Second Temple period has led to the 'new perspective on Paul'. It is now argued that the Reformation crisis resulted from failure on both sides to understand Paul's message. Similarly, work on the meaning of the Greek word for 'head' (*kephalē*) and on the import of Paul's words to Timothy on the place of women in the ministry, in the light of linguistic research and in view of a reconstruction of the situation Timothy faced at Ephesus, has created the impression that one cannot understand the text of Scripture unless one is able to view it through the appropriate scholarly lenses. Is not the approach to 1 Corinthians 7, which emphasises the need to take account of the Roman law background, similarly guilty of taking the Bible from the people and weakening the doctrine of Scripture's perspicuity? I do not think so, and I shall explain why.

One of the fullest statements of the evangelical and Reformed doctrine of Scripture is found in chapter 1 of the Westminster Confession of Faith. Paragraph 7 deals with Scripture's perspicuity. It states: 'All things in Scripture are not alike plain in themselves, nor alike clear unto all: yet those things which are necessary to be known, believed, and observed for salvation, are so clearly propounded, and opened in some place of Scripture or other, that not only the learned, but the unlearned, in a due sense of the ordinary means, may attain unto a sufficient understanding of them.' The statement acknowledges that all Scripture is not equally clear and that some Scriptures are not equally clear to all readers. 1 Corinthians chapter 7 is not as easy to understand as the Ten Commandments!

Secondly, while the Reformers were implacably opposed to a magisterium that took from the believer the right and duty of private judgement, and were equally opposed to the requirement of implicit faith in whatever the Church may teach, rather than faith in the explicit teaching of Scripture, this did not mean that they were opposed to helps in understanding Scripture. Luther's changed view of penance resulted from his discovery that *metanoia* meant 'repentance', not 'penance'. His use of Erasmus' Greek Testament—itself partly the product of the Renaissance learning—was crucial at this point. Tyndale 'invented' some words in his translation (e.g. 'scapegoat' in Leviticus chapter 16). Unless one has a very good command of Hebrew and Greek, one has to depend upon the work of other, uninspired—even though providentially directed—translators. Moreover, the Reformers and Puritans held a very high view of the ministry of the Word, and in their sermons and commentaries they used every help to get at the meaning of Scripture. This did not displace their belief that 'the infallible rule of interpretation of Scripture is Scripture itself', but it did testify to their determination to be clear as to what Scripture says and means.

Thirdly, the interpretation of 1 Corinthians 7 raises the question as to whether we understand that chapter in the light of the culture at that time or *in the light of the culture in which we find ourselves*. The contrast between a culture-less interpretation and an interpretation controlled by considerations of first-century Greek culture and Roman law is entirely fictitious. While marriage may rightly be termed a 'creation ordinance', and its essential nature and *raison d'être* are not culturally conditioned, marriage customs certainly are culturally conditioned. The fact that English law requires two witnesses and that the ceremony, in ordinary cases, be carried out on registered premises is clearly a cultural variable. That another society has different ceremonial requirements does not overthrow the biblical nature of marriage. It is the same with divorce. The fact that national law is involved at any point puts us on notice that there will be culturally variable factors. Thus, we come to the text of 1 Corinthians 7 aware that this culturally variable factor will be present. At this point there is a huge difference between this and the approach that wishes to reinterpret Paul's teaching of justification. The latter has to do with a sinner's standing before God and is not a culturally variable matter. Similarly, whatever cultural background needs to be borne in mind when Paul discusses the role of women in the church, it is nevertheless true that he refers back to the opening chapters of Genesis to demonstrate that he is dealing with principles that apply at all times and in all places.

Fourthly, study of the terms Paul uses and his reference back to Christ's teaching is sufficient to bring the interpreter to an understanding of 1 Corinthians 7 without knowledge of Roman law. That background knowledge confirms the interpretation.

Finally, the doctrine of Scripture's perspicuity does not mean that an understanding of the background to a passage is unnecessary or illegitimate in interpreting that passage, any more than it renders illegitimate the study of Hebrew and Greek grammar. What is being asserted by the idea that Scripture is perspicuous is that its teachings are declared sufficiently clearly for the individual believer to understand them. But even with respect to such fundamental doctrines as justification, it does not follow that the believer may not stand in need of help in understanding Scripture. The difference between the Protestant and the Catholic view of this matter is that the Protestant teacher does not appeal to his own authority or that of the Church but to Scripture itself, whereas Rome calls for allegiance to an interpretation *because* the Church teaches it.

Appendix 2
The Status and Application of Biblical Law

Two conclusions reached earlier in this study inevitably raise questions relating to the status and application of biblical law. In chapter 3, it was argued that the Mosaic law had an eschatological purpose that was fulfilled in Christ. This raises the question as to the present status of the Mosaic law and as to whether it still has any direct application. In chapter 4, the exegesis of 1 Corinthians 7:10-12 led to the conclusion that Jesus' teaching on divorce did not have unbelievers in mind. This raises the very important question as to whether Jesus' ethical teaching applies to the unbeliever. If it does not, enormous issues are raised, which relate not only to ethics but also to the content of the message that the Church is to preach to the unbeliever. This second concern is of vital importance and raises issues that justify a book devoted exclusively to them. I shall seek to articulate a number of principles that might help to identify the areas of concern and to clarify some of the issues raised.

The place of the Mosaic law in the New Testament is far from straightforward, and a vast amount of scholarly and popular literature has sought to address the issues. A wide range of views on this question affects evangelical belief and behaviour. While an adequate treatment of the question demands a major and substantial study, a number of fairly simple and obvious points should help to guide us through this minefield and clarify some of the difficult questions. Firstly, to believe that the Mosaic law has been fulfilled does not entail the corollary that moral absolutes and the category of law no longer apply to the Christian. The New Testament letters are replete with commandments addressed to Christians, obliging them to refrain from some actions and to practise others. There is a very real distinction between the antinomian heresy that personal justification, releasing us from condemnation, leaves us free to do what we want, and the belief that the place of the Mosaic law in salvation history is such that *that* law does not apply to New Testament Christians *as it did* to the Old Testament people of God. The Christian is to keep his Lord's commandments. The question that must be answered is, What are these commandments?

Secondly, while it is true that the Old Testament distinguishes different

195

laws within the Mosaic law and that Jesus himself graded rules within that law, it is nevertheless the case that the New Testament writers refer to 'the law' and not to 'the laws'. This means that the Mosaic law must be regarded as a totality: one may even say that the Mosaic law, *qua* Mosaic law, is a package and that the New Testament refers to it as a package. Two of the fullest New Testament treatments of the Mosaic law are found in Paul's letters to the Romans and to the Galatians. In both letters, he stresses that the Mosaic law had been given *at* a precise point in history *for* a specific period —and people (Romans 5:13-14,20*a*; 9:4*e*; Galatians 3:15-19; 3:23–4:7). The important point to bear in mind is that Paul is dealing with the total 'package' and its place in the history of redemption. As such, it no longer applies to the Christian. However, there are elements within that package which bound men before the giving of the Sinaitic law, continued to bind men outside of Israel after Sinai, and continue to bind all men today. These commands are not binding because they are in the Mosaic law, for they existed prior to the giving of that law. Likewise, they do not cease to apply because the Mosaic package has been fulfilled, precisely because they have an existence and authority that is independent of the Mosaic law. For the people of Israel under the Mosaic law, Moses confirmed the sanctity and authority of these rules. But for those who lived during the Old Testament outside the sphere of special revelation, the rules applied, as they still apply to all people today, who are living after the fulfilment of the Mosaic law. A number of biblical passages put this point beyond all dispute.

In Leviticus 18:24-28, the Lord warns the Israelites of the terrible consequences of disobeying the commands given earlier in that chapter. (That the commands referred to are those contained in chapter 18 is clear from the words with which the chapter begins: 'The Lord said to Moses, "Speak to the Israelites . . ."') What is instructive for our present purposes is to note that the Lord states that the pagan nations had defiled themselves by the sins detailed in the chapter, and that for that reason the land had 'vomited' them out (vv.24,25,27). Clearly, these commandments did not have a life span limited to theocratic Israel. However, there are theocratic elements within the chapter, since verse 29 refers to being cut off from one's people, and in verse 30, for example, the Lord reminds Israel that he is the Lord their God. While the Mosaic penal code, in dealing with those matters which are clearly timeless, expresses God's detestation of sin, it does not become a pattern upon which civil rulers are to rule today.

The reasons for this are fairly clear. The whole penal code is intimately bound up with the Tabernacle/Temple worship and the Levitical priesthood. That worship, together with its covenant and priesthood, would pass away with the coming of the Priest after the order of Melchizedek. Moreover, we saw in chapter 3 (p. 52, see also note 18, pp. 239-40) that Jesus taught that the death penalty would no longer apply for *porneia*, although

Leviticus 18 stipulates this penalty. It is essential to bear in mind that any legal system needs what Hart calls 'primary rules' and 'secondary rules'. Where the administration of the primary rules is dependent upon the type of secondary rules that are in place, then it is misguided to seek simply to isolate the primary rules and apply them in a context with different secondary rules. For example, the Mosaic death penalty for adultery is found in a system of laws which also prescribed for ritual cursing where a husband's suspicions as to his wife were proved to be well-founded. However, where the ritual—which was to be conducted by the Aaronic priest—can no longer be performed, it is grossly mistaken to seek to maintain other provisions such as the death penalty for adultery. Any careful reading of the Mosaic legislation leads inevitably to the conclusion that the primary and secondary rules are so intertwined that it is impossible simply to make Mosaic laws the basis of legislation today.

The New Testament also bears witness to the fact that God's timeless laws apply to those outside the pale of special revelation. Romans 1:18-21, 28,32 clearly testify to this fact. Romans 2:12-16 makes a similar point. Indeed, Romans 2:14-15 clearly indicates that the Mosaic law contains and commands things which are also impressed upon the consciences of those without the law of Moses, and that these elements must, therefore, constitute something of what is known as God's moral law. This may be contrasted with the reference to circumcision, later in the chapter, which—although commanded to Abraham as well as in the Mosaic covenant—is clearly shown, in its external sense, to be anything but timeless and universal. Care is needed, however, in assessing this aspect of biblical teaching, since Paul makes clear, later in Romans, that the knowledge of God's moral law—while not confined to those within the pale of special revelation—will, nevertheless, be more fully perceived by those with that revelation. This is hinted at in chapter 3:20*b*, and is then spelled out briefly in 5:20 and massively in chapter 7. Verses 7-12 of chapter 7 are crucial in emphasising this point.

Admittedly, Paul's usage of the term 'law' sometimes has a wider referent than the Mosaic law. However, his usage of a salvation-history grid through which to assess the total package of the Mosaic law makes clear that he held the Mosaic law to be fulfilled eschatologically in Christ. That he could, nevertheless, cite and apply to Christians principles and commandments from within that total package indicates that his approach was far more nuanced than that of some 'dispensational' approaches to the law. Moreover, that he could quote from outside the Decalogue in this way indicates that his approach was more complex than is sometimes allowed for by those who embrace the 'Puritan' view of the law.

The thesis thus far advanced safeguards against theological antinomianism, while doing justice to the theme of development within the history of redemption. Moral absolutes are safeguarded, while, on the basis of a principled theological argument, theonomy—with its plea that Mosaic punishments be imposed by the State—is shown to be fundamentally misconceived. The general approach to 'moral law' espoused by Christians such as the Puritans is found to be biblical, as long as certain caveats are borne in mind.

The second question that must be addressed in this section concerns the application of Jesus' ethical teaching to those who are not his disciples. This question arises from the conclusion reached in chapter 5 that Jesus' teaching on divorce did not bring unbelievers within its scope. Hence, for the believer married to the unbeliever Paul lays down principles somewhat different from those for the situation of a Christian husband and wife. The problem with this approach is that it appears to suggest that certain moral absolutes are not so absolute after all, and may change according to circumstances. Will not this suggest, at the very least, a 'two-lane' approach to ethics which is theologically akin to 'situation ethics', and will it not lead to great uncertainty as to precisely what the Church tells the unbeliever that God commands? Might it not either undercut the approach already advanced in this chapter, that God's moral law binds all men, or lead to the view that there is one law for Christians and another law for non-Christians? This will inevitably raise profound questions concerning the nature of moral obligation and the status of God's law, quite apart from leaving the Church unable to answer the agonising questions of conscience that may beset the unbeliever. Put quite simply, if something is a sin, the unbeliever is to repent of it. To do so, he must know whether or not it is sinful.

The following observations may help to unravel this tangled skein. Firstly, all of Jesus' teaching on divorce was either by way of explanation of the Mosaic teaching (which, as we have seen, was time-bound), or it constituted his instruction as to the behaviour required of one of his disciples married to a disciple. It was teaching, therefore, concerning a relationship. It was not given to one disciple in isolation, but it was teaching as to the behaviour of a disciple in a marriage relationship with another disciple. We should not, therefore, be surprised that there is a difference in the teaching given by Paul to a Christian married to an unbeliever. The Bible regularly adjusts its requirements as to our behaviour in relationships, according to the nature of the relationship and the type of person with whom we are in a relationship. For example, the command to love one's neighbour as oneself does not deny the requirement to treat one's family somewhat differently from those outside it. Furthermore, there are different obligations to different members of one's family: one's behaviour towards one's parents must be different in some respects from one's behaviour towards one's children. This is not situation ethics; rather, it is the recognition that different obligations arise and exist in different relationships. But those obligations are *obligations*; they are imposed upon us by God and cannot be simply swept aside by situational considerations.

The second observation, which is all too easily ignored, is that there is a sense in which the behaviour of a Christian married couple is expressive of the life of the people of God in a way that cannot be true of a 'mixed marriage'. If Christians do not behave as Christians in their marriages, what hope is there that they will behave as Christians in the fellowship of the church? And what kind of message will this give to those who are outside the kingdom of God? Now, while the Christian married to an unbeliever is to behave as a Christian, the same cannot be said of his spouse. While God's common grace is such that many a mixed marriage is very happy and successful—as is many a marriage of unbeliever to unbeliever—it is, nevertheless, true that such a marriage is not, nor can it be, expressive of the life of the kingdom of God. This is another point which, according to the Bible, applies in numerous realms of life. For example, although a Christian is always to demonstrate the same qualities of Christlike behaviour, he is not under the same obligation to maintain the unity of the political party to which he belongs as he is to maintain the unity of the church of which he is part. Although the Christian is to pursue peace with all men (Heb. 12:14), it is acknowledged that peace—involving another person beside the Christian—may not always be possible (Rom. 12:18). That person may not be interested in peace. But another Christian is under similar solemn obligation to pursue peace and, thus, the 'group dynamics' should be fundamentally different from the situation that obtains in a 'secular' body. Something of this distinction may be perceived in Matthew 5:23-26. In verses 23-24 Jesus is dealing with a relationship problem between two brothers, whereas verses 25-26 suggest that there is a problem with someone who is not one's brother. High standards are required of the believer in each case, but the response of the other party may well be different in the one situation from the other. Indeed, this appears to be implied in Matthew 18:17. The person is no longer to be regarded as a brother but as an outsider, precisely because he has behaved like an outsider.

The implications of all this should be obvious. If somewhat different considerations apply in a mixed marriage from those in a marriage of two Christians, *a fortiori* these different considerations will apply where two unbelievers are married. This does *not* mean that the unbeliever is not under obligation to obey God's moral law. It *does* mean that one cannot take Christ's teaching for one type of situation and apply it to a totally different situation. It may be objected that by going back to Genesis 1:27 and 2:24 Jesus is referring to the creation pattern, which must therefore bind all people. Thus, set in that context, Jesus intended his teaching on divorce to apply to all men. But this is a most naive objection, based on a superficial misreading of Jesus' words in Matthew 19:4-6. 'In the beginning' is a reference to the pre-Fall state. In such a state, sin did not exist and, therefore, the *porneia* referred to in verse 9 did not exist. If this objection to the position I have outlined were to be seriously entertained, one would also have to do away with all criminal legislation etc., because 'in the beginning it was not so'. What we can say is that life in the kingdom of God is bound up with restoring the image of God in man that was marred in the Fall. The ethics of the kingdom of God should thus, at the very least, be seen as restoring God's people to that which existed prior to the entrance of sin. Of course, ultimately, God's people will be restored to something even higher; for, as Augustine observed, in Eden it was possible for man to sin, but in heaven it will be impossible for God's people to sin. However, God's salvation is progressive in nature, in that, although believers are already saved, full deliverance from all sin awaits the consummation of all things. While the creation pattern continues to express God's ideal, this does not mean that in the present fallen state of the world one simply seeks to apply that ideal to people indiscriminately. Rather, it is the ideal to which life in the kingdom of God is to seek to be conformed.

As God's image-bearers, Adam and Eve were to live under God's rule in a perfect world. Their moral state allowed for the possibility of sin by going outside God's rule for them. Had they not sinned and had they continued to have the right to eat from the tree of life, they would have lived perfectly under God's rule and would have been incapable of sin. As a result of the Fall, it became impossible for them not to sin, although, because the divine image was not obliterated (albeit that it was marred), traces and echoes of the kind of life that they should have lived are still found in mankind. In Christ, the restoration of that image is begun and is completed when the new age—which has already partially broken in—comes in perfection and is completed. At that point, there will no longer be the possibility of sin. Thus, 'creation ethics' and 'kingdom ethics' are not two different realities but two different terms to denote the same type of reality viewed from differing temporal and theological perspectives. Passages such as Romans 8:18-27, 1 Corinthians 15 and Hebrews 2:5-18 clearly establish links between creation, the kingdom of God, and the new creation. Outside of the kingdom of God, those ethics are not fully possible because people are still governed by 'this age' and belong to 'the world'. The Christian belongs to 'the age to come' which has already broken into 'this present age', but he has to live in this present age. The most that one could say of the moral law of divorce as it affects the unbeliever is that he is obliged to show the same behaviour as the believer is obliged to show to the unbeliever. Christ's teaching on this issue is not to be universally applied to all men.

Appendix 3
The Teaching
of Romans 7:1-3

In chapter 3, the argument was presented that Jesus taught that the effecting of divorce terminates the one-flesh union of marriage. One of the main objections to this thesis is that in Romans 7:1-3 Paul teaches that only death severs the marriage bond. For some writers this teaching entails the further proposition that remarriage is always adulterous while the first spouse is still living. This interpretation is seriously flawed, as will be seen.

It is now fairly generally accepted that the purpose of chapter 7 of Romans is to expound the place and significance of the Mosaic law, and the place it occupies in God's plan. The law to which Paul refers in verse 1 is the Mosaic law. Earlier in the letter, Paul has referred to the giving of the law at a certain point in history (5:20); he has also made clear that the new covenant people of God are not under that law (6:14). Nevertheless, he has also spoken positively of the Mosaic law (3:21,31). In chapter 7 he gives an extended exposition of the place and purpose of the Mosaic law. He is *not* dealing with marriage and divorce, but with the place of the law. The general proposition in verse 1 is that the law is only authoritatively over a person while that person is still alive. In verses 2-3, Paul illustrates this fact from the sphere of marriage. For a number of reasons it is essential to remember that he is dealing with the Mosaic law and using an illustration. Firstly, the Mosaic law did *not* call a woman an adulteress if, having been divorced, she remarried. In chapter 2 (pp. 27-8; see also note 26, pp. 221-2) we noted that whatever abnormality the Mosaic law attached to divorce, it was also the case that it attached abnormality to death: the high priest was forbidden to marry a widow. Accordingly, if the Mosaic law did not regard a divorced woman who remarried as an adulteress, it follows that Paul cannot have that kind of situation in view in this passage. He is dealing with the general situation and, given that he is not writing a treatise on marriage and divorce but illustrating a point concerning the application and authority of the law, it is hardly surprising that he does not insert words of qualification. Nor is the situation any different if he is referring to the Roman law, for it was certainly not the case that the Roman law branded a divorced woman an adulteress if she remarried.

Secondly, Paul's illustration demonstrates how well he knew his Old

Testament. A man was *not* called an adulterer if he took a second wife. But a woman could not take a second husband. The way in which he applies his illustration in verses 4ff. has occasioned much controversy, but that need not concern us here since it is not at all relevant to the point at issue. The Mosaic law did not recognise polyandry in the way in which it recognised polygamy.

In fact, verse 3 confirms our understanding that Jesus taught that divorce would end a marriage. In this verse Paul brands a woman who marries another man an adulteress, if her husband is still alive. But if a divorce has taken place, she is no longer married to her first husband and, therefore, he is not her husband. Paul is not dealing with a divorce type of situation.

Appendix 4
The Teaching of
Dr David Instone Brewer

Dr Brewer's Background
David Instone Brewer is Research Librarian of Tyndale House, Cambridge, an evangelical research centre for biblical studies. He obtained his doctorate from Cambridge University, having submitted and defended a thesis that was concerned with Jewish techniques of exegesis prior to AD 70. His researches in that area have provided extremely useful and helpful background information to the New Testament teaching on marriage and divorce, as well as illuminating the Old Testament teaching. Dr Brewer has written articles at both the popular and academic level on this theme, and—at the time at which I am writing—he is writing both an academic and a non-academic work on the biblical teaching on divorce. I have spoken on the telephone with Dr Brewer on a number of occasions, and he has very generously given of his time to explain and discuss some of his ideas. Moreover, I have read articles by him, and his work-in-progress on his books which is available on the Internet. At various points in this book I have sought to interact with Dr Brewer's writings, although I was fairly well advanced in writing before I was made aware of his work. In the nature of the case I have, therefore, tended to interact throughout this book with Dr Brewer in a somewhat ad hoc manner. It will be useful here to seek to bring his views together in order to evaluate them. However, given that his work is not yet completed, there is the risk of misrepresenting his views until his full work on this subject is published. Given the importance of his work and the new ground that he has broken, however, it would be a great omission not to take it into account.

Dr Brewer's Thesis
Dr Brewer's essential position appears to be as follows. Since marriage is a covenant relationship, we need to take account of the fact that it thereby involves *contractual* obligations. Marriage contracts were a very important aspect of the Jewish understanding and custom of marriage. The amount of money to be settled upon a bride was an important aspect of this practice, as may be seen from the fact that the Old Testament refers to this on a number of occasions, and the Mishnah devotes an entire tractate to it,

Ketuboth. A commonplace of Jewish marriage contracts was the obligation of the husband to provide his wife with food, clothing and love, while the wife was to prepare meals, possibly to make clothing from cloth which the husband provided, and to honour and observe the sexual side of marriage. Failure on the part of the husband or the wife to honour these obligations would give grounds for a divorce. Thus a wife could obtain a divorce if her husband did not provide her with food, or with clothing, or with sexual relations. Exodus 21:9-10 is dealing with divorce for these reasons. The Mishnah refers to these verses as dealing with the law of marriage, and they figured largely in rabbinic discussions of divorce. It was a common-place of Jewish and rabbinic understanding that a breach of these obligations would give grounds for divorce. Similarly, the Old Testament represents the Lord as abiding by this law of marriage and divorce with his people. References to his provision of food, clothing and love evidently refer to this contractual aspect to marriage. The failure of Israel to recipro-cate—offering her food to false gods, decking herself out for other lovers—is a reference to her failure to honour the marriage covenant entered into with the Lord.

This, Brewer believes, is the background to 1 Corinthians 7. The early part of that chapter is concerned with marriage obligations: the reference to the need to maintain sexual relationships within marriage was a subject to which the rabbis gave attention, and, as we have noted in the body of the text, the Mishnah contains discussions as to the frequency with which sexual intercourse is to take place between a married couple. Paul, as an erstwhile Pharisee, was fully cognisant of, and conversant with, all this, and it is unthinkable that it did not inform his background thinking on this subject. 1 Corinthians 7 must, therefore, be read with this background in mind.

The Old Testament contained a fourth ground of divorce. It is referred to in Deuteronomy 24:1 as *'erwāṯ dābār*. Brewer believes that this refers to sexual infidelity. At the time of Jesus, the Hillelites and the Shammaites were divided on the meaning of this phrase. Both groups agreed that it dealt with sexual infidelity. However, whereas the Shammaites thus confined the meaning of the phrase, the Hillelites extended it to cover things such as the burning of food. Against that background, Jesus lined himself up with the Shammaite understanding. He did not teach that it was obligatory to divorce for sexual infidelity, but he did teach that it was permissible to do so, and that it was permissible to remarry. Moreover, Jesus' teaching concentrated on the reason for divorce given in Deuteronomy 24:1. Since the teaching found in Matthew 19 and Mark 10 is exclusively concerned with the debate about Deuteronomy 24:1, we should not think that Jesus would have dis-allowed divorce for the reasons given in Exodus 21.

Evaluation of Dr Brewer's Thesis

There are so many positive things to say about Dr Brewer's work that I shall have to be selective and confine myself to the most obvious things for which we are indebted to him.

First of all, he has begun to reverse a trend in academic circles, which has gradually been undermining a Protestant or Reformed understanding of divorce. Both Heth and Wenham and Cornes have displayed considerable scholarly ability and been influential in undermining the Reformed view of divorce and remarriage. Heth and Wenham comment in their book that the scholarly works are on their side, and that evangelical writers who espouse the Reformed view have ignored the scholarly literature. Dr Brewer has convincingly demonstrated that a scholarly approach undermines a fairly common approach amongst some Anglicans to this issue. Secondly, his studies in Jewish writings have been put to extremely profitable use when he demonstrates that Mark's treatment of the Pharisees' question in Mark 10:2 is highly condensed. Thirdly, his treatment of marriage contracts and Exodus 21 is extremely stimulating and valuable.

Since I find myself in substantial agreement with the results in practice of Dr Brewer's study, it may seem churlish to make any negative comments. However, I find myself in disagreement with a number of aspects of Dr Brewer's thesis. I shall confine myself to the most serious.

First, I do not think that Dr Brewer has properly understood the relationship between the new covenant and the Mosaic covenant. If some *over*emphasise the discontinuity between the two Testaments, it seems to me that Dr Brewer *under*emphasises the discontinuity. This failure mars his treatment of Christ's teaching and this, in turn, feeds a misunderstanding of the Mosaic teaching. Jesus emphatically *contrasts* his teaching with that of Moses, whereas Dr Brewer appears to want to see Jesus' teaching as a *continuation* of the Mosaic teaching.

Secondly, Dr Brewer does not sufficiently emphasise the contrast between Jesus and Paul, and rabbinic Judaism. Dr Brewer stands within a tradition which has gained in influence over the last twenty to thirty years, and which wishes to understand Christianity very much as a movement *within* Judaism, but which finally came to a parting of the ways. This has been a wholesome and necessary emphasis, which makes sense of much of the New Testament and throws light upon passages that had once been deemed somewhat obscure. Moreover, it has been a powerful corrective to the old liberal idea that Christianity is an essentially Hellenistic religion: Paul was the villain, who corrupted the simple teaching of Jesus—usually cast as a good, nineteenth-century, liberal romantic figure—by adding certain legalistic ideas and aspects of Greek religion, so that in time the human Jesus became the divine person of the Trinity. Understanding the Gospels and letters against the Jewish background of the time has put that approach very firmly to bed, if not laid it in its tomb. But the question must be asked if this approach has now gone too far. There are numerous examples in both the Gospels and Acts of Jesus and Paul standing over against their Jewish culture and its ideas, as well as standing within it. Jesus contrasted his teaching on divorce not only with that of Moses but also with that of his contemporaries. Indeed, given his understanding of himself as the climax of the Old Testament promises and law, by being their eschatological fulfilment, he was bound to differ from his contemporaries, since they were not seeking to understand and apply the Old Testament's meaning and significance as enlightened by the Person of Jesus. I fear that Brewer has not emphasised the significance of this fact. Moreover, the differences within Judaism were such that it was possible for Jesus and Paul to stand within it, and yet to be saying things significantly different from what anyone else was saying.

As an overrun of the previous point, the third thing to say is that Brewer attaches too much importance to the Jewish background to Paul's teaching in 1 Corinthians 7. While it is undoubtedly the case that the Jewish background to much of the New Testament has not been adequately grasped, and that treatments of the Jewish background to New Testament themes are yielding very positive results, there is the danger of this almost becoming a fixed hermeneutical principle which ignores some fairly obvious points. Firstly, Paul hardly lived in a hermetically sealed Jewish bubble, quarantined off from the Gentile world. His sermon to the Areopagites in Acts 17 demonstrates his ability to take Old Testament ideas and, with their eschatological fulfilment in Christ, to present them to a Gentile audience in terms that were readily intelligible to them. His sermon displays familiarity with Greek poetry, as does his letter to Titus. As a Roman citizen he appears in Acts to be fully aware of the implications of his citizenship and the correct procedures to follow within the existing Roman law. Moreover, he was a man who had travelled extremely widely. Given these facts, and the cosmopolitan nature of Corinthian society and the mix of Jews and Gentiles in the Corinthian church, is it not dangerous to read Paul's teaching on divorce in 1 Corinthians 7 against an exclusively Jewish background? Might it be the case that Brewer has been more influenced by Jewish writings, at this point, than was Paul?

The point may be illustrated in the following way. An English missionary goes to work amongst the English and Chinese community in Hong Kong. The missionary was brought up in an English public school, established on an Anglican foundation. Its prevailing ethos was that of Anglo-Catholicism. He studied theology at Oxford and chose a certain college because the theology tutor was a well-known Anglo-Catholic theologian. He noticed that many of the University lecturers had a high view of the theology found in the Creeds and discovered that the explanation for this was that more evangelicals were on the Faculty than had once been the case. In contact with these, he underwent an evangelical conversion. He believes that Anglo-Catholicism is fundamentally mistaken, though a number of its doctrines, for example on the Trinity, the Person of Christ, and the infallibility of Scripture, it shares with evangelicalism. Now, is it to be believed that when he is leading a Bible study or preaching in a congregation of expatriate English and Chinese in Hong Kong, his every theological utterance must be understood against the background of his Anglo-Catholic upbringing? As a well-educated missionary, he has been aware of many influences. Moreover, unless he is devoid of all common sense, he is bound to realise that even his English hearers who had a nominal acquaintance with the Anglican Church can hardly be expected to understand his teaching against his Anglo-Catholic background, and it would be idiotic to think that his Chinese hearers would.

Why must we think that Paul was possessed of less common sense than a typical missionary, and that he was culturally isolated in a way that no educated person is today? Brewer might respond that I am being unfair and that he is not suggesting this. But this is the net effect of wishing to read 1 Corinthians 7 against a Jewish and rabbinic background. In personal conversation, Brewer suggested to me that, as a lawyer, I would use the term 'consideration', aware of its specific meaning in English contract law, and that my background would be necessary to understand my use of the term. I think this proves the opposite of what Brewer wants to say. If I were writing a book on Contract Law for law students or practitioners, of course I would expect them to understand the specific meaning of the term. But if I am preaching to a congregation and start using the term 'consideration', I shall expect them to be quite ignorant of the meaning of the term in English law, and if I wish to convey that sort of information I shall have to explain the term. Paul was not writing 1 Corinthians 7 to a school of Jewish rabbis, but to a church of immature Christians, comprised of Jews and Gentiles.

Of course, Brewer is not alone. Others have written on, for example, the Stoic background to 1 Corinthians 7, and so on. Might it not be time to say that the background was multi-form, and that the apostle Paul was quite capable of being original, all the while realising that his readers had to operate in a society controlled by Roman law?

Specifically, Brewer's case would appear to imply that Jesus accepted the grounds for divorce found in Exodus 21, but that since he was either specifically responding to questions about Deuteronomy 24:1 or framing his teaching with that verse in mind, he did not pronounce upon Exodus 21. Had he done so, he would, presumably, have endorsed the passage as giving grounds for divorce. As it is, it was left for Paul to do this in 1 Corinthians 7. I have a number of problems with Brewer's argument.

Firstly, at the hermeneutical level, we are back to the problem of the relationship between the two Testaments. Since Jesus taught that with his eschatological fulfilment of the Law and the Prophets profound changes would take place with respect to the teaching on divorce, is it possible thus to confine his teaching, for example in Matthew 5, to the correct interpretation and application of Deuteronomy 24:1? If we accept that Jesus believed that the rabbinic understanding of Exodus 21 was correct, surely he is saying that the time for the provisions of that chapter has now reached its terminus. We have seen earlier that for a man to withhold those things which would justify a woman in obtaining a divorce under Exodus 21 was for him to be guilty of the hardness of heart which lay behind the divorce of Deuteronomy 24:1. But concessions to hardness of heart will no longer be made; life in the kingdom of God calls for a heart that is anything but hard. To the question as to what would happen if a man was thus hardhearted, it has to be replied that that hardness of heart must not exist in the Christian community. Were it to do so, it would necessitate the kind of discipline that would bring the case into the category of a mixed marriage. But in such a situation a different state of affairs exists, and it is to that that Paul applies himself in 1 Corinthians 7, *not* by citing Exodus 21 but by laying down, as an apostle of Jesus Christ, the revelation of God's will in such a case.

My second difficulty is related to my first. Exodus 21:10-11 is concerned with a slave wife whose husband has taken a second wife. Are we to understand Jesus as approving of this type of situation, or even recognising it in the way in which Moses recognised it? In the light of his teaching on the foundational principles of marriage found in Genesis 1–2, this is hardly likely. Of course, the reply may be made that it was on the basis of a passage like this that the rabbis developed the idea that a free wife could not be worse off than a slave wife, and that a sole wife could not be worse off than a wife whose husband had taken a second wife. However, it is precisely this kind of approach to Scripture that Jesus castigates. While it is true that in Matthew 5:18 he accords authority to the minutiae of Scripture, and that he certainly displays the ability to employ the minute details of Scripture to make theological points (e.g. Matt. 22:31-32; John 10:34-36— though it should be noted that he is really beating his opponents at their own game and did not minutely dissect the Old Testament when teaching the crowds or his disciples), it is nevertheless the case that he appears to have frowned upon the prevailing practice of his religious contemporaries to analyse minutely every nuance of the Old Testament, because it involved them in missing what was staring them in the face (John 5:39-40). In other words, we must not assume too readily that Jesus approved of the prevailing interpretation of Exodus 21:10-11.

I have made other criticisms of Brewer's work in the body of the text. I do so both reluctantly and fearfully: reluctantly, because his work is the most stimulating treatment I have read; fearfully, because he is possessed of a vast knowledge on the subject and, producing his work later than mine, will have the opportunity to respond to these strictures, possibly in a decisive manner! But given the importance of getting to grips with the biblical teaching on such a contentious subject, it is a risk worth taking.

Appendix 5
Divorce Law in
Scotland and Northern Ireland

The Family Law Act 1996 applies to England and Wales. 'The United Kingdom means the United Kingdom of Great Britain and Northern Ireland and its territorial waters';[1] 'England and Wales, Scotland and Northern Ireland form the United Kingdom of Great Britain and Northern Ireland'.[2] Neither the Channel Islands nor the Isle of Man are part of the United Kingdom, '. . . though in some legal contexts the term "United Kingdom is deemed to include them"'.[3] They do, however, form part of the British Isles. Their constitutional position is somewhat unique.

Although Scotland and Northern Ireland form part of the UK, their respective histories are such that the law of divorce that applies in them is different from that of England and Wales. Wales was annexed by the Crown in 1284, but still followed its own 'sinister usages and customs' until the Laws in Wales Acts 1535 and 1542 abrogated them and the legal position of the Welsh was integrated into that of the English. Separate courts existed until 1830, when a unified system of justice was introduced. 'From 1746 till 1967 the word "England" in an Act of Parliament was deemed to include Wales.'[4] Since the Welsh Language Act of 1967, reference is to England and Wales.

A United Kingdom of Great Britain was created in 1707 by the Acts of Union. Scotland, which thus became part of the UK, retained its judicial system and its civil law. This was heavily influenced by Roman Law, as distinct from the Common Law of England and Wales. In no two areas were the differences greater than in the law of property and in the law of marriage. Until the earlier part of this century, a marriage in Scotland could be either 'regular' or 'irregular'. The regular marriage was celebrated by a minister of religion after the proclamation of banns or after a notice of intention had been given to the Registrar. By contrast, irregular marriages required no such ceremony. They could be contracted in one of the following three ways.

First, a marriage by declaration *de praesenti* was created by mutual consent of the parties to be married at that time. Witnesses were not necessary, though advisable. 'Gretna Green marriages' were of this kind. Interestingly, there is an affinity between this kind of situation and that which obtained during the Roman Empire and which, I have argued, lay behind 1 Corinthians. It is not insignificant that Scots Law drew heavily upon Roman Law. Secondly, a promise of marriage followed by intercourse would constitute a valid marriage. The third method of contracting an irregular marriage was by habit and repute: that is, where a couple had lived together for some time as husband and wife, an irregular marriage would be inferred. This also had affinities with Roman Law during the New Testament period.

Today, Scotland does not recognise irregular marriages. Divorce law in Scotland is covered by the Divorce (Scotland) Act 1976. The law is very similar to that enacted for England and Wales by the Matrimonial Causes Act 1973. Divorce is on the basis of irretrievable breakdown of marriage, evidenced by one of the following facts: separation for a period of 5 years, or 2 years where the spouses consent to a divorce; desertion for a period of 2 years; adultery; unreasonable behaviour; insanity.

It can be seen that the Scottish law has been largely, though not entirely, assimilated to the law of England and Wales which applied before the Family Law Act 1996. At the date of writing (July 1998), I am informed by Mr Bruce Ritchie, Solicitor, who is the Deputy Secretary (Professional Practice) Law Society of Scotland, that there are no plans to bring the Scottish law into line with that of FLA 1996. Section 17 of that Act does apply to Scotland, by amending section 10 of the Family Law (Scotland) Act 1985. However, this is concerned with the ancillary matter of division of pension assets, rather than with the substantive issue of divorce.

The constitutional history and position of Northern Ireland is considerably more complex than that of Scotland. In brief, legislation dealing with divorce is covered by Orders in Council. At present, the Matrimonial Causes Order 1978 allows for divorce for identical reasons to the Matrimonial Causes Act 1973. Basically, the law for England and Wales is brought into Northern Ireland some years later by means of an Order in Council. In the normal course of events, this would mean that FLA 1996 would become the law in Northern Ireland some years later by means of a Family Law Order. Whether this will be so will depend upon the future of the body set up as a result of the 'Good Friday Agreement'. At present, that body has no legislative powers. However, should it do so, it would then be an interesting question as to whether the law of Northern Ireland would owe more to that of the Republic of Ireland than to that of England and Wales, or whether it would have a distinctively 'Ulster flavour' about it. The Republic of Ireland has a written constitution and, a number of years ago, a referendum was held in order to decide whether divorce would be allowed. The result, which was in the affirmative, indicated the weakening hold of Roman Catholicism in the Republic. Nevertheless, the divorce law there is not as liberal as in the UK. Given the strongly religious flavour of politics in Northern Ireland, and the position of the episcopalian church as well as that of many independent churches which adopt a more restrictive position than the position of the Westminster Confession of Faith, it may not be unreasonable to assume that, should legislative powers be accorded to the body set up as a result of the 'Good Friday Agreement' *before* FLA 1996 becomes the subject of an Order in Council, then a less liberal divorce law may be enacted there. Only time will tell. At the time of writing, the Secretary of the Family Law Association of Northern Ireland has expressed to me his belief that FLA 1996 will come on stream in a number of years' time.

Notes

Introduction

1. For example, see the following: Atkinson; Cornes; Crispin; Heth and Wenham; Murray; Stott.
2. That is, England and Wales: see Family Law Act 1996, s. 67 (4).
3. Family Law Act 1996.

Chapter 1
Divorce Law in England and Wales

1. *Field of Choice*, para. 21.
2. This refers to those situations where a couple agreed to divorce and where evidence would be 'manufactured', on the basis of the spouse staying in a hotel room with an 'accomplice' and a private detective on hand to confirm that the spouse did spend the night in the same hotel suite with another of the opposite sex. In ordinary 'hotel evidence', the name of this person would not be disclosed. This was the kind of evidence in the divorce which led to the marriage of Edward VIII to Mrs Wallis Simpson and the sensation of his abdication: see Montgomery Hyde, pp. 454-8. (This does not mean that there had not been adultery in this celebrated case, but that the type of evidence used could obviously be 'manufactured' in cases where there had not been adultery.)
3. *Putting Asunder.*
4. *Field of Choice*, para. 15.
5. Matrimonial Causes Act 1973 s. 1 (2) (a)-(e).
6. FLA 1996 s. 67 (3).
7. September 1996.
8. FLA 1996 s. 1.
9. cf. s. 5 and s. 20 (1).
10. s. 8 (2).
11. s. 7 (6).
12. s. 7 (1), (3).
13. s. 7 (2).
14. s. 7 (10), (13).
15. s. 7 (7)-(9).
16. s. 13.
17. s. 29
18. ss. 3, 5.

19. s. 7 (6) only applies to an application for a divorce.
20. s. 4.

Chapter 2
The Old Testament Teaching

1. It is not entirely clear if the words are those of Adam or Moses, although it is probably preferable to read them as Moses' inspired comment upon the nature of marriage. For the Christian, Christ's words in Matthew 19:4-5 are definitive: Jesus makes it clear that these words are the Creator's and that they declare his institution of the nature of marriage.

2. The entrance of sin which ruptured the relationship between Adam and Eve and their Creator also affected their relationship with each other: Genesis 3:12 is a tragic contrast with Genesis 2:23. The scene is set for the biblical perspective, which is that all tension and breakdown in human relationships results from man's fall into sin. The fact that the divine judgement included the sentence of physical death (Genesis 3:19) gives rise to the question as to what Adam's state and condition would have been had sin not entered the world, and how this would have related to his marriage. Clearly, death would end marriage; however, does it follow that marriages would have gone on and on had sin not entered the world? It is impossible to answer this question with any degree of certainty, and it may even be the case that it is an improper question to ask because of its hypothetical nature. The question revolves around a cluster of related questions. Was Adam's state of probation such that, were he to have successfully passed it, he would then be confirmed in a state of holiness? Is the condition of believers at the resurrection the same as Adam's would have been in a state of confirmed holiness, or are believers raised to a higher station? How these questions are answered will bear upon the point at issue. For stimulating treatments of these issues, see the following: Vos, pp. 27-40; Murray (1978), pp. 47-59; Blocher, pp. 111-34; Lloyd-Jones (1971), pp. 226-39.

3. Genesis 4:19-24.

4. Genesis 34:2; 38:15-18.

5. Genesis 19:4-5.

6. The standard Hebrew word for wife, *'iššâ*, is used twice in Genesis 16:3, the first time with reference to Sarai, and the second time with reference to Hagar. In spite of the tendency to regard Hagar as Sarai's concubine—e.g. NBD, p. 246—it is surely significant that nowhere is the usual Hebrew term for concubine, *pîlegeš*, applied to Hagar. The LXX also uses the usual Greek word for wife, *gynē*, for Hagar in this verse, while using the different word, *pallakē*, when referring to a concubine (e.g. Gen. 25:6). Calvin does not treat the arrangement as one of concubinage, but evidently struggles with the fact of Hagar being Abram's wife. He explains the language as being used to safeguard Sarai from the charge that she was turning her house into a brothel or making Hagar a pander to Abram. Notwithstanding these comments, Calvin states that Hagar is improperly called a wife, because she was brought into another person's bed. He opts for the view that the relationship was something between fornication and marriage. It is difficult to see how Calvin has not ended up by describing the relationship as concubinage, though he does not call it such (Calvin, p. 426).

216

7. Genesis 21:10-14. The passage is interesting for a number of reasons. The Hebrew verb *šālaḥ* is used in verse 14 to describe Abraham's act of sending Hagar away. While this word is used frequently in the Old Testament in the general sense of sending, it is also used to refer to the specific act of sending away that is associated with divorce (Deut. 22:19,29; 24:1,3-4; Is. 50:1; Jer. 3:1, 8; Mal. 2:16). The fact that Hagar has already been called Abraham's wife brings the use of the verb in this verse into the range of meaning where sending away is associated with divorce. The significant point is, of course, that Abraham does this because God specifically told him to listen to what Sarah had said (v.12). The conclusion seems inescapable that here is the first biblical reference to divorce and that it is one that God mandated.

8. See 6, above.

9. This kind of 'surrogate motherhood' was evidently not uncommon: Genesis 30:3,7,9-12. Evidence from the Code of Hammurabai and from the Nuzu tablets indicates that this kind of arrangement was legal in civilised Mesopotamia. On the Nuzu tablets, Harrison comments: 'The marriage contract provided that if the wife remained childless for any reason, she was obliged to give a handmaid to her husband, so that children might be born into the family circle' (Harrison (1957), p. 60). In such a situation, the slave's child was to be kept. The command to send Hagar away is inextricably linked with the requirement that Abram send away Ishmael, and thus break with the prevailing custom, so that it would be the child of promise who would have the inheritance rights, rather than Ishmael (Gen. 21:10; Galatians 4:30). It is probably the status of the child of such a surrogate mother that leads to her being called a wife rather than a concubine. Thus in Genesis 30:4,9 the word *'iššâ* is used to refer to Bilhah and Zilpah. The LXX uses *gynē*, which means wife. However, in Genesis 35:22 Bilhah is called a concubine. This is almost certainly because, having given birth to a son, Bilhah continued to have sexual relations with Jacob. At that point, the whole nature of their relationship changed and she was, therefore, called a concubine.

10. For example, Murray (1961) begins his examination of the Old Testament teaching with these verses, and the main part of his treatment of the Old Testament is taken up with the exegesis of this passage.

11. See Matthew 19:7-9. Mark 10:1-9 is an account of the same incident. Matthew 5:31-32 clearly refers to this passage, as is obvious from the reference to the certificate of divorce. The only place where Christ deals with divorce without specific reference to this passage is in Luke 16:18. However, even then his teaching follows immediately after teaching concerning the role of the Law and the Prophets, and the inviolability of the Law.

12. The reference to being 'cut off from their people' (Leviticus 18:29) would appear to refer to execution. This is confirmed by Leviticus 20:10-16.

13. The proof or evidence of the wife's premarital virginity consisted in the production of the blood-stained cloth (v.17). It may be wondered just how reliable and fair this would have been as evidence. However, the following points may help to place this legislation in perspective. Firstly, as designed to protect the wife from unfair accusations, the fact that such a cloth might be produced would be a powerful disincentive to a husband making unfair allegations. Secondly, the whole passage would seem to suggest that the girl had been quite young

when she married and, given the kind of society in which such a young girl would have been brought up, this kind of evidence would be more likely than in a society such as our own. Thirdly, the existence of such a law would have ensured that any situation which might lead to the girl being unable to produce this proof of her virginity would be relayed to her parents immediately.

Josephus has an interesting account of this procedure (Ant. IV. viii. 23). He writes: 'If the damsel obtain a sentence in her favour, that she had not been guilty, let her live with her husband that accused her: and let him not have any further power at all to put her away, unless she give him very great occasions of suspicion, and such as can no way be contradicted . . .' It would appear that Josephus regarded the prohibition of future divorce as being limited; evidently, he believed it possible that there might be situations where the husband could divorce her in future. This throws an interesting light upon the Pharisees' understanding of divorce around the time of Christ, but it may well obscure, rather than illuminate, the Mosaic teaching. The important words are, 'unless she give him very great occasions of suspicion, and such as can no way be contradicted'. This can only refer to one of two possible situations. First, it might have reference to a situation where the wife is guilty of a capital sexual crime, which has been witnessed. In such a situation, the Mosaic law—whatever was the Jewish practice in the time of Christ—was that she be executed. Alternatively, it might refer to the suspicions which give rise to the ritual prescribed in Numbers 5, and which was the subject of the Mishnaic tractate *Sotah*. However, should the wife be found guilty as a result of the ritual, the Mosaic law did not stipulate that divorce was to follow. This was the Mishnaic understanding, but it is important to distinguish between the Mosaic law and the later rabbinic traditions of understanding that law. It is possible that divorce might have followed the ritual; however, it is submitted that where the wife had already been compelled to prove her innocence of premarital sexual relations, the husband could not subsequently divorce her, even where the ritual of Numbers 5 had led to her coming under the curse. On Numbers 5, see the Excursus to chapter 2.

14. The NIV brings out this difference by using the word 'rapes' in Deuteronomy 22:28. There are good reasons for thus understanding it. While the Hebrew verb *tāp̄aś*, which NIV translates as 'rapes' and AV as 'lay hold', is not the same as that used in verse 25, which is clearly used elsewhere of rape (e.g. 2 Sam. 13:11), it is used frequently with the idea of forcibly taking hold of someone. By contrast, in Exodus 22:16, there is no physical forcing or overpowering, but an enticing, or a persuading that leads to the virgin consenting. The verb *pāṭâ*, translated by NIV as 'seduces', evidently carries the idea of persuading someone to agree to something. Thus it is used in Proverbs 1:10—'My son, if sinners entice you, do not give in to them.'

15. The fact that Deuteronomy 22:29 stipulates a set figure to be paid confirms that the situation envisaged in these verses is different from that of Exodus 22:16-17. The Exodus passage is dealing with dowry, and dowry evidently varied according to the status of the bride: compare, for example, 1 Samuel 18:18, 23-27. Although Deuteronomy 22:28-29 does not explicitly say so, we should infer from Exodus 22:17 that the father had the same right to prevent the marriage as in the non-rape situation. If this were not so, then the deuteronomic legislation—which was evidently aimed at the protection of the woman and the

218

deterrence of the man—would effectively be punishing the woman for the sin of the man. This having been said, we should not too readily assume that the woman would not wish to marry the man. Strange though it may appear in our social context, it is clear from 2 Samuel 13:16 that for Tamar a greater wrong would be suffered by being summarily dismissed by Amnon than by what he had already done to her. Deuteronomy 22:28-29 was therefore to safeguard the woman. The fact that she could never thereafter be divorced by her husband was added safeguard to her and, possibly, an added deterrence against men forcing virgins: if they then wanted to walk away from the situation, they could find that they were bound, for life, to the woman. The absence of this prohibition of subsequent divorce from Exodus 22:16-17 is quite significant. A virgin who had been seduced and then married the man could subsequently be divorced by him. Since she had consented, the situation differed from that found in Deuteronomy 22:28-29, presumably because she bore a measure of responsibility for the premarital intercourse. Her vulnerability to divorce from a man who sought to allure her might well strengthen her resolve to resist his approaches, just as his obligation to pay dowry—whether he married him or not—would be an encouragement to the man to exercise self-control. It will be noted from the Excursus to chapter 2 that the possibility of subsequent divorce in this situation may throw light upon the meaning of the words 'something indecent' in Deuteronomy 24:1.

16. See note 15, *supra*.

17. The fact that the adultery had not been witnessed and that the woman had not been caught in the act raises a number of interesting points. The Mosaic law contained important procedural and evidential requirements before the death penalty could be carried out. Deuteronomy 17:6 stipulates that no one was to be put to death on the testimony of only one witness. The testimony of two or three witnesses would be necessary. While this requirement is set in the context of a passage that deals with capital punishment for idolatry, by necessary implication this requirement would apply to any capital offence. But this raises the question as to what it was that had to be witnessed. This question is important for a number of reasons. Firstly, the witnesses to a capital offence were to be the first in carrying out the execution (Deuteronomy 17:7). However, a false witness was to be dealt with in the same way as he intended to deal with the accused. Accordingly, a witness who falsely accused someone of adultery ran the risk of the death penalty. Had Ruth been a married woman, would the fact that someone had seen her sleeping near to Boaz have been sufficient evidence that adultery had taken place? Evidently not, according to Numbers 5:13. The presence of the Hebrew word *zera'* indicates that full-blown sexual intercourse has taken place. BDB understand the term, in this context, as 'flow of semen', and a literal translation would be along the following lines: 'a man lies with her with semen'. It would seem that more than a compromising situation needed to be witnessed. However, this raises the question as to who would be likely to witness such adultery and in which circumstances. Apart from the situation where a couple were unbelievably careless and a number of witnesses stumbled across them at the precise moment when the sexual act was itself being consummated, when would anyone be likely to be a witness to such an event? It would seem almost certain that witnesses would have to be planted to see such a thing and keep

quiet until the guilty moment. Presumably, it was to prevent a suspicious husband from resorting to such degrading measures that the Lord laid down the ritual in the verses in question. The evidential requirements were such that the ritual of Numbers 5:11-31 may have been far more significant than may, at first, be realised. Failure to relate procedural and evidential requirements to the substantive laws in question will inevitably lead to serious misunderstanding of the Mosaic teaching.

18. Verses 21-27 state what will be the effects of the curse. Various attempts have been made to identify precisely the disease that would ensue, but Wenham is probably on surest ground when he quotes the Mishnaic comment, 'In the member she sinned with, she will be punished', and goes on to note from verse 28 that she will be childless (Wenham, G.J. (1981), p. 84). Verse 28 would appear to indicate that barrenness would certainly be a result of the curse.

19. Exodus 21:9-10 and Deuteronomy 21:15-17 touch upon the whole question of bigamy. Exodus 21:10 is concerned to safeguard the marital rights of a woman where her husband has married a second wife, while Deuteronomy 21:15-17 is concerned to protect the inheritance rights of a firstborn son by a wife who is loved less than a second wife. Neither passage specifically approves of bigamy, but it is fairly clear from them that the Mosaic law did not outlaw bigamy. It tolerated or endured it. The Exodus legislation was given at Sinai soon after the Israelites' deliverance from Egypt. There may, therefore, have been bigamous marriages already in existence. However, the deuteronomic legislation contemplates the entrance of the Israelites into the Promised Land and, given many years later, is anticipating the situations that will obtain when the Israelites are settled in the land. This being so, the legislation dealing with bigamy cannot be explained by saying that it was only dealing with already existing, bigamous marriages. For example, Dabney says concerning these verses: 'Both these cases are explained by the admitted principle, that there may be relations which it was sin to form, and which yet it is sinful to break when formed . . . There appears, then, no evidence that polygamy was allowed in the laws of Moses' (Dabney, p. 412). On the contrary, by regulating difficulties that might arise in bigamous marriages, the Mosaic legislation was implicitly tolerating, though not approving of, such marriages. In terms of the institution of marriage in Genesis 2:24, bigamy is clearly contrary to the will of God and is sinful. But in terms of the Mosaic legislation, it was not outlawed.

    The Exodus passage makes explicit what one would assume might have been a common reason for a man taking a second wife, viz., that he preferred her to the first woman whom he had married. This is an important point to keep in mind when considering the Mosaic toleration of divorce.

20. The Gaming Act 1738, s. 2; Gaming Acts 1739 and 1744 made illegal certain games which depended upon chance and all games played with dice, except backgammon. The law was changed by the Betting and Gaming Act 1960, Schedule 6.

21. All gaming contracts were rendered void by s. 18 of the Gaming Act 1845.

22. See note 19, *supra*. The toleration of divorce in Deuteronomy 24:1-4 is similar to the toleration of bigamy.

23. For example, the AV, RV, ARV.

24. Presumably, the prohibition of Deuteronomy 24:4 applied equally to subsequent husbands. Thus, if husband number 2 divorced his wife she could return to him, but not if she had subsequently married a third husband and then been widowed or divorced. In such a case she could marry a fourth husband but not return to the first or second husbands.

25. For example, Heth and Wenham see the defilement of the woman as consisting in the fact that she has had sexual relations with a man other than her husband. The defilement is thus attributable not to the divorce but to the remarriage (Heth and Wenham, pp. 109-10). Similarly, commenting on this passage, Craigie understands the second marriage to have defiled the woman: 'the woman's remarriage after the first divorce is similar to adultery in that the woman cohabits with another man. However, if the woman were then to remarry her first husband, after divorcing the second, the analogy with adultery would become even more complete; the woman lives first with one man, then another, and finally returns to the first.'

26. A number of situations may be considered where a woman will have sexual relations with more than one man. A divorced woman who remarries comes into this category, as does a prostitute. But so does a widow who subsequently remarries. Although the widow is not morally blameworthy for her husband's death in the way in which a prostitute is morally blameworthy for sleeping with different men, it is nevertheless the case that she would not be a widow had sin not entered the human race (Gen. 2:17; 3:19; Rom. 5:12; 1 Cor. 15:22). The ending of marriage in any way—whether by divorce or death—is evidence of the abnormality introduced by sin. Thus, the high priest was forbidden to marry not only a prostitute or a divorcee, but also a widow (Lev. 21:14). A priest could marry a widow but could not marry a prostitute or a divorcee (Lev. 21:7). This means that a man who had divorced could marry anyone other than his divorced wife who had been subsequently married and then widowed or divorced. A single man was free to marry any woman within the permitted degrees, be she a prostitute, a widow, or a divorcee. A divorced woman could, therefore, return to her husband if she had not remarried. But it is not true that she was free to remarry any man, for she could not marry a priest or the high priest. In that sense, there was a defiling barrier between her and such men, even when she was not prevented from returning to her first husband. This fact and this range of regulations demonstrate the inadequacy of Heth and Wenham's treatment of the defilement referred to in Deuteronomy 24:4. Clearly, the remarriage of the divorced woman cannot be separated from the divorce itself; there is a complex of events initiated by the divorce. At differing stages within that complex of events, prohibitions of remarriage would apply, depending on the status of the intended husband. The whole theology underpinning these regulations is best understood in terms of the clean/unclean and 'poles of existence' symbolism found in the Book of Leviticus. (For an extremely stimulating exposition of this theology see the essay by G. J. Wenham, 'Christ's Healing Ministry and His Attitude to The Law' in Rowden.)

It is an interesting point to consider whether the prohibited degrees of marriage—which apply to all—are also the result of the abnormality introduced by sin. The old chestnut, Who was Cain's wife? received a very serious answer from R. L. Dabney. Dabney reasoned that Cain's wife must have been his sister.

However, there would have been no abnormality or sin involved in this if sin had not entered the race.

The command to replenish the earth was given to Adam and Eve in their pure estate, in which, had it continued, incest, like every other sin, would have been impossible. Who can deny, but that the marriages between the sons and daughters of the first parents, after the fall, were sinful in God's eyes? It is not unreasonable to suppose that, thus, the very propagation of the degraded race, to which its present earthly existence under the mercy of God is due, began in sin and shame; that its very perpetuation is the tolerated consequence of a flagrant crime (Dabney, p. 413).

27. See note 26, *supra*.

28. Christ's interpretation of the Old Testament is final and definitive, and it is clear that he taught that the divorce tolerated by Moses ended the one-flesh union. In Matthew 19:3, the Pharisees' question clearly has in view the Mosaic provision of divorce (cf. verse 7). (For a full discussion of this passage and demonstration of this point, the reader is referred to the discussion of this passage in the chapter on Christ's teaching, pp. 74ff.) In verses 4-6a, Jesus goes behind the Mosaic divorce legislation to the original institution of marriage. The all-important words are in verse 6b. There Jesus tells us that the one-flesh union which comes into being when a man leaves his parents and marries his wife (cf. verse 5) is, in one sense, effected by God: 'What God has joined together . . .' However, in the final clause of verse 6, Jesus says, 'let man not separate'. The word translated 'separate' is *chōrizetō*, from the verb *chōrizō*. As Thayer points out, in Matthew 19:6 this word is used as the opposite of *syzeugnymi*, the verb meaning 'join together', which is used in 6a. Thus, Jesus is forbidding the separation by man of what God has joined together. Implicit in this prohibition is the acknowledgement of the fact that it is possible—though wrong—for man to separate what God has joined together. Various attempts may be used to tone down what Jesus is saying, but such attempts fail. The word *chōrizetō* is the third person singular active imperative of *chōrizō*. The imperative mood is that which is used to express a command. Accordingly, Jesus is issuing a command in the form of a prohibition. This is no different from, for example, a commandment not to kill or not to steal: killing and stealing ought not to be done, but they are physical possibilities. It is the very possibility of these sins being committed that requires a prohibitory commandment. Likewise, man ought not to sunder the one-flesh union, but it is possible for that union to be sundered.

What is it, specifically, that separates the one-flesh union that God has effected? According to Jesus, it is the putting away accompanied by the certificate of divorce. Jesus has been asked, in verse 3, if one may put away (*apolysai* from *apolyō*) a wife for any and every reason. It is to that question that he is responding and, after having laid out the foundational theology of marriage, he gives his answer to that question in verse 6b: 'let man not separate'. The implication is irresistible that it is the 'putting away' which separates what God has joined together. The putting away is what takes place and is effected by divorce, as is clear from the Pharisees' next question, in verse 7, as to the reason why Moses gave a command concerning the certificate of divorce. The conclusion to be drawn from this is that Jesus taught that the putting away, accompanied by the certificate of divorce, ended the one-flesh union. The implications of this understanding are, indeed, very wide-ranging and are worked out elsewhere in this study. For present purposes, it is sufficient to note that this was the Old Testament provision, and it clearly undermines the whole kind of approach proposed by Heth and Wenham, as well as modifying considerably other approaches to the durability or otherwise of the one-flesh union. On the relevance of Romans 7:1-3 to the question as to whether the marriage bond is broken only by death, see Appendix 3.

29. See the Excursus on the meaning of 'something indecent' at the end of chapter 2.

30. As has frequently been observed, verses 1-3 form the protasis and verse 4 the apodosis. Verse 1, therefore, forms part of the protasis. Moses is here referring to an already existing practice. This having been said, it would appear that this is the only kind of divorce recognised by the Mosaic law, and the events recorded in verse 1 would have to take place for a valid divorce to have been effected. Thus, there would have to be 'something indecent' as a consequence of which the woman 'becomes displeasing to him' and which leads to him giving her a certificate of divorce and sending her from his house. Thus, Jesus referred to the process of divorce as something which Moses commanded (*eneteilato*) (Mark 10:3) and as a command (*entolē*) which he had written (verse 5). Jesus does not mean that Moses commanded divorce, but that the formal recognition of the elements that had to be present for a divorce to be effected amounted to a command that divorce could only be effected in such a way.

31. Verse 16 has been translated in a variety of ways. A helpful discussion and treatment of the issues is found in Moore.

    Brewer (Tyndale 47.1 [1996]) contends that it is not divorce against which the Lord inveighs but the treachery of the breaking of the marriage covenant by the husband. Brewer seeks to drive a wedge between the divorce allowed by Deuteronomy 24:1 and the divorce which was being practised in Malachi 2:14ff. In the former case, a man would have good reason to divorce his wife because of her unfaithfulness, whereas in the latter case the husband was guilty of treachery against his wife. However, in view of the understanding of '*erwat dābār* given above (note 29), it is preferable to understand Malachi 2 as dealing with the type of divorce envisaged in Deuteronomy 24:1. The people were failing to see that legislative toleration of a practice was not the same as divine approval of it, and that adherence to the formalities required under the legislation did not constitute the act as righteous in God's eyes. What Deuteronomy 24:1 implicitly allowed, Malachi 2 envisages as now endemic within the nation.

32. Verse 13 refers to the unacceptableness of the people's offerings. The reason for this is given in verse 14: the Lord was witness to the breaking of the marriage covenant and chastened the people for this. This is typical of the prophetic insistence that right relationships with one's fellow men and women were essential to the enjoyment of the covenant relationship with the Lord. See also Psalm 51:4.

33. The most recent advocate of this view is Brewer (ibid.). Brewer's thesis is that 'God is described as someone who subjects himself to his own law with regard to regulations concerning marriage, separation, divorce and remarriage.' In spite of his display of a vast and enviable knowledge of Jewish and Ancient Near Eastern marriage contracts and divorce procedures, Brewer has, in my

view, failed to make out his case. Essential to the establishment of his thesis is the proposition, '. . . the prophets did not regard this concept of God's marriage covenant as an interesting metaphor, but rather they examined it as a legal reality'. The evidence, however, does not support this proposition. For example, appeal is made to the marriage covenant in Hosea. Yet in the context of the inaugurating of the covenant, Hosea also refers to Israel as God's son (11:1). God's bride is his son! It is difficult, if not impossible, to see how this illustrates that God subjects himself to his own law with regard to regulations concerning marriage. Moreover, Hosea 1 describes the covenant people as split into two and then reuniting in the great day of Jezreel. In thus referring to the covenant people as God's bride, one is left wondering, If this is not metaphor, what is it? It may be argued, by way of response, that Hosea did not marry his son but Gomer, and that it is this that provides the thrust for the Book of Hosea. While this is true, it does not take from the fact that in Hosea the Lord refers to his relationship with his people as both that of a husband to his bride and that of a father to his son. It is the use of different models or pictures to describe the multi-faceted nature of the relationship of the Lord to his people which underlines the fact that these *are* metaphors rather than legal realities. If the reply be made that the covenant is a dominant Old Testament theme and covenant lies at the heart of Hosea, the point may be granted. But it would be unwarrantable to infer, from the dominance of the covenant motif in the Old Testament and from the fact that marriage is a covenant, that Hosea represents the Lord's marriage to Israel as a legal reality. For it is well established that the covenant as presented in Deuteronomy shares characteristic structural features with Ancient Near Eastern suzerainty treaties, but this does not mean that one elevates such a type of treaty into a position of exclusive dominance for interpreting the Lord's covenant with Israel. That the marriage covenant is a rich metaphor, rather than a legal reality, will become clear from a consideration of prophetic passages where the Lord's action is significantly different from that envisaged by the Mosaic law.

Brewer goes on to consider the themes of separation and divorce, as found in Isaiah, Jeremiah, and Ezekiel. However, close examination of the relevant passages does not allow us to draw the conclusion that the Lord obeyed his own law of marriage and divorce.

The background to Isaiah 50:1 is the prophet's anticipation of the mood of God's people when they would be in captivity. That mood would be one of anguish that the Lord had cast them off for ever and that he would not receive them again unto himself. Motyer comments on these verses as follows:

> The thrust of the two hypothetical situations, divorce and sale, is to ask if something irretrievable has happened, terminating a relationship. Marriage is a covenant motif (e.g. Jer. 2:1-3; 3:1-2; Ezek. 16). Behind it here lies the dreaded possibility that the Lord's covenant with his people may have suffered a final breach. According to Deuteronomy 24:1-4 a divorce could set in train a series of events making the reconstitution of the first marriage impossible. The absence of a *certificate*, however, would indicate that this process had not even been started and that, therefore, the door was open to a reconciliation (Motyer, p. 397; *his italics*).

Leupold's comments are helpful:

> A court hearing is being conducted by the Lord . . . Israel is guilty of miscon-
> duct but is not ready to admit it. She is behaving as though the Lord had put
> her aside and cancelled the covenant that he had made with the nation at
> Sinai. The Lord follows through on this situation treating Israel as though she
> were the wife and he her husband. The analogy leads to a striking refutation
> of the claim that he might have cast off his people. For according to basic
> Mosaic law (cf. Deut. 24:1) if a man did divorce his wife he was legally bound
> to give her a certificate to make the transaction legal. There is no such
> *certificate* in existence. Therefore no divorce has taken place. A separation? Yes,
> a temporary separation. But not a divorce . . .
>
> Now to sum up this somewhat difficult first verse—looking at Israel's pres-
> ent plight in her Captivity, is it thinkable that this all came about because the
> Lord, as a hot-tempered husband, cast off his wife and finalized the transac-
> tion by a writ of divorcement? Of course not. (Leupold, pp. 190-1.)

The import of this passage will become clearer upon an examination of
Jeremiah 3:1ff., to which we now turn. This is, in some respects, a difficult passage. Firstly, 3:8 states unequivocally that the Lord had given faithless Israel her
certificate of divorce. This appears to be in flat contradiction to what we read in
Isaiah 50:1. How are the two passages to be reconciled? Secondly, the same verse
states that the Lord sent faithless Israel away 'because of all her adulteries'. The
Hebrew verb *nāʾap̄* is the same one as is used, for example, in Leviticus 20:10,
where the death penalty is prescribed for the adulterer and the adulteress. Here,
then, is a case of the Lord effecting divorce for adultery. Ought this fact to mod-
ify our exegesis of the Mosaic legislation? The first thing to note is that there are
obvious differences between Israel's relationship with the Lord and the relationship of a wife to her husband. As Heth and Wenham point out, the very
verse which speaks of the divorce certificate also refers to Judah as Israel's sister
(verse 8). The Lord is married to two sisters! This should immediately alert us to
the fact that we are in a different type of situation from that which the whole
Mosaic legislation covered (cf. Lev. 18:18). This point is reinforced by the fact
that 3:4 also refers to the Lord as the Father of the people of Jerusalem (2:2
identifies the people of Jerusalem as those who are being addressed). Not only
has the Lord married two sisters but he has also married his daughter! The point
of all this is that, in certain respects, the Lord's relationship with his people can
be compared with that of a husband to his wife, and that of a father to his child,
but that we cannot press these analogies in every detail. Brewer's point that the
prophets treat the marriage covenant between the Lord and his people as a legal
reality utterly fails. This being the case, we have to see that Jeremiah 3:1ff. is, in
some respects, working out the implications of an extended simile and is not to
be used as providing us with an interpretive key with which to unlock some of
the difficulties found in Deuteronomy 24:1-4.

The whole point of Jeremiah 3:1ff. is to bring out the difference between the
Lord's treatment of his people and a husband's treatment of his divorced wife.
The first part of 3:1 deals with the kind of situation envisaged in Deuteronomy
24:1-4. By contrast, the Lord's people are compared with a woman who subsequently prostitutes herself with many men (v.1b). Moreover, prior to the

divorce, Israel had committed adultery against the Lord with many lovers (vv.6-7). The contrast with a typical divorce is being sustained; thus, the fact that the Lord divorces her for adultery is atypical of the situation in which a man would give his wife a certificate of divorce. This point is further reinforced in verse 14 and in 4:1ff., where the Lord calls upon his faithless bride to return to him, whereupon he assures her of a welcome and of reconciliation with him. It should now be clear how Isaiah can deny that a certificate of divorce had been given, whereas Jeremiah can refer to the certificate of divorce having been given by the Lord to Israel. Isaiah is dealing with a typical Mosaic type of divorce, where the wife is divorced not because of her fault but on account of her husband's caprice. This, Isaiah declares, has not happened, since Israel is in captivity because of her sins (Isaiah 50:1ff.). By contrast, Jeremiah is stressing that she has received a certificate of divorce for her unfaithfulness, which was not the type of situation envisaged by Deuteronomy 24:1-4. To reinforce that point, the Lord urges unfaithful Israel to return to him. Thus, commenting on the certificate of divorce in Jeremiah 3:8, Matthew Poole writes: 'God took from her the title of being His church, 2 Kings 16;5, 6, etc., which He calls here a bill of divorce; not such a one as the Jews were allowed to give upon every slight ground, (for such a one God denies that He ever gave them, and challengeth them to produce it, Is. 50:1) but upon just and great occasion, viz., her playing the adulteress against Him in her idolatries' (Poole, vol. 2, p. 500).

Brewer's treatment of these two passages is unconvincing. Having stated that the Old Testament is concerned to emphasise that God abides by his own law of marriage and divorce, his comment on Jeremiah 3:1ff. is, at the very least, surprising and disappointing: 'Jeremiah is clearly concerned by this [viz., that the Lord will take back his wife after, having divorced her, she has lived with many lovers], but appears not to come to any solution. He proclaims the fact that there will be a new covenant (3:16) and perhaps he thinks that this new covenant will not be subject to the law of Moses.' While Brewer is correct in noting that Jeremiah 3:1ff. is referring to Israel, whereas Isaiah 50:1ff. is concerned with Judah, it is difficult to see how this helps to establish the case he wishes to prove. Indeed, he may thus argue that a certificate of divorce was given to Israel but not to Judah. But this leaves unanswered the two pressing questions: first, how can the Lord take Israel back after her behaviour subsequent to her divorce? and, secondly, why does not the Lord divorce Judah as well as Israel, in the light of the fact that her behaviour was worse than that of the northern kingdom (Jer. 3:8ff.)?

Brewer also appeals to the Book of Ezekiel to support his thesis. Thus, 'When Ezekiel examines God's marriage and divorce, he goes to great lengths to show that God is just and law-abiding in his action.' Again, 'The conclusion of Ezekiel's deliberations is that God was perfectly justified and acting within the law when he divorced Israel.' But Ezekiel 23 will not bear out Brewer's case. For example, verses 22-27 speak of the Lord handing Oholibah (Jerusalem) over to the lovers from whom she had turned in disgust. Verse 25 explains that they will execute the Lord's jealous anger against Jerusalem: 'They will cut off your noses and your ears, and those of you who are left will fall by the sword. They will take away your sons and daughters, and those of you who are left will be consumed by fire.' A number of comments may be made. Firstly, the analogy with a bride obviously breaks down somewhat because of the collective nature of the Lord's people: that is to say, whereas in the human marriage covenant one man is married to one woman, the Lord is in covenant with a people made up of many individuals. Individuals within the covenant community may, for example, be executed, but the covenant community still exists and the covenant remains intact. However, if a wife were to be executed, the marriage would obviously be at an end. For this reason, the analogy between a husband and wife and the Lord and his people cannot be pressed in the way in which Brewer presses it. Some are carried away, some fall by the sword, while others are consumed by fire. It is both unwarrantable and impossible to reason that this passage illustrates that the Lord is abiding by his own law of marriage and divorce. Secondly, the Lord is not only sending his people away; he is inflicting judgement upon them. This becomes very clear in verses 42-47. Thus, verse 45 states: 'righteous men will sentence them [that is, both Oholah (Samaria) and Oholibah (Jerusalem)] to the punishment of women who commit adultery and shed blood'. That punishment is specified in verses 46-47: 'Bring a mob against them and give them over to terror and plunder. The mob will stone them and cut them down with their swords; they will kill their sons and daughters and burn down their houses.' We are here in the realm of capital execution—at points, almost lynching—rather than in the world of divorce encountered in Deuteronomy 24:1-4.

It should, by now, be clear that arguments based upon the Lord's divorce of his people are basically flawed. Firstly, the analogy between an individual woman and a nation—a nation which divided into two—is only an analogy, and the comparison cannot be pressed too far. Secondly, while both Jeremiah and Hosea refer to the Lord divorcing his people, the prophecies of Isaiah and Ezekiel describe God's chastening of his people in somewhat different terms. This confirms our observation that the marriage analogy is not a legal reality. While it is true that there are prophetic references (e.g. in Hosea) to the Lord divorcing his people for adultery, it does not follow that adultery was the kind of situation envisaged in Deuteronomy 24:1. As we have seen, Jeremiah distinguishes the divorce from the situation covered in Deuteronomy 24. Secondly, while capital punishment is referred to in Ezekiel 23, a moment's reflection should demonstrate that that analogy cannot be pursued all the way. If the Lord utterly exterminated the nation, what would then become of the covenant? Hence, a variety of metaphors are used to describe the Lord's treatment of his wayward people. At one point, he divorces them for their spiritual adultery. At another point, he is handing them over for execution.

A further point to bear in mind concerns the fact that even were it to be the case that the divorce certificate referred to in Deuteronomy 24:1 was, in the days of the major prophets, being given on the ground of a wife's adultery, and that this explains why some of the prophetic writings refer to the Lord's divorce of his people for adultery, it would not follow that such a practice would assist in interpreting the 'something indecent' of Deuteronomy 24:1. The reason why this is so is that God's people at this stage of their history were marked by disobedience to, and disregard of, the Mosaic law, rather than by strict adherence to it. Appeal to Israel's behaviour during the time of her apostasy as a basis for illustrating the Mosaic law is a flawed hermeneutical approach to Scripture.

227

In referring to Brewer's use of the prophetic writings, I do not mean to say that Brewer reasons backwards from them in order to interpret Deuteronomy 24:1-4. Rather, he appears to find his understanding confirmed by these passages. If, however, it can be shown—as I believe I have shown—that these passages cannot confirm Brewer's treatment of the deuteronomic passage, then one must surely ask whether a different understanding of the Mosaic legislation is consistent with, and confirmed by, the later prophetic writings.

34. There are clear indications in the book of Genesis that it was not good for the descendants of Abraham to consider themselves free to marry from any ethnic group (e.g. Gen. 24:3-4; 26:34-35). This is specifically dealt with in the Mosaic legislation. Deuteronomy 7:1-3 forbade the Israelites to marry the Hittites, Girgashites, Amorites, Canaanites, Perizzites, Hivites and Jebusites, and forbade them to allow their sons or daughters to marry them. The reason for this prohibition is given in verse 4: 'for they will turn your sons away from following me to serve other gods, and the Lord's anger will burn against you and will quickly destroy you.' Thus, intermarriage with these nations would lead to idolatry, which would be both an offence against the Lord and unfaithfulness to him. Furthermore, it is clear that the detailed regulations dealing with food, the Sabbath, etc., would also be compromised by intermarrying with such peoples, and there would be the ever-present danger of following them in those very abominations for which they were being driven out of the land (Lev. 18:24-25).

In addition to this prohibition, there were restrictions upon certain other nations, which could not but have implications relating to those whom the Israelites might marry. Thus, Deuteronomy 23:3 forbade an Ammonite or Moabite to enter the assembly of the Lord down to the tenth generation. (Craigie regards this as a permanent exclusion: 'Their permanent exclusion is given emphasis in v.4: to the tenth generation . . . for ever.' He also refers to Keil and Delitzsch who 'note that "ten" in vv.3,4 "is the number of complete exclusion"' (Craigie, p. 29).) By contrast, an Egyptian was only excluded in the first and second generation; the third generation might enter the assembly of the Lord (vv.7-8). This would appear to mean that children of a marriage between two Ammonites and Moabites would be forbidden down to the tenth generation, and children of a marriage of two Egyptians would be forbidden until the third generation. What would be the position of children of a mixed marriage between an Israelite and an Ammonite or Moabite, or between an Israelite and an Egyptian? It would appear that, for a child of a marriage between an Israelite *man* and a woman from one of these nations, a different answer must be given from the answer to be given if an Israelite *woman* married a man from one of these nations. The explanation of this statement lies in the fact that inheritance rights were acquired from the father and not the mother. (This can be clearly seen from the case of Zelophehad's daughters in Numbers 27:1-11 and 36:1-12.) The child's 'legal' nationality would, therefore, depend upon his father. (This typically Jewish way of thinking underpins the genealogy of Jesus in Matthew 1:1-17, where Jesus' descent is traced through his father's line, though Joseph was not his biological father.) Where the father was an Israelite, it would appear that the child would, for the purposes of this legislation, also be regarded as an Israelite. Where the woman was an Israelite, then the child would take the father's nationality. This would explain why David would not have come under the prohibition of Deuteronomy 23:3. By contrast, the prohibition of Deuteronomy 7:1-3 and 23:2 was absolute. However, although absolute, mercy could override it: this is the glory of the account of Rahab. As a woman possessed of true and penitent faith there was a place for her amongst the people of God. The reason for the stark language of Deuteronomy 7:1-3 was the threat that these pagan nations posed to the nation's religion, behaviour, and continuance. Where there was true faith and devotion to the Lord, that threat did not exist and the judgement would not apply. The Book of Ruth bears eloquent testimony to the fact that the Israelite concern about certain mixed marriages did not spring from xenophobia or from a separatism which was nationalistically, as distinct from religiouly, motivated. Furthermore, as Craigie points out, Moses was married to a non-Hebrew (Ex. 2:21), while Deuteronomy 21:10-14 laid down regulations for a Hebrew desiring to marry a foreign woman taken as a prisoner in war (op. cit. p. 178).

It is against this background that we must understand the behaviour of Ezra and Nehemiah with respect to those who had married foreign wives. The Exile had been a catastrophe for God's people and had happened because they had been guilty of idolatry and the sins that accompanied that idolatry. Having been restored to the land, God's people were purged of their idolatrous tendencies and a firm monotheistic faith was restored. Few things were more calculated to undermine this faith and lifestyle than intermarriage with foreigners who cared nothing for Israel's God and his law. Further judgement was intolerable to a devout Jew. This is the thrust of Ezra 9:10-15 and explains the actions recorded in Ezra 10, as well as what we read in Nehemiah 13:23-31. There had been widespread intermarrying which threatened the people of God in a number of ways. The putting away of these wives was something quite different from what was envisaged in Deuteronomy 24:1-4. That passage is essentially concerned with the effects of a man divorcing his wife. The situation dealt with in Ezra and Nehemiah is a more public matter. Moreover, Deuteronomy 24:1-4 is not commanding a man to divorce his wife but is simply dealing with the consequences of such a divorce. But in Ezra and Nehemiah, the people are compelled to put away their wives. It may be that a certificate of divorce was given. But it needs to be stressed that this situation was nothing like that envisaged in Deuteronomy 24:1-4, and to try to use this post-exilic material so as to give a more positive understanding of the Old Testament attitude to divorce would be quite unwarrantable, and would be to seek to draw out general Old Testament principles from what was very much a unique type of situation. This having been said, Heth and Wenham may well be going much too far in their treatment of this post-exilic material, which they regard as more the nullifying of contracts to enter into forbidden marriages, than the putting away of wives who should not have been married (Heth and Wenham, pp. 162, 164). The scale of the problem and the particular juncture at which the nation stood demanded drastic action, just as a modern state may adopt emergency measures when its security and very survival are at stake.

35. The origin of this belief is to be found in the fact that Deuteronomy 24:1-4 deals only with the husband divorcing his wife. Josephus clearly indicated that a woman could not divorce her husband, though she might leave him. She would only be free to remarry if the husband put her away. He writes: 'But some time

afterward, when Salome happened to quarrel with Costobarus, she sent him a bill of divorce, and dissolved her marriage with him, *though this was not according to the Jewish laws; for with us it is lawful for a husband to do so;* but a wife if she departs from her husband, cannot of herself be married to another, unless her former husband put her away' (Ant xv. vii. 10; *italics mine*). Josephus's words appear to make it perfectly clear that a wife could not initiate a divorce; however, it does appear that in the event of a woman leaving her husband, the husband might then give her a certificate of divorce which would leave her free to remarry. Of course, the ruling classes have often been guilty of taking liberties, and Salome is an example of this.

36. Brewer has drawn attention to the significance of Exodus 21:10-11 (Brewer, Tyndale Bulletin 47.1 [1996], pp. 7-12). I am not aware of treatments of divorce, from a Christian perspective, which consider the significance of these verses. In this respect, Brewer has broken new ground and has placed us greatly in his debt. He draws attention to the fact that these verses are referred to in several Jewish marriage contracts, and alluded to in most of them. Moreover, he demonstrates that the terms of the marriage contract found in these verses are referred to by biblical authors as well as by the early rabbis. Most significantly, the final words of verse 11, 'she is to go free', form the basis of Jewish divorce certificates. The passage has clearly figured in Jewish treatments of divorce, though not largely in Christian teaching. However, Christian commentators have long been aware that these verses are dealing with divorce. Thus Matthew Poole, the Puritan commentator, clearly regards these verses as giving the woman a right of divorce where she has not been provided with food, clothing, or conjugal duties (Poole, vol. 1, pp. 162-3). See also comments by Durham.

37. Craigie believes that Deuteronomy 21:14 is referring to divorce (Craigie, p. 282). Although, as with Exodus 21:7-11, these verses are not considered in works dealing with the Christian teaching on divorce—e.g. Murray, Heth and Wenham—the view that they may be dealing with divorce is not at all of recent origin. Matthew Poole considered the possibility that verse 14 was a reference to divorce, though he preferred to understand the verse to be teaching that the man may reject the woman after the month's mourning specified in verse 13, but before marrying her. However, he then appears to contradict his own exposition by interpreting the phrase 'because he has humbled her' as follows: 'i.e. lain with her, as this phrase is oft used, as Gen. 34:2; Deut. 22:24, 29; Judg. 19:24; Ezek. 23:10, 11' (Poole, vol 1, p. 376).

38. The main reason for believing this to be the case is that the end of the verse states, 'since you have dishonoured her'. The Hebrew verb for 'dishonour' bears the meaning 'to humble, to afflict' and is used, for example, in Deuteronomy 8:2 of God humbling his people, and in Psalm 35:13 of the psalmist humbling or afflicting himself. However, it can also be used with certain sexual connotations, where it is referring to a woman losing her virginity or being violated. This usage is found on a number of occasions in the Old Testament, and BDB group its usage in Deuteronomy 21:14 with these examples (Gen. 34:2; Deut. 24:22, 29; Judg. 19:24; 20:5; 2 Samuel 13:12, 14, 22, 32; Ezek. 22:10-11; Lam. 5:11). This being so, the words at the beginning of verse 14, 'If you are not pleased with her', must be understood as displeasure which arises after all the events of verse 13, i.e. after the marriage. Even if this argument is not accepted

and the view taken that the marriage had not taken place, one must neverthe-less regard the woman as in a similar position to a betrothed woman, in which case we are still dealing with a divorce or quasi-divorce situation.

39. The Hebrew verb is *šālaḥ.* This verb is used frequently in Exodus in connection with Moses' request, and Pharaoh's refusal, to let the people go. It is also used where an animal has been curtailed and is then released. It is used in this way, for example, in Leviticus 16 of the goat that is to be let go into the wilderness. It is also used of letting a slave go free. This word is used in Deuteronomy 22:19, 29: in the former verse, a man who has falsely accused his wife of having lost her virginity before marriage is forbidden to 'divorce' her (NIV) or 'put her away' (AV), while a similar prohibition applies in verse 29 to a man who has married an unbetrothed virgin whom he had raped. The verb is used in Deuteronomy 24:1,3, and in Jeremiah 3:1 and Malachi 2:16. In all of these examples, as BDB note, the meaning is equivalent to 'divorce'. Craigie, noting the Piel of the verb in Deuteronomy 22:19,29 as having a possibly technical meaning of 'divorce', argues that Deuteronomy 21:14 is referring to divorce.

40. The following considerations support this conclusion. Firstly, the emphasis is on the husband: it is he who finds his wife displeasing, rather than the wife who finds her husband displeasing. Therefore, the second part of verse 2 is probably epexegetic: that is to say, the words 'You must not sell her or treat her as a slave' explain the words 'let her go wherever she wishes'. The contrast is not, there-fore, between a wife wishing for a divorce instead of the husband but, rather, between her having no say in what happens to her—not being sold or treated as a slave—and having a say: 'let her go wherever she wishes'. Thus, she is a free woman on being divorced. Moreover, the idea is present that, in such circum-stances, she might wish to return to the area from which she was seized. The impression conveyed by the verses is that the husband becomes displeased with her soon after marriage. If we are meant to understand this, then these verses are another example of the Mosaic concession to men's hardness of heart.

41. See the quotation from Josephus in note 35, *supra.* On the judicial function of judges, see, e.g., Deuteronomy 17:8-13; 21:1ff. Rabbinic teaching on the woman's right to divorce 'is a complex matter' (Hilton and Marshall, p. 127). Hilton and Marshall's conclusions are the same as those of Hertz, who states: 'the wife might sue for a divorce in the Jewish Courts, which could for certain causes— e.g. loathsome occupation or disease—compel him to free her' (Hertz, p. 933). The reference to loathsome occupation or disease is a reference to the Mishnaic teaching that a woman was to be divorced from a man with polyps or who col-lected dog's excrement.

42. This is clear from verse 2, which heads the entire section, where it is stated that Hebrew servants are under consideration, and from verse 8, which forbids the master from selling his slave to a foreigner.

43. A comparison of this verse with Deuteronomy 21:14 should make clear that the master has not, at this stage, married her. If he had married her, the treatment of her required by verse 8 would differ significantly from the treatment of the foreign wife in Deuteronomy 21:14. While it is true that the foreign wife had not been purchased in the same way as the Hebrew servant had, it could be said that the provision of a home and husband for someone who was but a prisoner of war would have been equivalent to the purchase of a Hebrew slave. It would,

therefore, be remarkable if the foreign wife were treated on more favourable terms than the Hebrew wife. It makes far more sense of the legislation to understand Exodus 21:8 to refer to a state of affairs where the woman has not yet been married. This would seem to be confirmed by verse 11 where, on divorcing her, the husband receives no money. This would be in keeping with the principle that marriage would have obliterated her status as a slave, just as it did in the case of a foreign prisoner who was married.

It may be objected that verse 8 states that the master had already betrothed her to himself (AV) and that, therefore, given the importance attached to betrothal, verse 8 is dealing with a divorce type of situation. But this argument cannot be sustained. The usual Hebrew verb for 'betroth' is not used in verse 8. While it is true that the verb used may mean 'appoint, assign, especially of acquiring or designating as wife' (BDB), and that BDB refer to Exodus 21:8-9 as the acquiring or designating of a concubine, it would appear that, in the context, we should understand the verses to describe a master selecting a slave with the understanding or expectation that she would become his wife. This differs somewhat from the more definite betrothal of a free woman. This adequately explains what is meant by the words, 'he has broken faith with her'. The Israelites were forbidden to sell their slaves to foreigners. As Matthew Poole points out in commenting on this verse, the reason for this specific prohibition being found in verse 8 is that the master might be especially tempted to sell her to foreigners because, given the basis upon which she had entered the master's household, an Israelite would be unlikely to purchase her and, if he did, the price would have to be considerably lowered.

44. In verse 4, the woman and children are the master's servants. Verse 9 makes clear that the woman no longer stands in such a relation to him.

45. It is true that the word 'wife' or 'woman' is not found in the verse and that the verb translated by NIV as 'marries' is a frequently used word meaning 'to take'. Nevertheless, when this verb is used of taking a woman, it has the meaning 'to marry', and is so used in, e.g., Exodus 2:1; 6:20,23,25. The taking of another, therefore, refers to marrying another woman. It would appear that this does not mean that he takes another instead of, but in addition to, the slave wife. There are two reasons for saying this: firstly, if the slave were sold on the understanding that the master would marry her, it would appear sensible to assume that she would be married before, and not after, another woman. Secondly, the presence of the words 'marital rights' (NIV) or 'her duty of marriage' (AV) suggest that she is already married. The Hebrew term thus translated means 'habitation' or 'cohabitation', and is assigned in this verse by BDB the meaning of 'marriage rights'. Interestingly, the LXX rendering of verse 10 translates the Hebrew term rendered 'deprive' (BDB), with the Greek verb *apostereō*. While this verb carries the general meaning of 'defraud' and is so used in 1 Corinthians 6:8, it is the same verb which is used in 1 Corinthians 7:5, where Paul tells married couples not to deprive each other of sexual relations.

46. See note 45, above.

47. The claim that this verse is dealing with divorce depends, of course, on the fact that marriage has taken place. One would assume that if a wife who had been a slave had such rights, then a free woman who had been married would also have had such rights. If this were not so, the slave wife would be in a more

privileged position than a free wife. The passage in question is, however, dealing with the rights of slaves, and this is probably the reason why the principle is not specifically extended. Brewer notes: 'It was assumed that if a slave wife had these three rights [i.e. the rights referred to in verse 10], then a free woman should also have them.' Interestingly, he goes on to say: 'her husband should also have [these rights]. Therefore, from this short text the whole principle of the rights of each marriage partner was inferred as part of the law of God. It was concluded that each partner should find support from the other in terms of food, clothing and love' (Brewer, Tyndale Bulletin 47.1 [1996], p. 8).

Brewer's case proceeds on the basis that the prophets—especially Ezekiel, in Ezekiel 16—demonstrate that the Lord provided food and clothing for his bride, but that she gave herself to other lovers. Thus, the Lord kept his part of the contract, but Israel broke hers. This was the classic divorce situation. Brewer seeks further support for his thesis from the fact that most of chapter 5 of the tractate *Ketuboth*, in the Mishnah, is concerned with the details of the obligations within the marriage contract. He states:

> It was assumed that the man supported his wife by providing money for food and clothing, while the wife supported her husband by purchasing and preparing food and clothing. The exact amount of money and work involved was discussed at length. The frequency of conjugal acts was also discussed, with the Hillelites concluding that a husband may only abstain for one week and the Shammaites that two weeks were permitted.

Exodus 21:10-11 is clearly of considerable importance, but it is to be doubted whether it is safe to follow the rabbis in their development of it, or to regard it as shedding very much light upon grounds for the husband to divorce the wife. To begin with, verse 10 speaks of conjugal duties of a husband to a wife, rather than vice versa. As is clear from Paul's treatment of this matter in 1 Corinthians 7:3-5, the one-flesh union is such that each spouse's body is under the power of the other and, therefore, each should fulfil the conjugal duty to the other. However, Corinth was a different society from ancient Israel, and it was far more likely that the husband would deprive the wife than that the wife would refuse the husband in ancient Israel. The economic dependence of the wife on the husband in a largely agricultural society—a fact which is clearly indicated by the different 'economic values' of men and women found in Leviticus 27:3-5—led to a situation where there was greater risk of a man depriving his wife than vice versa. Moreover, the context of Exodus 21:10-11 is that of a man who now has a second wife and who is finding sexual fulfilment in her rather than in the first wife. This is exactly the kind of situation that obtained between Jacob and his two wives (Genesis 29:30; 30:14-16). Nowhere does the Old Testament refer to a wife depriving her husband. The only possible reference is the Song of Solomon 5:3ff. It is not certain that this is so and, in any event, the passage occurs in a book that celebrates the depth of love between two people. As for the argument that Ezekiel is dealing with Israel's failure to love the Lord, it is much more accurate to say that he portrays Israel's abominable unfaithfulness to the Lord by turning to her gods (Ezek. 23:14-21). It is unlikely, therefore, that Exodus 21:10 may be legitimately extended to cover a wife's depriving of her husband. The issue is important and is dealt with elsewhere, in 1 Corinthians 7:3-5.

However, a consideration of such an obligation is best grounded in the one-flesh union. Further comment on the question as to whether Paul had Exodus 21 in mind when he wrote 1 Corinthians 7 will be found in the chapter which deals with Paul's teaching.

Similarly, detailed consideration of the wife's duty in terms of preparing food and clothing takes us away from the biblical world of principles to be applied in life to the legalism which bedevilled so many rabbinic discussions. Certainly Proverbs 31:10-31 pictures a godly wife who purchased and provided food for her family (vv.14-15), and who made fine clothing for her household (vv.19,21,24) and was an extremely hard-working woman (vv.18,27). No doubt, in the kind of society in which she lived, there would be something of a distribution of labour between husband and wife along the lines found in this chapter. However, the mainspring of the woman's life was not adherence to a marriage contract but fear of the Lord (v.30). The kind of discussion in the Mishnah as to amounts of money and work, together with the Hillel/Shammai discussion as to the frequency of intercourse, is light years removed from the spirit which lies behind Proverbs 31. The context of Exodus 21:10-11 is surely that of a situation where a husband might exploit the position of his wife. The verses in question were intended to protect her and to build in safeguards against exploitation. Thus, the teaching could be similarly extended to other wives—who had not been purchased as slaves—who might be exploited. But to build up an elaborate case law on this verse would appear to be unwarrantable.

48. See notes 35 and 41, *supra*.

Chapter 3
The Teaching of the Gospels

1. There is a broad division between those who believe that Jesus allowed divorce and remarriage in certain situations and those who maintain that Jesus would not allow remarriage. Within the first group, opinion differs as to the situations where divorce and remarriage would be legitimate. Some hold that Jesus allowed divorce and remarriage only on the ground of adultery or some sexual sin. Murray is representative of this viewpoint, which is the position of the Westminster Confession: 'In the case of adultery after marriage, it is lawful for the innocent party to sue out a divorce: and, after the divorce, to marry another, as if the offending party were dead' (ch. xxiv, para. v). This is fairly typical of 'Reformed Protestantism', although many independent churches might take a different view. By contrast, Anglicanism will not allow remarriage after divorce. This view is articulated by Heth and Wenham and by Cornes.

2. Matt. 5:31-32; 19:3-12; Mark 10:2-12; Luke 16:18.

3. The phrase is that of my friend Keith Walker. It is, of course, concerned to bring out a positive emphasis, just as 'pro-life' is more positive than 'anti-abortion'. The phrase is mentioned in a paper on divorce and remarriage by Mr Walker, which has stimulated my own thinking and to which I am indebted at a number of points.

4. The exceptions are found in Matthew 5:32; 19:9. Numerous writers have

challenged the belief that exceptions are to be found in Christ's teaching. These base their challenge on a variety of foundations, some arguing on the basis of textual criticism, others on the basis of the proper translation of the 'exceptive clauses'. These arguments are considered later in the chapter. At this stage, where I am only concerned to give a general overview, I shall assume that these clauses are, indeed, exceptive.

5. Matthew 5:32 has been variously understood. Some believe Matthew states that the divorce causes the woman to become an adulteress, while others believe Jesus is saying that she suffers adultery. Detailed consideration is given later in this chapter as to the precise meaning of the verse. At this stage of the argument, the general case being presented is unaffected, whichever understanding is accepted.

6. The exception in both Matthean passages is on the basis of *porneia*. The meaning of this term will be examined later in this chapter. Suffice it to say, at this stage, that I believe it to refer to illicit sexual intercourse.

7. Christ's attitude to the Old Testament is a vast subject. Reference may be made to the relevant sections in Warfield, France, Wenham, and Carson and Woodbridge for the evidence that Christ regarded the books of our Old Testament as the inspired, infallible, inerrant and authoritative Word of God.

8. e.g. Matt. 4:4,7,10; 5:17-18; 15:3-6; 22:43-45; 26:54; Luke 24:25-27; John 10:34-35, etc.

9. e.g. Matt. 15:1-9; Mark 7:5-13.

10. This is an important point, which has often been overlooked. Christ's words in Matthew 5:17*a* clearly imply that there was the danger that his hearers would misunderstand his teaching as being an assault on the Old Testament. In his controversies with the religious authorities, it is clear that he differed from them not on the basis that they accepted the Old Testament and that he had rejected it, but rather, on the basis that he accepted its authority *in toto* and taught that it pointed to him, whereas they, blinded to its real import and overlaying it with their own traditions, were effectively nullifying its authority (e.g. Matt. 15:1-9; Mark 7:5-13; John 5:36-47). Thus, the repeated phrase in the Sermon on the Mount, 'You have heard that it was said', is not a reference to Scripture but to tradition. When Jesus referred to Scripture, he said, '*gegraptai*' (= it is written).

11. The word used in Matthew 5:17 is *plērōsai*. The verb *plēroō* is used in a variety of ways in the New Testament. Matthew is particularly fond of this word, and continually uses it of the fulfilment of the Old Testament in the life of Jesus (e.g. 1:22; 2:17; 2:23; 4:14). The Old Testament thus has a prophetic role in pointing forward to Christ, and he is the eschatological fulfilment of the Old Testament. We are thus prepared for the usage of this term in 5:17. It may be asked how *the law* as well as the prophets may be understood in this way. The answer is supplied in 11:13. Here Jesus teaches that the law as well as the prophets prophesied until John the Baptist. At that point, they reached something of a terminus. The reason for this is given in verse 12: from the days of John, the kingdom of heaven had been forcefully advancing. We are dealing here with what Carson (1996) has called the Bible's 'story line'. With eschatological fulfilment, the law and the prophets are not of the same significance as they were before that fulfilment. Matthew 5:18 is crucially important at this point. Until heaven and earth

disappear, not the smallest part of the law can disappear *'until everything is accomplished'*. Jesus is *not* saying that the smallest part of the law cannot pass away, but that this cannot occur unless *'everything'* is accomplished. There are good reasons for believing that Jesus is here referring to the entire Mosaic legislation, *qua* Mosaic legislation, and that he is not subdividing the law into moral, ceremonial, and civil categories. In the light of what Jesus says in Matthew 5:18, viz., that not even the slightest part can pass until all is fulfilled, the fact that a verse such as Hebrews 7:12 makes clear that parts are now obsolete must mean that all has been fulfilled. In this connection, it is highly instructive to compare Matthew 5:18 with Matthew 24:35. The latter verse, when set against the former, constitutes a glorious claim of staggering proportions. What all of this means is that Christ's fulfilment of the law inevitably entails continuity between Christ and the law, since *it is the law that he fulfils*. But it also entails discontinuity, *because the law, having been fulfilled, has achieved its purpose, and is therefore of different significance now*. Consequently, an interpretation of Matthew 5:17 which entails that Christ is simply reaffirming the teaching of Moses is inevitably wrong. Furthermore, *within* the Old Testament, the Mosaic legislation occupies a particular position. Thus, Jesus contrasts the teaching found in Genesis 1:27 and 2:24 with that found in Deuteronomy 24:1 (Matt. 19:4-8).

This hermeneutical approach to the law is developed throughout the New Testament. Mark hints at it in 7:19, while it is brought out frequently in Christ's healing ministry. It is introduced by John in John 1:17, and is then developed by him in 2:19-22; 4:21-24; 5:16-47; 6:32ff., etc., etc. The place of the law in the Pauline writings is a huge subject. Romans 3:21 is a good example and illustration of the point that is being made. The 'but now' is eschatological: hitherto, the Old Testament witnessed to a righteousness, but that righteousness has now been revealed. The point is developed, theologically, by Paul in Galatians 3:15–4:7.

On the meaning of 'fulfil' in Matthew 5:17, see Banks; Carson (1977). On the Pauline attitude to the law, see Moo (1983); Wright (1991); Eveson.

12. This mistake is made by Crispin.

13. There is a tendency for Heth and Wenham to do this.

14. In Matthew 5:31-32, Jesus is setting forth his teaching in contrast to that of the Pharisees and teachers of the law (cf. v.20). In Matthew 19:3-11 and Mark 10:2-12, his teaching on divorce is called forth by the questioning of the Pharisees. Luke 16:18 is set in the immediate context of teaching concerning the place of the Law and the Prophets and the eschatological kingdom of God, while the wider context is that of Pharisaic misunderstanding of the demands which God makes upon men. Thus, on each occasion Christ's teaching is against the background of the prevailing ideas of his day. If this is not borne in mind, we may go seriously astray in our understanding of his teaching.

15. The Mishnaic tract *Gittin* deals with these differences. *Gittin* 9.10 states:

> The House of Shammai says: 'A man must not divorce his wife unless he has found her unfaithful. As was said (Deuteronomy 24:1) *Because he has found some uncleanness in her.*' The House of Hillel says: 'He may divorce her if she only spoiled a dish for him because it was said: *Uncleanness is anything.*' Rabbi Akiba says: 'He may divorce her if he found another that is more beautiful

than his wife, because it was said: (Deut. 24:1) *If it come to pass that she find no favour in his eyes.'*

It is interesting to note that Hillel and Akiba were both interpreting Deuteronomy 24:1 as giving grounds for divorce: 'He *may* divorce her . . .' if such-and-such had happened. By contrast, Shammai took a more restrictive view of the verse: 'A man *must not divorce* . . .' unless a certain event has occurred. Nevertheless, the three rabbis approached Deuteronomy 24:1 on the basis that it afforded a ground for divorce. This is still the approach within Judaism. For example, Hilton and Marshall begin their consideration of rabbinic teaching with reference to Deuteronomy 24:1 and comment: 'Most translations make this verse only part of a sentence, but from the Hebrew it is clear that the verse can stand alone.' Interestingly, they go on to say,

> Our passage begins with another phrase—'if she finds no favour in his eyes'. From our text we cannot tell if this is an *alternative* reason for divorce or an *additional* reason for divorce: does it mean *either* she has done something wrong *or* she finds no favour in his eyes, or does it mean *both* she has committed adultery or incest *and* she finds no favour in his eyes? From the biblical text it is impossible to tell (Hilton and Marshall, p. 121).

(The reference to incest or adultery arises from the fact that Hilton and Marshall favour this understanding of the meaning of *'erwaṯ dāḇār*.) Hilton and Marshall go on to state that the remainder of Deuteronomy 24:1-4 was interpreted by the rabbis as a separate and second case.

The Mishnah provides extremely valuable background material to the Gospels and contains considerable material on the subject of divorce. For example, *Gittin* 4.7 states: 'If a man put away his wife because of her evil fame, he may not take her back.' *Gittin* 4.8 states: 'If a man put away his wife [i.e. with her Ketubah *Ket.* 11.6] because she was barren, Rabbi Judah says: "He may not take her back." But the sages say: he may take her back. If she then married another and had children by him, and he claimed her Ketubah, Rabbi Judah said, He should say to her, "Thy silence is fairer than thy speech!"' (Ketubah was money set aside by the husband at the time of a marriage and kept by the bride's father in safety, to ensure that it would be available for her in the event of a divorce.) The tractate *Ketuboth* also contains material concerning divorce. Thus 5.5 states: 'If a man put away his wife under a vow to do no work he should put her away and give her her Ketubah for idleness.' *Ketuboth* 7.10 states:

> The following are divorced without their marriage Ketubah: she who transgresses Mosaic or Jewish law. And what is meant here by Mosaic law? If she fed him food which had not been tithed, or slept with him during her period, or did not separate the dough, or made a vow and did not keep it. And what is meant here by Jewish law? If she goes out with her hair loose, or spins in the market-place, or speaks with all men. Abba Saul said, Also if she curses his parents before him. Rabbi Tarfon says, Also if she is loud-mouthed. What is meant here by loud-mouthed? One who speaks in her house so that her neighbours can hear her voice.

A number of comments are apposite. Firstly, it is important to note that Hillel and Shammai may have still been living during the time of Christ, and the difference between them is, therefore, extremely important background to Christ's teaching. Secondly, the emphasis is all the time upon the husband putting his wife away. *Ketuboth* 5.10 is a notable exception in its concern for the woman, since it is there laid down that a man was to put away his wife if he were afflicted with boils, polypus, or if he collected dog's excrement. Notwithstanding this provision, there is no doubt that the man is in a more powerful position than the woman. And the terms in which even this provision is couched indicate that it is the man who puts away, rather than the woman putting away the man. The last point to note is that the Mishnah clearly teaches that divorce left a woman free to remarry (*Kiddushin* 1.1).

16. Fundamental to Christ's teaching is his statement, 'Moses permitted you to divorce your wives because your hearts were hard' (Matt. 19:8; cf. Mark 10:5). The position appears to be that Moses was addressing an existing practice: men would divorce their wives, and then, after the wife had remarried and been subsequently divorced or widowed, would seek to take them back. It may even have been that the husband would seek to argue that he had never put his wife away in a manner that left her free for another man to marry. Moses tightened up this whole area in two ways. First, a divorce could only be effected with the giving of a certificate. This would indeed remove all doubt and leave the woman free to remarry. This explains the importance that the Jews attached to the certificate of divorce, and is the reason for Jesus referring, in Mark 10:5, to Moses' command. Secondly, the husband was unable to remarry the woman if she had been subsequently married and divorced or widowed. The point of Christ's interpretation of the Mosaic legislation is that he is asserting that Moses simply allowed the existing practice of divorce because of the hardness of men's hearts. To begin with that legislation, as though it were giving the grounds for divorce, was to be guilty of conferring a positive approval upon the practice, which Moses had never intended. Christ's disagreement with his contemporaries was not so much over the meaning of *'erwat dābār*—'something indecent'—as over their entire use of the Mosaic legislation. His approach was fundamentally different from theirs.

17. It is a commonplace of New Testament study that Messianic expectations ran high during the period in which Jesus lived in Palestine, and that these expectations were of a political nature. The fact that Palestine was under Roman domination fuelled the desire for a Messiah who would liberate God's people from political oppression. It was against this background that Jesus ministered, and this explains much of the misunderstanding of his mission, as well as throwing light upon the whole question of the so-called 'messianic secret', particularly as found in Mark's Gospel.

That Jesus was willing to function and minister in such a society, and to encourage and teach love for enemies, and that he was not hostile to those involved with the Roman authorities and even numbered tax collectors amongst his disciples, was itself a statement of far-reaching theological significance. To begin with, the theocratic nation envisaged in the Mosaic law could not function, as such, as long as it was an occupied nation and a subjugated people. Jesus' willingness to function and minister in such a society should be set against the withdrawal from such a society by the Qumran community. Not that Jesus approved of the religious establishment of his day. But precisely because he was the eschatological fulfilment of the Law and the Prophets (see note 11, above), it did not matter that the nation could no longer function as the theocratic state set up by the Mosaic legislation. The rise of the movement known as Theonomy, in recent years, which seeks to argue for the institution of the Old Testament civil law, all but fails to recognise the significance and importance of the fact that that law existed within the framework of the theocracy, together with institutions like the priesthood. It also fails to take account of the significance of the teaching found in Matthew 5:17 (see note 11, above). On the significance in Jesus' ministry of the Roman occupation of Palestine, see Wright (1996).

18. Christ's attitude to the death penalty found in the Mosaic law is part of the larger question of his view of the place of the Mosaic law. The argument already advanced as to his being the eschatological fulfilment of the law (see note 11, above) is relevant at this point. This does not mean that nothing in the Old Testament law is binding upon us today (see Appendix 1 for the treatment of the status of the Mosaic Law today). What it does mean is that one cannot simply make a straight equation and comparison between the Old Testament requirements and the New Testament. It is important to realise that Christ's view of the death penalty for sexual sin does not rest upon one or two isolated verses but upon a whole theological foundation.

Appeal is frequently made to the treatment of the woman taken in adultery, as found in John 8, as evidence for the proposition that Jesus did not approve of the death penalty for adultery. In fact, the incident recorded there is dealing with a range of complex questions. We are told that the teachers of the law and the Pharisees were seeking to trap Jesus and have a basis for accusing him (v.6). The trap arose from the fact that, at this particular time, the Jews did not have the authority to execute an individual for such a crime. Thus, Jesus was faced with the dilemma of siding with the Mosaic law and thus being liable to a charge of sedition or treason against Rome, or staying on the right side of the Roman authorities by disagreeing with Moses. It is almost certain that the decision being sought from him was not in the nature of a personal opinion but was tantamount to a legal verdict.

Jesus' response can be understood against the background of the Old Testament material relevant to capital punishment for adultery, and in the light of the requirements found in the Mishnaic tract *Sotah*. (These requirements are almost certainly very old. I am not suggesting that Jesus would have put these requirements on a par with the Old Testament, but that his would-be accusers would have required adherence to these requirements. This being so, he applies their own standards to themselves.) The failure of the accusers to have complied with the requirements of the Old Testament law and those found in *Sotah*, together with the fact that the witnesses were to be the first to cast the stone, obviously placed the woman's accusers in great difficulty, not only in terms of their own law but also with respect to Rome, since they themselves would be guilty of a seditious and treasonable act. Strictly, one cannot deduce Christ's attitude to the penalty for adultery from this passage, though the spirit he displays throughout contrasts sharply with that of the woman's accusers.

On the textual questions raised by this passage, see Morris. On the interpretation of the whole incident, a particularly valuable treatment may be found in

Derrett. (I do not agree with Derrett's treatment of divorce.) On the withdrawal of the power from the Jewish authorities to impose the death penalty at this period, see Derrett, pp. 156-88; Carson (1994), pp. 591-2; Morris, pp. 786-8.

19. The sentence reads: *ho nomos kai hoi prophētai mechri Iōannou*—literally, 'the Law and the Prophets until John'. The preposition *mechri* (until) means that with the coming of John, the Law and the Prophets reach their terminus. The terminus is reached because since that time *(apo tote)*, i.e. the time of John, the good news of the kingdom of heaven has been preached *(hē basileia tou theou euangelizetai)*. The Law and the Prophets reached their terminus with the proclamation of the good news of the kingdom of heaven, because the kingdom is the eschatological fulfilment of the Law and the Prophets. This is the clear teaching of Matthew 11:13, where Jesus says that all the Prophets and the Law *prophesied* until John: their prophetic witness is fulfilled in the kingdom of heaven.

20. See, for example, his words in John 5:36-47.

21. The LXX rendering of the words in our translation 'That would be detestable in the eyes of the Lord' is: *hoti bdelygma estin enantion kyriou tou theou sou*. The word 'detestable' *(bdelygma)* is exactly the same word as that used by Jesus in verse 15. Instead of the word *enantion* (neuter of *enantios* (opposite) which, followed by the genitive, has the force of a preposition meaning 'before, in the presence of'), he uses *enōpion*, which likewise means 'before, in the presence of'. (These two words are similarly used in Luke 1, in verses 6 and 19 respectively.) Thus Jesus' words in Luke 16:15, linked with his words in verse 18, clearly evoke echoes of Deuteronomy 24:4. Moreover, the LXX also uses *bdelygma* in, for example, Leviticus 18:22, and its plural form in verses 26 and 29.

22. The point is that the Pharisees specifically fastened upon Deuteronomy 24:1-4 and, in particular, upon the need for the giving of a certificate. The wider Old Testament teaching was conveniently ignored or forgotten. By being procedurally correct in the matter of the certificate, the Pharisees acquired a reputation for high standards, whereas Jesus condemns them as *detestable within the terms and requirements of the Old Testament as a whole*. The Hillelite school was clearly going well beyond what was permitted by Deuteronomy 24:1 (see note 29 in chapter 2, above). Even those who may rightly have understood the thrust of that permission, or those who interpreted the permission strictly—such as the Shammaites—were missing the purpose of Deuteronomy 24:1-4 in the context of the entire Old Testament.

23. Codex Bezae and nearly all the Syriac tradition, except for the Palestinian Syriac, omit the words *apo andros*. The existence of the words in other manuscripts, together with the fact that their absence might be explained as assimilating the verse to Matthew 5:32, means that it is more likely that Bezae et al. dropped the words, rather than that other manuscripts added them. Nestle and Kilpatrick retain the words, and relegate the shorter reading to the apparatus.

24. The Greek reads as follows: *pas ho apolyōn tēn gynaika autou kai gamōn heteran moicheuei, kai ho apolelymenēn [apo andros] gamōn moicheuei*.

25. The Talmud and the Mishnah reflect male dominance.

26. This is not a capitulation to a feminist hermeneutic. References in the Mishnah and Talmud indicate that women were somewhat subservient to men. This 'downgrading' of women was very different from the submission required of

women in the Old Testament and reaffirmed in the New Testament. Moreover, in condemning this wrong view of womanhood, Jesus was not overthrowing the distinction in gender roles found in the early chapters of Genesis, but was overturning the twisting of those distinctions which gave rise to a downgrading of women. 'Evangelical feminism' tends to view the Old Testament material on gender role differences as rooted in the Fall and the judgement that followed, and then goes on to assert that that is done away with in Christ who, in his kingdom, restores the pre-Fall position.

The Old Testament gave an honoured place to women: witness Sarah, Deborah, Ruth, Esther, Proverbs 31:10-31, the Song of Solomon, not to mention Genesis 1:26-31; 2:20-25. Luke, in particular, gives prominence to women. Thus, Elizabeth speaks out under the influence of the Holy Spirit, and Mary sings the Magnificat. Anna is a prophetess who spoke about the Christ child. It is Luke, alone, who records the incident of Mary sitting at the Lord's feet, listening to what he said. A similar emphasis is found in Acts. While we are meant to understand this emphasis upon women as being something counter-cultural to the society of Jesus' day, we must not assume that Jesus' attitude was totally revolutionary in this respect. The emphasis on women in the first two chapters of Luke makes it quite clear that there were godly women, according to the requirements of the Old Testament, who were endowed with the Holy Spirit and who exercised some kind of ministry without this being regarded as unusual. Much of the first two chapters of Luke has a specifically 'Jewish' feel to it. Elizabeth is singled out as one who was blameless and upright before the Lord (1:6). She is filled with the Spirit and makes an exclamation of praise (1:41-45). Anna spends her time in the Temple and is a prophetess; there is no hint of her having to face any kind of criticism for this.

At the same time, Jewish writings dating back to the period in question, and hints within the Gospels, demonstrate that there was a strong tendency for women to be downgraded. Luke 16:18 is particularly significant in this respect. It needs to be set in context:

> In our period, if a *get* [i.e. divorce certificate] was worded or delivered incorrectly, it was not valid, and this meant that any subsequent remarriage by the woman would also be considered invalid, and would have the status of an adulterous union. The man, however, was in theory permitted to have a second wife, as Jacob did, although one wife was the norm . . . So for a husband to remarry without correctly divorcing his first wife is not prohibited . . .
> Adultery in Jewish law is defined as follows: if a married woman has intercourse with a man who is not her husband, both parties commit adultery. If a married man has intercourse with a single woman, this is not technically adultery, since he is in theory allowed more than one wife. (Hilton and Marshall, p. 122.)

Against the above background, it is clear that in singling out the men and saying nothing about the women, Jesus was making a powerful statement concerning the way in which men were guilty of outrage.

On evangelical feminist interpretation, see the powerful critique in Piper and Grudem.

27. See note 28 in chapter 2 above, and the section in this chapter dealing with the

material found in Matthew 19.

28. A whole chapter in the Mishnah, *Gittin*, is devoted to the subject. See also the references in Matthew 5:31; 19:7, and note 26, above.

29. The references in the early chapters of Luke to Christ being presented at the Temple, and the description of Zechariah (1:5-6) are a good example of Luke's interest in the concern shown to comply with the Law. As the Gospel unfolds, we see Jesus touching a leper (5:13), healing a woman with a haemorrhage (8:43-48), and touching a dead body (8:54). In Acts, there are references to the Law (e.g. 1:12) which significantly change (chapters 10 and 11), climaxing in the Council of Jerusalem (chapter 15). It appears to be a major theme in Luke's writing, and probably arises from his recording of the spreading of the gospel to the Gentiles.

30. The danger which must be avoided is that of making the strongly absolutist statement of Jesus the 'baseline' against which every thing else must be judged. The Gospel material abounds in 'absolutist' language, which applies an underlying principle in a specific context that may not *necessarily* demand an identical application in every other context. To look no further than the Sermon on the Mount, he would be a singularly inept exegete and an incredibly dull conversation partner who would only ever say 'Yes' or 'No'. Yet Matthew 5:37 could be used to support such speech. Is Jesus saying that a Christian policeman is to allow the burglar he is about to apprehend to beat him up? Surely not, but a 'wooden' reading of the absolutist words found in Matthew 5:39 might be used to justify such behaviour. And what of giving to charity by cheque, in the light of Matthew 6:1-4, or of prayer meetings in the light of Matthew 6:5-6? Surely the all-important thing to say of much of Jesus' teaching is that, *in a specific context which controls and delimits the meaning of his words*, he teaches by way of dramatic examples of principles which are expressed in absolutist terms. So in Luke 16:18, the point he so forcefully makes, and states in absolutist language, is that the marriage commitment is intended to be paramount. By so doing, his teaching is dynamic and arresting and does not die the death of a thousand qualifications. But when one seeks to deduce principles that will apply in other contexts, it is essential to realise what has been going on, or one will be bound to 'misread' Jesus' teaching. Furthermore, Paul's words in 1 Corinthians 7:12 provide apostolic support for the view that Jesus was not setting out to cover every possible situation that might arise.

31. The evidence for this is overwhelming. The Beatitudes begin with the kingdom (5:3) and—if we regard verses 11-12 as unique within the Beatitudes—end with the kingdom (v.10). Those beatitudes which are sandwiched between are a description of life in the kingdom and are clearly 'subversive' of many messianic and kingdom expectations of Jesus' day. Verses 19-20 contrast the righteousness of the kingdom with that of the Scribes and Pharisees, while 5:21–7:12 is an exposition of this theme. The climax to the Sermon—or, to be precise, the material immediately preceding the climax—demonstrates how failure to obey the teaching Jesus has laid down will preclude many from entrance into the kingdom (7:21-23). On the interpretation of the Sermon, see Lloyd-Jones (1959), Wright (1996).

32. The approach to the Sermon which seeks to see it as no more than a series of ethical instructions with no real concern about Jesus himself—the so-called religion

of Jesus rather than *about* Jesus—is hopelessly inadequate. In 5:11-12, for example, Jesus speaks of his disciples suffering persecution 'because of me'. He goes on to compare such suffering disciples with the prophets. The point of the comparison is that the prophets suffered because of their faithfulness to Jehovah. Similarly, Jesus' disciples will suffer because of their faithfulness to him. He is implicitly distinguishing himself from the Old Testament prophets and identifying himself with Jehovah. In saying that he has come to fulfil the Old Testament Scriptures, he is effectively saying that the Law and the Prophets find their ultimate meaning and significance in him. It is against this background that his words 'But I say unto you' are to be understood.

33. Verses 21-24 are sufficient to establish that Jesus has his own day and age in view. He is envisaging a situation where the Temple is still standing and his disciples are still offering gifts. However, verses 17-18 clearly anticipate future developments. As the eschatological fulfilment of the Law and the Prophets, Jesus will supersede and replace the Temple and, with it, the Old Testament structures, etc. Thus while his teaching is expressed in the context of his time, underlying principles will apply in other contexts. This theme of Christ's eschatological fulfilment of the Old Testament and its structures is found throughout Matthew's Gospel: e.g. 2:15; 9:14-17; 11:28–12:8.

34. See notes 10 and 11 to this chapter, *supra*.

35. See notes 10 and 11, *supra*.

36. Jesus is *not* contrasting his teaching with that of the Old Testament. This would contradict what he says in verses 17-18. Verse 20 makes it quite clear that it is the Pharisaic misunderstanding which he is correcting. The repeated words, *ēkousate hoti errethē (tois archaiois)*—'you have heard that it was said (to the people long ago)'—(vv.21,27,33,38,43), are not the words which Jesus uses to quote from Scripture. When quoting Scripture, he says, *gegraptai* ('it is written') (Matt. 4:4,7,10). It is, therefore, instructive that in 5:21-48 the contrast is not, 'You have heard that it was said to the people long ago . . . but it is written'. Instead, in contrast to traditional misunderstanding Jesus says, 'But I say unto you'. The wording is emphatic, *Egō de legō hymin*, the first person singular pronoun being added for emphasis. The significance of the words Jesus uses are to be understood against the background of prophetic introductory formulae, such as 'The word of the Lord came to . . .' or 'Thus says the Lord . . .' Jesus' language is significantly different in these verses, as it also differs from other passages where he contrasts tradition with the Old Testament (e.g. Matt. 15:3-5). This confirms the general hermeneutical approach we are adopting to the Sermon on the Mount in general, and to verses 17-18, which is that Jesus is representing himself and the kingdom as the eschatological fulfilment of the Law and the Prophets.

37. The reference in verse 41 is to a Roman official who could compel someone to carry something (cf. 27:32). In a sermon expounding the theme of the kingdom of God, the Roman occupation of Palestine is never far from thought.

38. In verses 21 and 33, the longer words of introduction are used: *ēkousate hoti errethē tois archaiois* (= you have heard that it was said to the people long ago). In verses 27, 38 and 43, the shorter introduction is used: *ēkousate hoti errethē* (= you have heard that it was said). (It is true that some manuscripts and versions have the longer wording in verse 27, but the textual evidence for its inclusion here is

weak, and is to be accounted for by a copyist assimilating the words to that of verse 21.) However, verse 31 simply says, *errethē de* (= and it was said). The absence of *ēkousate* (= you have heard) and the presence of *de* suggest that verse 31 is continuing from verse 30. (This belief is strengthened by the fact that *de* functions, in this verse, strictly as a conjunction rather than as a stylistic connective. That this is the case may be inferred from the fact that *de* is not used as a connective to introduce any of the other antitheses.)

39. The verse reads as follows: *ho blepōn gynaika pros to epithymēsai autēn ēdē emoicheusen autēn en tē kardia autou.*

40. *Ho blepōn.*

41. It is true that *gynē* can mean 'wife' as well as 'woman'. Indeed, BAG assign this meaning of 'wife' to *gynē* in this particular verse. Certainly, as BAG indicate, it bears this meaning in verse 31. However, it is respectfully submitted that this is *not* the meaning in verse 28. In every other occurrence where the word clearly means 'wife', this is obvious either from the surrounding context or from the presence of a possessive pronoun or a genitive of possession. For example, in verse 31, the mention of a divorce certificate makes it clear that *gynaika* there denotes 'wife', and this is confirmed by the word *autou*. In 14:3, the words *tēn gynaika* are followed by *Philippou*. In 18:25, the context makes it abundantly clear that *tēn gynaika kai ta tekna* refers to his wife and children, and this is further underlined by the words *kai panta hosa echei*. The same holds true for the other references given by BAG. However, this is not the case with Matthew 5:28. Had Jesus been referring to another man's wife, we might have expected him to say *gynaika androu* or something similar. He does not. Nor may it be argued that, in speaking of adultery, it must be presumed that the woman was married, else according to his hearers' expectations and understanding, adultery would not have been committed: for the whole point of Jesus' teaching at this place is that he is challenging the prevailing understanding. In speaking of adultery in the heart, he is subverting his hearers' understanding and challenging the current belief.

It is, of course, true that there are a number of passages in the New Testament where *gynē* has been translated as 'woman', but the translation has been challenged. The two passages that have occasioned most difficulty are 1 Timothy 2:11 and 3:11. Some, such as Barnett, have argued that the reference in 2:11 is to a wife, while others such as Knight and Moo have argued that it refers to women in general. The point, however, is that whichever way one interprets the verse, there *are* contextual factors which demand that Barnett's position be seriously considered even if one disagrees with it, as I do. The same may be said for 3:11. But these contextual considerations are not present in Matthew 5:28. Indeed, the verse makes perfect sense if one understands Jesus to be referring to any woman. A man who looks after a woman to lust after her has committed adultery with her in his heart. Is it conceivable that, in a passage where he is distancing himself from that approach which immerses itself in legal niceties and technicalities, Jesus could have said something like this: if the man does not know the woman, then if she is married, he has committed adultery with her; though if she is single, he has not done so? Surely not. Nor can one say that Jesus is referring to a man who lusts after a woman *whom he knows to be another man's wife*. The verse does not say that. If *gynaika* denotes 'wife' in this verse, we are left with the absurd position that men who lust their eyes out in looking at women who happen to be single—though the men are unaware of the marital status of the women—are all right, but other men who look lustfully, though not as habitually, at married women are guilty of adultery. This is the very casuistry of the scribes and Pharisees that Jesus is seeking to counter!

42. Verse 30 is authentic. It is only missing from one uncial manuscript, Codex Bezae, and from a few unimportant manuscripts as well as from the Syriac version, sys.

43. The words *kai hos ean apolelymenēn gamēsē, moichatai* are omitted from Codex Bezae and some miniscules. The witnesses to the shorter reading are both few and of little weight, when compared with the evidence for the longer reading. Moreover, there are significant differences in the wording of verse 32 when compared with Luke 16:18, which make it virtually certain that the longer reading has not been added in Matthew to assimilate it to Luke.

44. BAG give as one of the uses of *de*, 'relating one teaching to another', citing Matthew 5:31 as an example.

45. Verse 31 reads: *Hos an apolysē tēn gynaika autou, dotō autē apostasion. Apolyein* is a standard term, which means 'to put away' in the sense of divorcing, while *apostasion* refers to the certificate of divorce, of which Deuteronomy 24:1 speaks. The fuller designation is *biblion apostasiou*.

46. The Mishnah tractate *Gittin* deals with certificates of divorce and is preoccupied with how and when these may be drawn up and given. Any legal system must, of course, address questions of procedure and formality, and there is nothing wrongly legalistic about this. What is wrong is to become so preoccupied with technical procedures that one loses sight of why those procedures are there. When following the correct procedures leads to manifest injustice, it is time to change the procedure. If the procedure was divinely stipulated, then only a divine edict can change it. If following the procedure works manifest immorality and sin, it may well mean that one has wrenched the procedure out of its context and is following it in isolation from wider and greater concerns about which God has spoken. This was precisely the situation Jesus was addressing.

47. We have already, in the previous chapter, noted the basis upon which a woman might request her husband to divorce her. Although we have also seen that rabbinic Judaism did not regard it as adulterous for a married man to have sexual relations with an unmarried woman, since the man was, in theory, permitted to have a second wife, it should be noted that 'there is not a single case of bigamy among the thousands of stories about the Rabbis in the Mishnah and the Talmud' (Hilton and Marshall, p. 122). It is possible—particularly in view of the preceding context—that two types of situation were leading to men divorcing their wives. Firstly, a man desired another woman and therefore divorced his wife. Secondly, having desired another woman, he treated his first wife in such a shameful way that she requested him to divorce her because of his breach of his marriage contract. Significantly, as Brewer notes, the Mishnaic tractate *Ketuboth* contains a discussion on the frequency of sexual relations within marriage, the Hillelites concluding that a husband may abstain for only one week, and the Shammaites allowing a man to abstain for two weeks (*Ketuboth* 5:6). It is not difficult to see how a man who was consumed with lust for another woman

might deprive his wife, and she in consequence request a divorce. The point would, however, be that it had been his behaviour which had forced the situation and, though divorcing her at his request, the situation was hardly different from that where he would divorce her before he would marry the woman for whom he was lusting.

48. The verb *poiei* indicates that the man, in divorcing her, is forcing her into a situation not of her own making.

49. *Moicheuthēnai.*

50. *Moichatai.* In verses 27-28, the verb *moicheuō* is in the active voice. In verse 32*a* it is in the passive voice (note 49, above), and in verse 32*b* it is in the middle voice. The contrast between verses 27-28 and 32*b* may lead one to assume that the middle voice is of significance in verse 32*b*. The following considerations indicate that the middle voice in verse 32*b* bears an active meaning. Firstly, as a very general rule, it is right to say that the middle is a kind-of-active rather than a kind-of-passive. Secondly, the situation envisaged in verse 32*b* is identical to that envisaged in Luke 16:18*b*. In that verse the active voice of the verb is used, while in this verse it is the middle. The reason for the middle voice in verse 32*b* is probably as follows. In verses 27-28, Jesus refers to a man committing adultery. In verse 32, he considers what happens when a man divorces his wife. Firstly, he forces her to suffer something done to her: he has created the situation. In remarrying she is something of a victim of her first husband's act. The first husband is *the* villain of the piece, and something of a distinction is made between him and the second man by placing the second man's action in the middle voice. However, because the middle bears an active meaning in this verse, the second husband is *not* a victim in the way in which the woman is a victim. Murray is right to reject Lenski's understanding of the second man's action. Lenski understands the second man to be stigmatised as an adulterer, whereas, in fact, something has been done against him.

The fact that the middle voice in verse 32*b* bears an active meaning stands in contrast, therefore, to the passive in verse 32*a*. Thayer gives the meaning of the passive of *moicheuō in* this verse as follows: 'to suffer adultery; to be debauched'. BAG differ somewhat from Thayer: referring to occasions where the verb has as object *tina (gynaika)* (= commit adultery with someone), it says: 'This explains the use of the passive in the case of the woman . . . *poiei autēn moicheuthēnai* he causes her to commit adultery [by contracting a subsequent marriage] Mt. 5:32; 19:9 v. 1 . . .' The point to be decided here is whether the woman is guilty of being an adulteress—albeit in a lesser way than the man who divorces her and the man who subsequently marries her—or whether she is an innocent victim. A number of factors indicate that Jesus means us to understand that she is a victim. First of all, we have already seen that the prevailing understanding of divorce and adultery was heavily weighted in the man's favour against the woman. Jesus' teaching must be understood in that context. Secondly, we have had cause to note the almost studied absence of reference to the woman's sin in Luke 16:18. Thirdly, Matthew 5:27-28 is dealing exclusively with the sin of the man. In verse 31, Jesus describes the prevailing practice, which, the men thought, left them perfectly acceptable before God. He now describes that practice as one in which the woman is forced to have something happen to her. This is the effect of linking *poieō* with the passive of *moicheuō*. In what way does she suffer the experience of adultery? There are two possible answers. First, her vulnerability is such that she will marry again. Support for this understanding may be found in two facts: the divorce certificate declared that a woman was free to marry another, and verse 32*b* envisages this as happening. Thus, she is in an adulterous relationship, but it is not really of her making: her first husband has created the situation. The second possible answer is that she has suffered the repudiation of her marriage relationship. Which understanding is to be preferred?

Although it is true that verse 32*b* clearly envisages the woman remarrying, there are weighty reasons for rejecting the first interpretation. The interpretation is built upon the understanding that the one-flesh union created at marriage is indissoluble; therefore to marry someone when one is already in a one-flesh union with someone is to be guilty of adultery. However, we have already seen that Jesus taught that divorce ended the one-flesh union. That being so, adultery does not consist in physically joining oneself to someone when one is already married to someone else. That is a species of adultery, but it is not the genus, as verse 28 has demonstrated. The essence of adultery consists in the attitude which undermines God's institution of marriage and expresses itself in acts which may undermine specific marriages or serve to disrupt marriage. This understanding makes perfect sense of verses 27-32, and is consistent with Jesus' teaching, in Matthew 19:6, that divorce severs that union. The lusting of verse 28 is a trampling upon the sanctity of marriage, in which sexual desire may legitimately be expressed. The man of verse 32 causes his wife to suffer the repudiation of her marriage. The man who subsequently marries her is part of an entire system, which exploited women and left them at the mercy of men: it was a system which effectively undermined and repudiated the divine intention of marriage. If Thayer's understanding of the passive is accepted, it is difficult to see how the woman can be anything other than a victim.

51. See note 50, above.

52. The English versions translate two Greek words, *parektos logou*. *Logou* poses no real problem, being the genitive of *logos*, which in this context bears the meaning 'matter of' or 'cause of'. This translates in English usage quite readily into 'in the case of'. How should *parektos* be translated? In Matthew 5:32 it is used as a preposition with the genitive. In such cases it means 'except', 'apart from'. Thus Thayer, referring to this verse and to Acts 26:29, gives the meaning 'except, with the exception of'. Abbott-Smith assigns the same meaning, while BAG give 'apart from, except for'. Used as a preposition followed by the genitive, the term is found in the New Testament only in Matthew 5:32 and Acts 26:29. Some manuscripts have the term in Matthew 19:9, but, as we shall see when considering that verse, it is almost certainly not the original reading. The only other occurrence of the word is in 2 Corinthians 11:28. It is used there as an adverb and has the meaning 'besides'. In addition to its use in the New Testament, it is found in a number of other writings. Heth and Wenham quote Kirsopp Lake's translation of *Didache* 6.1: 'See "that no one make thee to err" from the Way of the teaching, for he teacheth thee *without* God.' 'Without' is the rendering of *parektos*. Heth and Wenham quote Robertson, who states that *parektos* followed by the genitive means 'without'. However, it would seem that the use of the term in the *Didache* is similar to the meaning assigned by BAG to the term: 'apart

from, except for'. In support of this meaning is the usage of it in *The Testimony of the twelve patriarchs of Zebulun*, 1.4: 'I am not conscious that I have sinned all my days, *save* in thought.' 'Save' is the rendering of *parektos*. BAG also cite a Latin translation of the words *parektos emou* in *Dositheus* 45, 3. The Latin rendering is *praeter me*. *Praeter* = 'except, apart from, beyond'. This being the case, it is difficult to see how the 'preteritive' understanding of the exception can be sustained. This interpretation understands the phrase as a parenthesis or 'no comment'. Vawter's translation of verse 32 runs as follows: 'everyone who divorces his wife—setting aside the matter of *porneia*—makes her become an adulteress'. This means that *logou porneias* is completely excluded from consideration, rather than being an exception to the statement that whoever divorces his wife causes her to suffer adultery. The evidence adduced by BAG would indicate that the proper translation should be along the following lines: 'whoever divorces his wife *except for* [or, *apart from*] the cause of *porneia* . . .' Jesus is stating an exception to the statement that a woman who has been divorced by her husband is made to suffer adultery.

In view of the above, it is *a fortiori* illegitimate to assign an 'inclusivist' meaning to *parektos*. This would lead to the following translation: 'whoever divorces his wife, *even for the cause of porneia*, causes her to suffer adultery'. Hagner notes that while alteration of *mē* in Matthew 19:9 to *mēd(e)* could mean 'not even', and while Vawter's 'preteritive' understanding of 19:9—'passing over'—might be made out, this will not work in 5:32. (No comment is being made, at this point, on Hagner's treatment of Matthew 19:9.) Heth and Wenham—who canvass the preteritive view and the inclusivist understanding of the words as well as any—conclude that *parektos* in 5:32 'must be given an *exclusive*, not an *inclusive* sense'. They quote Moule, who says: '[it] occurs in the NT . . . as a preposition, with [the] Gen. = apart from, except'. The attempt to understand *parektos* in this verse as bearing a meaning other than 'except, apart from' must be judged a failure. Here is a genuine exception to the teaching that a man who divorces his wife causes her to suffer adultery.

53. See note 50, *supra*, for the reasons for understanding Jesus to be referring to the woman as 'suffering adultery'.

54. The name 'redaction criticism' has been used in a variety of ways for the study of the way in which the Gospels were written. In some hands, this is part and parcel of a thoroughly liberal approach to Scripture, while some evangelicals have used it somewhat inconsistently when it has suited their purpose, but dropped it when it might lead to unacceptable conclusions. However, it may be used in a perfectly consistent way by those with an evangelical doctrine of Scripture, when its use is limited to dealing with questions such as why one Gospel writer records an incident or saying which is passed over by another Evangelist; or when it is used to consider what purpose, if any, is being served by the same incident or saying being recorded in different words from the record in another Gospel. Furthermore, the way in which material is being organised may also have a significance in one Gospel which it might not have in another. My treatment of Luke 16:18 is a modest example of the way in which this approach may yield positive results. On the evangelical use of redaction criticism, see the excellent essay by D. A. Carson, 'Redaction Criticism: On the Legitimacy and Illegitimacy of a Literary Tool' in Carson and Woodbridge (1983).

55. Some of the reasons for holding this belief to be mistaken and unnecessary will be given when considering Paul's reference to Christ's teaching in 1 Corinthians 7.

56. Some understand Mishnah, *Gittin* 9.10, in this way. For example, Hilton and Marshall make this comment: 'Community pressure could prevent people treating divorce lightly: but the interpretation of the grounds for divorce was, except perhaps in cases of adultery, left in the hands of every husband. In other cases *there would be no obligation on him to divorce his wife . . .'* (p. 127; *italics mine*). The clear implication of this sentence is that there *was* an obligation to divorce where there was adultery. Hilton is rabbi of Menorah Synagogue, Cheadle, Cheshire. Thus, a present-day rabbi understands this part of the Mishnah as indicating the obligation to divorce in a case of adultery. See also Hertz, p. 931.

57. For example, Murray.

58. 'Perhaps the most characteristic feature of the Jewish Law of Divorce is its absolute prohibition of the adulterer to marry the adulteress' (Hertz, p. 933).

59. The wording is: *Kai egeneto hote etelesen ho lēsous tous logous toutous.* Codex Bezae and the Old Latin versions support the reading *hote elalesen*. This amounts to no real change of substance and is not to be preferred to the reading on which the English versions are based. Since there are a number of variant readings in this passage, most of them of no real significance, we shall not treat textual issues in this passage separately until we come to verse 9, where there are important variant readings.

60. 7:28; 11:1; 13:53; 26:1.

61. The behaviour of the disciples in, for example, Matthew 19:13 was something which they had not learned from Jesus. If Jesus' disciples could manifest an attitude so far from that of their Lord himself, it is not unreasonable to assume that those who were not his disciples would certainly express similar attitudes. This was an attitude which Jesus' disciples had to unlearn.

62. See note 61.

63. Josephus gives interesting information on this. In *Ant.* XVIII. v. 1, he relates Antipas' plan to divorce his wife and marry Herodias. In XVIII. v. 4, we are told that Herodias 'took upon her to confound the laws of our country, and divorce herself from her husband, while he was still alive, and was married to Herod [Antipas], her husband's brother by the father's side'. On the question as to whether Herodias 'divorced' her husband or merely separated from him and then married Antipas, see note 127, *infra*.

64. The English translates the Greek participle *peirazontes*. The verb *peirazō* is used a number of times in Matthew's Gospel of attempts to trap Jesus by what he says. For example, in Matthew 22:15, the Pharisees 'laid plans to trap [Jesus] in his words'. The verb used on that occasion is *pagideusōsin (pagideuō)*; this is a hunting term and is employed in the LXX of setting a snare or a trap. In verse 18, Jesus asks the Pharisees why they are trying to trap him, and the verb there is *peirazo*. The verb is used again in 22:35. Clearly, therefore, *peirazo*, which denotes trying and testing, also connotes the idea of trapping. The idea conveyed in Matthew 19:3 by *Kai proselthon autō Pharisaioi peirazontes auton kai legontes . . .* is that the Pharisees were intent on trapping him.

I am not disputing the fact that the reference to 'testing' was part and parcel of rabbinic debate, where a question might be asked 'to try someone out', in order to see 'what they were made of'. However, on a number of occasions Matthew clearly indicates that the Pharisees, while using the language of rabbinic debate, were seeking to trap Jesus.

65. It is John who records the fact that Jesus was regarded as a rabbi: see John 1:38, 49; 3:2; 6:25; 20:16.

66. To begin with, Matthew has already recorded Jesus' teaching on divorce in 5:31-32. That teaching was given openly so that the crowds could hear (5:1; 7:28). It was hardly a trap to ask him to restate what he had already declared quite openly. On the basis of what Jesus had already said in 5:31-32, it may well have been that the Pharisees understood Jesus to be taking a Shammaite view. If so, they could hardly have expected him to appear exposed and vulnerable by endorsing a view which was held within established Judaism. It may be thought that the trap lay in the fact that, having endorsed a Shammaite position, Jesus could then be trapped by further questions, which might have exposed inconsistency in the Shammaite position. For the reasons given in the body of the text, I do not think that this exposes the real nature of the trap that was laid.

Brewer has said to me, in a personal conversation, that the significance of the location recorded in verse 1 may well reside in the fact that the Pharisees of Judea would be more sophisticated than those of Galilee and that Jesus was being presented with a greater test. Moreover, many of the population would have had relatives who had been divorced, and many would have followed Hillel. Accordingly, the test lay in seeking to elicit Jesus' views on this subject. I make the following reply. First, Matthew has, quite early on, presented Jesus as possessed of an authority that clearly set him apart from the teachers of his day (7:29). Secondly, Jesus was quite prepared to alienate a considerable portion of the religious society of his day: his words in Matthew 5:20 would have won him few friends amongst the Pharisees. Thirdly, Jesus did not adapt his message to court popularity with the masses. The uncompromising lifestyle set forth in the Sermon on the Mount makes that very clear. Fourthly, Jesus had already made an attack on the Hillelite view of divorce in Matthew 5:31-32. Given that the Pharisees well understood Jesus' fearlessness and boldness, and his imperviousness to popular opinion (Matt. 22:16), it is difficult to see how the question which they posed would have constituted much of a trap unless more lay behind it. Moreover, Jesus' words in Matthew 26:55 demonstrate that he did not wish to keep his teaching secret from the crowds, and that he was in no way intimidated by the religious teachers of Judea. If we credit the Pharisees with any measure of intelligence and cunning, we must conclude that more lies behind their question than an invitation for Jesus to speak upon a matter upon which he had already been pretty forthright.

67. Matthew 22:15 records the fact that the Pharisees sought to trap Jesus in his words. Verse 16 specifically states that they sent their disciples to him along with the Herodians.

68. For example, in Matthew 21:23 the question posed is not a sincere desire to be instructed, as becomes clear in verses 25-26. This is the reason for Jesus' counter-question in verse 25, and his refusal in verse 27 to answer the question put. Matthew 22:15-22 records the question concerning payment of taxes to Caesar. This was also a trap question, and elicited the devastating reply of verse 21.

69. Carson (1987), pp. 75-6.

70. The meaning is unaffected, whichever reading of the text one accepts. The text behind NIV reads, *Ouk anegnōte hoti ho ktisas ap' archēs* . . . A number of manuscripts, and Textus Receptus on which the AV is based, have *poiēsas* in place of *ktisas*. Little, if any, significance attaches to these different readings, since both are emphasising that it is the Creator (*ho ktisas*) who made them male and female (*ho poiēsas ap' archēs* being a clear reference to the Creator of Genesis 1).

71. The Temple Scroll refers to Genesis 1:27. On the Temple Scroll, see Yadin.

72. Brewer has called attention to the significance of marriage contracts (Tyndale Bulletin 1996; Non-Academic 1996). However, while agreeing with some of Brewer's conclusions with respect to divorce, I do not think he gives sufficient weight to the fact that Jesus' teaching was, in many ways, a contrast to this emphasis.

73. The New Testament use of Old Testament material, particularly when the New Testament *quotes* the Old Testament, is a huge and complex subject. Suffice it to say that there is evidence to indicate that quotations of verses were sometimes intended to evoke material associated with the verses quoted. In the present case, the quotation might well have evoked the teaching found in verses 28-30 of Genesis 1, which confers dignity upon the woman and equality between man and woman *in their standing before God.* On the New Testament use of the Old, see the essay by Moo, 'The Problem of Sensus Plenior' in Carson and Woodbridge (1986).

74. It is quite clear that the New Testament treats Adam's primogeniture as of ongoing significance for male/female relationships. 1 Corinthians 11:2-16, especially vv.7-12, deals with this matter, as does 1 Timothy 2:12-13. The influence of feminist hermeneutics, even within evangelicalism, has led to strenuous attempts to evacuate these passages of any reference to divinely ordained gender distinctive roles. While it is undoubtedly true that some treatments which have argued for divinely ordained gender distinctive roles have lacked exegetical sensitivity and, having assumed what they have sought to prove, have failed to respond adequately to feminist criticisms of 'traditional' exegesis, it has to be said that the feminist case has not only not been made out but has been shown to be untenable. However, in arguing from Scripture for divinely ordained gender distinctive roles, we must beware of failure to give equal prominence to the fact that *before* the creation account of man and woman in Genesis 2, we have the account of Genesis 1. This chapter asserts that gender differences were part of God's original plan and that the creation of woman was not some divine afterthought. Moreover, underlying the diversity entailed by male and female is the unity and equality specified by the fact that both male and female are God's image-bearers. On the biblical teaching on male/female relationships in general, see Piper and Grudem. For treatment of the Genesis passages and Pauline material which interacts with and criticises feminist interpretation, also see Piper and Grudem.

75. Jesus did not say *en archē* but *ap' archēs*. The NIV translates 'at the beginning', as does the AV. However, the idea conveyed is '*from* the beginning'. Thus BAG give as one of the uses of the preposition *apo*: 'To denote the point from which something begins, in literal and figurative meaning'. Of time, they give the meaning

as 'from—(on), since'. The point is that Jesus is saying that something which God began at the beginning is continuing at the present. The support for this reading is very strong, and the omission of the words from the Syriac version, Sinaiticus (not to be confused with the uncial manuscript Sinaiticus), and a number of minuscules, is of no real significance.

76. There is a very slight difference. The LXX has *heneken* whereas Matthew has *heneka*.

77. It has been argued, for example by Brown, that no significance attaches to the words 'she shall be called'. The argument is as follows. In 2:20, 'the man gave names to all the livestock'; in 3:20, we are told, 'Adam named his wife Eve'. Therefore, the naming of the woman occurs *after* the Fall, and any gender specific submission required of the woman is, therefore, rooted in human sin and not in the original creation. But this does not follow. In saying 'she shall be called', Adam *was* naming her, but the wording is significantly different from verse 20, for he is now naming his equal. In 3:20, Adam gives the woman an added name: in chapter 2 he has named woman *qua* woman, whereas in chapter 3 he names the specific woman to whom he is married. In the context, although this naming occurs after sin has entered, it is an act of faith on Adam's part reflecting upon God's grace contained in the promise of 3:15, and the announcement of blessing and judgement in 3:16.

78. The presence of the word *sarx* towards the end of the sentence means that Jesus is specifying that they are no longer two but one *flesh*.

79. The verb used is *syzeugnymi*.

80. The clause in Greek is *anthrōpos mē chōrizetō*. The verb is in the third person singular, and is in the active voice and imperative mood. As such it amounts to a command. A general sentence, 'Let man not separate', can be specifically applied to a given case as 'Do not separate', in the second person singular, active imperative. What needs to be stressed is that Jesus does *not* say that separating is a metaphysical impossibility, and that it *cannot* be done. Rather, he is saying that it is a metaphysical possibility which man is forbidden to do.

81. There is clearly in this verse a contrast between man as creature and God as Creator. Moreover, the word for man is *anthrōpos*, which is the generic word for man as human, rather than *anēr*, which is the term for man as distinct from woman. Nevertheless, this point should not be overemphasised, since in verse 5 *anthrōpos* has been used of the man leaving his father and mother and then being united to his wife. In that verse, *anthrōpos* must mean man as male. In verse 6, therefore, Jesus may be rebuking the Pharisees for asking the question which they did: it was men who were separating what God had joined by putting away their wives, and that was something that should not be done.

82. Thayer points out that the verb *chōrizō* is used in verse 6 as effecting the opposite of *syzeugnymi*. Moreover, this is effected by the *apolyō* of verse 3. It is important to bear in mind the interrelationship of these terms, particularly in order to understand aright the teaching in 1 Corinthians 7.

83. It might be thought that, although wording it as a 'why' question, they are still concerned with ascertaining the grounds of divorce. 'Why did Moses command the giving of a certificate of divorce?' is then essentially the same as 'For what reasons did Moses command that a certificate of divorce be given?' But this is

not the meaning of the question. What the Pharisees are asking is something like this: 'If man should not separate what God has joined together, and if such separation is effected by the giving of a divorce certificate, why on earth did Moses command the giving of a certificate of divorce, since that would effect what is contrary to the divine will?' This is clearly the import of the question, as may be inferred from the presence of the conjunction *oun* (then): 'why *then* did Moses command . . .?'

84. We saw in the previous chapter that the procedural requirement of the giving of the certificate was, if divorce was to take place, a mandatory requirement of the Mosaic law. Secondly, the Mishnah devotes an entire section, *Gittin*, to the formalities of the drawing up and delivery of the certificate.

85. That the Pharisees regarded themselves as 'disciples' of Moses is well attested in the Gospels. Jesus refers to this in Matthew 23:2. John 9:2-29 brings this out very clearly. The Pharisees claim to be Moses' disciples and contrast this with being Christ's disciples. In verse 29, they explain that they knew that God had spoken to Moses, but nobody even knew where 'this fellow' came from. This claim to follow Moses, and the contrast the Pharisees drew between Moses and Jesus, clearly lie behind the question in Matthew 19:7. It is against this background that we are to understand Jesus' teaching in passages such as Matthew 15:1-7 and John 5:45-47, where Jesus says that the Pharisees do not really follow Moses, but that he does understand Moses' teaching. In Matthew 19 we are very much in the same world of thought as we find in Matthew 5:31-32 and Luke 16:16-18.

86. The words are *sklērokardian hymōn*. I have referred earlier to the view that Jesus was reproducing the Mosaic teaching on divorce. These words indicate that Jesus is contrasting his teaching with that of Moses. We are not to think that Jesus is making concessions to human hard-heartedness. The fact that he is not making such a concession demonstrates that something different from the Mosaic teaching is now being presented. However, Brewer (1996) has argued that Deuteronomy 24:1 refers to marital unfaithfulness and, in a personal conversation, has related the hard-heartedness to the unfaithfulness of the wife: thus Moses allowed divorce because of the sin of the woman. But this position is demonstrably unsustainable. The sentence reads: *hoti Mōüsēs pros tēn sklērokardian hymō n epetrepsen hymin apolysai tas gynaikas hymōn* (Moses on account of the hardness of *your* hearts permitted *you* to put away *your* wives). The personal pronoun used here is the second person plural. The first occasion it is in the genitive, to indicate that it was because of *your* hardness of heart that Moses gave the permission. The second occasion it is in the dative because Moses was giving permission *to you*. The third time it is again in the genitive because Moses had given permission to you to put away *your wives*. The reference must, therefore, be to the husbands, since it is the wives who are being put away. Jesus is saying that Moses allowed divorce precisely because of the hardness of heart of the men. And this must mean that if Jesus were allowing divorce for the same reason, he too would be making a concession to hard-heartedness. It makes much better sense to say that he is now removing this concession.

87. This, of course, had been made clear by Moses: Deuteronomy 7:7.

88. The classic treatments of this theme are found in Romans and Galatians. Romans 3:2 emphasises the privilege of being entrusted with God's Word, and

3:21 testifies to the law's positive role in bearing witness to the righteousness of God which came in Jesus Christ. However, 5:13-20 draws attention to an immediately more negative effect of the law, and this theme is developed in chapter 7. The argument in Galatians 3 proceeds on the basis that the promise was given to Abraham not by law. The law was added later and could not annul the promise. It was added because of transgressions until the promised Seed had come. The immediately negative effect of the law was ultimately positive by being preparatory to the coming of Christ and the coming of faith. However, with the coming of Christ it had fulfilled its purpose, and to return to it was in effect to return to the principles of the world (4:9).

It is appropriate to note, 'It is sometimes stated in rabbinic arguments that God gave various laws as a concession to man's weakness . . . Rabbinic thought more often regards subsequent generations as gradually getting worse, rather than better, and requiring more concessions rather than less' (Hilton and Marshall, p. 132). This observation gives added significance to Jesus' words in verse 9.

89. God's dealings with the antediluvian saints and with the patriarchs confirm that grace and mercy and covenant existed apart from, and prior to, the Mosaic law.

90. Carson, 1996.

91. The verse bristles with textual problems. The Nestle Kilpatrick (1958) edition of the Greek New Testament reads: *legō de hymin hoti hos an apolysē tēn gynaika autou mē epi porneia kai gamēsē allēn, moichatai.* This reading has been accepted by numerous editors of critical editions of the New Testament. The first variant readings within the verse relate to the words *mē epi porneia.* The weight of evidence supports this reading. *Parektos logou porneias* is found in Vaticanus and Codex Bezae, and is supported by most of the Old Latin versions. We shall see later that the *meaning* is unaffected, whether the words are *mē epi porneia* or *parektos logou porneias.* However, the former reading is to be preferred. The latter reading is almost certainly an assimilation to the wording of Matthew 5:32, as will become even clearer when we consider further variants within this verse. Bengel's first principle, that the form of the text that best explains all other forms is most likely to be the original, leads, as we shall see, to the reading accepted by Nestle Kilpatrick, which was also accepted by Tischendorf, Westcott and Hort, von Soden, and Souter. A small number of manuscripts read *ei mē epi.* This is the reading found in Textus Receptus. As we shall see when we consider the meaning of the exceptive clause, this reading would make the clause somewhat more straightforward and would certainly rule out the preterite understanding of these words. However, the paucity of evidence for it, coupled with the fact that it more completely assimilates the *meaning* of the words of exception to Matthew 5:32 and that *mē epi porneia* is a slightly more difficult reading, all suggest that *ei* was added at some stage and should not, therefore, be accepted.

The next variant reading in the text undoubtedly has the most important implications. Vaticanus, and a large number of manuscripts, omit the words *kai gamēsē allēn.* This is the *only* occasion where the Gospels record Jesus referring to a man who has been justified in divorcing his wife, going on to remarry. (The evidence that Jesus is justifying the divorce in this verse will be adduced later.) Accordingly, as Murray notes, it might be thought that acceptance of the reading which omits these words would help to resolve some of the apparent difficulties in the Gospel accounts of Christ's teaching. Moreover, it might be argued that Paul's citation of Christ's teaching in 1 Corinthians 7:11 emphatically rules out remarriage. Since Paul would have faithfully recorded Christ's teaching, it might be argued that the text found in Vaticanus is that which is nearest to the original. Attractive as this proposal might appear, there are overwhelming arguments against it. To begin with, the great textual scholars who were agreed in accepting the reading which includes *kai gamēsē allēn* must have felt there were good reasons for retaining these words. Chief among these reasons may well have been the fact that Vaticanus and those manuscripts which omit these words also have the reading *parektos logou porneias* and, in place of *moichatai*, have *poiei autēn moicheuthēnai*. This, of course, is a clear assimilation to Matthew 5:32. The reading we have accepted can account for this variant in terms of such assimilation. Moreover, particularly in the light of the uniqueness of the express mention of remarriage, this reading is the more difficult and is, therefore, more likely to be the original. Furthermore, as Murray points out, the impressive witnesses which support Vaticanus in the reading *parektos logou porneias* do *not* agree with it in the omission of the words *kai gamēsē allēn*. Thus Codex Bezae retains the words. As Murray says,

> It should be noted that, as far as the sense of the passage is concerned, it is not the reading *parektos logou porneias* that is crucial; as far as meaning is concerned this has the same effect as *mē epi porneia*. It is the second clause, *poiei autēn moicheuthēnai*, that makes the crucial difference. And it is surely significant that, although [Vaticanus] enlists a good deal of collateral support in the clause that makes no difference to the sense, it decidedly loses support in the clause that introduces crucial divergence in the meaning of the passage. In other words, the reading of [Vaticanus] weakens the farther it goes in assimilation to Matthew 5:32 and the farther it proceeds in changing the entire force of the passage.

The weight of manuscript evidence in favour of retaining the words, together with the fact that the omission of them is almost certainly an assimilation to Matthew 5:32, and the fact that the retention of the words gives the more difficult reading which can best explain the history of the text, are powerful reasons for holding to the genuineness of the words. As for the argument from Paul's words in 1 Corinthians, consideration of Paul's teaching will be found in the next chapter. Suffice it to say at this point, that while this may be the only *express* reference by Jesus to remarriage, we have already seen in Matthew 5:32 that the *concept* of divorce employed by Jesus entails the possibility of remarriage. This being so, an exception to his prohibition of divorce implies the possibility of remarriage and, therefore, omission of the reference to remarriage in this verse does not necessarily resolve apparent difficulties.

There is one other part of the verse which has variant readings. The Nestle Kilpatrick text ends with the word *moichatai*. This reading is attested by Codex Sinaiticus and Codex Bezae, as well as by a large number of manuscripts, and is supported by the Old Latin versions and the Syriac versions Sinaiticus and Nitriensis. However, a number of uncials, including Vaticanus, together with other minuscules and the Vulgate, support the reading *kai ho apolelymenēn gamēsas moichatai*. Some of these witnesses have *gamōn* instead of *gamēsas*. This reading is found in Textus Receptus. It seems fairly clear that this reading is an assimilation to Matthew 5:32, and that different witnesses are assimilated to varying degrees to that verse, Vaticanus being assimilated most of all. The Nestle Kilpatrick text should be accepted as representing the best reading. However, even were there to be dispute on this point, *the* crucial element which is specific to Matthew 19:9 concerns the reference to remarriage. The evidence for omitting that reference is extremely weak and should not be accepted. If, instead of the Nestle Kilpatrick text, a reading were accepted based on the manuscripts which assimilate to Matthew 5:32 and which contain the reference to remarriage, the teaching found in this verse would not be affected, since the new element in the verse would be retained, and the longer reading would simply repeat or duplicate what is found in Matthew 5:32.

92. The AV translates it, while the NIV omits it.

93. This is a huge subject, which is well beyond the scope and purpose of the present work. But these points are so important that they dare not be missed. Matthew's Gospel is dominated by the theme of Jesus fulfilling the Old Testament. This is frequently expressed, but it is just as frequently entailed or implied by things Jesus says. The fulfilment inevitably has implications for the Temple, the worship of the Temple, the Sabbath, the nation of Israel, etc. John and Matthew develop these themes. It is noteworthy that sandwiched between the question of Jesus' authority and the questions on 'the day of questions' is the counter-question of Matthew 21:28, and the Parables of the Two Sons, the Wicked Tenants, and the Wedding Banquet. Matthew 22:8-10 is a clear reference to the rejection of Israel and to the Gentile mission, while 21:43 specifically states that the kingdom will be taken from the nation of Israel and given to those who will produce fruit: their hearts will not be hard. Likewise, in Matthew 19 Jesus concludes his words to the Pharisees in reply to a trap question with an implied reference to the redefining of the people of God.

Wright (1996) has some extremely penetrating observations on these words. While certainly not agreeing with everything Wright says in this work, and not agreeing with everything in the following quotation (the reference to Exile is, I believe, somewhat misconceived: see Eveson's critique of Wright's use of the Exile motif in the New Testament), he has, nevertheless, said something of considerable importance:

> Deuteronomy . . . is part of a *temporary phase* in the purposes of YHWH. It was necessary because of the ambiguous situation, in which Israel was called to be the people of God, but was still a people with *hard hearts*. Israel cannot be affirmed as she stands. She is still in exile, still hard-hearted; but the new day is dawning in which the 'Mosaic dispensation is not adequate', since 'Jesus expected there to be a better order' [the words quoted are from Sanders, 1985] . . .
>
> Granted that the original permission to divorce was given because of the nation's hard-heartedness, Jesus' refusal of that permission only makes sense if he envisaged his hearers' hard-heartedness somehow being dealt with. The only explanation for that, which fits like a glove with the rest of Jesus' kingdom story, is that he believed himself to be inaugurating the great time of

renewal spoken of in the prophets, when the law would be written on the hearts of YHWH's people.

When this motif is set against the rabbinic thinking referred to at the end of note 89, it is clear that Jesus was making a staggering claim: the kingdom he had come to inaugurate would reverse the downhill trend of those who would belong to it.

Brewer's work on divorce, while ground-breaking in some respects, suffers from the serious flaw that insufficient emphasis is given to this theme of eschatological fulfilment and to the contrast between Jesus' teaching and that of the Old Testament. Yet that contrast lies at the very heart of what Jesus says in this verse.

94. BAG, under the figurative meaning of *epi*, state: '2. b. (gamma) of that upon which a state of being, an action, or a result is based.' Matthew 19:9 is then given as an example of this usage. Similarly, Thayer, treating metaphorical usages of the word, gives the meaning: 'of that upon which any action, effect, condition, rests as a basis or support; prop. *upon the ground of*. Examples are then given of subdivisions of this meaning and use of the term. Thayer goes on: '(delta) of the reason or motive underlying words and deeds, so that *epi* is equivalent to *for, on account of* . . . Matth. 19:9'. The exception then means something like this: 'whoever divorces his wife, not on the ground of *porneia*, and marries another, commits adultery.' This sounds a little clumsy in English, which is why it is rendered 'except for', which is equivalent in meaning but smoother English.

However, as Heth and Wenham point out, advocates of the preteritive view argue that *mē* (not) 'should be understood simply as the negative particle nullifying *epi*, the latter signifying the basis or grounds for the action, so the phrase should be translated "*porneia* is not involved"'. Support for this understanding is sought in Matthew 26:5, where the words *mē en tē heortē* (= not during the festival) are considered in relation to the whole preceding verse. However, this does not follow. As Heth and Wenham point out, '*mē* is not here a simple negative particle, but is governed by the introductory conditional formula and thus no different than *ean mē* (= if not, unless).' Heth and Wenham draw attention to the fact that BAG list *mē* in Matthew 19:9 under AI1 (= a negative particle, negativing clauses, in conditional clauses) and Matt. 26:5 is placed under AIII6 (= in a prohibitive sense in abrupt expressions without a verb). Heth and Wenham go on to quote M. Zerwick on the meaning of this phrase: 'In this . . . *mē* not only may but should mean "except", not that *mē* = "except" is of itself admissible, but because *mē* is here dependent upon the introductory *hosoi an* which is equivalent to *ean tis* . . . and thus we have *ean mē*—"unless", i.e., "except". Both expressions [i.e. *parektos logou porneias* and *mē epi*] lay down the same true exception.' Indeed, it would be strange if, having allowed an exception in Matthew 5:32, Jesus were specifically to express 'no comment' in this verse.

95. The exceptive words are *mē epi porneia*. They come after the words rendered 'divorces his wife' (*apolyse tēn gynaika*) but before the words 'and marries another' (*kai gamēsē allēn*). It will be useful to address the import of the exceptive words by comparing the arguments adduced by Murray, in support of the proposition that the words apply both to the divorce and the remarriage, with

the critique of Murray's arguments offered by Heth and Wenham. I shall then make my own observations upon this hotly contested matter.

Murray adduces six reasons for his understanding of the exceptive words.

i) If the exceptive words applied only to the divorce, then the whole statement should first have been given, and then the exception. However, the insertion of the exceptive words before the statement is completed indicates that the divorce and the remarriage are covered by the exception.

ii) Murray notes that the burden of the sentence falls on divorce *and* remarriage; it is with both that Jesus is concerned. The concern of the sentence is that whoever puts away his wife and marries another commits adultery. Since that is the concern of the sentence, then the exception must apply to both. If not, then one is left with the following: whoever divorces his wife, except for marital unfaithfulness, commits adultery; and whoever divorces and remarries, commits adultery. Murray claims that it is patent nonsense to say that whoever puts away his wife commits adultery. But confining the exception to the divorce would lead to such a result.

ii) Murray's third point is similar to his second. Since Jesus co-ordinates the divorce with the remarriage, the exception must apply to both.

iv) Jesus' hearers understood divorce to allow remarriage. While Jesus is drastically changing the situation when divorce is permissible, there is nothing to suggest that he is changing the concept of divorce. Accordingly, since he allowed divorce for *porneia*, it follows that he allowed remarriage.

v) Murray's fifth argument is that it is against the analogy of Scripture to permit 'divorce' where the marriage bond is still intact. This would mean that a man may live separately from someone who is still his wife. While acknowledging that Paul permits separation in 1 Corinthians 7:10-11, this was very much a less-than-ideal response to a contingency rather than a provision and sanctioning of permanent separation. What Murray is saying is that divorce is allowed where the marriage bond is no longer intact: *porneia* constitutes a breach in the bond, and divorce declares this to be so. Since the marriage bond is no longer intact, it must be permissible not only to divorce, but also to remarry.

vi) If the marriage bond itself is not severed in such a case, then a believer may find himself permanently united with a woman abandoned to the most shameless prostitution. This would be contrary to the demands of a passage such as 1 Corinthians 6:15-17. (Murray, 1961, pp. 39-43.)

Heth and Wenham are not at all impressed by Murray's arguments. As to the word order of the sentence, Heth and Wenham contend as follows. There are three possibilities:

i) Matthew could have placed the exceptive words after 'whoever' and before 'puts away'. This would have had the effect of making the sentence read like this: 'Whoever does not put away his wife for unchastity and does not marry another, commits adultery.'

ii) The words could be where they are in the sentence. Heth and Wenham contend that this leaves the sentence reading something like this: whoever puts away his wife, if it is not for unchastity that he puts her away, and marries another, commits adultery.

iii) Matthew could have placed the words after 'and marries another' but before 'commits adultery'. This would then read as follows: whoever puts away his wife and marries another, if it is not for unchastity that he puts her away and marries another, commits adultery. (Heth and Wenham, pp. 113-20.)

Heth and Wenham—as does Cornes—accept that there is ambiguity in the existing word order, but contend that the meaning Murray argues for would be virtually demanded if the exceptive words were placed after 'marries another' but before 'commits adultery'. Since Matthew chose not to put the words there, it must be because he did not want to convey the meaning for which Murray contends; rather, divorce was allowed for marital unfaithfulness but remarriage was absolutely forbidden. Heth and Wenham go on to argue that each time *ei mē* is used in Matthew's Gospel with reference to a statement which precedes it, it does not pick up the subsequent verbal statement. They state that Murray should have sought to understand the function of the negated prepositional phrase in the protasis alone ('Whoever divorces his wife, *except for immorality*, and marries another'). They state: 'It would indeed be grammatically harsh to force another verb – "marries another"—into this elliptical clause that is clearly, by the nature of its position in the protasis, linked only with "put away".' They believe that Jesus is saying that a man may not put away his wife unless she is guilty of adultery and that whoever marries another after having put away his wife commits adultery.

Heth and Wenham then go on to assert the following:

In a study of the function of all the negated prepositional phrases in the New Testament (about forty with *mē* preceding), the following norm emerged: it appears that every time a prepositional phrase immediately follows the negative particle *mē* (unless a postpositive particle intervenes), the negative particle negates the verb which the prepositional phrase *follows* unless the qualification is emphatic, in which case it precedes the verb it qualifies. Similarly, in an examination of over 250 prepositional phrases in the first seven chapters of Matthew's Gospel, it is clear that Matthew usually has a qualifying prepositional phrase *follow* its intended object (ratio 4:1). Those which precede the unit to which they add precision are usually emphatic phrases moved forward, quotes from the Septuagint or phrases beginning new sections or movements in Matthew's Gospel.

All of this seems to mean that on the grounds of New Testament word order in general and Matthean style in particular, the elliptical negated prepositional phrase, 'except for immorality', is intended as a simple limitation of the verbal action that immediately precedes it: 'put away'. Matthew did not intend the phrase also to qualify the action which follows: 'marries another' ... Therefore, when Murray insists that the co-ordination of putting away and remarriage must not be broken, and that this co-ordination must not be disturbed in any way, it is evident that he is assuming what he wants to prove . . . That Murray did not consider other syntactical options possible for Jesus' divorce saying in Matthew is evident from the comment at the close of his discussion of the syntax of the passage: 'Where else could the exceptive clause be placed if it applies to all three elements [to put away, marry another and commit adultery] of the situation expressed?

In the light of these considerations it appears that Murray was basically misinformed when he attempted to sort out the syntactical and grammatical implications of verse 9 (pp. 118-19).

Clearly, this is a fairly technical debate, but it is essential to evaluate the relative strengths and weaknesses of the various arguments. It may be as well to begin by noting that Murray, on the one hand, and Heth and Wenham and Cornes, on the other, are all agreed that the sentence is not entirely straightforward. Thus, of the rendering which Heth and Wenham favour, Murray comments, 'Such a rendering does in itself make good sense' (Murray, 1961, p. 39). Heth and Wenham note, 'Matthew 19:9 is admittedly difficult' (p. 116). They are prepared to concede the possibility of Murray's understanding: 'It is not denied that this dual qualification is somewhat possible—which may even be allowing too much' (p. 118). Cornes' comment on Murray's understanding is, 'This is a strong argument and is a perfectly natural way to understand the verse seen in isolation.' A little later Cornes says, 'So both interpretations of Matthew 19:9 are possible and the syntax of the sentence, taken by itself, might lead us to believe that Jesus allows remarriage . . . in the case of divorce for adultery.' Heth and Wenham's point, and Cornes's point also, is that although the sentence is not entirely straightforward, Matthew could have expressed the meaning for which Murray contends in a more straightforward way by placing the exceptive words after 'and marries another'. By placing them where he did, the more natural way of understanding the exception is in the way in which they understand it.

However, the matter is not as straightforward as these writers contend. Firstly, had Matthew placed the exception clause after 'and marries another', then, on Heth and Wenham's own translation of the verse, problems arise. They render the meaning of the verse, so worded, as follows: 'Whoever puts away his wife *and* marries another, if it is not for unchastity that he puts her away and marries another, commits adultery.' This suggests that he not only puts her away for her unchastity, but that he also remarries because of his first wife's unchastity. But that leads to a nonsensical situation. It is suggesting that the reason the man remarries is because his first wife was unfaithful. But surely, the meaning for which Murray contends is that unchastity is the reason for *the divorce* and that, having *divorced for this reason*, he is free to remarry. He does not remarry because of the unchastity, but because he is divorced. But he may only remarry where the divorce is on the ground of unchastity. So to have placed the exceptive words after 'and marries another' would not have removed all ambiguity. Moreover, had Jesus intended to convey the meaning for which Heth and Wenham and Cornes argue, then Matthew could have put the matter beyond all doubt by wording the sentence as follows: *Hos an apolysē tēn gynaika autou mē epi porneia, moichatai. kai hos an gamēsē allēn, moichatai* (= Whoever puts away his wife, except for *porneia*, commits adultery; and whoever marries another, commits adultery). This gives the precise meaning for which Heth and Wenham contend, without creating the problems which arise by putting the exception after 'and marries another'. So the argument that Matthew could have arranged the word order differently to convey Murray's understanding, but could not have worded it differently to convey Heth and Wenham's understanding, is not correct.

All are surely agreed that the burden of this verse does not fall on the exception but on the fact that the action referred to will involve adultery. Without the exception, the action consists of *two* elements: putting away *and* remarrying. It is with the two actions that Jesus is concerned. The reason for this is almost certainly due to the fact that men put away their wives in order to remarry, and the Mosaic legislation allowed this. Divorce for a Jew denoted the possibility of remarriage. So Jesus co-ordinates the two actions. He is emphatic that divorce and remarriage entail adultery. However, where the divorce is on account of *porneia*, the subsequent remarriage will not entail adultery. It is perhaps unfortunate to formulate the question as to whether the exception clause applies only to the divorce or also to the remarriage. Rather, it would be more accurate to say that the exception applies to the divorce *and thereby* causes the remarriage to be free of adultery. In other words, since the two actions are co-ordinated, an exception to the one inevitably affects the other. There is the danger of making too much hang on the question as to whether the exception modifies the whole clause or only part of it.

This, of course, raises the whole question of what Jesus considered to be the effect of the putting away. Murray contends that there is nothing in the context to indicate that Jesus is suggesting a different understanding of the effects of divorce from that held by his interlocutors. Similarly, Carson (1984), having noted that in verses 3, 7 and 8, *apolyō* means the type of divorce understood by the Jews, goes on to say: 'It is unwarranted to understand the same verb a few verses later in some other way, unless there is some compelling contextual reason for the change.' Cornes believes that the whole point of verse 9 is that there is a compelling contextual reason for the change. He writes:

> Jesus' principal concern in 9 is not with the exception but with the man who divorces for a reason other than adultery and remarries. There is no disputing the fact that Jesus calls this remarriage adultery. That means that his divorcing (*apolyō*, 9) does not effect full divorce but only 'separation divorce' (a shorthand for: legal divorce which does not break the marriage bond and therefore does not confer the right to remarry). Those who want to argue for full divorce in the case of a divorce that is justified (i.e. for adultery) point out (rightly) that *apolyō* means full divorce in 3, 7 and 8 and, in their opponent's view, means separation divorce in 9; they maintain that there is no justification for this change of meaning.
>
> But Heth and Wenham rightly point out that these same people actually require Jesus to use *apolyō* with two different meanings in the same verse! They must maintain that *apolyō* in 9 means full divorce where *porneia* is involved, and separation where *porneia* is not involved.

What Cornes and Heth and Wenham are saying is this: if divorce and remarriage, according to verse 9, constitute adultery, then the marriage bond with the first wife must still be intact, and hence the marriage still exists. However, in response to this it may be said that if there is no adultery when the divorce has been because of unchastity and the man then remarries, then the marriage bond has been broken and the first marriage no longer exists. It makes more sense to assume that Jesus is using *apolyō* differently in verse 9 from its use in verses 3, 7 and 8, than to believe that he is using the same word in the same verse in two different ways. But this does not follow. It is possible to argue that Jesus is teaching that divorce does not break the marriage bond but that unchastity does. Accordingly, divorce and remarriage will entail adultery except where it is for unchastity, because in that case the marriage bond is broken. However, while this can make sense of the verse, there is another way of understanding what Jesus is saying. We have already seen that in verse 6 Jesus has said that the putting away of one's wife separates what God has joined together. Divorce breaks the marriage bond. This is contrary to the divine will and, as we have seen earlier, Jesus taught that repudiation of a marriage—and divorce is an example of such repudiation—is an example of adultery. However, where a wife is guilty of unchastity, she is herself repudiating the very heart of the marriage and is thereby guilty of adultery. In such a case, a man may put away his wife *without* being guilty of adultery. The 'official' breaking of the marriage bond is permissible because the wife has *in essence* already broken it. In such a case, the man is *permitted to remarry because the divorce was justified*. This interpretation means that in each verse Jesus understands the nature and effects of divorce in the same way as his interlocutors. There is no change of meaning from verses 3, 7 and 8 to verse 9. But neither is there any change within verse 9. Divorce always means and effects the rupture of the divinely constituted unit. But in the one case covered by Jesus' exception, it is justified: in the others it is not.

It may be objected that the real evil is, therefore, in the divorce rather than in the remarriage. There is a sense in which this is both true and untrue. It is true in that Jesus specifically forbids divorce in verse 6. It is untrue in that, in verse 9, he categorises the remarriage as adultery. The divorce was a repudiation of the specific marriage; the remarriage carried that repudiation one step further and, often being the reason for the divorce, was part and parcel of a practice that was inimical to the true meaning of marriage.

Thus, both the syntax and the meaning of *apolyō* indicate that Jesus is saying that divorce, for unchastity, followed by remarriage, would not entail adultery. There is no need to give serious attention to the argument that the exception could have been placed at the end of the entire sentence. Cornes suggests that this would make Murray's understanding unassailable. It would be a most unusual and unnecessary way of expressing matters. Heth and Wenham's surprise at this suggestion, put forward for other reasons by Duty, is conveyed in the following: 'It can be at the . . . end [by which he means after 'commit adultery'!] . . .'

96. The *lex Julia de adulteriis*.

97. Heth and Wenham are an example.

98. e.g. Cornes, Heth and Wenham.

99. The Greek reads, *Ei houtos estin hē aitia tou anthropou meta tēs gynaikos*. A literal rendering would be along the following lines: 'if this is the case of the man with the woman/wife'.

100. To begin with, Jesus' prohibition of divorce and remarriage, except for sexual infidelity, is set in the context of his having expounded the temporary nature of the deuteronomic legislation on divorce, and having laid down on his own authority his teaching on divorce. The context and perspective of his teaching were, therefore, fundamentally different from that of Shammai, who was only

concerned to explain the significance of the 'indecent thing' of Deuteronomy 24:1. However, this does not adequately account for the disciples' surprise. It is probably to be understood against the background to the Shammai/Hillel debate, to which Brewer has drawn attention. Brewer has pointed out (Non Academic 1996) that while debate focused on the interpretation of Deuteronomy 24:1, the Pharisees as a whole accepted other reasons for divorce. It appears that Brewer is here referring to the rabbinic understanding of marriage contracts and of divorce for breach of them based on Exodus 21:11. Jesus' teaching in Matthew 19 involves a contrast with the Mosaic teaching, and it would appear that he is insistent that there is now only one ground for divorce. Thus, he is not only disagreeing with the Hillelites over Deuteronomy 24:1, but is also disagreeing with both the Shammaites and the Hillelites by ruling out any other ground for divorce The fact that his reply in verse 4 to the question posed in verse 3 is in terms of the foundational principles of marriage found in Genesis 1 and 2 makes clear that, as far as he was concerned, he was not only speaking about the meaning of the 'indecent thing' of Deuteronomy 24:1, but was dealing with divorce somewhat comprehensively.

101. The Greek reads: *ou sympherei gamēsai*. Thayer renders *sympherei*, 'It is expedient, profitable', while BAG state: 'It is well translated, "It is better not to marry".'

102. Certainly the phrase *ton logon touton* (= this word, this saying) has affinities with *tous logous toutous* (= these sayings) which occurs frequently in Matthew's Gospel, and is found at the beginning of this chapter in verse 1. However, as our treatment of verse 12 should demonstrate, verse 12 will not really make sense unless 'this saying' refers to the disciples' words. Furthermore, although I have argued that treating Christ's words as Matthean additions which are presented as Christ's words is inconsistent with an evangelical—and biblical—doctrine of the inspiration of Scripture, it does not follow that the Gospel writers were purporting to record Christ's words verbatim. There is evidence in the pastoral letters that there were memorable 'sayings' which were used in the early church, which are not presented as sayings of Christ though they may well have been based upon his words. Thus 1 Timothy 1:15 is one such saying, which clearly has affinities with Luke 19:10. Similarly, 2 Timothy 2:11 has affinities with Matthew 10:32-33. It is not impossible that some 'saying' about the single state was circulating in the early church, and that it may well have been misunderstood. We know from John 21:22-24 that a misunderstanding of Christ's words led to a wrong idea circulating in the early church, and that John had to deal with that. It is possible that this had happened with Jesus' words about singleness, and that this accounts for Matthew referring to the disciples' words as 'this saying', precisely because it had attained that status in the early church. The second clause Jesus utters in verse 11 rescues the 'saying' from misunderstanding. Of course, this is speculation; but given that verse 12 requires the interpretation I shall suggest, it is not a work of supererogation to supply a satisfactory explanation of the fact that Matthew here applies 'this saying' to words of the disciples, when a similar type of phrase is regularly used by him to describe words of Jesus.

103. Hilton and Marshall, p. 135.

104. The Greek reads: *kai eisin eunouchoi hoitines eunouchisan heautous*. Three times

Jesus refers to those who have been made eunuchs. On each occasion he uses the same word to denote eunuchs: *eunouchoi*. When referring to those who are 'made eunuchs', as distinct from being born that way, he uses similar wording: *eunouchoi . . . eunouchisthēsan* and *eunouchoi . . . eunouchisan*.

105. The noun is *eunouchos* and the verb *eunouchizō*. BAG, after noting classical references and references in Philo and Josephus, where the noun denotes an emasculated person, a eunuch, go on to give three usages of the word. Physically castrated men is the first usage, and they cite, *inter alia*, Matthew 19:12*b* as an example of this usage. The second usage is that of those who, without a physical operation, are by nature incapable of marrying or of having children. *Wisdom of Solomon* 3:14 and Matthew 19:12*a* are cited as examples of this usage. The third usage refers to those who abstain from marriage, without being impotent. The only example cited is Matthew 19:12*c*. Thayer treats the term in a similar way.

In the LXX, *eunouchos* translates the Hebrew *sārîs*. The Hebrew term includes within its semantic range those who have been castrated, but also denotes certain officials. For example, in Esther the term is used on a number of occasions to refer to those officials who looked after the harem or who served the queen; in these instances, it almost certainly denotes those who have been castrated: 1:10,12,15; 2:3,14,15; 4:4 5. In all of these examples, the LXX translates with the noun *eunouchos*. There are other usages in Esther where the Hebrew term *sārîs* is translated by *eunouchos* and the word may simply denote a royal official: 2:21; 6:2,14; 7:9. There are other examples in the Old Testament where *sā rîs* almost certainly does *not* denote a castrated person, e.g. Genesis 37:36. In this case, the LXX does not use *eunouchos*.

In the prophets, the word is used both of castrated people and of royal officials. Thus, Isaiah 56:3-4 is a clear reference to a castrated person, while 39:7 probably does not refer to castrated persons but to exiles who would serve a foreign king. As Young points out, Theodoret was correct to suggest that Daniel 1:3 is a fulfilment of Isaiah 39:7, but Josephus was misguided in assuming that the Jewish youths were castrated. The Targum on Isaiah renders the word as 'nobles'. The LXX does not render *sārîs* in Isaiah 39:7 with *eunouchos*.

Of the verb *eunouchizō* BAG give the meaning, 'castrate, emasculate, make a eunuch of *heauton* oneself Mt. 19:12*b* . . .' They then go on to state: 'From ancient times it has been disputed whether the word is to be taken literally in both occurrences, fig. in both, or fig. in the first and lit. in the second . . . The context requires the fig. interpr. . . . for the second occurrence, and the lit. for the first.'

106. See the final paragraph of note 105, above.

107. This understanding fails to take account of the following. First, the arguments adduced when considering verse 9 are such that Jesus allowed remarriage after divorce where the divorce was for unchastity. If the meaning that is here being suggested were valid, then verse 9 would have to be reinterpreted. But we have already seen that there is good reason for accepting verse 9 as we have done. Secondly, this understanding requires that the disciples gave all their attention to the question of remarriage. But by forbidding divorce in every case except one, Jesus was, *a fortiori*, forbidding remarriage except in that one case. But the interpretation which, for example, Heth and Wenham contend for, only makes

sense if the disciples completely ignore Jesus' prohibition of divorce but latch on to the one case where he does allow it, since, according to this interpretation, this would be the only occasion when the question of remarriage would become an issue. Thirdly, as we have seen, the disciples' exclamation in verse 10 makes no sense at all if they are referring to the fact that Jesus forbade remarriage in the one case where he allowed divorce. Their exclamation only makes sense in view of the fact that, in all cases except one, Jesus forbade divorce. It was that which stunned them and led to their remark that it would be better to remain unmarried. It is to that remark that Jesus replies in verse 11 and gives an explanation in verse 12. The interpretation of Heth and Wenham disturbs the whole flow of the conversation.

108. The foundational teaching found in Genesis 1:27-28 assumes the goodness of the God-given sexual instinct and, in conjunction with Genesis 2:23-24, teaches that marriage is the context in which that instinct is to be expressed. Proverbs 5:15-23 indicates that the sexual drive may legitimately be expressed within marriage, but not outside of it. 1 Corinthians 7:8-9 makes it abundantly clear that the sexual drive is stronger in some than in others. Those in whom it is particularly strong should marry.

109. The arguments are as follows. Firstly, Dupont notes that the words, 'Not all men can accept this statement, but only those to whom it has been given', are reminiscent of Jesus' words in Matthew 13:11: 'To you it has been granted to know the mysteries of the kingdom of heaven, but to them it has not been granted.' Heth and Wenham note the similarity with the parallel in Mark 4:11: 'To you has been given the mystery of the kingdom of God; but those who are outside get everything in parables.' Heth and Wenham comment:

> The outsiders, those who have not been granted an insight into God's divine rule, are 'the broad mass of the people not amongst the disciples of Jesus'. In other words, 'to understand' or 'comprehend' or 'gain insight' (*syniēmi*) into the message of Jesus is a privilege accorded only to his disciples (cf. John 6:65; 8:43). This means that those who do not accept Jesus' teaching are the unbelieving outsiders. In Matthew 19:11 they are set over against Jesus' disciples who *have* been granted this ability.

Heth and Wenham go on to note Dupont's observation that whereas Mark emphasises the disciples' misunderstanding in certain situations, 'Matthew over and over again stresses the disciples' comprehension of the truths revealed by Jesus (cf. Matt. 13:51). This bringing together in Matthew 19:11 of those who do not "accept" (*chōreō*) or make room in their hearts for Jesus' teaching and those who have been accorded this privilege, once again reminds the reader of this common gospel theme' (Heth and Wenham, pp. 59-60). Heth and Wenham conclude this part of the argument by observing that concerted effort is still required by the disciples to put this teaching into practice, and that the words in verse 12d are similar to what we find in Matthew 11:15; 13:9, 43; 24:15.

The parallels and similarities which Heth and Wenham note do not work. Fundamental to their thesis is the belief that Jesus is *not* referring to two groups of disciples in verses 11-12. The interpretation I have offered entails the belief that there *are* two groups of disciples envisaged: those with the gift to remain single, and those without that gift. Heth and Wenham are arguing that the two groups are disciples and those who are not disciples. They believe that this is consistent with Matthean teaching elsewhere that there are two groups, disciples and non-disciples, and only the disciples can understand or accept Jesus' 'hard sayings'. But analysis of the other Matthean passages reveals how different are verses 11-12 of chapter 19. In the other cases, it is *all* the disciples who speak with Jesus who are admitted into the knowledge of the secrets of the kingdom of heaven and can grasp his teaching. It is they who will be able to implement it. But even if verse 9 were to be forbidding remarriage after divorce, that saying would not need to be accepted by every disciple, in the sense that not every disciple gets divorced. Comparison of verses 11 and 12 puts this matter beyond all dispute. In verse 11, Jesus says that not everyone can accept the saying, but only those to whom it has been given. He explains who they are, in verse 12. Verse 12 is linked to verse 11 by the conjunction *gar* (= for). The people who can accept the saying are the eunuchs. But everyone is agreed that they are a subset of all the disciples, and that there are many disciples who do not come within this category. But this is to say that there are two groups of disciples. Q.E.D. This argument cannot be overthrown by saying that *all* disciples are called upon to accept that this is Jesus' teaching: only some—i.e. those who have been divorced—will have to live it out, but all are called upon to accept it and, therefore, Jesus is distinguishing between disciples and non-disciples. This argument will not work precisely because those who can accept the teaching (verse 11) and who are called upon to accept it (verse 12*d*) are the eunuchs of verse 12, not all disciples. In any event, this argument would lead to three groups, not two: unbelievers, disciples, and disciples who have to implement the teaching.

The second argument advanced by Heth and Wenham, based on Matthean usage and style, builds on a comparison of verses 10-12 with Matthew 19:23-26. The 'this' (= *touto*) of verse 26 cannot refer back to the disciples' question of verse 25, but to Jesus' words in verses 23-24. Similarly, it is argued, 'this word' (= *ton logon touton*) should not refer back to the disciples' words of verse 10, but to Jesus' saying in verse 9. Jesus' words in 19:23-24 are 'hard words' and so is his teaching in 19:11. Hence the parallel. With respect, this is a very weak argument. Why should the fact that a reference later in the chapter must be back to Jesus' words rather than to the disciples' words demand that this be so in the present case? If there were twenty other such usages, then admittedly this would present a prima facie case. Even then, the immediate context would have to support the argument, but it would be a strong factor to be considered. But this is hardly the case when there is only one other instance.

Heth and Wenham adduce three other arguments, which have been advanced by Quesnell, to support the view that verses 10-12 are an extension of Jesus' absolute prohibition of remarriage after divorce. The first argument builds on the fact that thus far in Matthew the disciples' speeches serve the purpose of asking questions, misunderstanding or objecting, or simply advancing the action dramatically. 'Their objections are not accepted and confirmed by the Master, but are refuted or made the occasion for stronger restatements of the original teaching.' The only exception to this is found in 16:15-17, and even in that case Jesus makes it clear that Peter has come to this understanding by way of divine revelation to him. The argument goes that if verses 10-12 are understood as a call to consecrated virginity, they present a great anomaly:

> the disciples' objection in verse 10 to Jesus' teaching on the permanence of marriage (despite legal divorce) would result in a complete reversal of the argument of verses 3-9. The whole argument that has been developing in verses 4-8 is that man and wife are not to separate . . . This culminates in Jesus' precept that man and wife, if separated for some reason, are never to marry another (v. 9). Then in verse 10 the disciples reject this conception of life and marriage. Quesnell argues that if verses 11-12 really do constitute a call to celibacy, then Jesus suddenly backs off, agrees with the disciples' objection and begins to teach that it may well be advantageous not to marry; that it is a good thing to give up marriage for the sake of the kingdom. Let him accept it who can. (Heth and Wenham, p. 62.)

I must confess that I find this argument almost incomprehensible and certainly inconsequential. Let us accept Quesnell's analysis of the purpose of the disciples' speeches. On that analysis, verses 10-12 fit perfectly with the interpretation I have offered. In verse 10, the disciples express their belief that it is expedient not to marry if one is limited in the cases where divorce may take place. Jesus does not 'back off' at all. He disagrees with what the disciples are saying. They are making a call for everyone to refrain from marriage; Jesus explains that only certain people are able to refrain and these are the ones who should. He does correct them. He is *not* saying that people who have the gift should refrain from marriage because they will subsequently be limited in their opportunity to divorce. Rather, he is differing from the argument of the disciples and explaining that the only people who should choose to remain single are those who have both the gift to do so and who do so for the sake of the kingdom. In verses 4-6, Jesus sets forth the divine ideal with respect to marriage. In verse 10, the disciples call this into question by suggesting it is best to remain single. In verses 11-12, Jesus corrects their misunderstanding, and in doing so indicates that not all will marry. This is similar to the high view of marriage found elsewhere in Paul's writings, which nevertheless accord a place to the single life (cf. Ephesians 5:22-33; 1 Corinthians 7).

Quesnell's second argument is equally inconsequential. He observes that whereas Luke calls for the disciple to forsake all, including one's wife, for Christ (Luke 14:26; 18:29; also, 20:27-40), Matthew omits these references (10:37-39; 16:25; 19:29; see also 22:23-33). On this basis, Quesnell argues that a call to celibacy would be incongruous in Matthew's Gospel. But this is a classic non sequitur. Luke is recording demands which would be made on *all* disciples, not only some. His call is *not* that everyone has to abandon every family tie and possessions to follow Christ, but that *everyone* who will be a disciple must put Christ first; there is an inner reappraisal of all for Jesus' sake. Secondly, the call to forsake one's wife demands that one is already married. Now, in Matthew, Jesus' words in 19:11-12 are not incongruous with his teaching elsewhere in this Gospel, precisely because he is addressing a very different situation from that addressed in 10:37-39 etc. and that addressed in the passages cited from Luke. There, he refers to *all* disciples: here he refers to *some*. There, he refers to those who are *already married*: here he refers to those who forgo marriage. It is a different universe of discourse, and Quesnell's analysis fails to recognise this.

The third argument advanced by Quesnell concerns Paul's treatment of 'virgins' in 1 Corinthians 7:25. In verses 10-11, Paul had appealed to the authority of the Lord. In verse 25, he specifically says that he has no command from the Lord. 'If Paul knew of the sayings now recorded in Matthew 19:11-12, it would have been to his advantage to appeal to them in support of his teaching on the benefits of the single life.' The conclusion drawn by Quesnell is that Matthew 19:10-12 cannot, therefore, be referring to singleness of life, but to no remarriage after divorce. This is the strongest of Quesnell's three arguments, but—as Heth and Wenham themselves note, for they give a negative evaluation of this third point—on closer inspection it cannot be sustained. To begin with, as everyone is agreed, 1 Corinthians 7:25ff. is one of the most difficult sections—possibly *the* most difficult—of the letter, particularly in terms of ascertaining who are 'the virgins' and the type of situation with which Paul is dealing. Fee presents as good a case as possible that 'the virgins' were female. If so, that immediately distinguishes the situation from that dealt with in Matthew 19:12. Secondly, as Fee observes in a footnote to verse 25, 'Since this is such unusual talk for Paul, some have argued that the Corinthians themselves have been using some of the sayings of Jesus circulating in their Q form (esp. Luke 20:34-36) and have turned them into support for their asceticism. Paul would then be opposing their use of Jesus in this way by saying that there is not a commandment of the Lord on this matter.' Fee goes on to comment on the verse: 'the issue itself lies in the category of concerns for which there are no commands of any kind, just advice or judgements (cf. v.40). The Corinthian pneumatics apparently had turned their slogan into something close to law, the net result of which is that the betrothed would sin against the Spirit if they consummated their marriages. But the Lord did not give commands on this kind of issue; therefore Paul can only give advice' (pp. 327-8).

It might be thought that in verse 9 Jesus allows some to remarry after divorce for *porneia*, but that those who are gifted to be eunuchs for the kingdom of heaven's sake may not remarry. There are at least two reasons why this understanding cannot be sustained. First of all, Jesus is replying in verses 11-12 to the disciples' words in verse 10. As we have already seen, the disciples are there referring to a man not marrying at all. This is 'the saying' with which Jesus deals in verses 11-12. Secondly, in verse 9 Jesus is not so much giving a ground for divorce as allowing an exception to his teaching that divorce and remarriage will entail adultery.

The positive reasoning found in the body of the text and in this note, together with the criticisms of the view that Matthew 19:10-12 is dealing with remarriage after divorce, justify the belief that those verses are, rather, dealing with the case of celibacy, and that such a case fits the context. That being so, no support can be found in verses 10-12 for the argument that verse 9 is forbidding remarriage after divorce.

110. Since various textual questions arise, they will be dealt with either in the treatment of context or in the exegesis.

111. Lane addresses the textual questions raised in connection with the location. The reading given in the text of Nestle and Kilpatrick is that upon which ASV, RSV, and NIV are based: *ta horia tēs Ioudaias kai peran tou Iordanou*. This reading is found in Sinaiticus and Vaticanus and a small number of other witnesses,

almost all of which are Alexandrian. Caesarean and Western witnesses, including Codex Bezae, omit *kai* in the phrase, *Ioudaias kai peran*, giving the sense, 'the territories of Judea *beyond* Jordan'. Lane comments that this reading 'reflects the geographical situation in the days of Ptolemy the astronomer (ca. AD 130-160)', and represents, therefore, a later stage in the manuscript tradition, while the third reading, which is not well attested and which is found in Textus Receptus and, therefore, underlies the AV, 'the coasts of Judea by the farther side of Jordan [*Ioudaias dia tou peran tou Iordanou*] belongs to a later stage of the tradition when it has come to be thought that Perea was no more than a bridge between Galilee and Jerusalem'.

112. Lane, p. 352.

113. ibid., p. 353.

114. Nestle Kilpatrick has *ochloi* and this reading is very well attested. However, there is a variant reading, supported by Codex Bezae and other manuscripts, which have *ho ochlos*. Lane observes that Mark nowhere else uses the plural. Although the singular has been defended, it is more likely that the unique *ochloi* should be accepted and, as Lane comments, 'If the plural is correct, it may be intended to suggest the different crowds which gathered on different occasions' (p. 351).

115. op. cit., *supra*, p. 353.

116. The omission of the words *proselthontes Pharisaioi* is not well attested (Codex Bezae, some Western manuscripts, and the Syriac version Sinaiticus), and they should be accepted as original. There is no strong argument for accepting Lane's comment that the words may well have come into other manuscripts through the influence of the parallel in Matthew 19:3. This fails to come to terms with the fact that Jesus was being invited to take part in a current rabbinic debate by a recognised religious group.

117. See note 64, above.

118. The wording of the question is, *ei exestin andri gynaika apolysai* (= if it is lawful for a man to put away a wife).

119. Brewer (EN).

120. ibid.

121. Accepting the traditional authorship of the Gospel, Mark was 'a Jewish Christian whose mother Mary owned a home in Jerusalem where the nucleus of the original Christian community met' (Lane, op. cit., *supra*, p. 21) and was both a relative of Barnabas and colleague of Paul (Col. 4:10; Acts 13:4,13; 2 Tim. 4:11), and a fellow labourer with Peter (1 Pet. 5:13). Accordingly, one would expect him to be familiar with the Jewish rabbinic debates of his day and with the way in which they might be summarised or abbreviated. There are indications within the Gospel of his familiarity with Jewish customs. However, there is both good internal and external evidence to support the belief that he wrote his Gospel for a largely Gentile readership, unfamiliar with the Jewish customs prevalent in Palestinian Judaism. In 7:3, he explains the hand-washing custom of 'the Pharisees and all the Jews'. In 14:12, he explains that the first day of the Feast of Unleavened Bread was the day when it was customary to sacrifice the Passover lamb. In 15:42, he has to explain that the Preparation Day is the day

before the Sabbath. If this was necessary, it is unlikely that he would expect his readers to understand why he had omitted certain words from the Pharisees' question in 10:2, and assume that they would mentally add those words.

Lane gives a very full account of the reasons for believing that the Gospel was originally addressed to persecuted Christians in Rome and that the Gospel was written in Rome (Lane, pp. 12-17, 24-5). While the Letter to the Romans indicates that the church at Rome included Jews as well as Gentiles, there is much to be said for Wright's argument that if Galatians was written to warn largely Gentile Christians of the folly and dangers of allowing themselves to be Judaised, part of the message of Romans is concerned to prevent Gentile Christians from disparaging their Jewish brothers and the Jewish roots of the Gospel (Wright, 1991). This suggests a predominantly Gentile membership and, presumably, it was likely that the Gentile:Jew ratio within the church at Rome would increase in time. This being so, the arguments are strengthened for the belief that Mark would not expect his readers to be able to supply the missing words of the Pharisees' question.

122. I am accepting Lane's reconstruction of the life setting to which Mark addressed his Gospel. This provides a very helpful background to 10:1-10 and sharpens somewhat the political edge to the question put to Jesus in verse 2. As Lane observes, the readers would have been familiar with the LXX. Furthermore, one of the recurring themes in the Letter to the Romans is the way in which elements of the Mosaic law apply in a New Testament context to a largely Gentile church (e.g. 10:5-9; 13:9-10; 15:4).

123. In verse 3, Jesus had asked what Moses had commanded: *Ti hymin eneteilato Mōüsēs?* In verse 4, the Pharisees' reply refers to what Moses had permitted: *Mōüsēs epetrepsen.* This is quite different from the wording used in Matthew's account. In Matthew's account, it is the Pharisees who ask why Moses 'commanded' the giving of a certificate of divorce: *Ti oun Mōüsēs eneteilato?* (19:7), while it is Jesus who uses the language of permission: *Mōüsēs epetrepsen* (19:8). In Matthew, the Pharisees pose their question in response to Jesus' exposition of the Genesis material. Jesus has just said that man ought not to put asunder what God has joined together. The Pharisees' question is a counter-thrust to what Jesus has said. The Mosaic teaching in Deuteronomy 24 clearly envisages the giving of a divorce certificate as the means of effecting the divorce. In that sense, the giving of the certificate was a legislative requirement and could, therefore, be construed as a commandment. Certainly, there is evidence within Matthew's Gospel and in the Mishnah that great attention was paid to ensure that the certificate of divorce was properly drawn and delivered. Matthew 5:31 indicates that the Pharisees focused on the certificate; the Mishnaic tract *Gittin* is devoted to this issue. Since Matthew 5:31 indicates that the Pharisees' understanding was that divorce was quite in order provided that a certificate were given, it follows that their question in Matthew 19:7 as to why Moses commanded the giving of a certificate of divorce is tantamount to asking why Moses commanded divorce. Jesus corrects this misunderstanding in Matthew 19:8 by focusing attention not on the *certificate*—which was mandatory if divorce were to be effected—but on the divorce itself: 'Moses permitted you to divorce your wives . . .'

Crucial to a proper understanding of Mark's account is Brewer's observation, which has already been noted, that the Pharisees' question in verse 2 is highly condensed. They are concerned to ascertain if it is lawful to divorce for any and every reason. Jesus' reply in verse 3 may be understood in a number of possible ways. Firstly, as Murray argues, it is possible that Jesus' question is not intended to focus on the deuteronomic material exclusively, but on the whole of the Mosaic corpus, Genesis 1 and 2 included. The thrust of Jesus' question would then be as follows: Taking the entire Mosaic teaching together, what is the Mosaic legislation on this issue? The fact that Jesus goes on to quote from Genesis in verses 6-9 makes this a distinctly possible understanding. Alternatively, Jesus may be referring exclusively to Deuteronomy 24:1-4. This is possibly the more likely interpretation for the following reasons. Jesus is replying to the Pharisees' question, and that question certainly would be understood as referring to the debate between Shammai and Hillel over the interpretation of 'the indecent thing' of Deuteronomy 24:1. Jesus' question concerns the totality of the legislation found in Deuteronomy 24:1-4. It is to be noted that those verses do contain mandatory legislation, both as to the need for a certificate to be given if divorce is to be effected, and as to the primary purpose of the verses which is, in certain cases, to prevent remarriage to the original divorcing spouse. Thus, Jesus is forcing the Pharisees to consider what it was with which Moses really was concerned. Their reply in verse 4 indicates their complete failure to understand what Jesus is driving at, and prepares for Jesus' positive teaching in verses 5-9. Given the flow of the conversation in verses 2-3, the Pharisees' reference to 'permission' must be understood as indicating their belief that it is lawful to divorce for any and every reason. But that was certainly not the purpose of the Mosaic legislation, as Jesus makes clear in verse 5. Jesus' words in verse 5 put beyond all dispute the fact that Jesus' reference to 'command' in verses 3 and 5 cannot be interpreted in the sense that he is teaching that Moses commanded divorce in certain circumstances. The Mosaic legislation on divorce was necessitated by men's hardness of heart. In effect, the Pharisees were understanding Moses to have given them carte blanche in the matter of divorce. By contrast, Jesus states that the Mosaic legislation was a necessary response to the men's hard-heartedness. This being the case, no real significance attaches to the changed wording in Mark.

124. See note 91, *supra*, of this chapter. There is another slight difference in Mark 10:11. Jesus says that the man who puts his wife away and marries another 'commits adultery against her' (*moichatai ep' autēn*), whereas in Matthew 19:9 Jesus simply says 'commits adultery' (*moichatai*). Whether Jesus is referring to adultery being committed against the former wife or the new wife, it is abundantly clear that he is saying something very different from what his contemporaries had come to regard as the position. Lane expresses the point thus: '. . . to rabbinic law a man could commit adultery against another married man by seducing his wife (Deut. 22:13-29) and a wife could commit adultery against her husband by infidelity, but a husband could not be said to commit adultery against his wife. The unconditional form of Jesus' statement served to reinforce the abrogation of the Mosaic permission in Deut. 24:1' (Lane, p. 357).

125. The Nestle-Kilpatrick text reads: *kai ean autē apolysasa ton andra autēs gamēsē allon, moichatai*. This reading uses *apolyō*, the same verb as is used of the man putting away his wife. This reading is found in Sinaiticus, Vaticanus and other

manuscripts in the Alexandrian family. The Byzantine reading, which is found in Textus Receptus, is very similar but specifically mentions the woman (*gynē*). A different reading is supported by Codex Bezae, a ninth-century manuscript, together with a small number of the Old Latin versions. This reading is as follows: *exelthē apo tou andros kai allon gamēsē*. The chief difference between this reading and that represented in the Alexandrian tradition and the Byzantine tradition lies in the fact that a different verb from *c* is used. *Exelthē* in this reading denotes the fact of the wife leaving her husband and marrying another. Lane accepts this as the original, authentic reading, and bases his decision on the fact that this reading represents a textual tradition current at Antioch, Caesarea, Carthage, Italy and Gaul at least as early as AD 150. 'Moreover, the situation envisioned (desertion and remarriage) is precisely that of Herodias and is appropriate to the importance this issue assumed in connection with John the Baptist' (Lane, n. 5, p. 352). Most commentators favour the reading found in the Nestle-Kilpatrick text. However, there is much to be said for Lane's position. Firstly, as we have observed, the background to this passage is the marriage of Antipas to Herodias. Herodias had left her husband to marry Antipas. Thus, it is natural that Jesus would have had that situation in view when speaking to his disciples in the house. However, as I make clear in the chapter dealing with 1 Corinthians 7, for a woman to leave her husband would, in the usual course of matters in the Graeco-Roman world, constitute divorce. Mark's readers in Rome would understand Jesus to be referring to an act of divorce, even if the verb *apolyō* is not used. Thus, Mark accurately reports the conversation between Jesus and his disciples, *and* records teaching which is highly relevant for Mark's readers.

126. The phrase *katharizōn panta ta brōmata* (= cleansing all meats) 'is almost certainly an interpretative comment of the evangelist which drew out the implications of Jesus' statement' (Lane, p. 255).

127. The discussion of food in Romans 14 is almost certainly to be understood against the background of the food laws contained in the Mosaic law. Jewish Christians might have been unhappy to eat meat at a Gentile Christian's house because it would not be kosher. The linking of food with holy days, which we find in this chapter, is found also in Colossians 2:16, while Galatians deals with the whole question of table fellowship in chapter 2:11-13, and treats of holy days in 4:10. The fact that in Galatians 2:1-3 Paul deals with circumcision, just before dealing with the question of table fellowship; that in Colossians 2:11-13, just before dealing with food and holy days, he deals with circumcision; and that chapters 2-4 of Romans deal at length with circumcision—should alert us to the fact that there is a reason why he groups these three things together. The reason is almost certainly that they were the hallmarks of Judaism in a pagan society. While not agreeing with all that he says—his theological treatment of justification by faith only is calamitous—Dunn has much to say that is thought-provoking and stimulating on the tensions between Jewish and Gentile Christians and how the food issue could be the focus of those tensions (Dunn, 1991). Wright makes similar observations (Wright, 1986).

128. Reference should be made to the standard commentaries on Mark for details concerning the evidence of dependence upon Peter. Lane gives a good summary. The link between Paul and Mark is established by Acts 12:25; Colossians 4:10; 2 Timothy 4:11.

129. Wright's remarks are apposite: 'There are two passages in particular in which the theme of the heart becomes prominent. The first of these is Mark 7:14-23/Matthew 15:10-20 . . .This is strongly supported by the second passage which speaks, again cryptically, of a renewed heart: Mark 10:2-12/Matthew 19:3-12 . . . The saying about hard hearts [in Matthew 19 and Mark 10] thus coheres well with Mark 7. Covenant renewal would bring about a new phase in the divine plan' (Wright, 1996, pp. 284, 286).

130. The *lex Julia de adulteriis* was enacted by Augustus in 18 BC, in an attempt to remedy—without much success, it should be said—the state of affairs resulting from fairly free and easy divorce The adulterous wife was to be divorced after having received notification before seven witnesses. As Thomas observes, 'Infidelity by a wife . . . [was] comprehensively legislated for by Augustus' (Thomas, p. 425). Augustus's legislation did *not* deal with adultery by a husband 'unless as the paramour and thus accomplice of a married woman' (Thomas, p. 425, n. 55). For discussions of this legislation see: Jolowicz, p 245; Thomas, pp. 425-6; Corbett, ch. V.

131. See note 125, *supra*.

132. See chapter 4.

133. Quoted by Heth and Wenham (p.158) from Bruce (1972), pp. 287-8.

134. Cited by Heth and Wenham (p. 159) from Fitzmyer (1976), pp. 177-226.

135. Nicholas, pp. 32-3.

136. ibid., p.36.

137. ibid., p. 36.

138. ibid., p. 35.

139. ibid., p. 40.

140. ibid., p. 40.

141. Buckland, Manual, p. 69.

142. op. cit., p. 319.

143. 'Owing to the influence of Akiba, in the first thirty or so years of the 2nd century AD, there became predominant a school of Rabbinic interpretation which laid emphasis upon every letter of the sacred text, and which drew the most far-fetched and often the most singular conclusions from the most unimportant of details. In this context we need only mention one instance of Akiba's methods; and this only because we shall have cause to refer to it again later. He interpreted the accusative particle . . . appearing in Genesis 1:1 . . . as meaning 'with'. Thence he inferred that God created 'along with the heaven and the earth' other things as well, namely, with the heaven the sun, the moon, and the constellations, and with the earth trees, plants, and the Garden of Eden' (Rahlfs p. lviii).

Chapter 4

1. For example, Murray, Richards, Stott.

2. For example, Pink, Shaw (ed.).

3. Murray, for example, criticises the Westminster Confession of Faith for its lack of precision in applying 1 Corinthians 7:15. Murray understands it to refer to

desertion by an unbeliever of a believer; as he points out, the Westminster Confession is somewhat wider in its understanding of this verse: Murray, pp 76-7, note 13.

4. Specific references to, and quotations from, 'the Law' to establish or to buttress positions contended for by Paul are found, for example, in the following: 9:8-9; 14:21,34. Quotations introduced by the formula *gegraptai* (= it is written) are found, for example, in the following: 1:19; 2:9. Quotations that are not formally introduced are found as follows: 2:16; 5:13. Chapter 10 records important events from Israel's journey in the wilderness, and the reference to 'forefathers' in 10:1 establishes the continuity of the New Testament Church with the Old Testament people of God.

   1 Corinthians 7:17 records a general principle which Paul laid down in all the churches, and verses 18ff. give specific illustrations and examples of this. Verse 18 evidently assumes that some of the Corinthians had been circumcised before conversion, while others had not been circumcised.

5. In this connection 6:9-11 is important. Much of the attraction and appeal of Diaspora Judaism lay in its strong monotheism and its avoidance of some of the grosser aspects of pagan life. Verse 9, in particular, lists some of these gross sins in conjunction with idolatry, and verse 11 informs us that some of the Corinthian Christians had, in their pre-conversion days, been guilty of these gross sins. The clear implication of verse 11 is that they had turned from such a lifestyle when they came to Christ. Accordingly, it is not the case that they abandoned paganism for Judaism and that this became a stepping stone to Christ. Rather, they went straight from paganism to Christ, without being Judaised in any way. The discussion in verses 8-10 clearly assumes that the church was composed of Jews and Gentiles.

6. See the verses cited in 5 above.

7. See 1:26-29; 11:21-22. At the same time, these verses indicate that there were some people of influence. See also the reference to Erastus in Romans 16:23.

8. 1 Corinthians was probably written about AD 54-55. Fee places the letter about three years after Paul left Corinth some time in AD 51-52, and comments: 'This is one of the few certain dates in the NT, and the one from which most Pauline dates are ultimately derived. That this is so is the result of the Gallio inscription . . . and the references in Acts 18:12, which place Paul and Gallio in Corinth at some point between AD 50 and 52' (Fee, pp. 4-5, note 13).

   The period of the Roman Empire may be dated from 27 BC, and succeeded the period of the Republic. The Empire is divided into two periods: the Principate (27 BC–AD 284) and the Dominate which followed.

9. Nicholas, pp. 80-1.

10. Justinian summarised the position thus: 'A civil law marriage is contracted by Roman citizens who are united according to law, males having reached years of puberty, females being of marriageable age, whether they be *sui iuris* or in power, provided that children in power must have the consent of the paterfamilias.' From this statement we learn what were the requirements as to capacity. They were three. First, the law of marriage related to those who were citizens. Someone who was not a citizen could contract a civil law marriage with

274

a citizen if granted the right of *conubium* or *ius conubii*. (See below.) Secondly, both parties had to have reached marriageable age: this was fourteen for a boy and twelve for a girl. The third requirement as to capacity was that those who were under the power—*patria potestas*—of a *paterfamilias* had to have the consent of the *paterfamilias*.

It may be thought that the application of the Roman law of marriage to the Corinthian Christians would have been very limited in view of the requirement that the parties to the marriage had to be citizens or those who had been granted the right of *conubium*. After all, Paul's words in 1 Corinthians 1:26 would make it unlikely that many in the church would have had Roman citizenship; 7:21 suggests that there were slaves in the church and these would certainly not have been citizens. Roman citizenship was highly prized and people were willing to pay a high price to get it (Acts 22:28). The fact that magistrates and a centurion assumed, incorrectly, that Paul was not a Roman citizen might suggest that it was not at all a common privilege to have. However, this needs to be balanced somewhat. Nicholas sums up the position in the following way: 'Very early . . . the Romans found it convenient to accord limited rights under the *ius civile* to their immediate neighbours, the Latins, and a similar status was later allowed to the growing number of colonies which the Romans established as their rule spread' (p. 64). This status, which was called Latinity, conferred one or more of three privileges, one of which was *conubium*. Nicholas observes that few Latins were granted *conubium*. He then continues:

> Latinity was not, however, the most that the non-Roman could aspire to. Although grants of citizenship were rare until the last years of the Republic, the Romans then relented. By the end of the Republic the citizenship had been extended to all Italy, and grants were frequently made by the Emperors either to whole communities or to individuals. *Moreover the slave population provided a never-failing source of new citizens. For, with rather surprising generosity, the Romans conceded to their manumitted slaves the privilege which as late as 91 BC at the cost of a bitter war they refused to their Italian allies.*
>
> A new class was created by a *lex Junia* (? AD 19), which accorded Latinity, but without *conubium* . . . to imperfectly manumitted slaves (Junian Latins). In the early years of the Empire the promise of citizenship was increasingly used as an instrument of policy to attract these and other Latins into activities in the public interest—the building of houses . . . and so forth. In the result, any enterprising Latin must have been able to raise himself to the citizenship (p. 65, *italics mine*).

It must be borne in mind, as Nicholas observes, that Latinity had ceased to be of geographical or ethnical significance by the end of the Republic. In view of the foregoing, Paul's words towards the end of 1 Corinthians 7:21 may well indicate his belief that Christian slaves had a good chance of obtaining their freedom; it would then be possible for them to obtain citizenship.

11. Justinian stated that marriage had to be 'according to law'. This referred, amongst other things, to the prohibited degrees of marriage. The prohibited degrees of consanguinity were as follows. Marriage was forbidden in the direct line between an ascendant and a descendant of any degree. As between collaterals, there could be no marriage if one party was only one degree removed

from the common ancestor. Thus, first cousins could marry, but an uncle could not marry a niece or an aunt a nephew. The prohibited degrees of affinity were as follows. A complete ban existed on the direct line, so that a man could not marry his former mother-in-law or daughter-in-law, stepdaughter and so forth. Laterally, there was no ban: a stepbrother could marry his stepsister.

In addition to the above, there were others who were prohibited from marrying. Castrati could not marry: this was probably because they lacked capacity. The *lex Julia de adulteriis* enacted by Augustus forbade an adulteress to marry her paramour after divorce.

On the above, reference should be made to the discussion found in Thomas and in Buckland on the material in the *Digest*. See also Corbett, chapter v.

12. By the time of the Empire, the parties to the marriage had to consent to it.

13. Nicholas gives a very helpful summary. For a densely detailed treatment, see Buckland, *Textbook*. The leading textbook on the Roman law of marriage is *The Roman Law of Marriage,* Corbett.

14. The Twelve Tables refers to the [? legendary] source of law, being a code which was set up in the market-place on ten bronze tablets.

15. Grimal, p. 123.

16. Nicholas p. 85.

17. ibid., p. 81.

18. ibid., p. 86.

19. Grimal pp. 123, 124.

20. D. 24.1.35; 24.2.9; 38.11.1.1. See Thomas, p. 425.

21. I fear that Fee is guilty of this. He understands chapter 7 very much against the background of the over-realised eschatology which lies behind much of this letter. He sees that there is a real problem arising from those whom he calls 'eschatological women'. Obviously, this is an important insight. However, in view of what we have noted of the status and behaviour of many women in the society of that period, it is quite possible that some were suffering from an 'under-realised eschatology'. When reviewing one of the volumes in Lloyd-Jones's series on Romans, Howard Marshall observed that sometimes the pastor may see things which are quite lost on the scholar. I cannot help feeling that Fee has so concentrated on a sanctified 'reading between the lines' of 1 Corinthians that he has missed what is obvious to any pastor, viz., that the Corinthians did not find it easy to live for Christ in a pagan setting and to shake off their former, immoral lives.

22. Chapters 8–10 illustrate this point.

23. In 1:11-12 Paul refers to the report from Chloe's household that the Corinthians were aligning themselves with various personalities. He begins to respond to this in 1:13 and concludes his treatment of this issue in 4:21. In 5:1, he refers to another matter raised in the report he has received: 'It is actually reported . . . '; 6:1ff. makes it clear that he is still dealing with matters reported to him; 7:1 marks the transition: 'Now for the matters you wrote about'. Each new matter raised in the Corinthians' letter to Paul and to which he responds is introduced by the words, 'Now about' (= *peri de*) (7:25; 8:1; 12:1; 16:1). While the letter, therefore, divides naturally into two parts, it is obviously not the case that there are

two watertight sections. Is his treatment of head coverings and the Lord's Supper occasioned by their letter or by the report he received? Certainly, 11:18 refers to the report. But this passage occurs in the second part of the letter. What has happened, it seems, is that the Corinthians have written to Paul with their questions, but he also has background information on the church situation from the report he has received, and this background information informs, somewhat, his response to their questions.

24. Fee, p. 7.

25. The better view is that the reference in 5:9 is to an earlier letter written by Paul. See Fee pp. 6-7, and p. 222, note 12.

26. Fee observes that this view is at least as old as Origen in the early third century, and that it first appeared in English in 1879 (p. 273, note 25). Paul almost certainly quotes from the Corinthians' letter in 6:12, 7:1*b*, and 8:1*b*. Carson notes that quotations from their letter are characterised by three things: they are short; they are followed by substantial modification; Paul's response is unambiguous, even sharp (Piper and Grudem, p. 148). In 7:2 Paul does not so much give a sharp response as what Carson has called Paul's 'Yes, but' response (Carson [Baker] 1987).

27. The word used is *kalos* not *agathos*. Both have the meaning good, but *kalos* also carries the idea of beautiful. Edwards comments that it has the 'notion of the morally beautiful' (Edwards, p. 157). The word translated by NIV 'to marry' is *haptesthai*. Fee demonstrates conclusively that the verb denotes sexual intercourse and cannot be toned down to refer to getting married (Fee, p. 275).

28. It is, of course, true that Paul quotes Genesis 2:24 in 6:16 as well as in Ephesians 5:31. However, the contexts and the quotations are significantly different. In 6:16, Paul quotes from that part of Genesis 2:24 which refers to the physical unity that exists in the act of sexual intercourse. Paul is *not* saying there that this constitutes the union that is effected in marriage. If sexual intercourse constituted marriage, then the Old Testament would not, in various places, refer to men later marrying those with whom they had had sexual intercourse (e.g. Gen. 34:1-12; Deut. 22:28-29). Secondly, Jesus taught that God joins husband and wife together. Admittedly, this joining by God is not completed nor consummated unless and until the couple are sexually united, but it does not follow that sexual union constitutes marriage. If it did, we should have to say that God joins together in marriage a prostitute with every man with whom she sleeps. This creates absurd anomalies. Furthermore, in Ephesians 5:31, Paul gives the full quotation from Genesis 2:24. In 1 Corinthians 6:16, by only quoting part, Paul is pointing out the tragic anomaly of Christian men consorting with prostitutes to engage in that which is one aspect of marriage and which must only ever occur within marriage. For a thought-provoking and very stimulating treatment of 1 Corinthians 6:16, reference should be made to Holland, pp. 249-68.

29. This equality does not involve denial of roles within the marriage relationship. Thus, the husband is the head of the wife.

30. See note, above.

31. Brewer argues this in chapter 5, 'Paul's Teaching on Divorce and Remarriage', in Brewer Non Academic 1996. Brewer has certainly done a real service in drawing attention to the significance of Exodus 21:10 for Jewish marriage contracts.

Certainly he is not the first writer from a Christian perspective to be aware of the significance of Exodus 21:10 for Jewish marriage contracts. Danby's translation of the Mishnah refers to Exodus 21:10 to explain the words in *Ketuboth* 5.6, 'The *duty of marriage* enjoined in the Law . . .' Nevertheless, it is Brewer who is bringing this to the attention of the wider Christian public as well as to the academic Christian community. The fact that many Christian writers on divorce do not refer to that verse is evidence of the fact that Brewer is breaking new ground and putting us all in his debt. However, he is probably going too far in asserting that Paul is applying Old Testament law to the Corinthian situation. My reasons for saying so are as follows.

First of all, the Corinthian church was made up of Gentiles as well as Jews. While some of those Gentiles would have had contact with the synagogue, others would not. Accordingly, while Paul would have been very familiar with the rabbinic discussions on marriage contracts, and while the ideas and language which informed those discussions would have been very much part of Paul's mental furniture and vocabulary, it is straining the point to assume that all his readers would have picked up these allusions. If I say, in the course of a sermon, that 'conscience doth make cowards of us all', I would certainly expect Shakespearean scholars to catch the allusion, as I would expect any reasonably well-read English speaker to do so. But I would not expect an average congregation to realise that I am quoting from one of Hamlet's soliloquies, and still less would I expect them to realise that Hamlet is saying that uncertainty as to one's standing at the future judgement is a powerful deterrent to committing suicide. I am simply using Shakespeare's language to express my point—perhaps the same point as is made in the play—but I would most certainly not be quoting Shakespeare as my authority for the point I would be making. If I were to do that, then I should need to make the point clear. Since there is no indication that Paul is applying his remarks only to that section of the population reasonably informed about matters Jewish, then I do not think the case can be sustained that Paul is building an argument upon Exodus 21:10.

Secondly, when Paul makes a point that is supported by the Old Testament or based on it, he is quite ready to quote from it. We have already seen that he specifically uses the formula 'It is written', and he also quotes specifically from 'the Law'. On an issue like this, is it likely that Paul would be building a case on Exodus 21:10 without saying so? It may be said that Paul's readers would have been sufficiently *au fait* with the use of this text within Judaism for it to have been unnecessary for him to quote it. But this raises a number of problems. Why does he quote on other occasions? Does this imply that his readers were not *au fait* with those matters? Furthermore, that generations of Christian writers on marriage and divorce—some of whom have been reasonably informed on Jewish rabbinic literature as well as steeped in the Old Testament—have not picked up any allusion to Exodus 21:10 in 1 Corinthians 7 ought to make us at least a little hesitant about crediting a fairly muddled Christian congregation with greater perception than some of the leading minds in the history of the Church.

Thirdly, if Paul is building a case on Exodus 21:10, does this not raise the question as to how much else of the Mosaic law on marriage is applicable to Christians? The discussions recorded in the Mishnah are, after all, very much concerned with the way in which the Old Testament law was to be applied. But he would be a bold man who would argue that the Mosaic provisions as to dowry are to apply today. Is it not a better hermeneutical procedure to say that Genesis 1 and 2 contain foundational material on marriage which is always applicable? Later chapters in the book of Genesis contain illustrations and examples of marriage customs in the Ancient Near East, while the Mosaic Law stipulated certain provisions relating to marriage which applied to the theocratic nation of Israel. With the inauguration of the new covenant era, the foundational principles still apply, but those provisions that were specific to Israel under the Mosaic covenant do not apply. In a chapter where Paul goes out of his way to tell us when he is quoting Jesus, and in a letter where he frequently cites the Old Testament, I think that more compelling evidence would be needed to substantiate Brewer's case.

Fourthly, while it is not disputed that that there are strongly 'Jewish' elements in the chapter—e.g. the call to live in peace in verse 15—all this means is that Paul was influenced by his background. But that is very different from saying that he is applying the Old Testament teaching to the matter in hand.

Finally, it may not be without significance that *Ketuboth* 5.6 deals with the question of frequency of sexual intercourse. Paul's words in 7:2-5 contain a studied absence of reference to the question, How often? precisely because each belongs to the other, and it is, therefore, for them to decide together upon such a matter. Thus, while Paul is concerned with some of the same issues as the Pharisees of his day, his treatment of those issues demonstrates that he is moving in a very different thought world. Of course, one needs to avoid what one wit has called 'parallelomania'. Certainly there are parallels between the issues raised by Paul and those raised by Jewish rabbis (see note 32, below), but one can also find parallels with other cultural backgrounds. Of course, the fact that Paul was a Jew and erstwhile Pharisee strengthens the argument that there will be a strong Jewish background to what he is writing. But, as his sermon to the Areopagites demonstrates, Paul was very well aware of the cultural background of his readers and hearers, and we should therefore look for allusions that would strike chords with them.

32. Paul's refusal to state the period of time confirms the point made in the final paragraph of note 31, above. The fact that it is to be by mutual consent and for the purpose of prayer contrasts sharply with *Ketuboth* 5.6: 'Disciples [of the Sages] may continue absent for thirty days against the will [of their wives] while they occupy themselves in the study of the Law . . .'

33. See note 26, supra.

34. *Tois agamois.*

35. *Agamos* occurs only four times in the New Testament, and all four occurrences appear in 1 Corinthians 7 (verses 8,11,32,34). (The NIV rendering of verse 27 is positively unhelpful and misleading, since 'unmarried' in that verse translates *lelysai apo gynaikos?* The AV 'Art thou loosed from a wife?' is a much better rendering. However, even this confuses the matter somewhat by using the word 'wife'. For the interpretation of this verse, see the comments in the section, 'Wider Issues Arising', in the body of this chapter.) The word has quite a wide semantic range. BAG give the following meaning: '*an unmarried man or woman*:

of both 1 Cor. 7:8 (opp. *gegamēkotes* vs. 10, as X . . . Of men vs. 32; Agr. 18; of women (Hyperid. 2, 12) 1 Cor. 7:34; . . . of divorced women 1 Cor. 7:11.' Thayer gives the meaning *unmarried* and cites 1 Co. vii. 8, 32, and then adds: 'used even of women, 1 Co. vii. 11, 34 (Eur. Hel. 690 [and elsewhere]), where the Gks. commonly said *anandros*.'

I am indebted to John Kendall, lecturer in New Testament Greek at the Evangelical Theological College of Wales, for drawing my attention to 'B Greek', a discussion site on the Internet, and for giving me access to a discussion initiated on this site by Ward Powers of Australia on the meaning of the term *agamos* in 1 Corinthians 7. Most of what appears in the following paragraphs was written before I had access to this discussion. The discussion served to confirm my conclusions, which were based on the *usage* of the term in 1 Corinthians 7. What follows in the next paragraph is a summary of the salient points relating to the matter in hand, while the paragraph following the next makes a number of observations on these points.

Jeffrey Gibson made a search of the *Thesaurus Linguae Graecae* (TLG) for the occurrences of *agamos*. In total, 81 references were noted. David Moore surveyed 22 of these references, ranging from Homer in the seventh or sixth century BC through to Pausanias in the second century AD. Moore concluded that the unanimous testimony for the referent being 'never having been married' came from the seventh to the fifth centuries BC. We know that Paul uses it of someone who has been married (1 Cor. 7:11) and Pausanias's use appears to support this meaning. From this data, Moore concluded that between the fifth century BC and the koine period there was a change in the meaning to bring within its scope those who had previously been married. Ward Powers was in agreement with Moore's conclusions.

Four comments are in order. First, Moore noted that he had not surveyed all of the references in TLG. It is possible that some of the classical references might have a wider referent than 'never before married', though this is probably unlikely. Secondly, however, none of the Internet discussion considered the point raised by Thayer that the usual classical word for an unmarried woman was *anandros*. Is it possible that this fact allowed for the development of *agamos* in koine Greek to cover those who had been married? Thirdly, since Paul is responding to the Corinthians' letter to him, it is quite possible that Paul's terminology is influenced by the Corinthians' terminology, and that when addressing the unmarried in verse 8, he is either picking up their word or is using this word to include the various possibilities raised by them. Whether this be so or not, the fourth thing to say is that the usage of the term by Paul in this chapter is all-important for ascertaining the meaning *in this chapter*. To that extent, the various classical usages of this term may not be of much use in helping us to determine Paul's meaning.

To what does *tois agamois* refer in verse 8? There is a broad division amongst commentators between those who wish to restrict the reference and those who wish to understand the term fairly widely. Fee is representative of the former group of commentators and assigns the meaning 'to the widowers'. His arguments in favour of this understanding are as follows. First, he makes the general observation that since to be widowed in antiquity created special problems for women, most cultures had a word for widows, but they did not always have a word for widowers. After noting that Greek did have a word for widowers, Fee goes on to say: 'but it appears seldom to have been used, and never in the koine period, in which *agamos* served in its place.' Secondly, Fee notes that Paul deals in mutuality with husbands and wives throughout the entire passage, and the understanding of *tois agamois* to be referring to widowers would fit naturally into the total argument of the passage. To reinforce this point, Fee asks, 'if *agamois* refers to all the unmarried, then why add widows?' Finally, Fee notes that the word appears again in verse 11 for a woman who is separated from her husband, and in verse 34 in contrast to a virgin. Fee concludes that in Paul's regular usage, 'it denotes not the "unmarried" in general, but the "demarried", those formerly but not now married. On balance, "widower" seems to be the best understanding of the word here. That would also help to explain the presence of these verses in this context, where all of the cases in vv.1-16 deal with those presently or formerly married, while vv.25-38 take up the issue of the never-before married.'

Edwards and Hodge wish to give a wider meaning to the word in this verse. Edwards dismisses the narrower meaning of widowers, and argues that the term is not to be understood simply as corresponding to *tais chērais* in verse 8, but in contrast to *tois gegamēkosi* in verse 10. Hodge takes the same view.

Fee is on strong ground when he says that Paul deals even-handedly with men and women and that *agamois* balances *chērais*. However, since verses 10-14 clearly deal with Paul's instructions to married couples, verses 10-11 with those who are both believers, and verses 12ff. with a believer married to an unbeliever, Edwards's point is well made that *agamois* is a contrast to 'the married' of verses 10-11 and 'the rest' of verses 12ff. Furthermore, Fee's use of verse 11 can hardly be used to support an argument to confine the meaning in verse 8 to widowers. The use of the term in verse 11 is of considerable importance, given its proximity to verse 8, and Fee is right to appeal to it. However, while it refers there to someone who has been married, it does not—as Fee readily acknowledges—refer to someone whose marriage has been terminated by death. What is demonstrated by the usage of the term in that verse is that the word is not to be confined to refer to those who have never been married. Furthermore, Fee's argument fails to address the significance of the use of the term in verses 32-34. In verse 32 *ho agamos* is clearly to be understood in contrast to *ho . . . gamēsas* of verse 33: the contrast is *not* between someone who is a widower and someone who is not widowed, but between someone unmarried and someone who is married. Moreover, there are good reasons for holding that 'an unmarried woman' in verse 34 is not to be confined to a widow. There was a perfectly good word for widow, *chēra*, which the New Testament uses regularly and which Paul himself uses in verse 8. By using the words *hē gynē hē agamos* Paul is referring to a wider group than to widows. Just as in verses 32-34, the contrast Paul makes is between an unmarried man and a married man, and between an unmarried woman and a married woman, so in the contrast between verses 8-9 and verses 10ff. the contrast is between unmarried people and married people, verses 10ff. further contrasting those who are married to believers and those who are in a mixed marriage.

It should be noted that there are considerable differences between the different readings which exist for verse 34. The reading which I am following is that which is adopted by Nestle Kilpatrick and reads as follows: *kai hē gynē hē agamos kai hē parthenos* . . . As Fee notes, this reading distinguishes between the unmarried and the virgin. While other readings repeat *ho agamos*, so that it modifies both 'woman' and 'virgin', the significant variant readings, for our present purposes, are those which place *ho agamos* after *parthenos*. This reading is followed by the Majority Text and the Western MSS. The effect of this, as Fee notes, is a new clause, which might lead to the following reading: 'There is also a distinction . . . between the wife and the virgin. The unmarried woman', etc. This reading does not have 'unmarried woman' and 'virgin', but simply makes a contrast between 'married woman' or 'wife' and the 'virgin'. Clearly, since the usage of *agamos* in this verse is not without importance to our present purpose, it is necessary to reach some conclusions upon this textual question.

The evidence is surveyed helpfully by Fee. He rejects the reading behind the Majority Text and the Western MSS on the following grounds.

(1) It requires a most unnatural sense to the verb *memeristai* . . . (2) It simply cannot account for the reading of B et al. Given the nice balance provided by the Western text, who would have created from that the text of B? Furthermore, the *kai* before *memeristai* is too well attested across the board to be a later addition; and its presence makes the verb go with v. 33. Its omission came about when Paul's distinction between the 'unmarried woman' and the 'virgin' was no longer understood and the compound subject with a singular verb was troublesome.

The main point here is that the more difficult reading is the one to be preferred, and that most certainly is not the reading adopted by the Majority Text and the Western MSS. This being so, we should read verse 34 as *hē agamos kai hē parthenos*; thus, Paul is distinguishing the virgin from the unmarried, and his use of the term *agamos* in this verse is not irrelevant to our consideration of the use of the term in verse 8.

If *tois agamois* in verse 8 has a wider referent than the widowers, two questions need to be answered. First, why does Paul distinguish the unmarried woman from the virgin in verse 34? After all, if a broad meaning were assigned to *hē agamos* in that verse, then would not *hē parthenos* be included? Fee poses questions like this to argue for 'widowers' in verse 8. However, even if Fee's point is conceded, all that he establishes by appeal to verse 34 is that there is a distinction between 'the unmarried' and 'the virgin'. But that distinction does not demand that 'the unmarried' be confined to 'the widow'. Indeed, given the fact that there was a perfectly good and commonly used Greek word for widow, the most that Fee's case proves is that verse 34 might *include* a widow. But it could also include someone who had been divorced. In other words, if the term in verse 34 is not to include all unmarried women, neither must it be confined to widows.

The second question to be answered is, Why does Paul refer to the unmarried and the widows in verse 8? Fee's point is that the 'unmarried' would include widows, and therefore the term must be assigned a narrow meaning in verse 8. Edwards' explanation is as follows: 'Hence *kai* is not "and also", but "and especially", *et quidem*. Cf. Mark xvi. 7; Hartung, *Partikell*. I. p. 145.' This usage of *kai* is well attested. BAG, when noting the various connective uses of this term, include the following: 'adding a (specially important) part to the whole *and especially*'. They cite LXX rendering of 2 Ch. 35:24; cf. 32:33, and 1 Macc. 2:6 from outside the New Testament, and then give Mk. 16:7 as an example of this usage. Thayer has a similar entry for the copulative use of this word: 'it joins to a general idea something particular, which is already comprised indeed in that general notion but by this form of expression is brought out more emphatically . . . so that it is equiv. to *and especially* . . . Mt. viii. 33 . . . Mk. xvi. 7 . . . Acts i. 14 . . . 1 Macc. ii. 6 . . . 2 Chr. xxxv. 24, cf. xxxii. 33 . . .' Although neither Thayer nor BAG cite 1 Corinthians 7:8 as an example of this use of *kai*, clearly not every example of a common occurrence can be cited and, given that both lexicons assign to *agamois* in verse 8 the meaning 'unmarried', rather than simply 'widowers', this usage of *kai* would be demanded by their understanding of *agamois* in that verse. This would then mean that Paul is singling out the widows for special mention in this verse. Since he goes on to speak in verse 9 of 'burning', it is not unreasonable to infer that he has younger widows in mind. This would then be consistent with what he counsels the younger widows in 1 Timothy 5:14. Indeed, the reference to 'burning' in verse 9 would appear to support a wider meaning of *agamois*. If 'burning' is adduced as a reason for marrying, this would apply to other unmarried people besides widowers. A divorced person could be subject to burning as much as a widower; likewise, a single person can be subject to burning.

It is *possible* that *kai* bears a similar meaning in verse 34. Although verses 25ff. are specifically concerned with virgins (*peri de tōn parthenōn*), the contrast in verses 32-34 is between the unmarried and the married. However, in verse 34— as we have already seen—*agamos* should not be confined to widow. What is the meaning of *kai* in this verse? Both NIV and RSV translate with the conjunction 'or'. Yet the conjunction could mean 'and especially' in this verse. The meaning would then be that an unmarried woman—and especially a virgin—cares for the things of the Lord. This would make good sense in the flow of the argument, because Paul is specifically concerned with virgins (verse 25). Fee's comments are apposite:

> Why does Paul begin the women's side by distinguishing two kinds of unmarried women? The answer to that must lie with the issue that was raised in vv.25-28. This is sure evidence that 'virgin' does not mean any unmarried woman, but must have a special sense in this section . . . Paul is making some general statements about the nature of married and unmarried existence in the present age. But as he starts the present section on the 'unmarried woman', he is brought back specifically to the issue at hand, so he adds 'and the virgin', meaning the 'virgins' who are the subject under consideration.

Thus, in verse 34 the virgins are a subset of the unmarried, and therefore *kai* functions as 'and especially'. Someone who had not been married might well be more undivided in devotion to the Lord than someone divorced or widowed.

The semantic range of *agamos*, the usage of the term by Paul in verses 11 and 32, together with the contrast which he sets up between *tois agamois* in verse 8 and *tois gegamēkosin* in verse 10, lead me to conclude that Fee is mistaken in confining the meaning in verse 8 to 'widowers'. The contextual factors incline me to the view that in verse 8 all the unmarried are included. To the objection that Paul deals with those who have never been married in verses 25ff., and that they should not, therefore, be regarded as included in verses 8-9, two possible replies may be made. First—as Fee himself convincingly argues—the virgins of this section are quite likely to be those who were already betrothed. If this be the case, then verses 25ff. are not dealing with those who had never been married per se, but with those who were engaged to be married. They were a very specific subset of those who had never been married and required special consideration. Alternatively, if they included those who were not engaged, they still represented a subset of the unmarried of verse 8. Since verse 8 would encompass a wider group, verses 25ff. give specific instruction on a specific issue raised by the Corinthians' letter to Paul. There is then an interesting parallel between verses 8-15 and 32-34. Verses 8-15 note contrasts between the unmarried and the married and, when dealing with the unmarried, Paul makes a special reference to one group within the unmarried, viz., the widows. In verses 32-34 Paul notes contrasts between the unmarried and the married, and then makes a special reference to one group amongst the unmarried, viz., the virgins. This observation holds good, whether 'virgins' denotes all who have never been married or only those who are betrothed.

However, even if Fee's argument were accepted that verse 8 cannot include all the unmarried, it would include all the 'demarried' (the term is Fee's) and, this would include the divorced. It is unthinkable that, in a passage which deals with the subject of divorce, in a letter to a church which existed in a society where immorality was fairly commonplace and divorce was a common phenomenon, the correspondence between the Corinthians and Paul would make no reference to the phenomenon of Christians who had been divorced before they became Christians. Thus, in verses 10-11, Paul deals with the subject of divorce between Christians: in verses 12-15, he considers the subject of divorce in a mixed marriage. The only other situation where the subject of divorce would press forcefully upon the Christian's conscience and thinking would be where he had been divorced before conversion. It is submitted that verses 8-9 deal, *inter alia*, with this type of situation.

The discussion initiated by Ward Powers specifically addressed the question whether, in 1 Corinthians 7—and particularly in view of the fact that verses 25ff. deal with the subject of virgins—*agamos* refers *only* to the demarried, or whether it also includes the 'never before married'. The significant point for our purposes is that whichever way this question is answered, the argument that Paul allowed those divorced before conversion to be remarried after conversion is unaffected. That argument would only be affected if *agamos* could only refer to the 'never before married'; but we have seen that this is not so. I think that on balance, given the background use of the term in the classical writings, and given the possibility that *kai* in verses 8 and 34 can carry the idea 'and especially' and should be understood in this way rather than as 'and, in addition', that the term in verse 8 should include all the unmarried, and that the word has a similar meaning to our 'unmarried'. However, as has been noted, the argument is unaffected even if the term is confined to the 'demarried'.

It may be worth considering the question, If Paul had wanted to make a reference to divorced people, was there any other way of doing so? Two possibilities spring to mind. In the LXX, Leviticus 21:7 refers to a divorced woman as *gynaika ekbeblēmenēn*. However, there are strong reasons why Paul would not use some cognate or form of *ekballō* to denote a divorced person. To begin with, as was noted in the Excursus on *porneia* at the end of chapter 3, the New Testament terminology relating to divorce is significantly different from that of the LXX. Secondly, the Old Testament vocabulary reflects somewhat the fact that the man sent the wife away. The situation which lies behind 1 Corinthians is significantly different.

The second possibility is that Paul may have used some cognate or form of *apolyō*. Thus, in Luke 16:18, the divorced woman is denoted by the word *apolelymenēn*. As with the LXX terminology, there are good reasons why Paul would not have used such a term to denote a divorced person. To begin with, Paul does not use *apolyō* in 1 Corinthians 7. This being so, it is unlikely that he would use some form or cognate of that word to denote a divorced person.

It should be noted that were there a term that Paul could have used to denote a divorced person, the problem might have been that what he wanted to say would have been limited. As we have seen, there is good reason to believe that Paul wished to include divorcees in verse 8, as well as others who were unmarried. *Agamois* perfectly suited this purpose and it is, therefore, submitted that verse 8 is, *inter alia*, addressing divorcees.

In conclusion, it is interesting to note that whereas Fee argues for a specific meaning arising from the fact that the people addressed in verse 8 were 'demarried', Fee does not appear even to consider the inclusion within the term of those who were already divorced. On the other hand, those who argue for a wider meaning also overlook any reference to divorcees and confine their attention to the widowed and those who had never been married. It is interesting to consider why this should be so. It is as if this possibility is so far removed from the horizon of the interpreter that exegesis becomes cramped and hampered by the outlook the interpreter brings to the text. That the interpretation I am suggesting may be rejected by some is one thing: that commentators fail to consider divorced people as possibly coming within the scope of verse 8 is a very different matter.

36. See note 26, *supra*.

37. The only exception is the discussion found on the Internet and referred to in note 35, *supra*.

38. The word is *parangellō*. BAG give the meaning as: 'give orders, command, instruct, direct of all kinds of persons in authority'.

39. See the discussion in Fee, Hodge, and Murray (1957) pp. 69 ff.

40. In Mark 10:2-8, the discussion is about divorce; which discussion is continued in verses 10-12, and in verses 11-12. As noted when dealing with Mark 10, some manuscripts have the verb *apolyō* in verse 12, while some—judged by numerous writers to be the original reading—have *exerchomai*. If the latter, it is still a reference to divorce, the word possibly bringing out the fact that a Jewish wife could not 'send away' her husband. Moreover, this is exactly what Herodias had done. But it amounted to divorce, and Paul's use of the verb *chōrizō* in 7:11, while bringing out the emphasis that the wife was 'separating' from her husband, is nevertheless a reference to divorce, as may be gathered from the fact that separation would usually constitute divorce in Roman law, and from the fact that the

verb *chōrizō* is used in Matthew 19:6 and in Mark 10:9, where it is obviously referring to divorce. Incidentally, that Paul can quote and apply Jesus' teaching to the case of a woman not separating from her husband indicates that Mark 10:12 is original to Jesus and is not Mark's editorial addition or comment.

41. See note 35, above.

42. Heth and Wenham, and Cornes, take this position.

43. There are a number of reasons why Paul's words cannot be fitted into the hermeneutical framework that insists that Jesus never allowed remarriage after divorce, and that Paul is, therefore, allowing divorce for *porneia* but no remarriage thereafter. To begin with, those writers who believe that the exceptive words in Matthew's Gospel are Matthean editorial comments cannot consistently hold that Paul is repeating the exception allowed by Jesus, for, according to their understanding, it was not Jesus who permitted the exception but Matthew.

    More significant is the following criticism of this view. It is generally held by those who take the 'no remarriage after divorce' position, that Matthew records the exceptive material because the Jewish law at that time demanded that the adulteress be put away. But, this being so, the husband would be forbidden to remarry the adulteress. Yet Paul specifically allows for the wife to return to the husband. But if that is the case, it makes a nonsense of the argument that Matthew's exceptive material was to make it easier for Christians to relate to their Jewish context. However, we have seen that the *lex Julia de adulteriis* also required that the adulterer put away his wife. So if Paul is allowing an exception for adultery and then speaking of the possibility of reconciliation, he is telling the Corinthians to ignore the law enacted by Augustus. Moreover, if Paul is re-affirming the teaching found in the Gospels—which is the position argued for by writers such as Cornes, and Heth and Wenham—then, to say the least, he expresses it in a most extraordinary way. The Gospel record contains no material that says a woman may not divorce except for *porneia*, but it does contain such exceptive material relative to a man divorcing his wife. Now, admittedly, the fact that, in Mark 10:12, Jesus applies the same prohibition of a woman divorcing as he does of a man divorcing, surely means that the exception in the Matthean material may be regarded as applicable to a woman in the same way as to a man. But for Paul expressly to deal first with the woman, and to go on to deal with an exception to the rule against her divorcing, is hardly what one would expect if he were reproducing the teaching of Jesus, for he does not state any exception when prohibiting the man from divorcing his wife.

    These considerations, together with those listed in the body of the text, render impossible that interpretation which says that Paul is stating an identical exception to that which Jesus gave. Moreover, as is argued in the body of the text, in verse 11 Paul is going out of his way to stress that the marriage is still intact. As we have seen, Jesus taught that divorce ended the marriage.

44. op. cit., chapter 5.

45. This is Fee's understanding of the verse.

46. To begin with, it would hardly seem necessary to tell people who separate because of an ascetic view, which flowed from an over-realised eschatology, that they must not then marry. Such people would hardly need such a warning. Fee

argues that Paul is here widening out the discussion, but this is quite unnecessary. Why should Paul widen out what he is saying? Secondly, as we observed when dealing with the background of Roman law, at this period of the Empire it was the women, more than the men, who were taking the initiative in divorce. It is perfectly possible that while some women had succumbed to an over-realised eschatology, others were suffering from under-realised eschatology and were simply being affected by their background. Paul has to caution them against this. Rather than commit adultery, they may have divorced their husbands in order to marry another man. Paul puts the lid on any such ideas.

Fee's treatment of 1 Corinthians 7 is marred by the fact that he probably overplays the significance of the over-realised eschatology which was damaging the Corinthian church. Certainly, the letter gives plenty of evidence that this was a major problem. But the discussion in 7:2-5 may have a more complex background than that of just over-realised eschatology. It is a commonplace of pastoral practice that Christians who may have distorted one of God's good gifts in their pre-Christian life may well acquire a negative view of that gift after their conversion. Augustine of Hippo is a classic example of a Christian who adopted negative views of sex as a result of his somewhat lax lifestyle in his pre-Christian days. Corinth was notoriously wicked. It is perfectly possible that some believers were reacting against their sexually promiscuous past. Others, who had not had such a lifestyle, may nevertheless have acquired a negative view of sex from seeing its perversion in the surrounding society. Whenever there are extreme views, there is the danger of some going to the opposite extreme. Some—with a warped view of Christian freedom—may have been tempted to abandon their spouses. Accordingly, both over-realised and under-realised eschatology may lie behind verse 11. Significantly, in Christian marriages, the problem appears to be the opposite of what Jesus encountered. He has to deal with men being lax in their view of marriage. In Corinth, it appears that the problem may have been greater with the women.

The question must be asked as to why Paul says nothing about the man reconciling or remaining unmarried. Brewer presents an argument on the basis of the different words used in verses 10 and 11 (Brewer, Non Academic, chapter 5). The verb used of the woman divorcing is *chōrizō*, whereas the verb used of the man is *aphiēmi*. If the woman separates, she has taken the initiative and, therefore, it is for her to reconcile. However, if the man sends her away, it is not for her to seek the reconciliation, since she is the victim. But all this does is to raise the question as to why Paul says nothing about the man seeking reconciliation, particularly in view of the fact that, in verses 12, 13 and 15, he deals even-handedly with the man and the woman. It might be thought that the woman could return to the man, who would be staying in the same dwelling, but that the man would not know where to find the woman. But this is pure speculation. In any event, this may well be reading too much into the different words used. We have seen that in Matthew 19 and Mark 10, the verb *chōrizō*—which is used here of the woman—is used there of the man. Moreover, in verses 12-13, *aphiēmi* is used of both the man and the woman.

There is a sense in which it is true to say that we simply do not know, and that the concession is expressed for the woman and not for the man because of factors specific to the situation about which we are ignorant. It may well have had something to do with the Corinthians' letter to Paul. However, we are warranted in drawing the inference that the same concession would apply to the man. But it may not be far from the truth to suggest that both the background of the society and the fact that the women are mentioned first indicate that there was far greater likelihood of the Christian women divorcing the Christian husbands, and therefore Paul addresses them more fully. He does not do so in the case of mixed marriages, because the reason why they were tempted to divorce was as strong for the men as for the women, and both were equally tempted.

47. Paul is not proposing an either/or. As will become clear, there are strong arguments for believing that reconciliation was what Paul regarded as the norm where a separation would occur.

48. See note 41, above, for the differences in the two words used of the woman divorcing and the man divorcing.

49. It is true that Jesus gave his teaching in Matthew 19, Mark 10, and Luke 16 as applicable to his contemporaries, whether his disciples or not. But the Gospels record material in what has been called the 'trans-covenantal era', when the old covenant was passing and the new covenant was dawning. Accordingly, this does not affect the proposition that Jesus' teaching was intended for his disciples; indeed, this is demanded by the fact that it was intended for those whose hardness of heart had been cured.

50. The verb used is *aphiēmi*. BAG give the meaning in this verse as 'in a legal sense *divorce*'.

51. The words translated 'willing to live' are *syneudokei oikein*. BAG say of the first word that it means, 'to agree with, approve of, consent to, sympathise with'. Fee comments that it 'implies more than simply "being willing" in a rather passive sense; it also means "agreeing with" it or "consenting to" it.' In view of Paul's view of marriage touched on in verses 2-5, he obviously means more than simply being willing to live under the same roof. It is this, as well as the entire context, which leads to the view that he is referring to 'living as a spouse'.

52. Reference should be made to the standard works on Roman law referred to in the bibliography for further information on this point. Fee lists a number of interesting interpretations of this verse, as does Edwards. One possibility is that Paul is transposing the Old Testament teaching on mixed racial marriages to mixed marriages between believer and unbeliever, and that he is assuring his readers that they are not in the situation in which the Jews of Nehemiah's day found themselves, when they had to put aside their foreign wives. This would explain the reference to the children not being unclean and be another example of the shifts that occur in the New Testament era.

53. The verb *chōrizō* is the same, though in Matthew and Mark it is *chōrizetō*, and in verse 15b it is *chōrizesthō*. In the Gospel material, the verb is third person singular, present active imperative. In verse 15a it is *chōrizetai*, which, though middle/passive in form, has an active meaning. Fee argues in a footnote that the verb refers to a mutual agreement to dissolve a marriage. But given the uses of the verb in the Gospel material, this is unnecessarily to restrict the word's meaning. Edwards brings out the force thus: 'if he is bent on departing'. In verse 15b, the verb is in the third person singular, present, middle/passive imperative. Again, Edwards brings out the meaning: 'let him begone'. However, comparing

Matthew 19:6 with this verse, we have *mē chōrizetō* and *chōrizesthō*. The contrast is obvious and, presumably, deliberate.

54. The words translated 'not bound' are *ou dedoulōtai*. Numerous writers, of differing persuasions as to the meaning of the phrase, have pointed out that in Romans 7:2 and 1 Corinthians 7:39, when speaking of the marriage bond, Paul uses a different verb, *deō*. Murray argues that since the verb *douloō*, which is used in 1 Corinthians 7:15, is stronger than *deō*, it must follow that the marriage bond is broken. Others, such as Fee and Cornes, argue that the use of a different word demonstrates the fact that Paul cannot mean that the marriage bond is broken. The fact that two opposite interpretations are built upon the word Paul uses suggests that too much weight is being placed on the meaning of a word and too much is being read out of it. *Deō* is used in a wide variety of contexts. It is used of the binding of the demoniac with chains in Mark 5:3, and of the binding of prisoners in Acts 12:6; 21:33. It is used of the binding of those who will be thrown into outer darkness in Matthew 22:13. Satan 'bound' the deformed woman: Luke 13:16. BAG give another, metaphorical meaning: what was forbidden was regarded as 'bound'. This meaning was based on the Aramaic and had as its background the language of the rabbis. It is used thus, for example, in Matthew 16:19; 18:18.

Douloō, the verb used in 1 Corinthians 7:15, carries the idea of enslaving. It is used in Acts 7:6 of the Israelites being in slavery to the Egyptians. It is used in 2 Peter 2:19 of those who are enslaved to depravity, and is used more positively in Romans 6:18 of being enslaved to righteousness and, in verse 22, of being enslaved to God. Paul uses it in 1 Corinthians 9:19, where he tells us that he becomes a slave of everyone.

From the above data, it is unwarrantable to draw any conclusions either way. The fact that Paul uses *deō* on only two other occasions hardly justifies the conclusion that he cannot be referring to being not bound to the marriage. This sounds too much like assuming what is to be proved and begging the question. Equally, *deō* is quite a strong term, and Murray is trying to squeeze too much out of the word the other way.

The interpretation of Paul's meaning is best arrived at by a consideration of the surrounding context and of the alternative interpretations. We consider the context first. In verse 12, Paul tells us that he is going to address a subject on which Jesus had made no pronouncement. In verses 10-11, he had repeated Jesus' teaching. Where a separation had taken place, it was to fall short of full-blown divorce: the believer was to reconcile or to remain unmarried. The reason—and I believe that all interpreters agree at this point—was that the marriage bond was still intact. If the marriage bond is still intact in verse 15, after the unbeliever has departed, then Paul is *not* saying anything different from what he has said in verses 10-11. But he has put us on notice that he *is* going to say something new. In the context of the Roman law, as we have seen, his words in verse 11 are such that he is going out of his way to explain that the separation must not be viewed as divorce. But, in verse 15, the divorce has already been effected by the unbeliever's departure. This would be viewed, in the context of the time, as the end of the marriage. Paul confirms this by saying that he is going further in this section than he had in verses 10-12.

The alternative interpretations cannot negate this conclusion. One interpretation claims that the believer is not bound by the obligations of verses 2-5. But this is to state the obvious. How can you have sexual relations with someone who has left, and is perhaps living where you do not know, possibly hundreds of miles away? In verses 2-5, the emphasis is on not depriving the other spouse. Implicit in such teaching is the recognition of the fact that the other spouse wants sexual relations with the spouse who is told not to abstain. But if the other spouse has divorced, the remaining spouse is hardly under the obligation not to abstain, and to say that Paul is telling the believer that he is free from this obligation is to make Paul write nonsense! In any event, why is the obligation no longer there, given that each spouse's body belongs to the other? The answer would be because the marriage bond is broken. But that is precisely what I am arguing for.

Another interpretation states that Paul means that the believer is not bound by the teaching he has given in verses 10-11. But again, this must mean that there is an added dimension, and that can only mean that whereas in verse 11 the marriage is intact, it has been dissolved in verse 15. A variation on this understanding is to say that the believer is not bound by the command in verses 12-13 to keep the marriage together. But this is an improbable interpretation. It makes a nonsense of the fact that verse 15 is dealing with divorce by repudiation, and it hardly makes sense that the believer is not bound to keep a marriage together when the unbeliever has dissolved it by his departure. Fee seeks to argue, on the basis of papyrus evidence adduced by Moulton and Milligan, that *chōrizetai* refers to divorce by mutual consent. Therefore, in verse 15, Paul is saying that the wife is not bound by the teaching in verses 12-13 that she must maintain the marriage and not initiate divorce. Where the other, unbelieving spouse wants a divorce, the believer can agree. But Fee is building too much on the meaning of *chōrizetai*. Whatever papyrus evidence exists, the fact remains that Matthew and Mark use the same verb in conjunction with—indeed, almost synonymously with—the word which denotes the sending away of the wife by the husband (*apolyō*). It is illegitimate to confine the meaning of the term in this verse to denote divorce by mutual consent. Moreover, as we have seen, verses 12-13 certainly imply the possibility of divorce by consent and, this being the case, it is all the more clear that verse 15 is dealing with a case of *repudium*. In verses 12-13 the verb used is *aphiēmi*. The simple fact is that there was a fluidity about the divorce terminology: indeed, Fee himself acknowledges this when he notes that verses 10-11 use *chōrizō* of the woman and *aphiēmi* of the man; verses 12-13 use *aphiēmi* of the man and the woman; while verse 15 uses *chōrizō* of the man and the woman. Matthew and Mark had used *apolyō*, and in verses 10-11 Paul is reproducing Jesus' teaching. So Fee's argument cannot be sustained.

Another interpretation is that the believer is not bound by the encumbrances of the married state. Paul refers to these considerations in verses 28*e*, 32-35. As an encouragement to those who have thus been abandoned, Paul says that they are now free to serve the Lord in a more wholehearted way. In a sense, this proves too much. Why is the believer thus free? Precisely because the marriage bond is broken *in a way that it is not broken in verse 11*. But this means that the divorce has ended the marriage, and this is just the position that I am arguing for. However, it is unlikely that Paul means that the believer is no longer bound by the encumbrances of the married state, since he introduces a fresh section in verse 25 which, while not unrelated to what has gone before, makes it unlikely that he would allude in verse 15 to encumbrances which he has not yet specifically mentioned, and to which he will not refer until the next section.

The context, the meaning of divorce, and the weakness of the alternative interpretations are such that it is clear that Paul is saying that the marriage is over and that the believer is to accept this.

55. The call to peace is expressed thus: *en de eirēnē keklēken hymas ho Theos*. Much ink has been used in seeking to relate the words to verses 12-13 or, alternatively, to the earlier part of verse 15. Fee and Hodge are examples of the former, while Edwards exhibits the latter tendency. But why may the verse not relate to the entire section? It then makes perfect sense. The believer should not initiate a divorce if the unbeliever is happy to live with him: God has called us in peace. The believer should not obstruct an unbeliever who wants a divorce: God has called us in peace. The believer should not continue to be compelled to sin, to be deprived sexually and thus to burn, or be treated like a slave by the other spouse: God has called us in peace. The believer should not struggle against an unbeliever who is departing: God has called us in peace. The *de*, contrary to what Fee says, can be left untranslated and be regarded as simply connecting the words with the foregoing.

56. An evangelical approach to hermeneutics cannot accept that meaning is *exclusively* in the eye of the beholder. The influence of deconstructionist ideas and reader response theories on hermeneutics in general, and on biblical hermeneutics in particular, is very helpfully analysed by Carson (1996). See also Vanhoozer.

57. John's writings are rightly famed for their 'double meanings'. A good example is John 1:5. John is saying *both* that the darkness has not understood the light *and* that it has not overcome it. We might say, in English, 'The darkness has not mastered it.' This brings out the double meaning. 1 John 1:1 is another example.

58. Moule's comment is apposite: 'It is uncertain whether the direct question implied is intended to expect the answer *yes* or *no*' (p. 154).

59. Hebrews 12:14; James 3:18.

60. Consideration of this is beyond the scope of this study, but the reader is referred to the standard works on Roman aw listed in the bibliography. The slave could have freedom conferred on him, or steps could be taken which would gain him his freedom.

61. I am grateful to John Kendall, of the Evangelical Theological College of Wales, for drawing my attention to the fact that one argument for a new paragraph is the asyndeton in verse 39.

62. There is a link between the verb *deō* in verses 27 and 39. Secondly, *gnōmēn* appears in verse 25—the beginning of the section—and reappears in the last verse of the section, verse 40.

63. *Tōn parthenōn*. Throughout the remainder of the section, the noun is singular and feminine. It is *possible* that in this verse the term could include men and women. One reason for favouring such an understanding is that Paul deals with both men and women in this section, and there is nothing to suggest that his focus is exclusively on difficulties faced by the female virgins. On the other hand, such

an understanding would require him to use the term differently here from the way in which he uses it in the remainder of the section, and this seems unlikely. A resolution of the problem may be found by confining the referent of the term in verse 25 to the female virgins, but understanding that term to be the signal that Paul is now moving on to deal with male and female who are betrothed.

64. There are four possibilities. First, that it refers to a 'spiritual marriage' that is not sexually consummated. This would be a flat contradiction of the biblical teaching in general, and of the teaching of verses 1-7 of this chapter in particular. The second option is to understand the term as referring to a virgin daughter who is to be given in marriage. This understanding seeks support from the terminology of verses 36-38. For the arguments against this view, see note 76 *infra*. This leaves two possibilities: virgins pure and simple, or virgins who are betrothed to be married. Fee points out that verses 34 and 36-38 create too many problems for the view that it refers to virgins pure and simple. Verses 36-38 seem to demand something more than a virgin. Clearly, the term includes that meaning within its semantic range but, as is clear from Matthew 1:18, 23 and Luke 1:27, it could also include those who were betrothed. Verses 36-38 seem to support the idea that there is a relationship between a man and a woman and, since I believe that these verses are still dealing with the same issue introduced in verse 25 (see note 77 *infra*), this would require that the virgins are those in a betrothal-type situation.

65. In verse 10, Paul uses the verb *parangellō*, which very much conveys the idea of giving an order or a command. In verse 25, he says: *epitagēn kuriou ouk echō* (=I do not have a command from [of] the Lord). He goes on to say: *gnōmēn de didōmi* . . . (= but I give an opinion [judgement] . . .). Both the word *gnōmēn* and the fact that Paul is contrasting it with *epitagēn*, together with the contrast with *parangellō* in verse 10, make it abundantly clear that we are here in the realm of counsel rather than commandment.

66. The words *ponēros* and *kakos* do not appear at all in this section. The word *kalos* (probably the word used by the Corinthians in their letter to Paul) does not denote so much 'right' (in the sense of 'absolutely good'—as the NIV appears to imply), but more the sense of 'good, morally beautiful or appropriate'. This appears from the fact that Paul can compare an action that is *kalōs* with one which is *kreisson* (=better).

67. The reference to *adelphoi* (=brothers) in verse 29 signals that in the subsection, verses 29-31, Paul is addressing *all* the church.

68. *dia tēn enestōsan anagkēn.*

69. *Anagkē* has a wide semantic range. BAG give three main meanings: necessity or compulsion of any kind; distress or calamity; means of compulsion or (instruments of) torture. It is within the second range of meaning that the reference in 1 Corinthians 7:26 is to be found. Paul uses the word in the singular in 1 Thessalonians 3:7 and in the plural in 2 Corinthians 6:4 and 12:10. In the Thessalonian reference, Paul uses it in the context of being encouraged with good news of the Thessalonians' faith and love 'in all our distress and persecution'. In this verse, it appears to be a fairly comprehensive term for the difficulties Paul faced in his ministry. In 2 Corinthians 6:4 it is likewise used of great difficulties attending Paul's service of Christ, and this appears to be the meaning

again in 12:10. BAG, noting its occurrence in LXX and in Josephus, state that it is a loanword in rabbinic writings of the distress of the last days: Luke 21:23.

There are a number of reasons why it should not be understood in 1 Corinthians 7:26 of eschatological woes immediately preceding the End. To begin with, this would necessitate the belief that Paul believed that the End would come in the lifetime of the Corinthians. There is not a shred of evidence to support this belief. Such an understanding of Paul's teaching would also entail consequences for one's view of the inspiration and infallibility of Scripture. Moreover, Paul's Thessalonian correspondence indicates the importance of getting on with the business of living in this world as one awaits the Lord's return. Secondly, the fact that the word occurs in Luke in the context of the End does not require it to assume the same context of the End in 1 Corinthians 7. Thirdly, as Fee observes, the eschatological perspective of verse 31 is not of what is yet to be but, rather, is of the present passing of the world in its present form.

A more satisfactory understanding of the term would relate it to the difficulties which will be the lot of God's people throughout this entire era until Christ comes. Certainly, Paul viewed the present age as one marked by sufferings, which would not cease until the new heaven and new earth are constituted (Rom. 8:18-25, especially verse 18). Moreover, in verses 29ff. Paul elaborates and explains what he means in verses 25-28. It is quite clear that verse 29 refers to this present age in the light of the consummation of all things, and verse 31 spells out the effect of the inaugurating of the new age: the world in its present form is passing away. The meaning of Paul's words would then be along the following lines: the troubles for God's people during this present gospel age are such that it is best to stay as you are, and that means that it is wiser not to marry.

However, there are considerable difficulties with this view. As I argue in the exegesis in the body of the text, Paul is dealing in verses 26-28 with a couple who are betrothed. To stay as you are in such circumstances is not the same as breaking off the betrothal: Paul forbids that in verse 27. Rather, it is to remain betrothed. But if this is so, then the meaning of the passage, if the distress refers to this entire period, is that those Corinthians who were engaged had only two options: stay engaged but unmarried, or marry. This would entail the position that if they did not marry, they were to remain betrothed throughout their lives. To say the least, this would be an odd state of affairs. If this were the case, one can hardly understand why Paul does not tell them to break off the betrothal. But since he forbids this, it would appear sensible to search for an understanding that both suits the context and flow of the argument without entailing the odd proposition that couples were to remain permanently betrothed. After all, this leaves them in a not very different position from that envisaged by those who believe that the entire section is dealing with 'spiritual marriages'. We have already seen that there are decisive arguments against that understanding.

From earlier in this letter—especially 4:8-13—it appears fairly clear that although not many of the Corinthians were what might be termed 'upper crust' (cf. 1:26), they were certainly not exposed to the kinds of rigours experienced not only by Paul but by all the apostles (v.9). Persecution and the suffering of the people of God are major themes in the New Testament, but it is fairly clear that the Corinthians had bought into an understanding—rather, a misunderstanding—of the Christian life which led them to denigrate somewhat those who experienced such difficulties and deprivations. Certainly, this is fairly clear from 4:8-13. This being the case, it hardly makes sense to understand the participle *enestōs* in this verse to denote 'present'. Apart from the reference in 11:30 to those who were weak and who had fallen asleep, there is not a hint in the entire letter that the Corinthians were experiencing suffering. That verse is a reference to the disciplinary or chastening hand of God upon many in the Corinthian church. It is possible that Paul is telling those who were engaged to those who had become weak to wait and see whether to go through with their marriage, but this would appear an extraordinarily strained way of understanding 7:25ff. To say the least, if Paul were referring in 7:26 to the chastening of 11:30, one would expect some indication of this in the text. Rather, Paul's reference to the distress is in the context of the new age having arrived, rather than in the context of the chastening hand of God.

The position appears to be this. The era inaugurated by the coming of the kingdom of God is one that will be marked by certain periods which will indeed be terrible: cf. 2 Timothy 3:1ff. Moreover, the dawning of the new age which guarantees that this present age will pass away also provokes an 'antichrist response': 1 John 2:15-18. Thus, in 1 Corinthians 7:29ff. Paul is dealing with this eschatological age and how believers should live in it. But he introduces this theme in order to elaborate and explain what he has said in verses 25ff. The point to grasp is that 'the present crisis' is *not synonymous* with this eschatological period but is *'triggered'* by it; the 'present crisis' arises during this present period and as a result of this age having dawned. A distress was impending at the time when Paul was writing. What was the distress? Any answer can only be tentative, because Paul does not specifically tell us. Indeed, it is not impossible that the matter was referred to in the Corinthians' letter to him. However, in view of what we have already noted, it would appear that the distress was that which would be experienced by Christians as a result of being believers during this eschatological era. Paul had already had experience of distress; when the Corinthians would start living as they should, and would have shed their warped, triumphalist misunderstanding of the Christian life, then they too could expect to face suffering. But Paul's words suggest something fairly ominous on the horizon. Given that this letter may safely be dated around AD 53-55, it is surely significant to note that Nero succeeded Claudius as emperor in AD 54. The observations of the eminent historian V. H. H. Green might serve to underline the significance of the fact that Nero had become emperor:

> He was to be the first emperor whom the senate would declare to be a public enemy . . . from the very start of his reign there were indications not merely of vicious propensities but of mental instability. He roamed the streets of Rome with a gang of like-minded toughs, robbing passers-by and committing acts of violence.
>
> (Green, V. H. H. *The Madness of Kings: Personal Trauma and the Fate of Nations*, 1993 [reprinted 1994], Alan Sutton Publishing Ltd, Stroud, pp. 30-1.)

How the new emperor's behaviour and policies would bear on the infant church, only time would tell; but the early signs noted by Green were such that it is not unreasonable that Paul may well have seen these to be the gathering clouds which would, in time, burst as a time of distress for the people of God. Nero's subsequent behaviour, which would lead Pliny to describe him as 'the destroyer of the human race' and 'the poison of the world' (ibid. p. 30), would serve only to confirm fears which Paul might have entertained at this point. The possibility that Paul might well have had Nero in mind is not weakened by the fact that Paul himself appealed to Nero, nor by the fact that he wrote as he did in Romans 13:1ff. With respect to his appeal to the emperor, it must be remembered that Paul had already been a victim of injustice at the hands of Felix, and was to fare no better under Festus (Acts 24:27; 25:9). In these circumstances he stood to lose nothing by appealing to the emperor. To the argument that Paul could not have had serious misgivings concerning Nero at this early stage, given that he subsequently wrote so positively about the powers that be in Romans 13:1ff., the following must be said. First, Paul is dealing with *all* in authority, not just the emperor. He had already suffered at the hands of the Jewish authorities and the Roman authorities, yet he still writes positively of the institutions (*exousiai*) that God has ordained. Secondly, Paul was nothing if not a realist. Nero's predecessor-but-one, Caligula, had been a fairly unlikeable character, to say the least. Paul knew what the Roman hierarchy could be like and, given Nero's early behaviour, the fact that Paul could write as he did in Romans 13:1ff. should not be taken to mean that he had a wholly positive and optimistic view of Nero.

70. *anthrōpō to houtōs einai.*

71. *Dedesai gynaiki? mē zētei lysin. lelysai apo gynaikos? mē zētei gynaika.* If Paul were referring to marriage, one would have expected him to have used the verb *gameō*. It may be responded that he uses *deō* in a marriage situation in Romans 7:2. This much may be granted, but this does not answer the question as to why he should use *lyō* when referring to divorce. Earlier in this chapter he uses the words *chōrizō* and *aphiēmi*. The other New Testament terminology relevant to divorce includes *apolyō, apostasion*, and *biblion apostasiou*. Nowhere else in the New Testament is *lyō* used of divorce, nor is it thus employed in LXX. I do not know whether anyone has searched TLG and analysed all usages of the term. However, Fee writes: 'The . . . word "loosed" . . . is otherwise unknown to denote divorce.' Fee goes on to write: 'The . . . word "loosed", which is found throughout the papyri as a technical term for discharging someone from the obligations of a contract." This fits perfectly with the interpretation that Paul is referring to a betrothal-type situation.

72. It will be noted that Paul does not use *parthenos* in verse 27 but *gynē*. For a number of reasons, this does not mean that Paul is not dealing with the subject of betrothal. To begin with, the 'you' of verse 28*a* refers back to the 'you' of verse 27. But the 'you' of verse 28*a* is balanced by the 'virgin' of verse 28*b*. Accordingly, the man who is bound in verse 27 may be a male equivalent of a female virgin, but the woman to whom he is betrothed may be a widow. However, this need not be so. As Thayer notes, the word is used in Matthew 1:20 and 24 of Mary. Verse 25 makes it abundantly clear that she was a *parthenos* as well as a *gynē*. Perhaps we get nearest to the meaning in Matthew 1 by translating it as 'bride'. This would be the meaning conveyed in 1 Corinthians 7:28*b*: 'Do not seek a bride.' The use of the word there would explain the presence of the word in verse 27*a*. That this verse occurs in a context where virgins are being considered;

that *lyō* denotes discharge from an obligation rather than divorce from a spouse; that mutuality is maintained between male and female in verse 28 where verse 28b is referring to a virgin; that the term is used of Mary before she had consummated her marriage with Joseph—all these considerations are such that the change of word from *parthenos* does not entail the proposition that Paul is dealing with anything other than a betrothed couple.

73. Lee, pp. 65-6.

74. See note 72, *supra*, for the arguments in favour of understanding Paul to be referring to a 'bride'.

75. *mē zētei lysin . . . mē zētei gynaika.*

76. BAG note that *phēmi* in verse 29 denotes what Paul *means*: that is, he is explaining what he has been saying. It seems fairly clear that the reference to the time being shortened (*ho kairos synestalmenos*) is introduced to explain both the significance of 'the present crisis' and, in view of what he says in verses 29-31, to explain that the kind of advice he gives in verses 25-28 is a species or example of the general kind of behaviour requisite of all believers during these last days, as spelled out in verses 29-31. Paul does *not* mean that the last days are synonymous with 'the present crisis' of verse 26 but, rather, that that crisis is a result of the last days having arrived: see note 69, *supra*.

77. The NIV translates verse 36 as a reference to the man and the virgin to whom he is engaged. However, it gives the alternative understanding at the foot of the page. The AV preserves the uncertainty by opting for a more literal translation: 'his virgin'.

The main argument in favour of the father/daughter understanding is the use of the verb *gamizō* in verse 38. Thus Paul changes from the usual word which means, 'I marry' (*gameō*) to this other word which, in Mark 12:25 and parallels, means 'to give in marriage'. However, this fact has to be considered in the light of the following. First, in verse 38 Paul is summing up the discussion thus far; but there has been nothing hitherto—not even in verses 36-37—to suggest that he has been dealing with a father/daughter situation. Two courses of action are considered in verses 36-37. In verse 36, Paul deals with the couple marrying; this is clear from the word he uses: *gameitōsan. Gameō* is the verb that is being used, and it must be the engaged couple who are in view. As Fee points out, if Paul were dealing with the father/daughter relationship, this would be a nonsensical thing to say. Then, in verse 37 the alternative is considered. Since verse 36 deals with the man and his fiancée, the alternative must do so likewise. Then in verse 38 Paul sums up what he has been saying. Secondly, the idea that verses 36-38 are dealing with a father/daughter needs refining. The *paterfamilias* who had *patria potestas* was not necessarily the girl's father. But the significant thing to note is that a man could also be in the *potestas* of a *paterfamilias* and, if so, his consent was needed for the man, just as much as a woman who was not *sui iuris* needed the consent of her *paterfamilias*.

What of the change of verb? As Fee points out, there 'is sufficient evidence that the classical distinctions between -*eō* and -*izō* verbs had broken down in the koine period'. Fee observes that the change of verb might well be accounted for by the fact that this is the only case in the chapter where the verb 'to marry' has an object. It is, therefore, possible that *gamizō* carried a transitive nuance for Paul.

This leaves the difficult phrase 'his virgin'. Fee is somewhat misleading in his observation that 'there is no known evidence for one's speaking of a father-daughter relationship in terms of her being "his virgin"' (p. 326). Strictly speaking, this is so. However, Edwards notes that Sophocles in *Oed. Tyr.* 1462 has Oedipus speaking of his daughters as *parthenoin emain* (p.200). Clearly, if this phrase may denote 'my maiden daughters', then *parthenon autou* in verse 36 can denote 'his maiden daughter'. However, the structure and flow of the argument demand that Paul is here referring to a man and the woman to whom he is betrothed. It will be noted later why Paul uses the unusual clause, 'to keep his own virgin'.

78. Verse 36 simply refers to 'his virgin' (*tēn parthenon autou*). This phrase makes clear that there is a relationship between the man and the virgin, but it does not specify what that relationship is. For the reasons given in 77 *supra*, it appears that it must be referring to the man and the virgin to whom he is engaged.

79. 'If she is getting on in years' (NIV) translates the words *ean ē hyperakmos*. Fee has an interesting discussion of *hyperakmos*. It is possible that it refers to the man, in which case it carries the idea of having strong passions. If so, then the 'acting improperly' (*aschēmonein*) would possibly be referring to the difficulty the man had in controlling his passions. This would then mean that the advice to marry would be similar to Paul's teaching in verse 9. If it relates to the woman, then it means that she is of marriageable age and, possibly, passing her bloom. The impropriety would then refer to the fact that it would be inappropriate to keep such a woman waiting for marriage. Whichever way the words are understood, the argument which I am advancing as the background to the interpretation of verses 39-40 is unaffected.

80. *houtōs opheilei ginesthai.*

81. *ho thelei poieitō.*

82. *tērein tēn heautou parthenon.* This is an unusual phrase. Clearly, in the context in which it is found, it must bear the same meaning as *mē gamizōn* in verse 38b and be the opposite of *gameitōsan* in verse 36. But given that Paul uses *gameō* in verse 36 and *gamizō* in verse 38, the question must be asked as to why Paul makes this unusual choice of words. The answer surely lies in the fact that Paul has already forbidden a breaking of the engagement: verse 27. This being so, the opposite of not marrying in verse 37 is *not* to revert to the pre-engagement situation but, rather, to stay engaged though unmarried. We have already seen that Paul is using the term *parthenos* in this entire section to refer to a virgin who is engaged. 'To keep his virgin' would, therefore, denote in this context 'to keep her as his fiancée'. We have already seen that Paul is not envisaging that this situation continue indefinitely: it is very much a 'wait and see' policy, which is dictated by the impending distress referred to in verse 26. Fee refers to evidence that the phrase could refer to a man not violating or taking away a maiden's virginity.

83. The words are *gynē dedetai.* The Received Text reading, on which AV is based, has the word *nomō* (= by law) after *dedetai*. The evidence for this reading is not at all strong and is almost certainly to be accounted for by way of assimilation to Romans 7:2. The significance of the use of *gynē* instead of *parthenos* should not be exaggerated. There is a clear verbal link with verse 27, where Paul uses *deō* and *gynē* together. The 'you' of verse 28 is clearly the same 'you' of verse 27. But

verse 28 balances nicely the woman with the man, and in that verse Paul uses *parthenos*. Thus, having used *gynē* in verse 27 of someone who is engaged, it is not at all surprising that he uses the term again in verse 39. Furthermore, the use of the term could include a widow who was engaged or, for that matter, a divorcee who was engaged. As was noted earlier, 'bride' might best convey the meaning.

84. *ho anēr autēs*. 'Her man' is a perfectly possible translation of these words and, in the context, is that which is demanded.

85. I am indebted to John Kendall for this insight.

Appendix 5

1. De Smith and Brazier, p. 50
2. Wade and Bradley, p. 416
3. De Smith and Brazier, p. 59
4. ibid. p. 50

ABBREVIATIONS

(For full titles of works listed under this heading, refer to Bibliography)

1. AV: The Authorized (King James) Version of the Bible (1611)
2. BAG: Bauer, Arndt, Gingrich
3. BDB: Brown, Driver, Briggs
4. D: Digest of Justinian
5. *EN*: Evangelicals Now
6. LXX: The Old Testament in Greek according to the Septuagint, third century BC
7. NIV: The New International Version of the Bible (1973, 1978, 1984, 1995)
8. RSV: The Revised Standard Version of the Bible (NT 1946, second edition 1971; OT 1952)

EDITIONS OF GREEK TEXT

1. *Septuaginta*, ed. A. Rahlfs, Deutsche Bibelgesellschaft, Stuttgart (1935, 1979)
2. *The Greek New Testament*, ed. E. Nestle and G. D. Kilpatrick, The British & Foreign Bible Society (London, 1958)

Bibliography

A. LEGAL

Legal Reference Works
1. Baker, J. H. *Introduction to English Legal History*, Butterworths (London, 1971)
2. Buckland, W. W. *Manual of Roman Private Law*, Cambridge University Press (London, second edition, 1939)
3. Buckland, W. W. *Textbook of Roman Law from Augustus to Justinian*, Cambridge University Press (London, 1921); reprinted William W. Gaunt & Sons (Holmes Beach, Florida, 1990)
4. Corbett, P. E. *The Roman Law of Marriage*, Clarendon Press (Oxford, 1930; reprinted 1969)
5. Cretney, S. M. and Masson, J. M. *Principles of Family Law*, Sweet & Maxwell (London, sixth edition, 1997)
6. Grimal, P. *Roman Civilisation*, George Allen & Unwin (London, 1963)
7. Hart, H. L. A. *The Concept of Law*, Oxford University Press (London, 1961)
8. Honoré, A. M. *Justinian's Digest: Work in Progress*. An Inaugural Lecture delivered before the University of Oxford on 12th May 1971, Clarendon Press (Oxford)
9. Hyde, H. M. *Lord Birkett of Ulverston*, The Reprint Society Ltd by arrangement with Hamish Hamilton Ltd (1965)
10. Jolowicz, H. F. *Historical Introduction to the Study of Roman Law*, Cambridge University Press (second edition, 1952)
11. Lee, R. W. *The Elements of Roman Law*, Sweet & Maxwell Ltd (London, 1956)
12. Nicholas, B. *An Introduction to Roman Law*, Clarendon Press (Oxford, 1962)
13. de Smith, S. and Brazier, R. *Constitutional and Administrative Law*, Penguin Books (London, seventh edition, 1994)
14. Thomas, J. A. C. *Textbook of Roman Law*, North Holland (Oxford, 1976)
15. Wade, E. C. S. and Bradley, A. W. *Constitutional Law*, Longman Group Ltd (London, eighth edition, 1973)

Legal Sources
English Law: Statutes
1. Matrimonial Causes Act 1973
2. Family Law Act 1996

English Law: Other
1. *The Law Commission. Reform of the Grounds of Divorce. The Field of Choice.* Report on a reference under section 3 (1) (e) of the Law Commissions Act 1965, 1966, Cmnd. 3123
2. *Putting Asunder, A Divorce Law for Contemporary Society.* The Report of a group appointed by the Archbishop of Canterbury in January 1964 (SPCK, 1966)

299

Roman Law
1. *The Digest of Justinian*: Latin text ed. Theodor Mommsen and Paul Krueger; English translation ed. Alan Watson, University of Pennsylvania Press (Philadelphia, 1985 [4 volumes]) (For Latin text, see below.)
2. *Digesta Iustiniani Augusti*: in association with Paul Kreuger and Theodor Mommsen, Weidmann (Berlin, 1870)
3. *Institutes of Gaius*: Latin text ed. and trans. F. de Zulueta, Clarendon Press (Oxford, 1946-53 [2 volumes])

B. BIBLICAL
Lexicons
1. Abbot-Smith, G. *A Manual Greek-English Lexicon of the Old Lexicon of the New Testament*, T. & T. Clark (Edinburgh, 1937, reprinted 1977)
2. Bauer, W., Arndt, W. F., Gingrich F. W, *Greek-English Lexicon of the New Testament*, University of Chicago Press (Chicago, second edition, 1957)
3. Brown, F., Driver, S. R., Briggs, C. A. *Hebrew and Testament*, Oxford University Press (1929)
4. Thayer, J. H. *The New Thayer's Greek-English Lexicon of the New Testament* (copyright by Jay P. Green Sr.), Hendrickson Publishers (Peabody, Mass. [01961-3473], 1979, 1981)

Reference works
1. Danby, H. (trans.) *Mishnah*, Oxford University Press (London, 1933)
2. Douglas, J. D. *The New Bible Dictionary*, Inter Varsity Press (Leicester, 1962; reprinted 1976)
3. *Encyclopaedia Judaica*, volume 6, Keter Publishing (Jerusalem, Israel, 1971)
4. Hertz, J. H. (ed.) *The Soncino Edition of the Pentateuch and Haftorales* (one-volume edition), Soncino Press, (London, 1936; reprinted 1958)
5. Moule, C. F. D. *An Idiom Book of New Testament Greek*, Cambridge University Press (Cambridge, second edition, 1963)
6. Vermes, G. *The Dead Sea Scrolls in English*, Penguin Books (London, 1962; reprinted 1987)
7. Whiston, W. (trans.) *The Complete Works of Josephus*, Kregel Publications (Grand Rapids, USA, 1960, 1978, 1981)

Biblical background and studies, commentaries and theological works
1. Bahnsen, G. *Theonomy in Christian Ethics*, Presbyterian & Reformed (Nutley, 1977)
2. Banks, R. *Jesus and the Law in the Synoptic Tradition*, Cambridge University Press (1975)
3. Barnett, P. 'Wives and Women's Ministry (1 Timothy 2:11-15)', *The Evangelical Quarterly* (ed. I. H. Marshall) LXI 3 (July 1989), The Paternoster Press (Exeter), pp. 225-37
4. Blocher, H. (trans. by D. G. Preston) *In The Beginning: The Opening Chapters of Genesis*, Inter-Varsity Press (Leicester, 1984)
5. Brown, A. *Apology to Women: Christian Images of the Female Sex*, Inter-Varsity Press (Leicester, 1991)
6. Bruce, F. F. *Commentary on the Book of Acts*, Eerdmans (Grand Rapids, USA, 1954)

7. Bruce, F. F. *New Testament History*, Thomas Nelson (1969; reprinted Doubleday, Garden City, New York, 1972)

8. Calvin, J. *Genesis*, The Banner of Truth Trust (Edinburgh, 1979; reprint of 1847 edition)

9. Carr, G. L. *The Song of Solomon: An Introduction and Commentary*, Inter-Varsity Press (Leicester & Grand Rapids, USA, 1984)

10. Carson, D. A. *Matthew* (The Expositor's Bible Commentary, 8), The Zondervan Corporation (Grand Rapids, Michigan, USA, 1984)

11. Carson, D. A. (ed.) *From Sabbath to Lord's Day: A Biblical, Historical, and Theological Investigation*, The Zondervan Corporation (Grand Rapids, Michigan, USA, 1982)

12. Carson, D. A. *When Jesus Confronts The World: An Exposition of Matthew 8–10*, Inter-Varsity Press (Leicester; copyright 1987, Baker Book House Company)

13. Carson, D. A. *Showing the Spirit: a theological exposition of 1 Corinthians 12–14* (1987; third printing 1989)

14 Carson, D. A. *The Gospel of John*, Inter-Varsity Press (Leicester, 1991)

15. Carson, D. A. *The Gagging of God: Christianity Confronts Pluralism*, Apollos [imprint of Inter-Varsity Press] (Leicester, 1996)

16 Carson, D. A. and Woodbridge, J. D. (ed.) *Scripture and Truth*, Inter-Varsity Press, Leicester (1983; copyright 1983, The Zondervan Corporation, Grand Rapids, USA)

17. Carson, D. A. and Woodbridge, J. D. (ed.) *Hermeneutics, Authority and Canon*, Inter-Varsity Press (1986; copyright 1986 D. A. Carson and J. D. Woodbridge)

18. Clark, S. 'Headship in Ephesians: An examination of the meaning of **kephale** in Ephesians 5:23', *Foundations* (ed. E. Davies) 35 (Autumn 1995), British Evangelical Council (St Albans), pp. 15-20

19. Craigie, P. C. *The Book of Deuteronomy*, William B. Eerdmans (Grand Rapids, USA, 1976)

20. Dabney, R. L. *Lectures in Systematic Theology*, Zondervan (Grand Rapids, USA, 1972)

21. Derrett, J. D. M. *Law in the New Testament*, Darton, Longman & Todd (London, 1970)

22. Dunn, J. D. G. *Romans 1–8*, Word Incorporated (Dallas, Texas, USA, 1988)

23. Durham, J. I. *Exodus*, Word Incorporated (Dallas, Texas, USA, 1987)

24. Edwards, T. C. *A Commentary on the First Epistle to the Corinthians*, Hodder & Stoughton (London, 1897)

25. Eveson, P. H. *The Great Exchange: Justification by faith alone in the light of recent thought*, Day One Publications (Bromley, 1996)

26. Fee, G. D. *The First Epistle to the Corinthians*, Eerdmans (Grand Rapids, USA, 1987; reprinted 1993)

27. France, R. T. *Jesus and the Old Testament*, Baker Book House (Grand Rapids, USA, 1982)

28. Hagner, D. A. *Matthew 1–13*, Word Incorporated (Dallas, Texas, 1993)

29. Hagner, D.A. *Matthew 14–28*, Word Incorporated, (Dallas, Texas, 1995)

30. Harrison, R. K. *History of Old Testament Times*, Marshall, Morgan & Scott, (Edinburgh, 1957)

31. Hilton, M. with Marshall, G. *The Gospels and Rabbinic Judaism: A Study Guide*, SCM Press Ltd (London, 1988; out of print)

32. Hodge, C. *A Commentary on 1 and 2 Corinthians* [1 volume edition], The Banner of Truth Trust (Edinburgh, 1974)

33. Holland, T. S. 'Romans and the New Exodus: A Study in the Paschal New Exodus Theology of the Apostle Paul' (University of Wales, Lampeter, Ph.D. thesis 1996)
34. Lane, W. L. *The Gospel according to Mark: The English Text with Introduction, Exposition and Notes* Eerdmans (Grand Rapids, USA, 1974; reprinted 1993)
35. Leupold, H. C. *Exposition of Isaiah* (1 volume edition), Evangelical Press (1977; copyright 1968, 1971 by Baker Book House Company)
36. Liefeld, W. L. *Luke* (The Expositor's Bible Commentary, 8), The Zondervan Corporation (Grand Rapids, Michigan, USA, 1984)
37. Lloyd-Jones, D. M. *Studies in the Sermon on the Mount*, vol. 1, Inter-Varsity Press (1960)
38. Lloyd-Jones, D. M. *Romans, An Exposition of Chapter 5: Assurance*, The Banner of Truth Trust (Edinburgh, 1971; reprinted 1976)
39. Lloyd-Jones, D. M. *Romans, An Exposition of Chapter 7:1–8:4: The Law: Its Function and Limits*, The Banner of Truth Trust (Edinburgh, 1973; reprinted 1975)
40. Moo, D. J. '"Law", "Works of the Law", and Legalism in Paul', *Westminster Theological Journal*, 45 (1983), pp. 73-100
41. Moo, D. J. *The Epistle to the Romans*, William B. Eerdmans (1996)
42. Moore, T. V. *A Commentary on Haggai, Zechariah, and Malachi* [1 volume edition], The Banner of Truth Trust (Edinburgh, 1979)
43. Morris, L. *The Gospel according to John: The English Text with Introduction, Exposition and Notes*, William B. Eerdmans Publishing Co. (Grand Rapids, USA, 1971; reprinted 1989)
44. Motyer, J. A. *The Prophecy of Isaiah*, Inter-Varsity Press (Leicester, 1993; reprinted 1994)
45. Murray, J. *The Epistle to the Romans: The English Text with Introduction, Exposition and Notes*, Eerdmans (1974)
46. Murray, J. *Collected Writings, Volume 2: Systematic Theology*, The Banner of Truth Trust (Edinburgh, 1977)
47. Piper, J. *The Justification of God: An Exegetical and Theological Study of Romans 9:1-23*, Baker (1993; second edition)
48. Piper, J. and Grudem, W. *Recovering Biblical Manhood and Womanhood: A Response to Evangelical Feminism*, Crossway Books (a division of Good News Publishers, Wheaton, Illinois, USA, 1991)
49. Poole, M. *A Commentary on the Holy Bible*, vol. 1, The Banner of Truth Trust (London, 1963; reprinted 1969; first edition published 1685)
50. Rowdon, H. H. (ed.) *Christ the Lord: Studies in Christology presented to Donald Guthrie*, Inter-Varsity Press (Leicester, 1982)
51. Vos, G. *Biblical Theology: Old and New Testaments*, The Banner of Truth Trust (Edinburgh, 1975; copyright William B. Eerdmans Publishing Co., 1948)
52. Warfield, B. B. *The Inspiration and Authority of the Bible*, Presbyterian & Reformed (1948)
53. Wenham, G. J. *Numbers: An Introduction and Commentary*, Inter-Varsity Press (Leicester, 1981; reprinted 1985; copyright G. J. Wenham 1981)
54. Wenham, J. *Christ and the Bible*
55. Wright, N. T. *The Climax of the Covenant*, T. & T. Clark (Edinburgh, 1993)
56. Wright, N. T. *Jesus and the Victory of God*, SPCK (1996)
57. Yadin, Y. *Message of the Scrolls*, Crossroad Pub. Co. USA (1991)

58. Yamauchi, E. M. *The Stones and the Scriptures*, Inter-Varsity Press (Leicester, 1973; copyright Edwin M. Yamauchi 1972)
59. Young, E. J. *A Commentary on Daniel*, The Banner of Truth Trust (London, 1972)

Works on biblical teaching on divorce
1. Adams, J. *Marriage, Divorce and Remarriage in the Bible*, Presbyterian & Reformed Publishing Company (Phillipsburg, New Jersey, USA, 1980)
2. Atkinson, D. *To Have and to Hold*, Collins (London, 1979)
3. Brewer, D. I. 'Three Weddings and a Divorce: God's Covenant with Israel, Judah and the Church', *Tyndale Bulletin* 47.1 (1996), Tyndale House (Cambridge), pp. 1-25
4. Brewer, D. I. 'Biblical Divorce and Remarriage: the Jewish background to the New Testament teaching on divorce', Academic Version 1996, 1997, 1998 (copyright D. I. Brewer: not published, but work in progress available on the Internet)
5. Brewer, D. I. 'Biblical Divorce and Remarriage: the Jewish background to the New Testament teaching on divorce', Non-academic Version 1996, 1997, 1998 (copyright D. I. Brewer: not published, but work in progress available on the Internet)
6. Brewer, D. I. 'Marriage after Divorce?', *Evangelicals Now* (June 1997), p. 17
7. Cornes, A. *Divorce and Remarriage: Biblical Principles and Pastoral Practice* Hodder & Stoughton (1993)
8. Crispin, K. *Divorce: The Forgivable Sin?*, Hodder & Stoughton (London, 1989)
9. Heth, W. A. and Wenham, G. J. *Jesus and Divorce*, Hodder & Stoughton (London, 1984; copyright 1984 William A. Heth and Gordon J. Wenham)
10. Murray, J. *Divorce*, Presbyterian & Reformed Publishing Co. (Phillipsburg, New Jersey, USA, 1961)
11. Okorie, A. M. 'Divorce and Remarriage: An Exegetical Analysis of 1 Corinthians 7:10-16', *Evangel* 15.1 (1997), pp. 28-32
12. Pink, A. W. *Studies in the Scriptures 1947*, The Banner of Truth Trust (Edinburgh, 1982), pp. 205-11; 229-35; 252-8; 276-85)
13. Stott, J. *Issues Facing Christians Today*, chapter 14: 'Marriage and Divorce', Marshalls Paperbacks (Basingstoke 1984; copyright 1984 John Stott)
14. Shaw, I. (ed.) *Christian Family Matters*, chapter 8: 'Divorce' by Neil Richards, and the Appendix (Evangelical Press of Wales, 1985)

Indexes

V. INDEX OF AUTHORS

(Ancient authors or individuals whose words are cited in ancient works are indicated in italic)